CorelDRAW!™ 2

SELF-TEACHING GUIDE

Wiley SELF-TEACHING GUIDES (STG's) are designed for first time users of computer applications and programming languages. They feature concept-reinforcing drills, exercises, and illustrations that enable you to measure your progress, and learn at your own pace. Other Wiley Self-Teaching Guides:

DOS 5 STG, Ruth Ashley and Judi N. Fernandez
INTRODUCTION TO PERSONAL COMPUTERS STG, Peter Stephenson
QUATTRO PRO 3 STG, Jennifer Meyer
LOTUS 1-2-3 FOR WINDOWS STG, Douglas J. Wolf
PARADOX 3.5 STG, Gloria Wheeler
Q&A 4 STG, Corey Sandler and Tom Badgett
FOXPRO 2.0 STG, Ellen Sander
ALDUS PERSUASION FOR IBM PC'S AND COMPATIBLES STG, Karen Brown and Diane Stielstra
PERFORM STG, Peter Stephenson
MICROSOFT WORD 5.5 FOR THE PC STG, Ruth Ashley and Judi Fernandez
WORDPERFECT 5.0/5.1 STG, Neil Salkind
WORDPERFECT FOR WINDOWS STG, Neil Salkind
MICROSOFT WINDOWS 3.0 STG, Keith Weiskamp and Saul Aguiar
PC DOS 4 STG, Ruth Ashley and Judi Fernandez
PC DOS 3.3 STG, Ruth Ashley and Judi Fernandez
MASTERING MICROSOFT WORKS STG, David Sachs, Babette Kronstadt, Judith Van Wormer, and Barbara Farrell
QUICKPASCAL STG, Keith Weiskamp and Saul Aguiar
GW BASIC STG, Ruth Ashley and Judi Fernandez
TURBO C++ STG, Bryan Flamig
SQL STG, Peter Stephenson
QUICKEN STG, Peter Aitken
HARVARD GRAPHICS 3 STG, David Harrison and John W. Yu
EXCEL 3 STG, Ruth Witken
AMI PRO 2 FOR WINDOWS STG, Pamela S. Beason and Stephen Guild

To order our STG's, you can call Wiley directly at (201) 469-4400, or check your local bookstores.

"Mastering computers was never this easy, rewarding, and fun!"

CorelDRAW!™ 2

SELF-TEACHING GUIDE

Robert Bixby

John Wiley & Sons, Inc.
New York ▲ Chichester ▲ Brisbane ▲ Toronto ▲ Singapore

In recognition of the importance of preserving what has been written, it is a policy of John Wiley & Sons, Inc. to have books of enduring value published in the United States printed on acid-free paper, and we exert our best efforts to that end.

Copyright ©1992 by John Wiley & Sons, Inc.

Published simultaneously in Canada

All rights reserved.

Reproduction or translation of any part of this work beyond that permitted by section 107 or 108 of the 1976 United States Copyright Act without the permission of the copyright owner is unlawful. Requests for permission or further information should be addressed to the Permission Department, John Wiley & Sons, Inc.

This publication is designed to provide accurate and authoritative information in regard to the subject matter covered. It is sold with the understanding that the publisher is not engaged in rendering legal, accounting, or other professional service. If legal advice or other expert assistance is required, the services of a competent professional person should be sought. FROM A DECLARATION OF PRINCIPLES JOINTLY ADOPTED BY A COMMITTEE OF THE AMERICAN BAR ASSOCIATION AND A COMMITTEE OF PUBLISHERS.

ISBN 0-471-54892-8

Printed in the United States of America

10 9 8 7 6 5 4 3 2 1

Acknowledgments

I offer my thanks to Corel Systems and Jennifer Poulsen in particular. Bill Gladstone and Matt Wagner of Waterside Productions, my literary agency. Laura Lewin, my editor at John Wiley & Sons. Chinon America, for the use of the scanner that produced the scanned images in this book. Star Micronics, for the use of the laser printer that produced the graphics in this book (and has generated thousands of pages of camera-ready text and graphics for several book and magazine projects without a hitch). COMPUTE Magazine and General Media, Inc. And most of all my wife Kathy and my children Jennifer and Steve.

Trademarks

Arts & Letters is a registered trademark of Computer Support Corporation.
Micrografx Charisma is a trademark of Micrografx, Inc.
Micrografx Designer is a trademark of Micrografx, Inc.
DrawPerfect is a registered trademark of WordPerfect Corporation.
MS-DOS is a registered trademark of Microsoft Corporation.
Pantone is a registered trademark of Pantone, Inc.
Ventura Publisher is a registered trademark of Ventura Software, Inc.
Windows is a trademark of Microsoft Corporation.
WordPerfect is a registered trademark of WordPerfect Corporation.
Other product names mentioned in passing may be trademarks or registered trademarks of their manufacturers or publishers.

Contents Overview

1. Preparing to Use *CorelDRAW!*
2. Editing the Drawing
3. Printing
4. Managing Files
5. Views
6. Node Editing
7. Lines and Fills
8. Corel Trace
9. Text
10. Advanced Topics

Contents

Introduction, 1

What *CorelDRAW!* Is For	4
Who Needs to Use It	6
Equipment Needed to Run *CorelDRAW!*	6
Mouse Commands	6
Clicking	7
Double Clicking	7
Dragging	8
If You Are Left-Handed	8
Keyboard Commands	11
Conventions for Special Formatting in the Book	14
What Comes in the *CorelDRAW!* Box?	15

1 Preparing to Use *CorelDRAW!*, 19

Copying the Disks onto Backups	20
Registering	23
Safeguarding Work	24
Setting Up *CorelDRAW!*	26
The Basics of *Windows* Operation	28
Starting and Exiting *CorelDRAW!*	30
The Elements on the *CorelDRAW!* Screen	35
Toolbox	35
Palette	47
Page Area	47
CorelDRAW! Window	48
Status Line	48
Title Bar	50
Menu Bar	50
Backing Out of a Decision with Cancel and Undo	51
Exercises	52

2 Editing the Drawing, 55

Creating a Drawing	56
Saving a Drawing	60
Getting Rid of a Drawing	63
Loading a Drawing	64
Editing an Object	66
Editing an Existing Rectangle	66
Editing Multiple Objects	67
Making Precise Adjustments	69
Creating a Drop Shadow	71
Changing Precedence	72
Changing Outline Color	73
Changing Fill Color	74
Aligning Objects	75
Using the Grid	76
Drawing	78
Open and Closed Objects	80
Solid Fills	82
Editing Nodes	83
Bezier	84
Straight Line to Curve	86
Curve to Straight Line	87
Other Node Editing Tools	87
Cutting and Pasting	92
Using Text	95
Editing Existing Text	95
Adjusting Text Spacing	96
Making Your Text Fit in the Text Rectangle	98
Getting Text from the Clipboard	100
Getting Text from a File	102
Changing the Appearance of a Block of Text	104
Changing the Appearance of Individual Characters	105
Using the Zoom Tool	107
Changing the Preview Arrangement	111
Exercises	112

3 Printing, 115

Installing a New Printer	118
Changing Printers	119
Printing with *CorelDRAW!*	124
Preparing Files for a Typesetter	135
Merge Printing	138
Exercises	143

4 Managing Files, 145

Backups	146
Importing and Exporting Art	147
Importing Art	147
Exporting Art	151
Using Autotrace	152
Using Clip Art	158
Using Symbols	161
Using Mosaic	162
Exercises	164

5 Views, 167

Magnification	168
Zoom In	168
Zoom Out	171
Actual Size (1:1)	172
Fit in Window	173
Show Page	174
Previews	174
Full Screen Preview	176
Preview Toolbox	177
Preview Selected Only	178
Auto Update	179
Show Bitmaps and Refresh Wire Screen	179
Grids and Snap	180
Guidelines and Snap	185
Rulers, Status Line, Palette	189
Exercises	191

6 Node Editing, 195

Delete Nodes	199
Control Points	201
Smooth Curves Through Nodes	203
Break Nodes	204
Attach Nodes	206
Turn Curves into Lines	208
Cusp Nodes	209
Add Nodes	210
Turn Lines into Curves	210
Make Nodes Symmetrical	210
More Node Editing Features	211
Crop Bitmaps	211
Exercises	211

7 Lines and Fills, 215

Vector and Raster Patterns	216
Vector Fills	216
Raster Fills	225
Fountain Fills	229
Spot Color	236
Process Color	238
PostScript Patterns	240
Pen Points	243
Putting Fills to Work	250
Brush Color	254
Color and Shape Blends	256
Mixing Colors	260
How and Why to Use Pantone Colors	261
Exercises	262

8 Corel Trace, 265

Starting *Corel Trace*	266
Create Color and Grayscale Tracings	272
The Batch Feature	273

9 Text, 275

Creating and Displaying Text	276
Fitting Text to Path	277
Altering the Baseline	278
Interactive Kerning	281
Interactive Kerning with Multiple Characters	286
Changing the Character Attributes	287
Editing Character Outlines	290
Exercises	294

10 Advanced Topics, 297

Blends	298
Manipulating Envelopes	302
Perspective	306
Extruding	310
Programming the Right Mouse Button	312
Repeat	314
Exercises	315

Appendix

Quick Keyboard Commands	319

Glossary, 323

Index, 333

Introduction

▲ What *CorelDRAW!* Is For
▲ Who Needs to Use It
▲ Equipment Needed to Run *CorelDRAW!*
▲ Mouse Commands
▲ Keyboard Commands
▲ Conventions for Special Formatting in the Book
▲ What Comes in the *CorelDRAW!* Box?

You are about to embark on learning the basics of one of the most powerful PC graphics packages ever conceived: *CorelDRAW!*. A list of this program's features could go on for pages. During the course of this book, you will see each of these features in action.

CorelDRAW! didn't come out of nowhere. It belongs to a class of graphics packages that includes paint programs, draw programs, presentation programs, illustration programs, and computer-aided design (CAD) programs. Although the differences among these programs go much deeper, they are most easily explained in terms of their products.

There are two basic approaches to creating an image on the computer screen. The first is painting to the screen, also known as *raster* or *bit-map graphics,* the approach used by *PC Paintbrush* and *Deluxe Paint.* Painting is dependent on the resolution of the computer screen itself. When you alter the color or shape of something on the screen, you are actually changing the pixels, or picture elements, that appear on the computer screen. (If you look closely at the screen, you can see that it's made up of tiny dots of light. Each of these dots is a pixel.)

The other approach is called *vector* or *object-oriented graphics* (OOG). This is the approach used by draw programs like *DrawPerfect*, presentation programs like *Charisma*, and illustration programs like *CorelDRAW!*. Instead of etching a circle or other object in the pixels of the computer screen, the object exists in memory in a sort of idealized, abstract formula from which a representation of a circle is rendered on the screen to the best of the computer's ability.

The difference is subtle in concept, but when it comes time to place the artwork on paper, it becomes much more important because printers are capable of far higher resolution than computer screens. Most laser printers are capable of placing 300 dots per inch (dpi) on paper, resulting in very fine printing. By contrast, the computer screen typically provides no more than 72 dpi. If you print a circle created with a paint program, the curves that make it up would be made up of "jaggies"—straight lines arranged to resemble a curve, as shown in Figure I.1.

But a circle created with a draw program can be printed at the highest resolution the printer is capable of, as shown in Figure I.2.

There are even higher resolution devices, like Linotronic machines, that can create printouts with over 2000 dpi resolution. The

▼ *Figure I.1. Circle created at screen resolution*

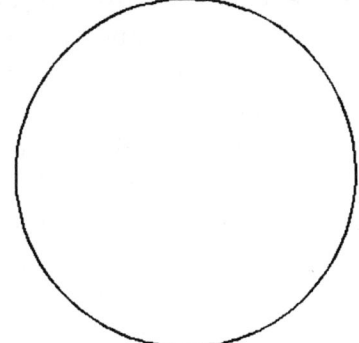

▼ *Figure I.2. Circle created at 300 dpi printer resolution*

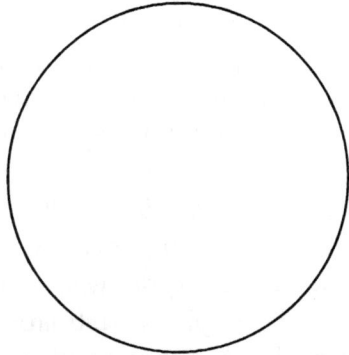

circle in Figure I.1 printed on one of these machines would look pretty much the same as the circle you see in the figure, while a printout of the circle depicted in Figure I.2 would look perfectly smooth, even if examined with a magnifying glass.

There are other differences besides resolution. The product of a paint program like *Deluxe Paint II Enhanced* is a single layer of color. You can edit a painting, but the changes must be made pixel-by-pixel. In a painting of a boy and his dog, if you want to make the dog's ears longer, you must erase the existing ears and painstakingly repaint the ears. In the process, you could accidentally affect the part of the painting that contains the boy. Paint programs typically contain tools that make working with individual pixels simple: built-in microscopes called *zoom tools*, and an easily used palette.

By contrast, the product of an object-oriented draw program is a collection of independent objects. A drawing of a boy and his dog could consist of two objects or hundreds of objects carefully grouped. For example, the dog could be composed of a group of independent objects representing his body, his four legs, his neck, his tail, his head, and his two ears. To alter his ears, you would ungroup the dog (which means to "unstick" the independent objects so they can be manipulated), change to node-editing mode, move the control points that determine the size and shape of the ears, return to object-editing mode, and regroup the objects that compose the dog. During this process, there would be no way to accidentally damage any part of the drawing that was not related to the dog's ears.

The parallel between the shapes on the screen and a group of objects on a shelf is almost perfect. The objects are all arranged in order of precendence. They can be selected and moved, sized, colored, or deleted at will. You can even save out items from a drawing and use them in other drawings. This is useful for commercial artists who spend much of their time creating nearly identical drawings for logos or form design. It is this nearly perfect control that makes illustration programs so valuable.

With its ability to load bitmap graphics, to turn them into vector graphics, and then save the graphics as bitmaps again, *CorelDRAW!* might be seen as a bridge between paint programs and vector graphic programs. In fact, the distinctions among the various types of programs in terms of power are becoming less important over time. Paint programs can exhibit a great deal of power, for example, providing scaling and perspective. If you use a range of programs as I do, you will quickly learn to recognize the superiority of illustration packages over their cousins the paint and presentation programs.

What *CorelDRAW!* Is For

As mentioned, *CorelDRAW!* is an object-oriented drawing program. It is equipped with tools that multiply your drawing power. It's the appropriate tool for any illustration job, including lettering,

What CorelDRAW! Is For

and is particularly suited to publication graphics. It combines the features you would find in several competing packages, including *Arts & Letters* and *Micrografx Designer*. The competition among these three packages is intense but so far *CorelDRAW!* has maintained the upper hand both in features and in sales.

If you are not a talented artist, you can still produce accomplished work with *CorelDRAW!* because it is shipped with over 3500 pieces of clip art and symbols. All you will have to do is select the appropriate components and arrange them in a pleasing composition to create the necessary graphic art. However, after you are finished with the lessons in this book, you will probably not be satisfied with this easy way out and you may find yourself creating clip art for your own purposes.

PRACTICE WHAT YOU'VE LEARNED

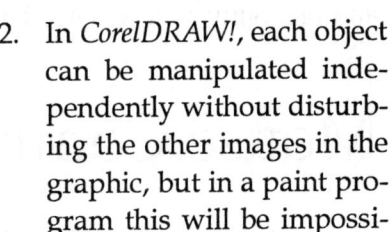

What You Should Do

1. If you have a paint program, try to adjust the size of a graphic image created with that paint program (most programs allow you to adjust the size and shape of an image). You can also import a raster graphic into *CorelDRAW!* and use the pick tool to make it twice its size. Print it out.

2. Using a paint program, draw several overlapping shapes. Try to adjust the size and shape of the first shape you painted in the paint program (you won't be able to do this checkup with *CorelDRAW!*).

How the Computer Responds

1. The picture is distorted, resulting in a blocky, jagged appearance.

2. In *CorelDRAW!*, each object can be manipulated independently without disturbing the other images in the graphic, but in a paint program this will be impossible.

Who Needs to Use It

Who needs *CorelDRAW!*? Anybody doing graphic art and anyone interested in getting involved in graphic art needs it. *CorelDRAW!*, like much computer software, offers much more than its simple list of features. It offers the opportunity to explore and learn. Because it is a professional tool, a curious beginner will find exploring the menus and capabilities of *CorelDRAW!* will add to his or her storehouse of ideas.

Equipment Needed to Run *CorelDRAW!*

The list of equipment required to run *CorelDRAW!* is very similar to the equipment list for *Windows* operation. It can run on any PC-compatible with an 80286 or higher-numbered central processing unit, *Windows,* Hercules, EGA, VGA or higher-level video, and a mouse or similar pointing device. Naturally, the higher the level of your equipment, the more satisfied you will be with *CorelDRAW!* operation. Some users warn that the 80286 (286) computer should be considered a minimal platform, which will provide minimal performance and may result in unexpected crashes (although my experience with a 286 running *CorelDRAW!* has not borne this out). Hercules and EGA graphics should likewise be considered a bare minimum. If you want to use *CorelDRAW!* to its maximum power and flexibility, you will need a 80386 (386) and VGA graphics.

Mouse Commands

There are certain mouse operations that are specialized, such as node editing, which will be described in depth when it is appropriate, but there are three generic mouse commands that you must understand before venturing into this book. If you are already an accomplished mouse wrangler and you understand the terms *clicking*, *double clicking*, and *dragging*, feel free to skip over this section. If these are new terms, please read on.

Mouse Commands

A mouse is a computer input device that is approximately the size of a pack of cigarettes or a bar of soap. It communicates with the computer either through a serial port or through a special mouse port. Although there are cordless mice that operate like infrared VCR remote controls or by way of weak radio transmissions, most mice are attached to the computer by a wire. Mice for the PC generally have two or three buttons. Generally speaking, we will concern ourselves with the left button. If you hold the mouse in the palm of your right hand, this button should be directly under your index finger. Later in this section, we'll cover how to switch the right and left buttons of your mouse, for southpaw operation.

Clicking

When you read the instruction to click on an item, you should move the mouse until the mouse pointer on the screen is located over the specified item and quickly press and release the left mouse button. Most mice have click switches under their buttons, so there should be an unmistakable clicking sound or tactile click inside the mouse. This action is typically used to select an item. It should be carefully distinguished from double clicking, which will be covered next.

Double Clicking

Double clicking is an action used to start applications, open windows, and enter the node-editing mode within *CorelDRAW!*. To double click, place your index finger on the left mouse button and press and release it twice in rapid succession. The speed of the click necessary to make a double click is adjustable by using the control panel, which will be covered in a later section of this introduction.

Dragging

Dragging is a process used to move and size objects and windows. To drag, place the mouse pointer on the object you want to drag (*CorelDRAW!* requires that you place the mouse pointer on the *outline* of an object) and press the left mouse button. Hold the button down until you have moved the object to the position where you would like to place it and then release it. You can see the difference between clicking and dragging. To click, you press the mouse button and release it immediately. To drag, you press the mouse button and hold it down.

If You Are Left-Handed

Windows contains an option for changing the operation of the right and left mouse buttons. In the main *Windows* screen (the Program Manager appears at the top), you should have a collection of icons with names like Accessories, Main, Games, and so on. Double click on the Main icon. A window will open with the name Main on the title bar (the bar at the top is known alternately as the title bar and the move bar because it contains the window title and because dragging this bar allows you to drag the window; you can move any window that isn't maximized—that is, any window that isn't filling the whole screen). The window is full of icons that can be used to customize the operation of your copy of *Windows*.

Double click on the Control Panel icon and the Control Panel window will open. This window is also full of icons. Double click on the Mouse icon to see the Mouse dialog box. Figure I.3 shows the *Windows* screen with the Program Manager, Main, and Control Panel windows and the Mouse dialog box all open. They probably won't look like this when you open them. Instead they will overlap, obscuring each other.

To adjust the double click speed, click on the arrows on either end of the slidebar in the Double Click Speed section of the Mouse dialog box. If you want to see how slow the click is, double click on

Mouse Commands

▼ *Figure I.3. Program Manager, Main, and Control Panel windows and Mouse dialog*

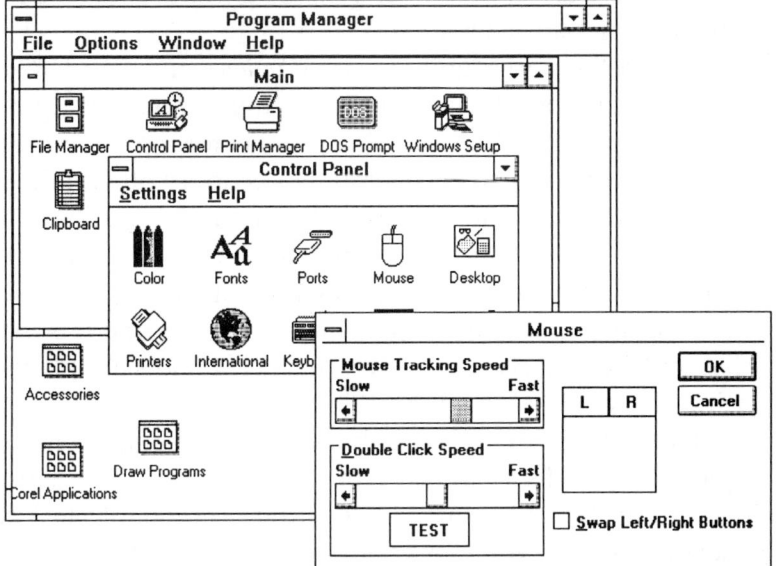

the box marked TEST in the bottom of this section. When it registers a double click, it turns from white to black or back again.

Turning to the purpose of this brief section, if you are left handed, it may not be natural for you to click on the left button. By clicking on the small box in the lower right of the Mouse dialog box, you can reverse the buttons on your mouse so that the right button is the active mouse button.

The Multitalented Mouse

Is that all there is to working with the mouse? Not by a long shot. You will be amazed at how versatile this little creature can be in creating art. By the time you have finished reading the first nine chapters of this book, you might think that you know everything there is to know about using the mouse with *CorelDRAW!*, but you would be wrong. In Chapter 10 there is a section on advanced use of the mouse. The right mouse button (or left button, if you have switched them) is programmable. You can select among five high-powered commands to assign to the little-used right mouse button.

I have received word that newer versions of *Windows* (3.1 and beyond) will use a completely different method of controlling the mouse. If you are using a *Windows* version newer than 3.0, refer to your manual for instructions.

I have had the opportunity to use *Windows* and *CorelDRAW!* with a variety of input devices, but I have found nothing superior to the mouse or Appoint's MousePen product for input. This is an opinion, of course, and you are certainly free to try other gadgets. Light pens would seem to be perfect for computer graphics, but they have to sample the screen several times to figure out where the pen point is, which slows *Windows* to a maddening crawl. Some pens continue sampling the screen when they can't find the raster location, making *Windows* slow even further. Tablets are plagued by their own troublesome quirks. With some tablets it's difficult to press a button without accidentally moving the stylus point, for example. Some tablets also slow operations when the stylus is removed from the tablet surface. Be sure to thoroughly test any unusual input device you purchase to use with *CorelDRAW!*. Some people have been able to make peace with a track ball as an input device. On its surface, it looks like a natural partner for a *Windows* illustration program. Try drawing with one for half an hour before making the purchase. Many track balls have their buttons in unusual locations that will force you to hold your hand in an odd position that quickly becomes tiresome (and may actually be hazardous to your carpal tunnel). For all its drawbacks, the mouse is probably your best bet for *Windows* input.

PRACTICE WHAT YOU'VE LEARNED

What You Should Do	How the Computer Responds
1. Place the mouse pointer on a menu name on the *CorelDRAW!* screen and press and release the left mouse button once.	1. The menu will appear. This is called *clicking*.

2. Place the mouse pointer on the outline of an object on the *CorelDRAW!* screen and press and hold the left mouse button, then move the mouse.

2. The object will follow the mouse pointer as you move the mouse until you release the button. This is called *dragging*.

Mouse Commands

Keyboard Commands

We will assume that you are passingly familiar with the PC keyboard. Rather than waste a lot of effort explaining what the function keys are or where you can locate the cursor keys, I will assume that you use your computer for other things and can identify the various keys. You will want to enter certain commands from the keyboard even though *CorelDRAW!*, as well as *Windows*, can be entirely mouse-driven.

In this book, you will occasionally be told to press a key combination like Alt-F4. This means that you should press and hold down the Alt key and press and release the F4 function key. By coincidence, this is the command to close the currently active window. Within *CorelDRAW!*, you will issue certain commands from a menu bar arranged along the top of the screen (shown in Figure I.4). If you are told to press Ctrl-C, you should press and hold down the Ctrl or Control key and tap the C key. To activate the menu bar from the keyboard, press either the Alt key or the F10 key and then press the first letter of the menu you want to see.

Once the menu bar is selected, to pull down a menu from the keyboard, press the down-arrow key. Use the up- and down-arrow key to move the highlight within a menu. To move right or left to the next menu, use the right- and left-arrow keys.

If there is a dialog box visible on the screen, some part of that dialog box will be active. For example, in Figure I.5, the Open Drawing dialog box is open. The Files area of the dialog box is the active area. If you press the down-arrow key, you could move the highlight through all the CDR files in the current directory. To load the highlighted file, simply press Enter. (Note that a simple repre-

12 ▲ CorelDRAW! 2

▼ *Figure I.4.* The **CorelDRAW!** *work screen*

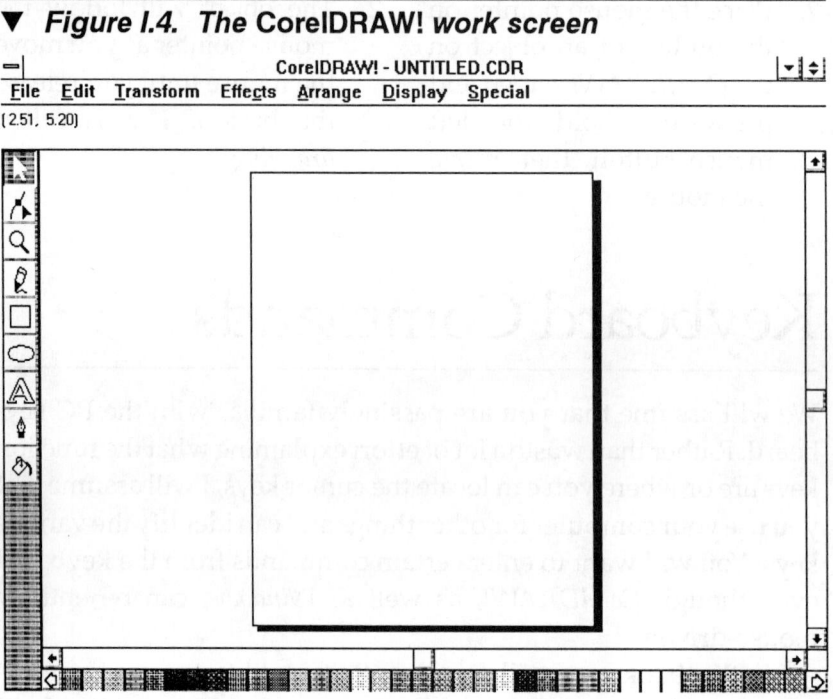

▼ *Figure I.5.* The Open Drawing dialog box

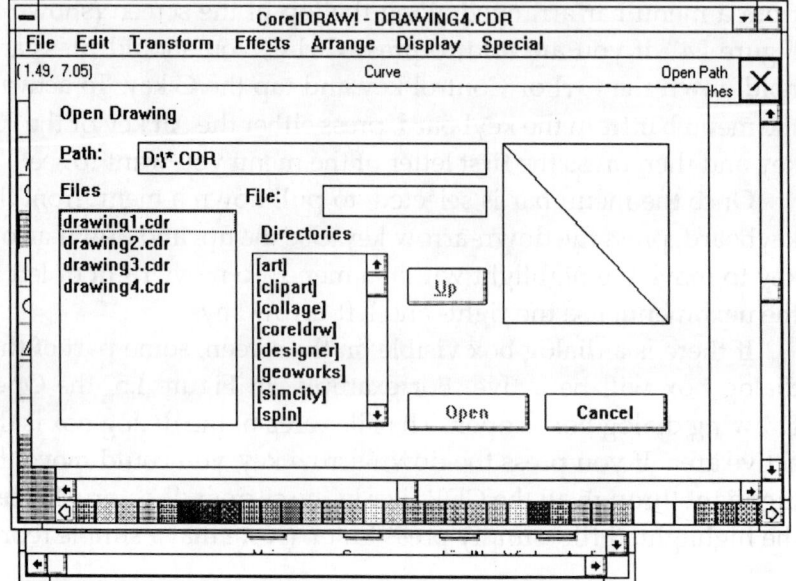

Keyboard Commands

sentation of the drawing in the file is shown in the large box at the right, just above the Cancel button.)

To move to the next area in the dialog box, use the Tab key. Tapping it once takes you to the Directories area (next to the Files area) where you can use the cursor keys to select a different directory.

Tapping the Tab key again takes you to the Path area, where you can simply type in the path of the file to be loaded.

Pressing the Tab key again takes the selection to the File box, where you can type the name of the file you want to load.

Press Tab again and you are moved to the Cancel button, which takes on a thick border to indicate that it's selected. If you press Enter at this point, the dialog box will close and no file will be loaded.

Finally, you can press Tab to return to the Files area of the dialog box.

All dialog boxes work this way, allowing you to maneuver either with the keyboard or the mouse.

You will learn many keyboard shortcuts in this book. They will be summarized in the appendix for easy reference. Some people feel more comfortable working with the keyboard and others prefer the mouse. *CorelDRAW!* and *Windows* are flexible enough to allow you either option.

PRACTICE WHAT YOU'VE LEARNED

What You Should Do

1. Press Alt-F4 while *Corel-DRAW!* is running.

How the Computer Responds

1. The *CorelDRAW!* window will close. If anything has been drawn in the *CorelDRAW!* window, the program will pause and give you a chance to save it to disk.

2. Restart *CorelDRAW!*, draw a few objects on the screen and select Save from the File menu (or press Ctrl-S). Press the Tab key several times.

2. The Tab key cycles the selection through the various boxes and buttons within the dialog box. When the item in the box that you want to use is selected, you can operate that item. For example, you can type in a text box or press a button by hitting the Enter key.

Conventions for Special Formatting in the Book

You will note that the chapters are laid out in a particular way. There is a good reason for this. Each chapter is set up as a series of lessons that operate from beginning to end—not necessarily from beginning to end of the chapter, but with a logical flow. In fact the entire book was carefully arranged to take you through the simplest parts first so you would have a thorough grounding in the rudiments before you began your first forays into the more advanced areas. Naturally, you are free to meander through the book at random, picking up points here and there as you wish. I have no control over the way you use the book. However, if you want to get your money's worth out of it, you would be wiser to use it as it was intended.

Once you have worked through all the lessons, you may discover that you need to refresh your memory on some point or other. Use the index or table of contents to find the particular item you need help with. When you find the item, work through the lesson again to refresh your memory. Each of the lessons has been made completely discrete.

Each chapter will begin with an introduction to the major points to be made in the chapter. The chapter will follow the structure you see in the introduction, with added tips, lessons, and brief reviews to keep you up with what's going on in the chapter. Finally, the chapter will close with exercises.

The lessons are the heart and soul of this book. If you don't have your computer running and *CorelDRAW!* on the screen at all times, and if you don't follow along with the lessons, you will lose out completely on the value of this book. The lessons are not only designed to illustrate the processes involved in creating art with *CorelDRAW!*, but also show you tricks to use, design ideas, and provide an opportunity to practice skills.

There are a few more conventions used in this book. When DOS prompts you to do something, this will be shown in quotation marks, like "Copy another diskette (Y/N)?" Note that I will refer to all floppy disks as *disks* and DOS usually refers to them as *diskettes*.

When you are instructed to enter something at the command line, this will be shown all in uppercase letters. For example, to format a disk, you should type FORMAT A: and press Enter.

Conventions for Special Formatting in the Book

What Comes in the *CorelDRAW!* Box?

When you open the *CorelDRAW!* box, you may feel as if it's Christmas morning. Corel packs its product boxes chock full of goodies and unexpected surprises.

▲ First, there are the system disks. You will back them up and install *CorelDRAW!* in the next chapter. In the mean time, protect these disks carefully. They contain about 90 percent of the value of the whole package.

▲ Also of great importance is the registration card. This card is a standard postcard. Fill it out completely and make sure you put enough postage on it to get it to Canada (if you live in the U.S., remember that sending something to Canada is international mail and it will cost more than standard U.S. postcards). If you fail to register, you lose out on several benefits, including access to the technical support hot line, low-cost upgrades, and the Corel newsletter.

▲ A flier is included on the *CorelDRAW!* International Design Contest, your chance to recoup your investment in the package—and then some. Currently, the prizes amount to over $300,000. Check out the flier for details.

▲ There is a pamphlet called *Read This First* containing important information, including a condensed version of this list.

▲ You will find the *Typeface Conversion and Creation with WFN Boss* booklet. Although this highly technical area is beyond the scope of this beginner's book, you might take a look at this when your skills with the rest of the package have developed. *CorelDRAW!* has built its reputation, at least in part, on its ability to work with type.

▲ Another booklet included is called *Mosaic Visual File Manager*. Mosaic is an innovative way to keep your graphics straight. One of the more frustrating aspects of file management with graphics programs of the past was the fact that DOS allows you only eight characters for the filename and the graphics package takes control of the extension, so it's very difficult to provide clues as to the contents of a particular graphics file. For example, I have whole disks full of files with names like FACE1.CDR, FACE2.CDR, AUTOMOB1.CDR, AUTOMO12.CDR, and so on. Who knows what's in the files? It would take a very long time to go through them and find a particular face or automobile. Mosaic avoids this confusion by allowing you to see a simplified version of the drawing (called a *thumbnail*) when you highlight the filename. This improvement alone would make *CorelDRAW!* worth having, but Mosaic goes on to completely revolutionize graphics file management. This will be covered in full in Chapter 4.

▲ There is a booklet covering Corel Trace, the mechanism Corel uses to convert bit-map art into raster art. This will be covered in Chapter 8.

▲ A technical reference that explains how *CorelDRAW!* interacts with many different programs and graphics formats is included.

▲ Another item is a book covering the symbol and clipart libraries provided with *CorelDRAW!*. This will be covered in Chapter 4.

What Comes in the CorelDRAW! Box?

- ▲ There is a booklet called *Learning CorelDRAW!*. This is a brief set of eight lessons to get you started with the package.
- ▲ Also included is a typeface reference chart that allows you to see at a glance what the typefaces look like. When you look through this reference, note that not all typefaces are provided with both upper- and lowercase.
- ▲ You'll find a reference card that shows how you can access special symbols within various fonts. It also covers the extended character set, which will be useful when you turn to using accented vowels and foreign currency marks.
- ▲ A quick reference card covering process colors and various commands is included.
- ▲ There is a typescale—a very useful tool for judging the size of type, thickness of lines, and for general measurements.
- ▲ You'll find a sticker with the telephone and fax numbers of the technical support line.
- ▲ Included is an addendum sheet to cover changes in the program since the manual was produced.
- ▲ There is also a videotape that shows you how to use the *CorelDRAW!* tools and a card telling you the approximate playing times of the various sections of the tape.
- ▲ Lastly, there is a thick manual giving exhaustive explanations of everything you'll find in the program.

Preparing to Use *CorelDRAW!*

▲ Copying the Disks onto Backups
▲ Registering
▲ Safeguarding Work
▲ Setting Up *CorelDRAW!*
▲ The Basics of *Windows* Operation
▲ Starting and Exiting *CorelDRAW!*
▲ The Elements on the *CorelDRAW!* Screen
▲ Using Menus
▲ Backing Out of a Decision with Cancel and Undo

Copying the Disks onto Backups

CorelDRAW! is shipped in two different versions. The versions are identical except for the way they are stored. One version is shipped on 1.2Mb (megabyte) 5 1/4-inch disks and one is shipped on 1.44Mb 3 1/2-inch disks. In either case, it's crucial that you pause before installing *CorelDRAW!* to make a complete backup of the disks.

Why make a backup? You should always have at least one copy of everything—programs and files. (One copy of a program is the most you can legally make. Don't share your copies because that is illegal and you can be prosecuted for copyright infringement.) Computer use is fraught with hazards. Hard disks die at distressingly unpredictable intervals. Disks are lost, damaged, and stolen. Fires and floods occur (if you have a modern sprinkler system in your office, they can both happen at the same time), neither of which is beneficial to computer disks.

The smartest way to start is to purchase a brand new box of disks designed for high capacity or high density data storage. It's possible to punch or drill an extra hole in some 720K (kilobyte) 3 1/2-inch disks and format them at 1.44Mb, but this practice isn't recommended. After all, the purpose of the backup is to safeguard your investment. How safe is your investment stored on disks designed to hold half as much data as you have put on them? It's like hauling a ton of sand in a half-ton pickup: You might make it in one trip, but you'd take less risk using a sturdier truck.

I'll make the assumption that you have a drive installed as drive A. If you are copying the disks with a drive designated as B, simply substitute the drive letter B where you see the letter A in the examples.

Begin by formatting the disks.

1. Boot your computer (usually this involves simply turning it on and waiting a minute or two).

Copying the Disks onto Backups

2. When the boot process is completed and you see the DOS prompt on the screen (which probably looks like C:\) type FORMAT A: and press Enter.
3. DOS will prompt you with a message like "Insert new diskette for drive A: and press ENTER when ready..."
4. Put a new disk (NOT one of the *CorelDRAW!* disks, but a blank disk you have purchased) in the drive. Depending on your version of DOS, you will be shown either which head and cylinder is involved in the format process or what percentage of the disk has been formatted. If the latter is the case, when the disk is completely formatted, the formatting program will pause and ask you to enter a disk label. You can enter a disk name of up to 11 characters or simply press Enter. Again, if you were shown the percentage of the disk formatted, you will be shown how much of the disk formatted properly. If there are any bad tracks, put the disk aside. You will want to return it to the manufacturer and request a replacement disk.
5. You will see a prompt that says "Format another (Y/N)?" Type Y and replace the disk in drive A with another new disk. Continue formatting until you have ten or more formatted disks. You won't need that many to copy the *CorelDRAW!* disks, but you can never have too many formatted disks on hand.
6. When you are finished formatting the last disk and DOS asks you "Format another (Y/N)?" type N.

Now that you have a supply of formatted disks, it's time to copy the *CorelDRAW!* disks.

1. Type DISKCOPY A: A: and press Enter. DOS will prompt you with "Insert SOURCE diskette in drive A:." Remember that the *CorelDRAW!* disks are the SOURCE disks and the blank disks you just finished formatting are the TARGET disks.
2. Place the *CorelDRAW!* disk marked Disk 1 in the drive and press Enter.
3. After a few seconds DOS will prompt you to "Insert TARGET diskette in drive A:." Replace the *CorelDRAW!* disk in drive A with one of the disks you just finished formatting and press Enter.
4. You will have to repeat this process more than once. Remember that *CorelDRAW!* Disk 1 is the SOURCE disk and you should

continue to use the same newly formatted disk as the TARGET disk.

When the disk copying process is completed, you will see a prompt that says "Copy another diskette (Y/N)?" You have many disks to copy, but pause a moment to properly label the new copy you have just made. Usually labels are provided with new disks, but if not, I've found that address labels work well as disk labels. If you are copying 3 1/2-inch disks, cut the address labels in half so they will fit on one side of the disk. Be sure that the label doesn't cover any of the holes or notches in the disk and that it is completely on the disk enclosure and clear of the disk itself.

With a felt-tip pen, write the name of the *CorelDRAW!* disk you copied on the label you have affixed to the copy.

1. Set both disks—the *CorelDRAW!* original and the copy you just made—aside.
2. Make copies of the rest of the disks, following the same steps outlined above. Make sure to label each of the copies and don't confuse the SOURCE disk with the TARGET disk.
3. When your *CorelDRAW!* disks are all made, you have an important task. You must find a completely safe place for the original disks.

If you use *CorelDRAW!* at work, you should keep the original disks at home. If you use *CorelDRAW!* at home, keep the original disks at work. If you work with a lot of expensive software, it wouldn't be out of the question to rent a safe deposit box at a bank for your disks. After all, if you paid $300—$400 for *CorelDRAW!*, $600—$700 for *Ventura Publisher*, a couple of thousand dollars for *AutoCAD*, and have about one thousand dollars tied up in word processors, that's a significant investment in what amounts to a small pile of very fragile sheets of mylar.

Don't keep both sets of disks at the same location because disasters have a way of befalling whole buildings. On the other hand, if your business office burns to the ground or falls victim to a horde of wilding teenagers, it's unlikely that the same fate will happen to your house or bank, unless it's right next door.

Put the original disks away and install *CorelDRAW!* with the copies of the disks. That way you will save wear and tear on the original disks.

Copying the Disks onto Backups

CHECK YOURSELF

1. What's the point in making backups?
2. Why not use lower capacity disks formatted at a high capacity and save some money?

ANSWERS

1. To protect your investment in time and money.
2. Lower capacity disks are not reliable when formatted as high capacity disks. You might lose information from the disks without even knowing it.

Registering

You must register your software. This has a benefit both for you and for Corel Systems. Be sure to fill out the registration form completely, affix a stamp (remember that it is going to Canada, so it will require more than standard first-class postage).

The benefit to you is that you will be able to upgrade at low cost and (as perfect as *CorelDRAW!* is) there may be minor upgrades and bug fixes between now and the next major version release. Generally, these improvements are provided at no cost to the user. Registration also makes you eligible to enter the design contest Corel is holding. If you are particularly talented, you stand to win thousands of dollars worth of prizes.

The benefit to Corel Systems is that it can keep track of its software. When a Justice Department investigation uncovers a pirate selling illegal copies of a product, Corel can trace the serial number of the copies back to the registered owner and possibly locate the person who committed the first copyright infringement and prosecute him or her. Copyright infringement is serious business. Don't get involved in the trafficking of illegal copies. A copy thoughtlessly passed to a coworker may be the beginning of a chain of events that can result in a stiff fine or even a prison sentence.

TIP

In years past, software piracy was dealt with relatively lightly. But lately there have been heavy fines levied. A construction firm in Chicago had to pay a fine in the hundreds of thousands of dollars for illegally copying and using software.

Safeguarding Work

If it's important to safeguard your original disks, it's vital to protect your work files. After all, if you lose all your *CorelDRAW!* disks, you can request a replacement from Corel Systems. Additionally, if they refuse to replace them, you could go out and buy a new copy of *CorelDRAW!*. But where will you find new copies or replacements for the art you will painstakingly create with *CorelDRAW!*?

Because hard disks transfer information so much faster than floppies, most people keep their work files on their hard disks. This is a dangerous practice because hard disks are as prone to destruction as any other PC peripheral. An earthquake or a hyperactive cat could jar an operating computer, causing a head crash—causing the read/write head to come into contact with the disk surface, planing off layers of the magnetic material that holds your information (word processor documents, databases, and graphics) in the form of magnetic code.

You could turn off your computer, suffer a power failure, or brown-out while your computer is writing a vital file called the File Allocation Table, resulting in a bad byte of information that literally renders your hard disk unreadable. When mishaps occur you have few options. A head crash may mean you need a new disk or that you will need to do a surface analysis with *Spinrite* or *PC Tools Deluxe* to set aside the damaged sectors on the disk—sectors that may contain important parts of other files, meaning that you may wipe out whole subdirectories full of files when you repair the damage. A scrambled disk resulting from a power failure will require that you reformat the disk, thus losing all data on the disk. Hard disk controller cards can fail too. Your hard disk, in short, is a catastrophe waiting to happen, a sword of Damocles waiting to fall.

As you can see, failure to back up the files you create is bravery of the worst kind. The hour or two a week it would cost to maintain a complete backup of your hard disk balances against weeks or months of lost work if you lose the disk to one hazard or another.

If you aren't interested in purchasing *PC Tools Deluxe* to back up your hard disk at regular intervals, you can at least keep copies of all your work on floppy disks.

The best solution by far is to simply do your work on removable disks. You've seen how easy it is to back up floppies with the DISKCOPY command. Simply keep copies of all your files on two or more sets of floppy disks and remember to keep the one set apart from the other, as you did with the original *CorelDRAW!* disks.

Remember: Don't trust your hard drive any farther than you can throw it. And never throw your hard drive.

Safeguarding Work

CHECK YOURSELF

1. Why shouldn't you make dozens of copies of *CorelDRAW!* and distribute it to your friends?

2. Why is your personal artwork even more valuable than the *CorelDRAW!* disks?

ANSWERS

1. *CorelDRAW!*, like most commercial quality software, is protected by international copyrights. You could incur a fine or other penalty if you are convicted of violating the Copyright Act.

2. Because your artwork can only be replaced through hard work on your part, while *CorelDRAW!* can be purchased anywhere.

Setting Up *CorelDRAW!*

Before you can install *CorelDRAW!*, you must have *Windows* installed properly on your machine. This means that you must have the equipment necessary to run *Windows*—an AT-compatible or 80386-based PC with a hard disk, 640K or more of RAM, a graphics adapter capable of high resolution graphics (Hercules, EGA, VGA, or compatible; CGA is not supported). You will also need to have a mouse and you will want a printer, though a printer isn't necessary for *Windows* or *CorelDRAW!* operation.

Installation of *CorelDRAW!* is almost completely automatic.

1. Start up Windows by typing WIN and pressing Enter at the DOS prompt.
2. Open the Main program group by double clicking on the icon with "Main" written under it.
3. Insert the first installation disk in the floppy disk drive.
4. Double click on the File Manager icon to start the File Manager.
5. When the File Manager starts, you will see a window with an icon at its top representing each of your disk drives. Double click on the drive you will be installing from.
6. A new window will open with a little picture of a file folder in it. Double click on this folder to see what files are on the disk in that drive.
7. One of the files on the disk should be INSTALL.EXE (if that file isn't in the window, you probably inserted the wrong disk in step 2). Double click on the text INSTALL.EXE to start the installation program.
8. You will see a screen containing a box informing you that you are in the *CorelDRAW!* installation program. Click on the button marked Continue. *CorelDRAW!* does almost everything else for itself. The files are archived, which means that they have been severely compressed so huge files can be stored on very little disk space.
9. You will be asked where you would like *CorelDRAW!* to be installed. The default is C:\WINDOWS\CORELDRW. If that is where you want *CorelDRAW!* installed, press Enter. If you want

it installed elsewhere, enter the complete path to where you want it installed, including the disk designation. If you elect to place *CorelDRAW!* some other place than C:\WINDOWS\ CORELDRW, the next installation screen will request confirmation of the location

10. You will be asked from what drive you will be installing the program. The default is your A: drive. If that's the drive, just press Enter. Otherwise, type the designation of the drive you put the disk in when you followed step 2. Make sure the drive designation is followed by a colon. Click on the button marked Continue.

Setting Up CorelDRAW!

At this point the installation program begins unarchiving files and placing them on your hard drive.

More informative than most installation programs, *CorelDRAW!'s* installation will tell you what files are being unarchived.

Don't abandon your computer at this point. Eventually, you will be prompted to replace the first disk with the next. Computers can do a lot of things automatically, but no one has yet successfully marketed an automatic system for changing floppy disks.

Continue changing disks when prompted until you see the prompt that says, "Install the symbols library and/or samples files?" The symbol library takes up 1Mb with useful all-purpose graphics. The sample files take up 2Mb with files that illustrate the power of *CorelDRAW!*. Install both by clicking on the appropriate buttons. Follow the screen prompts for disk changes.

When the symbol library and sample files have been installed, the installation process is complete. The installation program does more than simply place files on the disk. It also creates a program group in *Windows* all set up with the four main *CorelDRAW!* programs: *CorelDRAW!*, Mosaic, CorelTRACE, and WFNBOSS. But you'll read more about that in the next section.

The remainder of the disks contain clip art that will probably be useful to you, but it wouldn't pay to place these files on your hard disk. You will occasionally need a piece of clip art, but you will probably only use it once. It's more efficient to leave the clip art on floppies against your occasional call for using it. This issue will be covered in Chapter 4.

The Basics of *Windows* Operation

A little bit about *Windows* operation has been covered in the introduction. If you are familiar with earlier versions of *Windows*, *Windows* 3.0 is a completely different animal. First, *Windows 286* and *386* and *Windows* version 2.x were much more text-oriented. This text orientation is still available within *Windows*, hidden away in the clunky and poorly designed File Manager, available in the Main program group (avoid using this part of *Windows* 3.0 if you can). Fortunately, *Windows* 3.1 will contain a much more modern file management system.

There is a good chance that at least a few people have bought *Windows* specifically to run *CorelDRAW!*, or are coming to the PC for the first time. Therefore, although the true resource for your *Windows* questions should be the *Windows* manual, a few important matters will be discussed here.

To start up *Windows*, enter WIN and press Enter.

In Figure 1.1 you can see the Program Manager window in *Windows*. This is the starting point. Note the icons along the bottom of this window: Main, Corel Applications, Games, and so on.

▼ *Figure 1.1. The Program Manager screen*

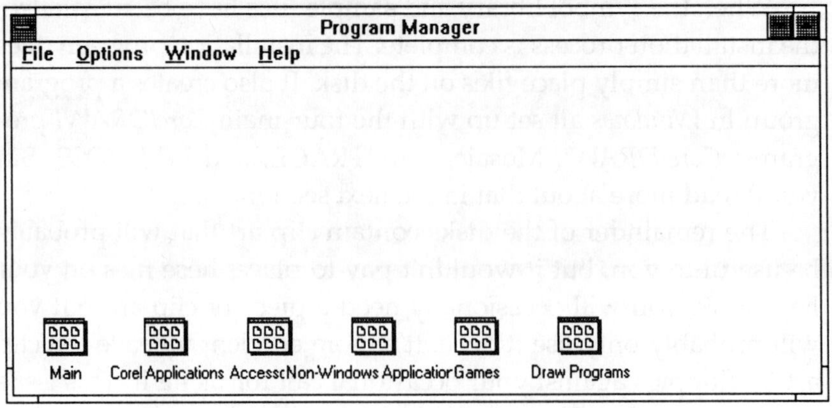

Each of the icons stands for a program group. It's wise to keep your related applications in the same program group. It's possible to create a new program group at any time by pulling down the File menu and selecting New, then Program Group. Fortunately, it isn't necessary to create a new program group. The *CorelDRAW!* installation program takes responsibility for creating its own program group.

Therefore, to keep this explanation as simple as possible, let's open the Corel Applications program group icon. Double-click on the Corel Applications icon. You will see the Corel Applications program group.

Because the size of windows can be changed, the Corel Applications program group on your screen—in fact any window displayed in the figures throughout this book—may be of a different size or in a different position.

Note that all the major *CorelDRAW!* applications are accounted for: *CorelDRAW!*, Mosaic, Corel Trace, and WFNBOSS. The latter three will be discussed in later chapters, but this chapter is specifically concerned with *CorelDRAW!*.

The Basics of Windows Operation

PRACTICE WHAT YOU'VE LEARNED

What You Should Do

1. Drag the icons of the programs in the Corel Applications program group so they are all mixed up in the window. Pull down the Window menu and select Arrange Icons.

2. Double click on the *CorelDRAW!* icon.

How the Computer Responds

1. The icons shift into an orderly pattern in the program group.

2. *CorelDRAW!* starts up.

Starting and Exiting *CorelDRAW!*

Explore *Windows* further by starting up the main application: *CorelDRAW!*. Double click on the first icon on the far left.

The *CorelDRAW!* program will start. For a moment, you will see an introductory screen containing a hot-air balloon and the *CorelDRAW!* logo. Then you will see the *CorelDRAW!* screen shown in Figure 1.2.

▼ **Figure 1.2. The CorelDRAW!** *screen*

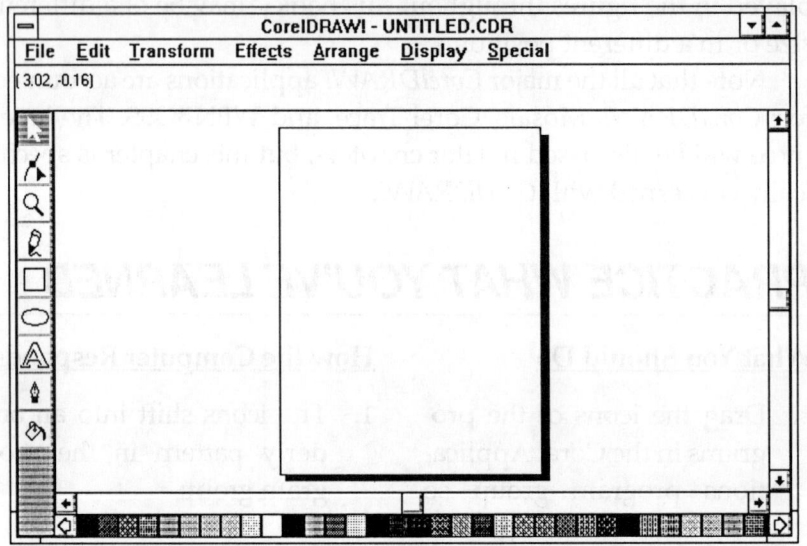

Figure 1.3 shows the same screen with the various items on the screen named. If you become confused when told to click on a given item, or drag a particular item, you can refer to Figure 1.3 and see what the text is talking about.

If you have any familiarity with *CorelDRAW!* 1.2 or earlier versions, you will note that there is a new menu on the menu bar: Effects. This menu contains a number of new and exciting features. The palette along the bottom of the screen is also new. Formerly, you would have had to call up the pen or fill menu from the toolbox

Preparing to Use *CoreIDRAW!* ▲ 31

▼ *Figure 1.3. The* CoreIDRAW! *screen explained*

Diagram labels: Close Button/System Menu, Title Bar/Move Bar, Maximize/Minimize Button, Maximize/Restore Button, Menu Bar, Status Line, Toolbox, Horizontal Scroll Bar, Palette, Page Area, Vertical Scroll Bar, CoreIDRAW! Window

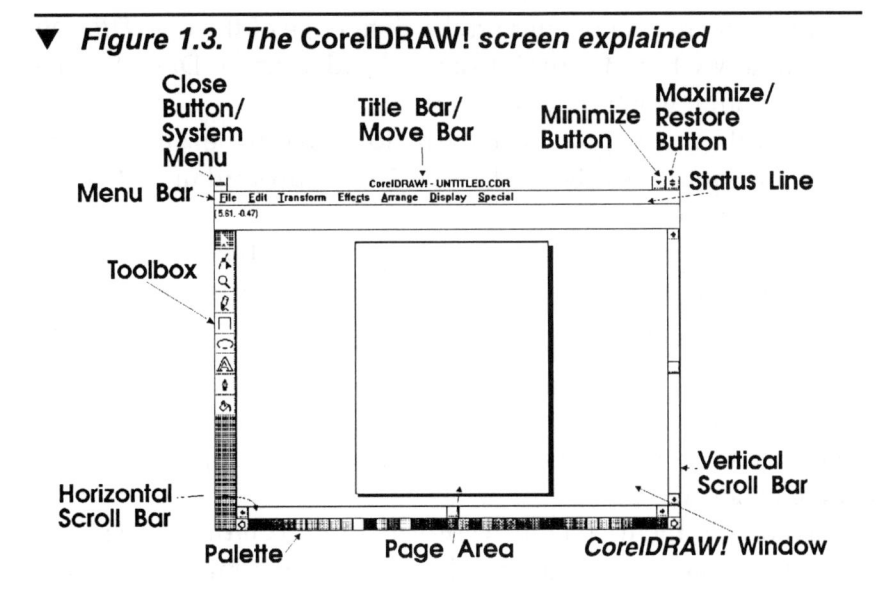

Starting and Exiting CoreIDRAW!

to effect a color change. As you can see, in its latest version *CorelDRAW!* has become both more innovative and more friendly.

There are two items that are of particular interest if you are not very familiar with *Windows*. The first item is the scroll bars along the bottom and right-hand side of the screen. The scroll bars allow you to move through a zoomed (magnified) screen easily. To move incrementally, click on the arrow in the direction you want to move. To move an entire screen in a given direction, click on the slide bar between the *thumb* (the small box on the scroll bar, also known as the scroll box or elevator) and the arrow pointing in the direction you want to move. To move proportionally through the graphic, drag the thumb. Dragging it halfway along the scroll bar will take you about halfway through a graphic.

The second item is the Minimize and Maximize/Restore button. In *Windows*, any window, including the *CorelDRAW!* window, can be one of three sizes: minimized (a very tiny icon), maximized (filling the whole screen), or in an intermediate size called its *restore size*. A restore screen can be sized (it can be made even larger than a maximized screen—or a tiny rectangle) and moved by dragging its title bar/move bar.

1. Click on the maximize/restore button.

2. Place the mouse pointer on the right edge of the *CorelDRAW!* window where it turns into a two-headed arrow. Drag it to the left until it won't move any farther.
3. Place the mouse pointer on the bottom edge of the screen where it turns into a two-headed arrow. Drag it upward until it won't move any farther.
4. You should be able to see a fragment of the window that contains the word "CorelD." Place your mouse pointer on it and drag it. You should be able to move it around the screen at will.

When *CorelDRAW!* is in its restore size, the toolbox always remains visible. No matter how tiny the window becomes, the toolbox always retains its position relative to the upper left corner of the window.

Naturally, there isn't much you can do with *CorelDRAW!* in this state other than move it around the screen. To minimize the screen, click on the minimize button.

1. To return the window to its restore size, double click on the icon of the minimized window (these gravitate to the lower left corner of the screen).
2. Drag the edges of the *CorelDRAW!* window to make it nearly fill the screen. Now click on the maximize/restore button. The window will expand to fill the screen.

Now take a look at the system menu. To get to the system menu, you can either click on the close button/system menu or press Alt-spacebar. The system menu is shown in Figure 1.4.

▼ *Figure 1.4. The system menu*

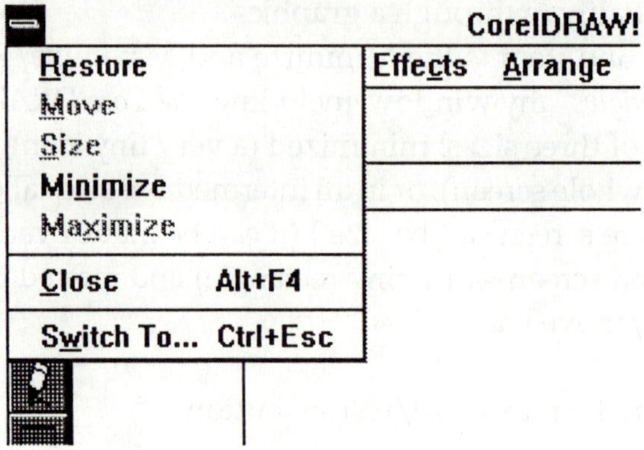

Starting and Exiting CorelDRAW!

Note that you can select options on this menu to restore, move, size, minimize, or close the window. You can also use Switch To... on this menu to switch to another *Windows* program. To get to this menu from a minimized window, click once on the window's icon. You can also shut down a program by pressing Alt-F4 (note in Figure 1.4, this key combination is on the same line as the Close option, to the right).

Finally, closing the window is discussed. Closing the window isn't the same as minimizing it. When you minimize a program, it continues to run. It's available on the Switch To... dialog box (*CorelDRAW!* may appear dormant when it is minimized, but technically, it's still running).

You can quit an application one of three ways. You can double click on the close button, you can click on the close button and select Close (either by clicking on Close or by pressing the C key on the keyboard), or you can pull down the File menu and select Exit.

TIP

Never quit a *Windows* application by shutting off the computer or rebooting. It's simple enough to quit a program, as you have seen. All *Windows* applications have a File menu and an Exit option on that menu. You can quit any program by pressing Alt-F, and then X or by double clicking on the close box. *Windows* reads and writes your hard disk frequently and if you turn off the power or reboot at an inopportune moment, you could trash your hard disk. You might think you know when your computer is accessing your hard disk because the drive light comes on, but sometimes the disk accesses are so brief and rapid that the LED indicating disk access doesn't have a chance to light up completely. On the other hand, sometimes *Windows* will quit *you*. If *Windows* freezes and no amount of mouse clicking or key pressing will get it to respond, your only recourse is to reboot with Ctrl-Alt-Del or the reset switch, or by turning your computer off and then on. If you see a dialog box stating that you have experienced a UAE (Unrecoverable Application Error), don't panic. *Windows* is smart enough to preserve your disk. Click on the OK button and it will close the offending program. Any changes in the open file since the last time you saved it will be lost but the file itself will remain intact.

Since you will need to understand how to use menus in *CorelDRAW!*, let's use the last option to quit the program.

1. Place your mouse pointer on the word File in the menu bar and click or press Alt-F. You will see the menu shown in Figure 1.5.

▼ **Figure 1.5. The File menu**

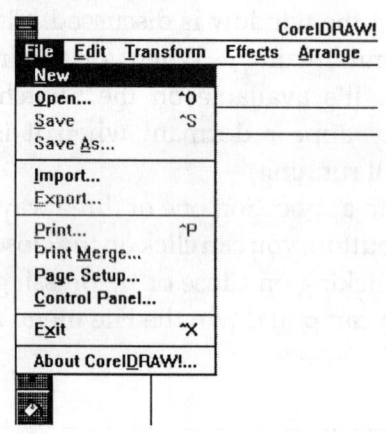

```
                              CorelDRAW!
File  Edit  Transform  Effects  Arrange
New
Open...            ^O
Save               ^S
Save As...

Import...
Export...

Print...           ^P
Print Merge...
Page Setup...
Control Panel...

Exit               ^X

About CorelDRAW!...
```

Most *Windows* applications have a File menu that is very similar to this one. Note that *CorelDRAW!* offers yet another way to exit the program. On the Exit option, at the right, you can see ^X. This means that if you type Ctrl-X at any time while *CorelDRAW!* is running, you will exit the program. Whenever you see a key combination in the right side of a menu, that is a hotkey option—an option that you can access directly from the keyboard without selecting the menu. In the appendices of this book, you will find an exhaustive list of hotkeys.

2. In order to exit the program, click on the word Exit, or type X on the keyboard.

The window will close and the application will quit running. If you have created or changed a graphic while *CorelDRAW!* was running and you have failed to save the sketch, *CorelDRAW!* will pause in its shut-down operation and ask whether you want to save the graphic. If so, simply click on the Yes button or press Enter (because the Yes button is highlighted in this dialog box, pressing

Enter will select it). Click on No to exit without saving the graphic. There is also a cancel button in this dialog box. If you don't want to exit, click on the cancel button to return the application to the screen.

Starting and Exiting CorelDRAW!

If the graphic was named, it will automatically be saved under its current filename. If it was unnamed, you will be shown the *CorelDRAW!* Save As... dialog box. Using this box, you can specify the filename and the location of the saved file.

CHECK YOURSELF

1. Load or save a drawing. Which menu did you use?
2. Draw something on the screen and select Exit from the File menu.

ANSWERS
1. The File menu.
2. *CorelDRAW!* prompts you to save your work.

The Elements on the *CorelDRAW!* Screen

There are several other items on the *CorelDRAW!* screen that haven't been discussed yet. You might want to refer back to Figure 1.3 during this discussion.

Toolbox

Like most graphics programs, *CorelDRAW!* offers the toolbox as a simple way to access the most commonly used tools. This is the part of the screen you will use most often. It contains the tools you will use for selecting objects, drawing lines and curves, magnifying sections of the screen, and performing other day-to-day tasks with your *CorelDRAW!* graphic.

The Pick Tool

The pick tool has three main purposes: selecting, moving, and editing objects. When you want to select an object, you have two options. You can click on the wire frame—the lines of the object on the page area—or you can drag a rectangle on the screen. To test these two operations, you need to have something on the *CorelDRAW!* screen, so skip ahead briefly to the rectangle tool.

1. Locate the rectangle tool on the toolbox (fifth from the top, appropriately enough, it's shaped like a rectangle; it's between the pencil tool and the ellipse tool). Click on the rectangle tool.
2. Place the mouse pointer somewhere in the upper left quarter of the page area.
3. Press the left mouse button and drag the mouse pointer to the lower right quadrant of the page area. Release the mouse button. A rectangle will be drawn there.

The rectangle is called a wire frame because no matter what color you make the rectangle or how thick you make its lines, it will still look like a thin wire outline of a rectangle. To see what the real rectangle will look like, you will need to display the preview screen. *CorelDRAW!* saves an enormous amount of time redrawing images on the screen by using only the wire frame in the page area.

Note that the rectangle is selected as soon as it is drawn. You can recognize a selected item because its *nodes* are visible. A node is a tiny rectangle that appears at the corners of polygons and along the curves of curved objects. Nodes can be used to adjust the shape of an object (this subject will be covered shortly).

1. Click on the pick tool. Note that eight *handles* (tiny black squares used to control the size and shape of the rectangle) appear all around the rectangle.

2. Deselect the rectangle by clicking in the *CorelDRAW!* window away from the rectangle. Note that the nodes and handles disappear.
3. Move the mouse pointer so its point is on the very edge of the rectangle. Click on the outline of the rectangle. The nodes and handles should reappear. If they don't, you probably didn't quite have the point of the mouse pointer directly on the wire frame. Go through the steps again until you are comfortable selecting an object by clicking on its wire frame.

The other method of selecting an object is to drag a selection rectangle around it. This method is less discriminating than clicking on the wire frame because you can select more than one object by dragging a selection rectangle. Any object that is completely enclosed by the selection rectangle will be selected. To prove this, draw an additional rectangle on the screen completely inside the first rectangle.

1. Locate the rectangle tool on the toolbox. Click on it.
2. Place the mouse pointer somewhere in the upper left quarter of the first rectangle.
3. Press the left mouse button and drag the mouse pointer to the lower right quadrant of the first rectangle. Release the mouse button. A rectangle will be drawn.
4. Click on the pick tool.
5. Deselect the rectangle by clicking in the *CorelDRAW!* window away from the rectangle. Note that the nodes and handles disappear.
6. Move the mouse pointer so its point is above and to the left of the first rectangle. Press the left mouse button and drag the mouse pointer until it is below and to the right of the first rectangle. When you release the mouse button, the handles should reappear around the large rectangle. If they appeared around the smaller rectangle, you probably didn't entirely enclose the larger rectangle in your *selection rectangle*. Go through the steps again until you are comfortable selecting objects by enclosing them in a selection rectangle.

The Elements on the CorelDRAW! Screen

You should now have handles all the way around the larger rectangle. So how do you know that both rectangles are selected? Note that each rectangle has a single node visible. This indicates that each is selected. But if you're still not sure, use the pick tool for sizing to show how having both rectangles selected gives you the power to affect both at the same time.

1. With both rectangles selected, place the mouse pointer on the lower left handle. Note that when the mouse pointer is on a handle, it turns into a cross. This makes it easier to tell when your mouse pointer is in contact with a handle.
2. Press the mouse button and drag this handle up and to the right.

When you release the mouse button, you will discover that both rectangles have been made proportionately smaller. The corner handles always maintain the proportionality of the shape. This is called *scaling*. For example, if you have a rectangle that is four inches long by two inches wide and you drag a corner handle so that the rectangle is two inches long, you are assured that the width is now one inch.

What if you want to adjust only the length or only the width of a rectangle? That's what the handles in the middles of the sides are for.

1. Place the mouse pointer on the handle in the middle of the right side of the rectangle.
2. Press the mouse button and drag this handle to the right. When you release the mouse button, you will discover that both selected rectangles are proportionately wider, but their heights have not changed. This is called *stretching*.

If you want to select certain objects within an area, but not all objects, you can do this by holding down the Shift key and clicking on the wire frames of objects you want to move or size. If you accidentally click on something you want to leave alone, click on that object again with the Shift key down. That will deselect the object.

Finally, the pick tool can be used to rotate objects.

1. Double click on the wire frame of an object and the handles will become tiny, two-ended arrows. Place your mouse pointer on one of the corner arrows. The mouse pointer will turn into a cross when you are in the right position.
2. Drag the corner arrow to rotate the object.

The Elements on the CorelDRAW! Screen

Note that there is a dot with a circle around it at the center of the object. This is the axis of rotation. You can drag it to any position in the *CorelDRAW!* window and then rotate the object around it.

Skewing an object turns its selection rectangle into a parallelogram. It makes an object look as if it is being buffeted by a severe wind or is on a plane at a different angle from the plane of the screen. It's easier to see this effect than to explain it.

1. To skew an object, select it, then click on it again to change its handles to rotate and skew handles.
2. Place your mouse pointer on one of the double-headed arrows located at the middle of one of the sides. The mouse pointer will turn into a cross when you are in the right position.
3. Drag the arrow and that side of the selection rectangle will follow your mouse movements while the opposite side remains fixed.

The pick tool has additional uses, which will be covered thoroughly in Chapter 2; but briefly, if you grab a handle on the right side and move it to the left of the left side of the selected object, you can flip the object horizontally.

Although it would be pointless to ascribe higher or lower values to the tools in the toolbox, the pick tool is certainly one of the most essential tools, and the one you will probably find yourself using most often. If you are the least bit unsure of its use, go through the exercises again until you are completely confident of your mastery of the pick tool.

PRACTICE WHAT YOU'VE LEARNED

What You Should Do	How the Computer Responds
1. Use the pick tool to select, move, size, and skew an object.	1. These actions are accomplished by clicking on the object for the first time (selecting), placing the mouse pointer on the outline of the object and dragging (moving), dragging a corner or side handle of the object (sizing), and clicking a second time, then dragging a side handle (skewing).
2. Create an object on your screen and click away from it so it isn't selected. Now click on the object's outline twice.	2. The rotate and skew handles appear. You can now rotate or skew the object. Note the arrows around its perimeter; these are the rotate and skew handles.

The Shape Tool

Sometimes you want to make more complex changes in a shape than simply changing its width or length or making it proportionately larger or smaller. The shape tool is intended for this. Although the shape tool won't be covered in depth here, you'll find a thorough discussion of it in Chapter 2.

The Zoom Tool

You will want to work on graphics in detail sometimes, and it can be difficult to see individual lines in complex drawings. The zoom tool will be very important in this work. To see what the zoom tool is capable of, select it. But first, there must be something on the screen to examine in detail. If there is anything on your page area, get rid of it. Click on the word File on the menu bar and then click on New. When *CorelDRAW!* pauses to ask whether you want to save the drawing to disk, click on the button marked No.

Now you must draw a squiggle on the page area.

1. Click on the pencil icon (the fourth icon from the top). Your mouse pointer will become a cross.
2. Place the mouse pointer on the page area and press the mouse button. Drag the mouse pointer in a random movement, making a squiggle on the page area.
3. Release the mouse button. *CorelDRAW!* will pause for a moment and your squiggle will be converted into a form called *Bezier curves* and it will be sprinkled with nodes.

TIP

There are two other ways to use the pencil tool. You can click in one location and then click again in another to create a straight line, or you can draw in Bezier curves. To draw in Bezier mode, Select Preferences from the Special menu, click on the button marked "Lines & Curves," and near the bottom of the Lines & Curves dialog box select Bezier as your drawing mode. With this selected, you will create a node each time you click. This mode is particularly useful when you are tracing an object on a drawing tablet. To switch back, select Preferences from the Special menu and click on Lines & Curves again. Then select Freehand as your drawing mode.

If your squiggle is very complex, it may be difficult to see various parts of it clearly. Use the zoom tool to see the squiggle in detail. Click on the zoom tool (it looks like a magnifying glass). You will see the menu associated with the zoom tool (Figure 1.6).

The magnifying glass with the plus sign will actually magnify part of the page area.

The magnifying glass with the minus sign will make the page area smaller, less detailed.

The Elements on the CorelDRAW! Screen

▼ *Figure 1.6. The zoom tool menu and the squiggle*

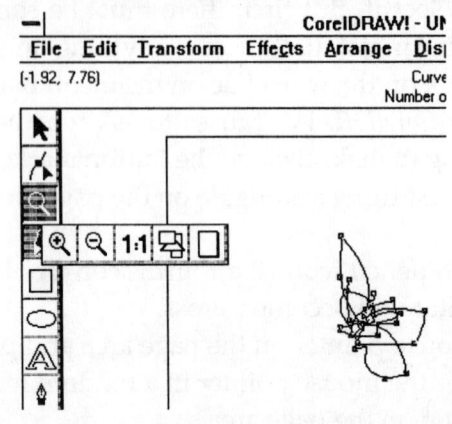

The section marked 1:1 will present the page area in approximately the size it will appear on the paper when it is printed.

The section with a group of shapes on it will expand whatever is drawn on the page area to fill the screen.

Finally, the section with a page drawn on it will cause the page area to appear as it has in all the figures up to now.

You will usually use the magnifying glass with the plus sign and the page tool, which returns the page to its normal (default) size. Now zoom in on the squiggle.

1. Click on the zoom tool. The zoom tool menu will appear.
2. Click on the magnifying glass with the plus sign. The mouse pointer will turn into a magnifying glass.
3. Place the magnifying glass at the upper left corner of the area to be magnified and drag it to the lower right corner of the area to be magnified. (This is the only tool in the zoom tool menu that uses a selection rectangle.)

When you release the mouse button, you will see the area within the selection rectangle expanded to fill the screen. How do you move around within the zoomed screen? Use the scroll bars at the bottom and right sides of the screen. This is called *panning*.

Now return to the normal screen.

1. Click on the zoom tool.

2. From the resulting menu, click on the item that represents a page. The page will return, as shown in Figure 1.5.

You probably noted that although you zoomed in on lines, the lines did not become thicker. They remained at their wire frame thickness. There is a limit to how close you can zoom, but you will undoubtedly find that the closest zoom is adequate for close work.

The Elements on the CorelDRAW! Screen

The Pencil Tool

You have already used the pencil tool. Basically, the pencil tool is capable of three different kinds of actions. It can create curves or straight lines or it can perform a powerful operation known as *autotrace*.

Draw a curve and a straight line. Autotrace has been left for Chapter 4 in the section on importing art.

1. To draw a curved line, click on the pencil tool. The mouse cursor will turn into a cross.
2. Place the cross on the page area.
3. Press the mouse button and drag the pointer in a curve. A line will follow your mouse pointer.

When you release the mouse button, the curve that you have drawn will be reworked by *CorelDRAW!* and turned into Bezier curves. You will note when this happens by the appearance of nodes along the line you have drawn.

Drawing a straight line is no trickier.

1. Click on the pencil tool. The mouse cursor will turn into a cross.
2. Place the cross on the page area.
3. While holding the mouse perfectly still, click the mouse button.
4. Move the mouse pointer to another location.
5. Click the mouse pointer again.

A straight line will appear linking the two places where you clicked.

The Rectangle Tool

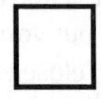

Most drawings are made up of normal geometric shapes like the square, rectangle, circle, or ellipse. This tool and the next provide simple ways to draw these objects. First you will learn how to draw a rectangle and then how to draw a square.

1. Click on the rectangle icon.
2. Move the mouse pointer to the page area. It will turn into a cross.
3. Place the pointer where the upper left corner of the rectangle should be.
4. Press the left mouse button.
5. Drag the mouse pointer down and to the right.
6. When the rectangle is roughly one inch by one inch, release the mouse button.

A rectangle will appear. This rectangle may be a square, but it's difficult to tell without printing it out and measuring it carefully. Sometimes that will be too much trouble. If you want to create a perfect square, you need a property called *constraint*. Constraint means that the shape is regularized, or more accurately, that it is prevented from deviating from the preferred shape.

1. Click on the rectangle icon.
2. Move the mouse pointer to the page area. It will turn into a cross.
3. Place the pointer where the upper left corner of the square should be.
4. Press the Control (Ctrl) key.
5. Press the left mouse button.
6. Drag the mouse pointer down and to the right.

7. When the square is about one inch by one inch, release the mouse button and the Ctrl key.

The Elements on the CorelDRAW! Screen

The resulting shape not only looks like a square; it *is* a square. You probably noticed that you didn't have to be careful when dragging the square. The shape remained a perfect square no matter where on the page you moved your mouse pointer.

There is a third action you can perform with the rectangle tool. Draw a rectangle while holding down the Shift key. Note that rather than drawing a rectangle from its corner, the place where you initially press the mouse button is the center of the rectangle. If you hold down the Shift and Ctrl keys, you can create a square from the center out. Try drawing a rectacgle and alternately pressing and releasing the Shift and Ctrl keys, alone or separately.

The Ellipse Tool

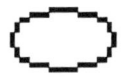

The other standard shape is the ellipse. As the name implies, you can create a rounded object of almost any width relative to its height using the ellipse tool. An ellipse can be constrained with the Ctrl key to form a circle.

1. Click on the ellipse tool.
2. Move the mouse pointer to the page area. The pointer turns into a cross.
3. Press the left mouse button.
4. Drag the mouse pointer down and to the right. An ellipse appears. You can create a very flat ellipse, even an ellipse that is indistinguishable from a line. But for the sake of this exercise, try to draw a circle.
5. When the ellipse looks roughly circular, release the mouse button.

Sometimes an almost perfect circle isn't good enough.

1. Click on the ellipse tool.

2. Move the mouse pointer to the page area. The pointer turns into a cross.
3. Hold down the Ctrl key.
4. Press the left mouse button.
5. Drag the mouse pointer down and to the right. A perfect circle appears. No matter how you move the mouse pointer, the ellipse that appears on the screen is a perfect circle.

There is a third action you can perform with the ellipse tool. Draw an ellipse while holding down the Shift key. Note that the place where you initially press the mouse button is the center of the ellipse. If you hold down the Shift and Ctrl keys, you can create a circle from the center out. This is very useful for drawing, for example, wheels around an axle or gears around a pinion shaft. Try drawing an ellipse and alternately pressing and releasing the Shift and Ctrl keys, alone or separately.

The Text Tool

Text is one of the most powerful parts of *CorelDRAW!*. So powerful, in fact, that it would be inappropriate to try to cover it here. It has its own chapter: Chapter 9.

PRACTICE WHAT YOU'VE LEARNED

What You Should Do

1. Click on the ellipse tool and hold down the Ctrl key. Drag the mouse pointer across the page area.

2. Create a perfect square and rotate it 45 degrees.

How the Computer Responds

1. You will create a perfect circle.

2. Click on the rectangle tool, hold down the Ctrl key and drag the mouse a short distance over the page area.

Click on the already-selected square and drag a corner rotate and skew handle until 45.0 degrees appears in the status line.

The Elements on the CorelDRAW! Screen

The Outline Tool

This tool is used to change the appearance of the outlines of objects. It's covered thoroughly in Chapter 7.

The Fill Tool

This tool is used to change the appearance of the interiors of objects. It's covered thoroughly in Chapter 7.

Palette

The palette can be seen along the bottom of the screen. In former versions of *CorelDRAW!*, you would have to access the fill tool menu in order to make use of the palette. Having the palette visible onscreen is a tremendous convenience. Note that, like the scroll bars, the palette has arrows at either end. Click on the arrow at the right end to scroll through the huge palette. The palette is actually about 2 1/2 times as wide as the screen. The arrow on the left end of the palette will scroll you back the other way.

Page Area

You've been using the page area in the earlier exercises in this chapter. It represents a page of paper. You can set up the page of paper to be tall or wide, or to be a different size than a standard sheet of typewriter paper by using the Page Setup on the File menu.

In Figure 1.7 the page is shown *wide* (or sideways to the normal orientation of typing paper, which would be called *tall*).

TIP

Although you can draw all the way to the edge of the page area, that doesn't mean that your printer will be able to print to the edge of the paper. Most laser printers must leave a border of about a quarter of an inch around the sheet. If part of the drawing impinges on this margin, it will be left out of the printout. There is an option in the Print dialog box (accessed by selecting Print on the File menu) called Fit to Page, which will shrink the image enough that it will all print on the page. If your drawing is actually smaller than the page area when this option is selected, the drawing will be expanded to fill the page.

CorelDRAW! Window

You may note that your drawings sometimes run off the edge of the page area. Having the page area smaller than the entire drawing area (which includes the whole *CorelDRAW!* window) allows you to ocasionally run off the edge and then size your drawing to fit on the page. At least one competing software package will crash if you draw too far off the edge of the screen. *CorelDRAW!* is much too friendly to do that.

Status Line

You may have noticed the status line while you were doing the exercises in this chapter. It is located directly beneath the menu bar and it is a fount of information (Figure 1.7).

Note the highlighted object—a rectangle. Also note that the word "Rectangle" appears at the center of the status line. The numbers that appear under the word tell you the size of the selected object (4.41 inches in width and 2.28 inches in height) and where its

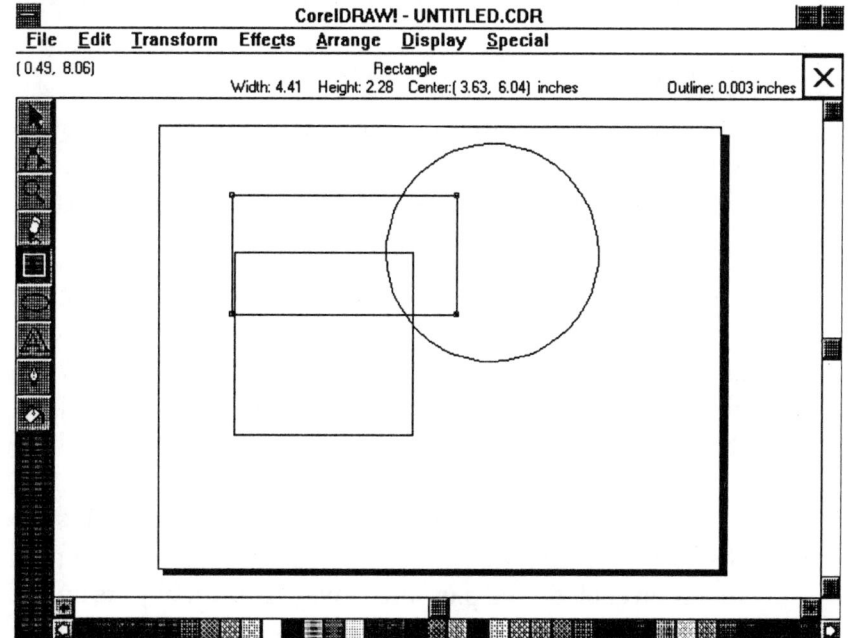

The Elements on the CorelDRAW! Screen

▼ **Figure 1.7. The status line**

can be found (at 3.63 inches from the left edge of the page and at 6.04 inches from the bottom of the page).

At the right edge of the status line is information about the outline (.003 inches thick) and the fill (none, as represented by the heavy X in the middle of the square at the extreme right of the status line).

At the left end of the status line is information about the location of the mouse pointer (.49 inches from the right edge of the screen and 8.06 inches from the bottom of the screen). The actual cursor is not shown onscreen because the capture software I am using cannot capture the cursor shape.

CHECK YOURSELF

1. Create a square with no fill. Look at the status line. How is it represented?

2. Change the default outline (the outline used when no outline is specified) to the thickest line available on the outline tool menu.

ANSWERS

1. At the right end of the status line you will see a rectangle with a large X in it, indicating no fill. At the center of the status line, you will see the word "Rectangle." Its width and height measurements will be identical.

2. Click on the pick tool, then click away from any object so that none is selected. Click on the outline tool and click on an outline thickness from the menu that appears. A dialog box will appear that allows you to specify to what objects the new default applies. Click on OK. That outline will be used in all objects you create from then on.

   Since this is a permanent change, you should reinstate the previous default before moving on. Click on the pick tool then click on the page area away from all objects on the screen to deselect all objects, then click on the outline menu and select the third item on the top row (the one with two arrows pointing toward each other). When the New Objects Outline Pen dialog box reappears, click on OK. The default is restored to its previous setting.

Title Bar

The title bar tells you the name of the graphic currently on the screen. If you haven't saved the drawing, the name will be UNTITLED.CDR. Use Save or Save As on the File menu to save your drawings.

Menu Bar

The menu bar offers a series of menus packed with commands. You have already seen the File menu in action.

Using Menus

To access a menu, place the mouse pointer on it and click. This will pull down the menu. When the menu is visible, place the mouse pointer on the item you want to use and click. The command will be issued.

The Elements on the CorelDRAW! Screen

Backing Out of a Decision with Cancel and Undo

Everyone makes mistakes, whether in *CorelDRAW!* or in life. The only difference is that just about any mistake you make in *CorelDRAW!* can be undone by selecting Undo from the Edit menu. There is a terrific advantage in this. Being able to undo an action takes a lot of the risk out of experimentation. Experimentation is the heart and soul of creativity. You need never fear doing the wrong thing if you save often and you have a powerful Undo option.

1. Draw a rectangle on the screen.
2. Click on the pick tool. Handles should appear around the rectangle. If they don't, click on the outline of the rectangle.
3. Drag one of the handles, changing the shape of the rectangle.
4. Pull down the Edit menu and select Undo. Note that the rectangle snaps back to its previous shape.

Did you ever hear this moldy joke? "I've only made one mistake. I thought I was wrong once, but I was mistaken." Sometimes you will discover that you really liked the change better after all. Will you have to painstakingly recreate the change you made to have it back after using the Undo command? No way. Simply select Redo from the Edit menu.

1. Draw a rectangle on the screen.
2. Click on the pick tool. Handles should appear around the rectangle. If they don't, click on the outline of the rectangle.
3. Drag one of the handles, changing the shape of the rectangle.

4. Pull down the Edit menu and select Undo. Note that the rectangle snaps back to its previous shape.
5. Pull down the Edit menu and select Redo (note that Undo is now gray and can't be selected). The rectangle will jump back to its previous shape.

By using these two commands, you can change the drawing back and forth between two states.

TIP

Using Undo *only* works on the last change to the drawing. If you make a mistake and then make any other change, selecting Undo won't help you. That's why it's important to save your work often, so that you will be able to return the drawing to a state before you made the mistake without losing too much work in the process.

You will often have need to use a command that calls up a dialog box. Almost all dialog boxes will have a Cancel button. For example, if you attempt to quit *CorelDRAW!* and you have made a change in your drawing that you haven't saved, *CorelDRAW!* will pause and show you a dialog box that gives you the option of saving the current graphic. It will say "UNTITLED.CDR (or whatever your graphic is named) Has Changed. Save Current Changes?" and it offers three buttons: Yes, which calls up the Save As dialog box; No, which shuts down *CorelDRAW!* without saving the graphic; and Cancel, which returns you to the program as if you had never selected Exit from the File menu. Always consider whether you want to cancel the action when you see the Cancel button. Someday it could save you a lot of work. Pressing the Escape (Esc) key automatically selects Cancel from the keyboard.

Exercises

You haven't see this feature of the book before. Exercises are intended to cement your knowledge of the topics covered in the chapter.

Preparing to Use CorelDRAW! ▲ 53

If *Windows* is currently running, shut it down. We're going to go from DOS to *CorelDRAW!* and back again. The exercise assumes that your computer is running in DOS, as if you had just started up the computer.

Exercises

What You Should Do	How the Computer Responds
1. Type WIN and press Enter.	1. Your computer should churn for a few seconds and the program manager should appear on the screen.
2. Pull down the Window menu and select Corel Applications.	2. The Corel Applications program group should open up and become foremost of the windows on your screen.
3. Double click on the *CorelDRAW!* icon. It is the icon with a hot-air balloon all by itself.	3. Once again your computer will churn for a few seconds while the *CorelDRAW!* screen is constructed.
4. Click on the fourth tool from the bottom of the toolbox, the ellipse tool. Place the mouse pointer in the page area and drag diagonally down the screen. Then release the mouse button.	4. An ellipse will appear on the screen.
5. Place your mouse pointer on the edge of the ellipse and drag the mouse to a new position.	5. The circle will follow your mouse movement.
6. Drag to the left the tiny black rectangle in the middle of the left side of the selection rectangle.	6. The ellipse will become wider.

7. Click again on the ellipse.	7. The handles will change to little arrows.
8. Press Alt-F4 to shut down *CorelDRAW!*.	8. A dialog box will appear stating "UNTITLED.CDR Has Changed. Save Current Changes?" and you will see buttons marked Yes, No, and Cancel.
9. Click on No.	9. You will return to the Program Manager screen in Windows. *CorelDRAW!* is shut down.
10. Press Alt-F4 again.	10. You will see a dialog box warning you "This will end your Windows session" and providing an OK and a Cancel button. The OK button is highlighted, meaning that it will be selected if you press Enter.
11. Press Enter.	11. You will return to DOS.

2 Editing the Drawing

- ▲ Creating a Drawing
- ▲ Saving a Drawing
- ▲ Getting Rid of a Drawing
- ▲ Loading a Drawing
- ▲ Editing an Object
- ▲ Drawing
- ▲ Open and Closed Objects
- ▲ Solid Fills
- ▲ Editing Nodes
- ▲ Cutting and Pasting
- ▲ Using Text

In this chapter you will spend some time with *CorelDRAW!* actually interacting with it, creating a drawing, saving it, loading it, and so on. This is really a watershed chapter. The rest of the book won't make much sense unless you have already worked through the exercises in this chapter. Therefore, it would be a good idea to take some time familiarizing yourself with the procedures discussed here.

Creating a Drawing

You won't tackle anything earth-shattering in this section. Later, you'll create interesting and attractive drawings, but for now all you really need is something on the page area of the screen.

Start up *CorelDRAW!*. If you are at the DOS command line, you will first have to start *Windows*. If *Windows* is already running, skip to step 2. If *CorelDRAW!* is already running, skip this entire sequence.

1. Type WIN and press Enter.
2. When the Program Manager window opens, there should be an icon or window visible called Corel Applications. If it is an icon, double click on it to open the window.
3. Identify the *CorelDRAW!* icon (it's a hot air balloon with "CorelDRAW!" written underneath it).
4. Double click on the *CorelDRAW!* icon.

When *CorelDRAW!* is finished loading, and before you draw anything in the page area, pull down the File menu. Note that some of the options are in black (New, Open, Import, Page Setup, Control Panel, Exit, and About *CorelDRAW!*). Other objects are "grayed" and unavailable to you (these include Save, Save As, Export, Print, and Print Merge). *CorelDRAW!* prevents you from saving a drawing until you have created something. Likewise, it would be pretty pointless to print a blank screen (though you can in some applications). That's why you have to create something before going on to the next section: "Saving a Drawing."

1. Click on the text tool in the toolbox (it looks like a capital A).

2. Click on the page area somewhere in the upper left quarter.

The Text dialog box opens up, as shown in Figure 2.1.

Creating a Drawing

▼ **Figure 2.1. The Text dialog box**

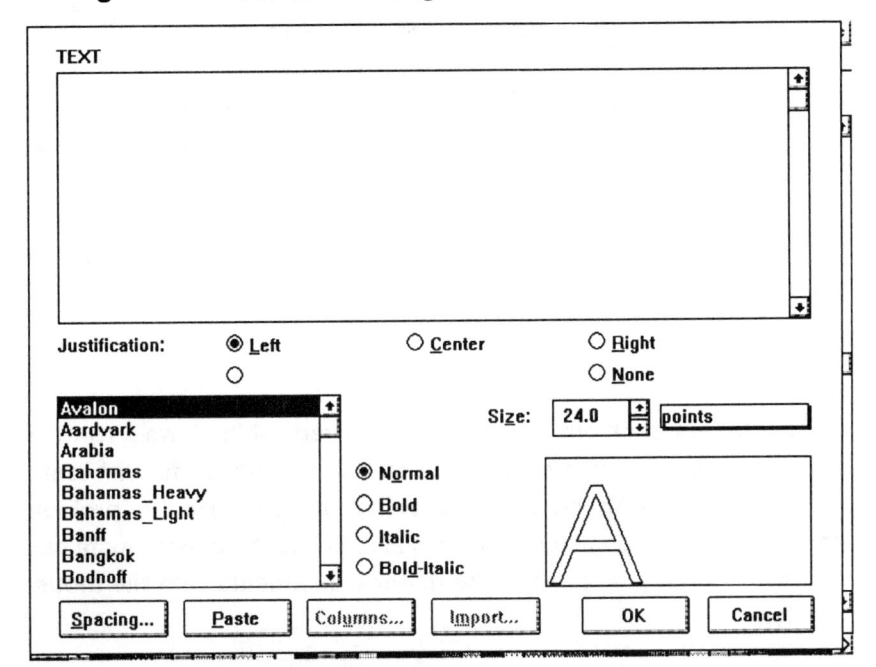

[Figure: The Text dialog box showing a text entry area at top; Justification options (Left, Center, Right, None); a font list box containing Avalon, Aardvark, Arabia, Bahamas, Bahamas_Heavy, Bahamas_Light, Banff, Bangkok, Bodnoff; Size: 24.0 points; style options Normal, Bold, Italic, Bold-Italic; a preview showing the letter A; and buttons Spacing..., Paste, Columns..., Import..., OK, Cancel.]

This is an interesting dialog box. Text will be covered in greater depth at the end of this chapter and again in Chapter 9.

1. Type in a name, a phrase, a nonsense word—anything you like. Note that the text appears in the text box at the top of the page.
2. Click on a name in the list box at the lower left of the screen (I recommend Arabia).

These are the names of fonts. Note how the letters in the box at the lower right of the screen change to show the first two letters that you typed in above the font you select in the list box. Other things you can select in this box are justification, size, and style (normal, bold, and so on). Buttons along the bottom of the box provide access to other dialog boxes that let you specify spacing and columns or allow you to paste or import text. You will cover these later.

3. Once you have the text typed in and your style and justification selected, click on the button marked OK.

When you return to the page area, your text will be displayed. It's in 24-point type, which is about 1/3 of an inch high—pretty tall for text, but not easy to see on the screen. Now make it really big.

1. Click on the pick tool. Handles will appear around the text.
2. Place the mouse pointer on one of the corner handles and drag until the text is as wide as the page.

Note that in the status line you can see the font name and the point size.

TIP

Although this problem has never occurred while I was running *CorelDRAW!*, some users state that stretching text too far can result in Unrecoverable Application Errors. If you experience this problem and you need to use text in a large size, specify the approximate size in the Text dialog box and make minor adjustments with the mouse pointer.

Now you will add one more enhancement to the drawing: Draw a rectangle around it.

1. Click on the rectangle tool.
2. Place the mouse pointer above and to the left of the text.
3. Press the left mouse button and drag the mouse down and to the right.
4. When the resulting rectangle completely encloses the text, release the mouse button. This process is called *dragging a selection rectangle*.

Unless you have a far steadier hand than mine, you probably drew a rectangle that was a little off-center. Even if it looks well centered, the screen is so much smaller than the paper we will eventually print that you can easily be fooled by appearances. Some people print out page after page, adjusting elements a little bit at a time until they are perfect. You can save paper, however, by using the Align command on the Arrange menu.

Creating a Drawing

1. Drag a selection rectangle to select the text and the rectangle: Click on the pick tool and place the mouse pointer above and to the left of the rectangle. Press the left mouse button and drag the pointer to a position beneath and to the right of the rectangle. When you release the mouse button, both items will be selected. The status line should say "2 objects selected."
2. Pull down the Arrange menu.
3. Select Align.

You will see the dialog box shown in Figure 2.2.

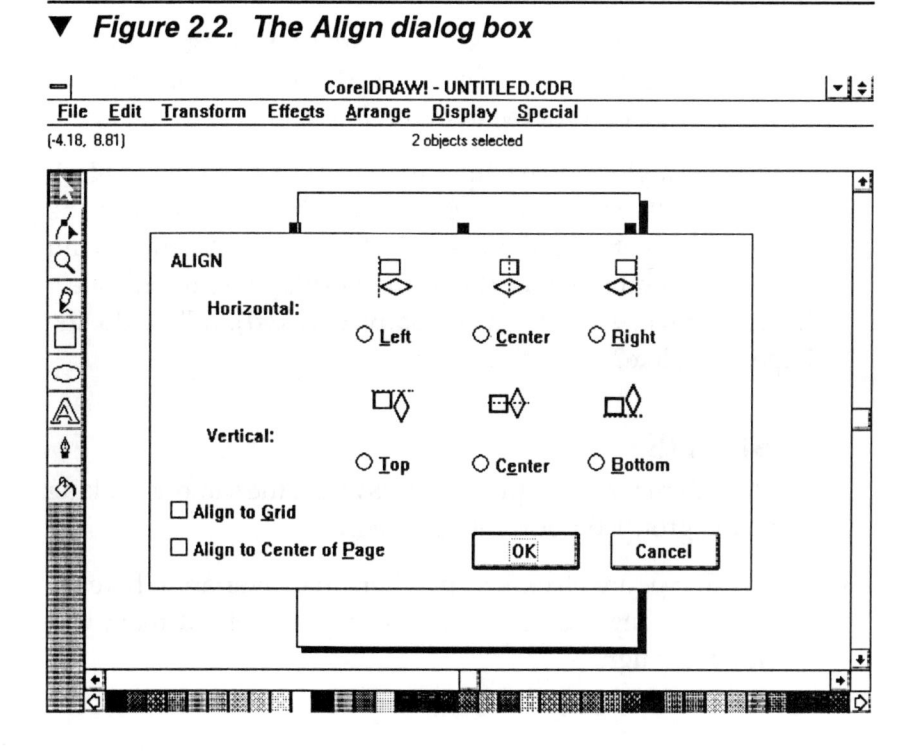

▼ *Figure 2.2. The Align dialog box*

You want to center the image both vertically and horizontally.

4. Click on both center options. You will learn more about aligning drawings, but you might want to look at your other options

now. If you would like, select one of the other options. You can always realign it later. When you have the alignment the way you want it, click on the button marked OK.

The result is a perfectly aligned drawing.

Next you will work with the drawing; saving it, loading it, and performing other tasks with it. If you would like, go through the last sequence of steps again, this time aligning the objects in some other way. The miracle of a product like *CorelDRAW!* is that you can experiment endlessly without fear because you can always come back to what you had before.

CHECK YOURSELF

1. Draw several items on the screen—circles, rectangles, lines—then select all of them and select Group from the Arrange menu. Try to move just one of the items on the screen.

2. Draw a rectangle and an ellipse that overlap. Color them black by selecting them both and clicking on the black color in the palette at the bottom of the screen. Pull down the Arrange menu and select Combine. Pull down the Display menu and select Display Preview (if it isn't already checked). What do the shapes look like?

ANSWERS

1. They all move. Grouping items is much the same as making all the grouped items into one item.

2. The shapes are black, except where they overlap. Where the overlap, they are not filled and objects behind them will show through.

Saving a Drawing

You should save your drawings early and often. If you create something particularly pleasing, you can save it under a different

Editing the Drawing ▲ 61

name to use later. But you should start out by simply saving what you have so far.

Saving a Drawing

TIP

In the words of a trusted advisor, *"CorelDRAW! does automatic backups, but are they ever enough? No way."* Take responsibility for making your own backups.

1. Pull down the File menu. Note that all the selections that were grayed earlier are now black and available to you.
2. Note the text to the right in the option on the File menu: ^S. This means that if you wanted to save the drawing without pulling down the File menu, you could simply press Ctrl-S and the file would be saved. Click on Save. You will see the Save dialog box (Figure 2.3).

▼ *Figure 2.3. The Save Drawing dialog box*

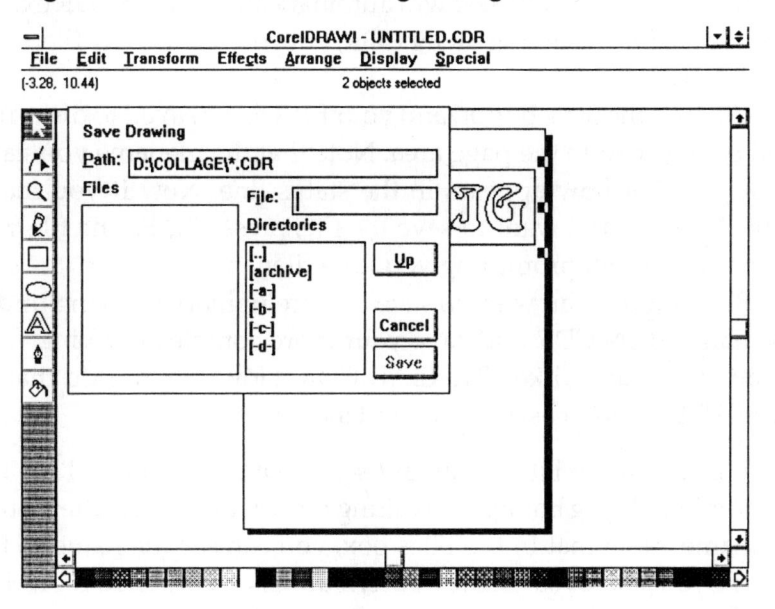

In the Save Drawing dialog box, you have your path laid out (in Figure 2.3, it is D:\COLLAGE*.CDR, but yours would probably be different). There are no CDR files (*CorelDRAW!* drawing files) in this subdirectory. If there were, their names would appear in the Files box. Your text cursor should be blinking in the File: text box at the center right of the dialog box. If you wanted to change directories, you could click on the name of a directory in the Directories box below the File: text box. In the Directory list box shown in Figure 2.3, [..] and [archive] are directories and [-a-], [-b-], [-c-], and [-d-] are disk drives. By double clicking on one of these, you could move to a different drive and directory.

The [..] refers to the parent directory of the current directory. Another way to move to this directory is to click on the Up button at the right of the dialog box. If you are not familiar with the directory structure DOS uses, you will need to refer to a book on DOS.

Once you have settled on which disk and directory to save the drawing, you should click on the File: text box and type a filename. A filename can be up to eight characters long. Filenames can use certain symbols beyond letters and numbers, but you should limit yourself to these and the hyphen and underscore character as a matter of style. *CorelDRAW!* will automatically add the CDR extension. I called my drawing SIGN.CDR, but you can use any filename you choose.

Click on the Save button and your file will be saved to disk. You will be returned to the page area. Note that the filename you gave your drawing now appears in the status line. Now if you make some changes and want to save the file, press Ctrl-S. The file will be saved without prompting you for a filename.

But suppose you want to save this preliminary drawing under the name SIGN.CDR and save your more complex drawing with some other name, like LTRHEAD.CDR. How can you do that, if *CorelDRAW!* won't ask you for a filename?

1. Pull down the File menu and select Save As. You will see the familiar dialog box again, waiting for you to enter an alternative name. Note that in the Files box, you can see the name of the file you just saved (in the figure, it's SIGN.CDR). LTRHEAD has already been typed into the dialog box File: text box.
2. Click on Save to save the file under the new filename.

Note that the name in the status line has changed to reflect the new name of your file.

Getting Rid of a Drawing

Getting Rid of a Drawing

The next step is to clear the screen. This is very simple, but before you do it you should always pause for a moment or two to make sure that you have saved it, if it is an important drawing, and if you have made any changes to it you don't want to discard. When you clear the screen, the drawing is gone, gone, gone.

TIP

Fortunately, *CorelDRAW!* is friendly enough to prompt you to save a drawing before it clears the screen. Pay heed to the prompt. It appears in the form of a dialog box that asks if you would like to save the drawing before moving on. If you want to discard it, click on No. If you want to save it, click on Yes. You can back out of the procedure by clicking on the button marked Cancel. This will take you back to the program with your drawing intact, as if you had never selected New.

1. Pull down the File menu.
2. Select New (it's the first item on the File menu).

   The drawing should now be gone.

CHECK YOURSELF

1. Click on the [-a-] listing in the Directories list in the Save Drawing dialog box. What files are available to you?
2. Click on the Up button in the Save Drawing dialog box. What is the equivalent of this action in DOS?

   ### ANSWERS
   1. You are logged to the A drive; any files that appear in the Files list box will be files on the disk in the A drive.

   2. Clicking on this button will take you to the parent directory of the current directory. The two-dot designation always

refers to the directory of which the current directory is a subdirectory. Therefore, clicking on the Up button is the equivalent of CD .. in DOS.

Loading a Drawing

You should have a couple of drawings saved to disk, if you've been following the exercises up to now. (If you don't, back up to the section called "Creating a Drawing" and go through the steps in that section and the next section, "Saving a Drawing.")

1. Pull down the File menu. Look at the Open option. Note the text off to the right of the word Open: ^O. This means that if you want to call up the Open Drawing dialog box from the keyboard, you can simply press Ctrl-O.
2. Select Open. You will see the dialog box shown in Figure 2.4.

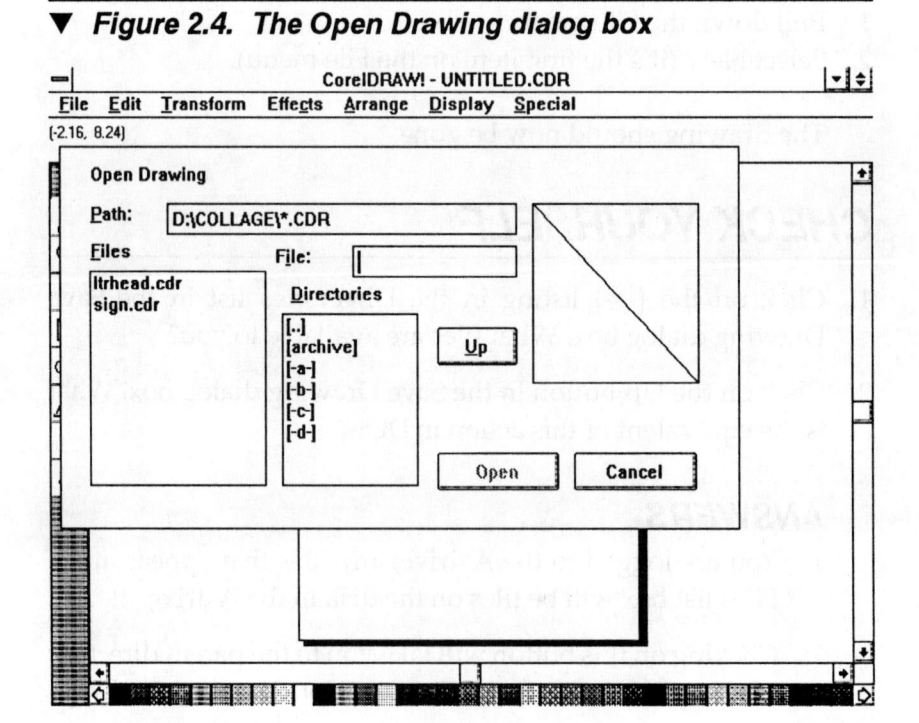

▼ *Figure 2.4. The Open Drawing dialog box*

Loading a Drawing

You can see that this dialog box is virtually identical to the Save Drawing dialog box seen earlier in Figure 2.3. The current path is shown in the Path text box; the drawing files are listed in the Files list box; the directories and disk drives immediately available are listed in the Directories list box. There is a text box marked File: where you can type a filename, if you wish.

The simplest way to open a drawing is by double clicking on its name in the Files list box. Load a file that way. But first, given the DOS limitation of eight characters for a filename, how will you know which file you want to load? Now, it's easy to recall the two drawings that you have saved so far in this chapter. But what if you had hundreds of drawings, or even a few dozen?

Allow me to reveal the future to you: Eventually, you will revert to the practice of using filenames like FACE1, FACE2, PIC1, and so on, in desperation, because it is simply too difficult to come up with really descriptive terms for essentially similar drawings, given the eight-character DOS maximum.

But don't despair. You will be able to tell your drawings apart as long as you are using *CorelDRAW!*. The reason is a remarkable new feature of the Open Drawing dialog that can be seen off at the right side of the dialog box. In Figure 2.4, this box, called the display box, is marked by a slash. This means that no filename is selected.

1. Now click on one of your filenames. You should see a "thumbnail" of the saved drawing: a small bitmap representation.
2. A representation of the contents of LTRHEAD.CDR opens in the display box. To load this graphic, either click on its name in the Files box and then click on the button marked Open or simply double click on the filename (most people's preference).

There are other ways to open a drawing, but none are so simple. First, you can enter the path in the Path: text box.

1. Click on the Path: text box and use the Backspace and Del key to edit out characters and type in replacement characters. When the path is the way you want it, press Enter.
2. Click on the File: text box and type in the name of the file you want to load. Press Enter and the file will be loaded.

As you can see, using the mouse to maneuver around the directories and to select the file to load is much simpler and easier.

Now that you have a drawing on the screen, you can move into editing an existing drawing.

CHECK YOURSELF

1. Pull down the File menu and select Open. What do you see in the display box in the Open dialog box?

   ANSWER
   1. The display box shows a thumbnail sketch of the drawing whose filename is currently selected. This eliminates most of the ambiguity in loading files.

Editing an Object

CorelDRAW! is such a massive and capable program that this part of the chapter could grow infinitely unless some strict discipline is exerted. As you go through the actions in this section, reference will be made to many options that you may or may not use. The options that are bypassed will be similar enough to the ones covered that you should be able to use them yourself simply by applying the steps provided for other actions.

Editing an Existing Rectangle

This action applies to nearly any object you might have on the screen, but since you boxed out text with a rectangle, this is the object you will edit.

Suppose that you have developed this letterhead for Brillig, maker of industrial solvents and slithy borogroves. The chairman of the board has looked over the letterhead and determined that the rectangle looks too loose. He would like less white space between the text and the box. Can you make the box slightly smaller? Of course you can.

Editing an Object

1. Click on the pick tool.
2. Place the point of the mouse pointer on the outline of the rectangle and click. It is selected and you will see the familiar handles all around it.
3. Place the mouse pointer on a corner handle and move it toward the center of the rectangle. The rectangle will shrink but maintain its aspect ratio—the relative length and height.

If you don't want to maintain the aspect ratio, drag one of the handles in the center of the sides of the rectangle. When you have the rectangle the size you want, remember to use the Align command on the Arrange menu to center the name in the rectangle again.

TIP

Rounded rectangles are also possible with *CorelDRAW!*. Select a rectangle, click on the Shape Tool and drag any corner of the rectangle toward the center of the rectangle. All the corners will become rounded.

Editing Multiple Objects

Now you take the graphic back to the chairman of the board and he says that he likes it better, but it looks staid, uninteresting. Is there some way you could make it bend a little? How about making the rectangle into a parallelogram? Sure, you can do that. Before you do, though, you should save your drawing. Use the Save As command to save the drawing with a slightly changed name, like LTRHEAD1.CDR.

TIP

Always save a drawing-in-progress before you make a major change.

This is the best kind of insurance: it's free, it's convenient, and it's virtually guaranteed to save you time. You'll discover that even on a good day you will regret about a quarter to a half of the changes you make. Using Save As will allow you to go back many changes, whereas the Undo/Redo options only allow you to go back one change.

1. Select the entire drawing by dragging a selection rectangle: Click on the pick tool, place the mouse pointer above and to the left of the letterhead rectangle, press the left mouse button, and drag down below and to the right of the letterhead. When you release the mouse button, you will have selected the entire graphic.
2. Click on the outline of any part of the drawing. The arrows will appear. These are special handles: the rotate/skew handles. You may recall from Chapter 1 that dragging the handles in the corners will rotate the drawing and dragging the handles on the sides of the drawing will skew, or bend, the graphic.
3. Place the mouse pointer on the arrow in the center of the top of the drawing and drag it to the right. Your drawing will look like the drawing in Figure 2.5.

▼ *Figure 2.5. The skewed drawing*

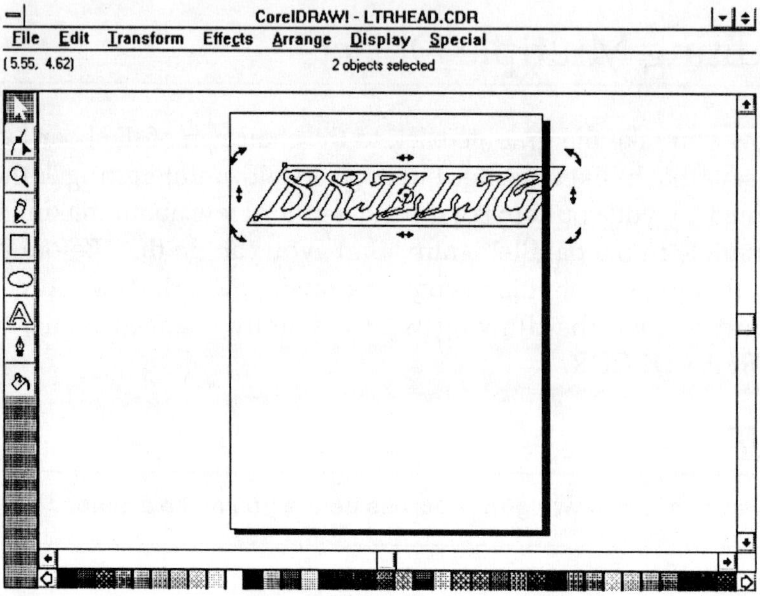

You may want to size the drawing slightly and drag it back to the center of the page area (or use the Align option on the Arrange menu and click on the box marked "Align to Center of Page").

Editing an Object

Making Precise Adjustments

"This looks pretty, good," the chairman of the board says. "What angle, exactly, is this? We prefer things to be at 45 degree angles." You wonder for a moment why he didn't specify this to begin with, and run back to your computer. You could use a protractor to measure the angle. Or you could skew the object with the mouse and keep a careful watch on the status line, which will tell you the angle of the skew, but there is an easier way. Since you saved your work before skewing it, you can simply reload it. But first, save the current drawing as LTRHEAD2.CDR.

1. Open the backup file you just saved as LTRHEAD1.CDR. Select the entire drawing. Now you need to specify the skew angle.
2. Pull down the Transform menu.

The options are Move, Rotate & Skew, Stretch & Mirror, and Clear Transformations. Note that you can call up the first three options from the keyboard by pressing Ctrl-L, Ctrl-N, and Ctrl-Q. The Move option allows you to specify in a text box the exact location of a drawing on the page. The Stretch & Mirror option allows you to flip a drawing left-for-right or right-for-left or specify, in percentage, how much larger or smaller to make the drawing both vertically and horizontally. But your immediate concern is the Rotate & Skew option.

1. Select Rotate & Skew from the Transform menu. You will see the dialog box shown in Figure 2.6.

TIP

You can constrain an object to moving only in a vertical or a horizontal direction by holding down the Ctrl key while dragging an object.

▼ **Figure 2.6. The Rotate & Skew dialog box**

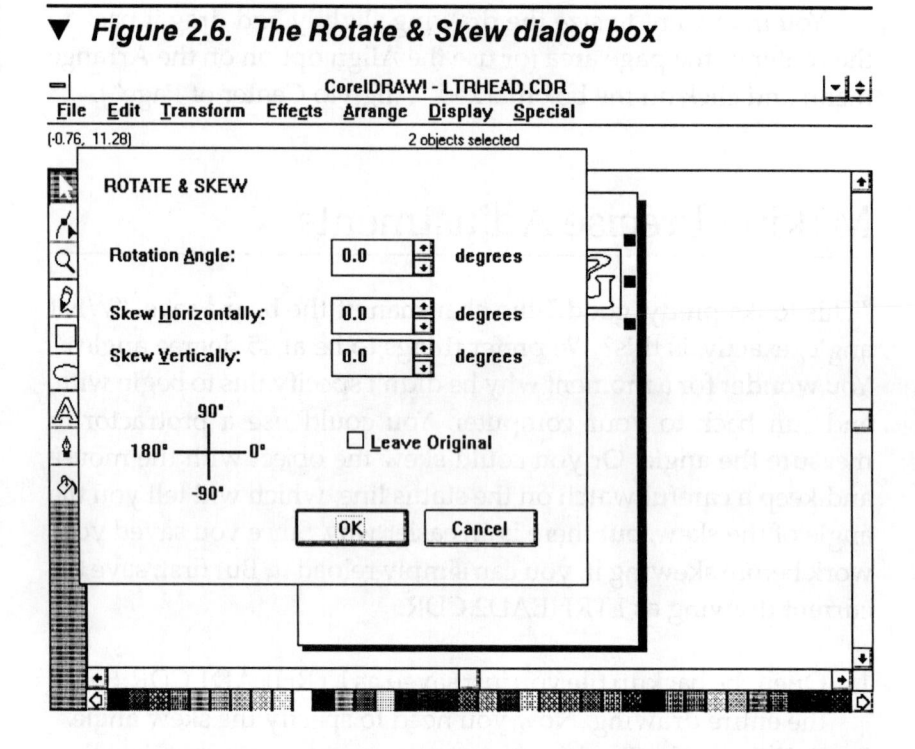

Note that you can rotate an object a specified angle or skew an object vertically or horizontally a specified angle. Arbitrarily, Corel Systems has determined that a skew to the left is a positive value and a skew to the right is a negative value. You want to skew your letterhead -45 degrees horizontally.

2. Click on the downward-pointing arrow next to the Skew Horizontally text box nine times, until the number -45.0 appears in the box. You could also drag the mouse pointer through the text in the box and type -45.0.

Before leaving the dialog box by clicking on OK, note that you have the option of leaving the original. Although you won't use it now, this is a very valuable option to use and you will learn about it in a moment. This leaves the currently selected object while rotating or skewing a duplicate. This option is also found in the other Transform dialog boxes.

3. Click on OK to skew the object exactly -45 degrees.

Creating a Drop Shadow

Editing an Object

This time the chairman of the board is perfectly pleased. But he wants a shadow. He says the shadow should make it look as if the letterhead is sitting on a horizontal plane. Simply accomplished, again using the Rotate and Skew option.

1. Save your work, then select the entire drawing and select Rotate & Skew from the Transform menu.
2. Click on the down arrow next to the Skew Horizontally text box until it reads -50.
3. Click on the box that says "Leave Original."
4. Click on OK. You will see the drawing shown in Figure 2.7.

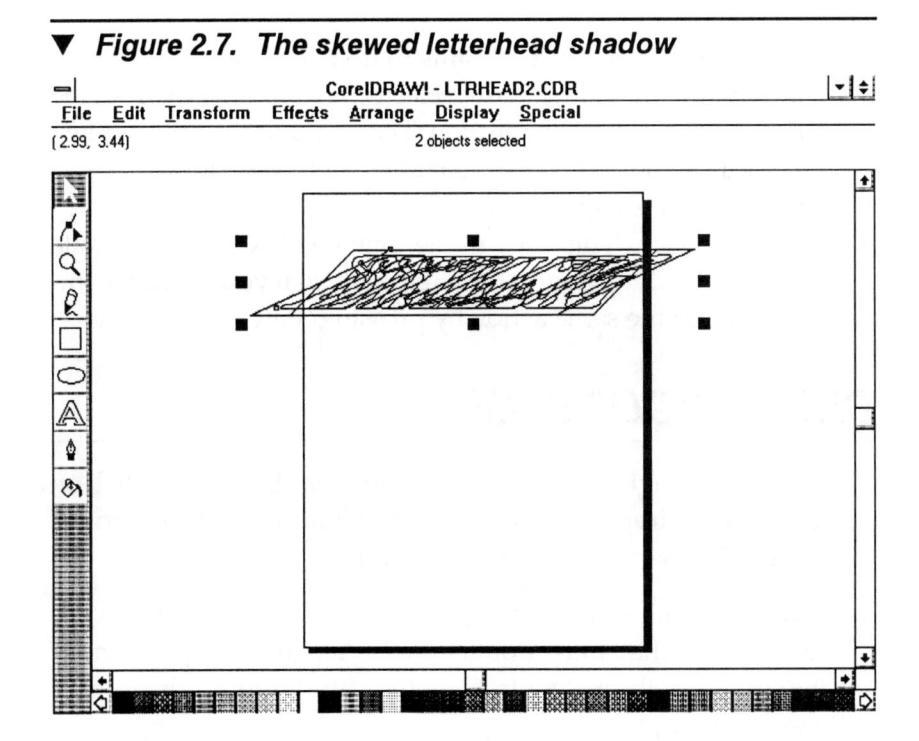

▼ **Figure 2.7. The skewed letterhead shadow**

It looks like a hopeless tangle of wireframes, but it is actually two versions of the skewed letterhead—one at -45 degrees (the original letterhead object) and one at a greater angle (the shadow). There are some problems with the shadow. For starters, since it is newer than the original, it has a precedence that is above the original—that is, it will appear in front of the original. A shadow should never be between you and the thing that is casting the shadow. Second, the shadow is the wrong color (all drawing up to now has been in black). By changing the color of the shadow to a light gray, it will appear more shadow-like. And finally, the bases of the two objects are not the same. You will need to move the shadow so that its base coincides with the base of the letterhead.

Changing Precedence

You can start by putting the shadow behind the letterhead object.

1. Select the shadow. The best thing to do to be sure you have the shadow, and only the shadow, selected is to click away from the drawings to remove all selection. Then hold down the Shift key and click on the text and the rectangle of the shadow
2. Pull down the Arrange menu.
3. Select To Back. This moves the shadow text and rectangle behind everything else on the page. Note that you could accomplish exactly the same action by pressing Shift-PgDn.

CHECK YOURSELF

1. Draw a rectangle and click away from it to deselect it. Click on it twice and drag the upper left corner handle down and to the right. What happens to the shape of the rectangle?

2. Looking at the same rectangle, note that there is a dot in the center. Place the mouse pointer on this dot and drag it to one of the corners of the rectangle. Drag the same handle as in number one. What happens?

ANSWERS
1. Nothing happens to the *shape* of the rectangle, but it rotates around its axis.

2. Instead of rotating around its center, the rectangle rotates around the corner where you moved the dot. This dot determines the axis of rotation.

Editing an Object

Changing Outline Color

Next, you must change the color of the outline of the rectangle and text, and the color of the fill of the text.

1. With the shadow still selected, click on the outline tool in the toolbox. You will see the outline tool menu as shown in Figure 2.8.

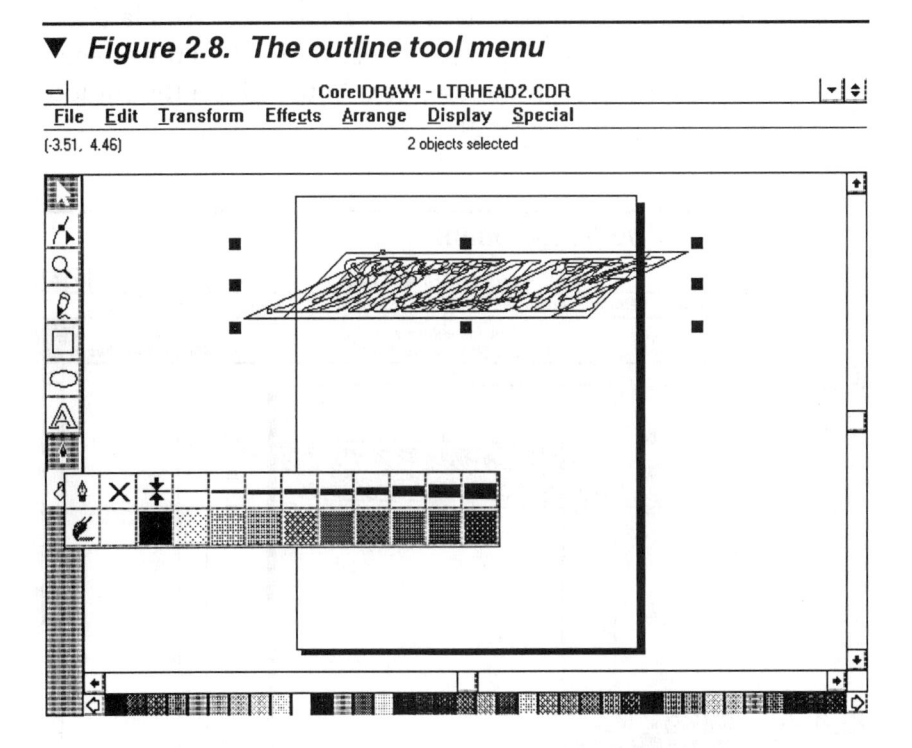

▼ *Figure 2.8. The outline tool menu*

The items along the top of the menu determine the thickness of the outline and the items along the bottom affect the color of the line. You will dive deeply into these items in Chapter 7.

2. Select a light gray color from the bottom part of the outline tool menu, such as the shade of gray seventh from the right.

Changing Fill Color

Now you must change the color of the fill of the text. You won't want to have the rectangle selected for this action because if you fill the rectangle and the text the same color, you will render the text invisible. Therefore, begin by deselecting the rectangle of the shadow.

1. Hold down the Shift key and click on the rectangle in the shadow. The status line should now read "Text: Arabia (Normal)," which should be the only selected object on the screen.
2. Click on the fill tool in the tool box. You will see the fill tool menu as shown in Figure 2.9.

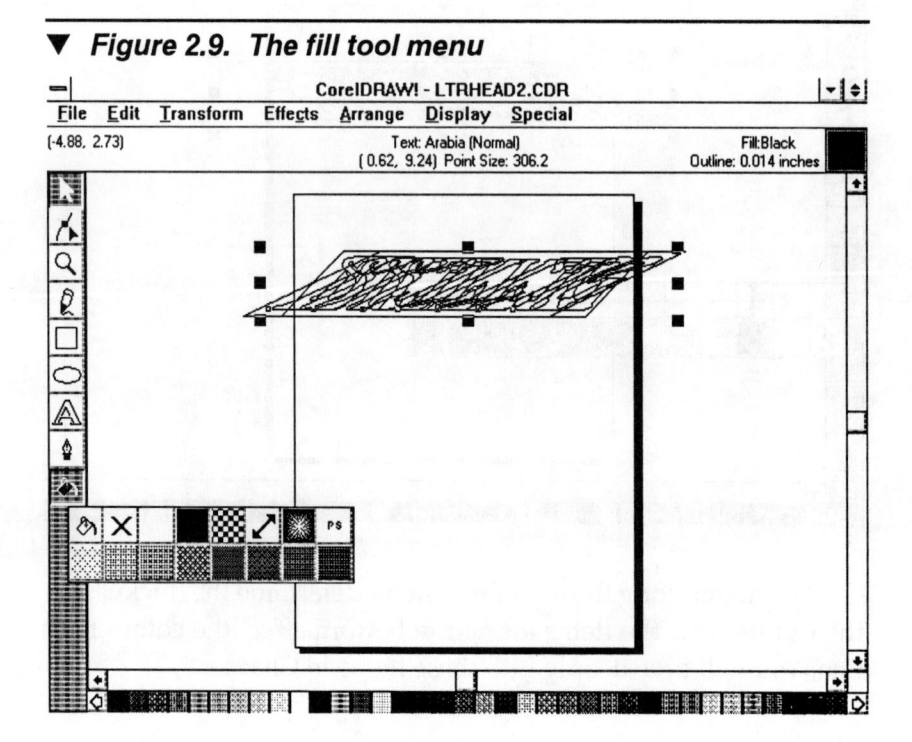

▼ **Figure 2.9. The fill tool menu**

Editing an Object

The top part of the fill tool menu provides access to various patterns. These will be covered in detail when you get to Chapter 7. The bottom part of the fill tool menu provides eight shades of gray. For now, select the same shade of gray as you used for the outline.

3. Click on the gray seventh from the right.

Aligning Objects

Finally, you must adjust the shadow so that its base coincides with the base of the original.

1 To begin, you must select the shadow rectangle again. Hold down the Shift key and click on the rectangle. The status line should now read "2 objects selected."

2. Place the mouse pointer on any part of the selected text or rectangle and drag the object to the right, being very careful to place its base visually on top of the letterhead's base.

After you have worked at this for a while, you will probably agree that it is not very efficient. Unless your hands and eye are very well coordinated, you will probably leave the shadow at least a little distance from the letterhead. Even when they look perfect, they may not be perfect when the drawing is printed out. Remember, the resolution of your screen is about 72 dots per inch (dpi), while your laser printer is able to print at 300 dpi. That means that you can have four times as much error on the paper as you can see on the screen.

There are two solutions to the situation: Snap and align. Either one will require that you group your objects.

1. Make sure you have both the text and rectangle of your shadow selected.
2. Pull down the Arrange menu and select Group. This effectively makes the two objects into a single object.

3. Click away from the selected object to deselect it.
4. Click on the outline of the text of the letterhead. Hold down the Shift key and click on the rectangle of the letterhead.
5. Pull down the Arrange menu and select Group.

You now have two groups of objects. You can treat the grouped objects as if they were two individual objects. Clicking anywhere on the outline of the rectangle or text of the shadow will now select the entire shadow. Rotating or skewing one part of the headline will rotate or skew the entire headline.

TIP

You may be wondering why you had to wait until now to group the objects. The answer is that if you had grouped them before changing the color of the shadow, you would have filled both components of the shadow—the text and the rectangle—with a solid, light gray. That would have made the text in the shadow invisible.

Now that the objects are grouped, you can use Align on the Arrange menu to align the two items.

1. Select both objects either by dragging a selection rectangle that includes both of them or by holding down the Shift key and clicking on the outline of both groups of objects. Another option, since there are only two objects on the page area, is to pull down the Edit menu and highlight the option Select All.
2. Press Ctrl-A or pull down the Arrange menu and select Align.
3. Click on Left and Bottom. This will perfectly align the objects at their bases.
4. Save your work.

Using the Grid

Another option is to use the grid. Personally, I don't like the grid because I forget it's on until I find myself trying to make fine adjustments with the mouse and discovering that the object I am moving is snapping all over the place—almost never where I want it to go. However, used properly, the grid can be a powerful tool.

Basically, the grid forces you to place an object in a given position. Imagine arranging marbles on a piece of hardware cloth or very coarse mesh. You can move the marbles from place to place, but they will always maintain their relationship to the grid. If you move a marble a certain distance, it will fall into the next square in the hardware cloth with a snapping motion. The marble will line up with either one or another square in the grid and cannot be left halfway between.

Turn on Snap to Grid by selecting this option in the Display menu.

Editing an Object

1. Pull down the Display menu and select Snap to Grid (or press Ctrl-Y, the keyboard equivalent).
2. Click on the outline of one part of the shadow outline toward the lower left corner of the shadow.

Where you click on an object determines the part of the outline that snaps to the grid.

3. Drag the shadow toward the bottom part of the page area.

You will want the shadow away from the letterhead so that you will be able to easily select the letterhead for the next step. Note that as you drag, the shadow jerks along, it doesn't move smoothly as it did in the past. This is the snap action referred to earlier.

4. Place the mouse pointer on the lower left corner of the outline of the letterhead and drag the letterhead down and match its base to the shadow base. Now when they look as if they match perfectly, you can be assured that they do match perfectly.

Figure 2.10 shows what the final drawing looks like, printed out on a Star LaserPrinter8-II equipped with LincPage, which is a PostScript emulation.

Printing will be covered in Chapter 3.

Is that all you can do editing a graphic? Not on your life. Unfortunately, this book isn't infinitely expandable, so it can only touch on the most creative aspects of *CorelDRAW!*. I hope that you will go back to the Transform menu and try out all the settings to see what they do.

▼ *Figure 2.10. Letterhead printout*

PRACTICE WHAT YOU'VE LEARNED

What You Should Do	How the Computer Responds
1. Click on the fill tool and click on the first item in the top row of the fill tool menu. In the right side of the resulting dialog box, click on the button marked Open. Select PURE225A.PAL in the files list box of the resulting dialog box and click on the button marked Load.	1. A new palette file is loaded, resulting in a completely different selection of colors. When you create a palette you want to keep, save it by calling up this dialog box and clicking on the Save As dialog box. If you want to discard this palette, click on the Cancel button in the Uniform Fill dialog box (which is the box that should be onscreen at this time).
2. Turn on the grid and drag an object by its upper left corner.	2. The upper left corner will snap to the grid as the object is dragged.

Drawing

So far, you have been working and reworking shapes provided with *CorelDRAW!*. There is no reason for you to stop there. Though you may have some limitations on your artistic abilities, everyone can create interesting drawings with *CorelDRAW!*. Think about it:

Drawing

one of the reasons people become frustrated with art is that once a line is on the page of Strathmore art paper, it's there for all eternity, whether it's perfect or a mistake. A relative few amount of people get over this hump and go on to become accomplished artists.

With *CorelDRAW!*, you can create art without fear of the blank page. Any line you create can be changed.

Now draw a cartoon face by way of illustration. You can follow the steps exactly and come up with a drawing radically different from the results you see in the figures, so don't worry about the appearance of your drawing; the whole point is to get used to using the pencil tool.

1. With *CorelDRAW!* running and the page area cleared, click on the pencil tool.
2. Generally, drawings of faces begin with ovals, so place the mouse pointer on the page area, press and hold down the left mouse button, and draw a rough oval (Figure 2.11). Make sure the place where you lift your finger from the button is at some distance from the place where you started or the next section won't make much sense.

▼ *Figure 2.11. Rough oval*

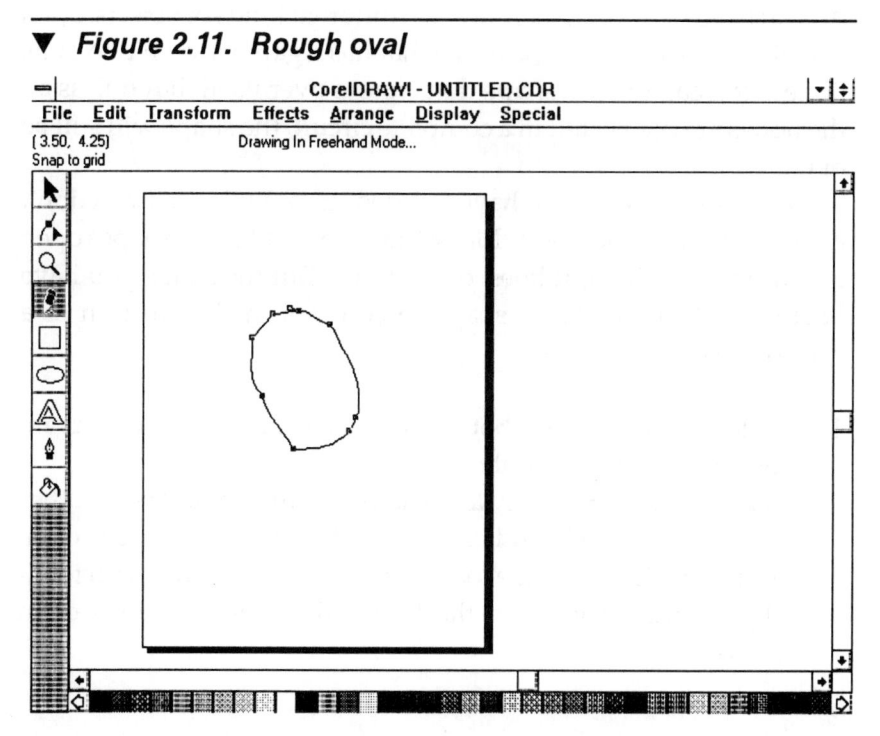

OK, maybe that oval is too rough even to call an oval. But notice the tiny box on the bottom of the oval. That box is called a *node* and it can be edited. You're going to read about nearly a dozen high-powered commands that relate to nodes in the next section, but for now, just drag it so your oval looks more uniform.

1. Click on the shape tool (second from the top in the toolbox).
2. Place the point of the mouse cursor on any node that seems a little out of line. Press the left mouse button and drag the node into a better position, then release the mouse button. I'd like to see Andy Wyeth do that with his sketch pad.

You need to fill this shape with some kind of coloring. Unfortunately, an open shape was drawn and only closed shapes can be filled. You need to close up the shape.

Open and Closed Objects

As you have surmised, there are two different kinds of objects: open and closed. An open shape is one that has a gap between two of its nodes. You can draw a shape that crosses over itself, but unless all the nodes are connected in a complete circuit, the shape will still be open.

Why is it important to have a closed shape? It isn't, if you don't care about filling the shape. Many times you will leave shapes open and use them as accent lines, or contours. But the shape you have begun has to be a closed shape to accomplish the creation of a cartoon face.

1. To close a shape, select both end nodes—the two nodes that are unconnected. Click on the shape tool.
2. Hold down the Shift key and click on both end nodes. Another way to select both end nodes would be to drag a selection rectangle with the shape tool. Just make sure you don't accidentally include more than the two end nodes in the selection rectangle.

Editing the Drawing ▲ 81

3. Double click on one of the selected nodes. You will see the dialog box shown in Figure 2.12.

Drawing

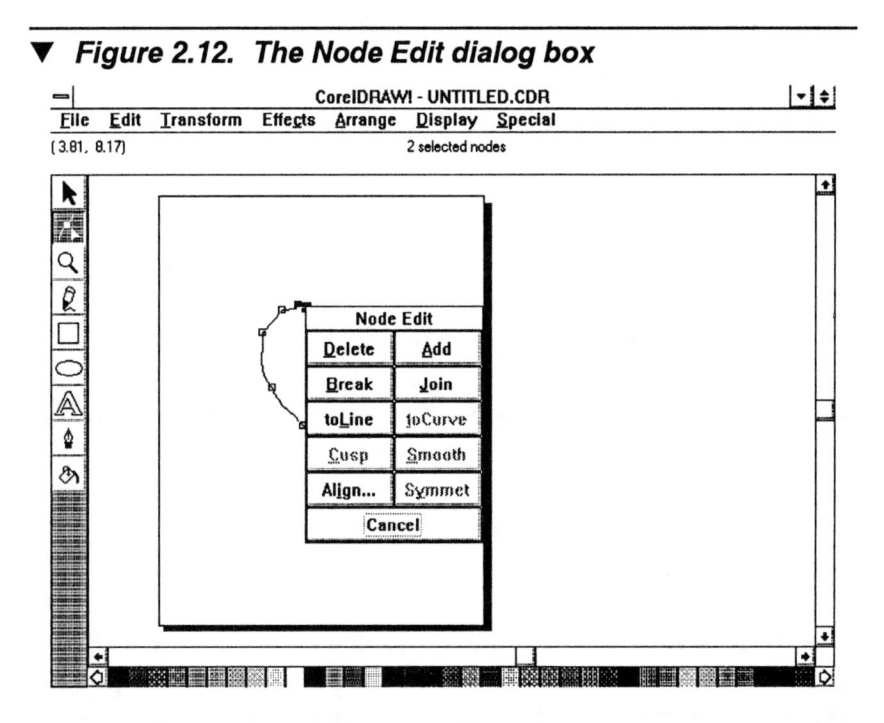

▼ *Figure 2.12. The Node Edit dialog box*

You'll be seeing a lot more of this dialog box later in the chapter. For now, however, you should only be concerned with one of its 11 buttons: Join.

4. Press the J key on your keyboard (when you see a letter underlined in a button, it means that pressing the key with that letter has the same effect as clicking on the button) or click on the Join button.

There is a more convenient and intuitive way to make closed shapes. As you are drawing your shape with the pencil tool, make sure your mouse pointer is exactly on top of your starting point when you lift your finger from the button. *CorelDRAW!* will automatically close the shape and you can fill it immediately without node editing.

The end nodes will be joined into one and you will have a closed shape. Now you can apply fills to the closed shape, including color and patterns, which will be covered in a later chapter. For now, however, you need to apply some color to the face. You can make it green.

Solid Fills

To color a closed shape green, you can take the easy way out and pick a green color from the palette you see running along the bottom of your screen, or you can go into the fill menu and mix a custom green. When you fill an object, it becomes opaque in the printout—that is, it completely covers all objects that coincide with it that have a lower precedence. To see this in operation, you need to be able to preview the printout. *CorelDRAW!* provides just such a preview screen.

1. Pull down the Display menu.
2. Select Show Preview.

The screen will divide in two, giving you access to your drawing area (the wire frames visible on the page area) and a preview that shows approximately what will print out on paper.

3. If the oval isn't currently selected (if the nodes or handles aren't visible), click on the pick tool and click on the oval.
4. Click on one of the green shades on the onscreen palette. You will see the oval in the preview screen turn green (Figure 2.13). Because you are restricted to black and white printing, the shape in the figure may appear dark gray or black, but onscreen it is green.

Now finish the face.

1. Click on the pencil tool and give your Martian lips, two or three noses, and an eye. Color them as you see fit.
2. Save your work.
3. Turn off Display Preview by selecting it again on the Display menu. You could leave it on, but it severely slows the *CorelDRAW!* display to show a preview all the time, and if you

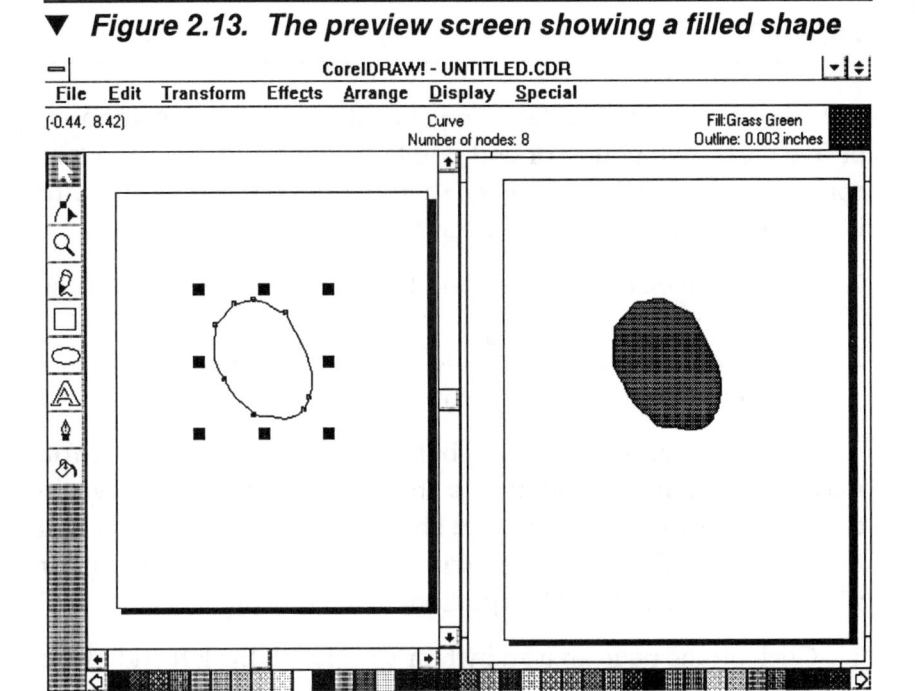

▼ **Figure 2.13. The preview screen showing a filled shape**

Solid Fills

display the preview constantly, you will quickly lose patience with it.

When you create something with curves that aren't regular, or with straight lines where curves should be, you should use node editing to make the curves correct.

Editing Nodes

What is a node? As you drew in the last section, perhaps you noticed something about the way *CorelDRAW!* handled your drawing. You would create a curve, then when you released the mouse button, *CorelDRAW!* would pause a moment and return the same curve with nodes sprinkled along it. *CorelDRAW!* operates entirely within the realm of a handy little item known as the Bezier curve. Everything you draw in *CorelDRAW!* is composed either of straight lines or Bezier curves.

Bezier

A Bezier curve, named after a French mathematician, is composed of five parts: two nodes, or end points, a connecting line, and two control points that determine the shape of the connecting curve. To illustrate, create a curve on the screen.

1. With *CorelDRAW!* running and the page area blank, select the pencil tool.
2. Place the mouse pointer on the left side of the screen. Press the left mouse button and drag to the right side of the screen.

When you release the mouse button, you will have a curve. You may recall that in order to draw a straight line, you should click in two positions on the screen. You should do that now, so you will have a straight line to contrast with the Bezier curve (and also for ulterior reasons that will be apparent in a moment).

1. Click on the page area an inch or so beneath the left end of the curve you created.
2. Click again on the page area an inch or so beneath the right end of the curve.

Your screen should now resemble Figure 2.14.

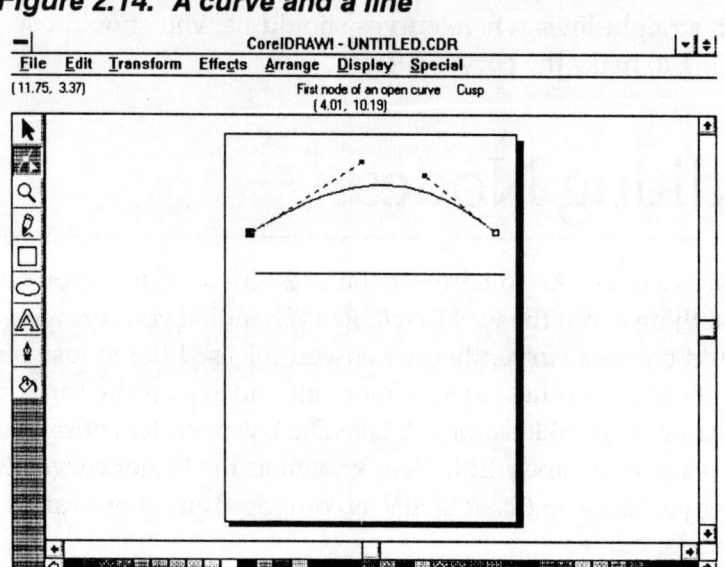

▼ *Figure 2.14. A curve and a line*

Editing Nodes

Your curve may have more than two nodes. You will need only two, so here's how to get rid of unwanted nodes:

1. Click on the shape tool.
2. Click on any node that appears between the nodes at the endpoints of the curve.
3. Press Del.

Repeat steps 2 and 3 until all the unwanted nodes have been eliminated. Now you have two nodes.

4. While the shape tool is selected, click on either of the remaining nodes to select it.

Note the lever-like devices that project from the nodes. On my screen, these levers are blue and at their ends are tiny squares called *control points*. The position of these control points determines the shape of the connecting line. Take a look at Figure 2.15. In the top of the figure, you can see the effect of moving these control points above the nodes and in converging directions. At the bottom of Figure 2.15, the right control point has been dragged below the nodes (unfortunately, it's impossible to show control points on two different objects at the same time).

▼ *Figure 2.15. The right control point above the node (top) and below (bottom)*

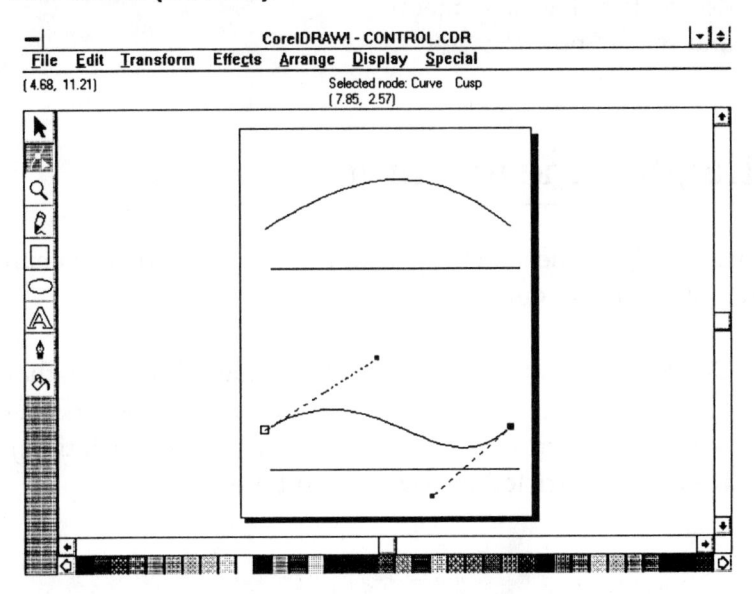

You can draw any possible curved line between these points by making the appropriate change in the control points.

Now try doing that with the straight lines. When you click on the nodes of a straight line, no control points appear. The only adjustments you can make are in the length and angle of the straight line.

PRACTICE WHAT YOU'VE LEARNED

What You Should Do	How the Computer Responds
1. Create an open object. Fill it with a blue color from the palette at the bottom of the screen.	1. You can't fill an open object. CorelDRAW! wouldn't know where to stop filling. Only closed objects can be filled.
2. Click away from any existing object so no object is selected. Click on a red color in the palette at the bottom of the screen. Now draw a rectangle. If the preview screen isn't visible, pull down the Display menu and select Show Preview.	2. The rectangle will have no color, and no fill, unless you have selected a default color.

Straight Line to Curve

True, a straight line isn't very flexible. However, you can change a straight line into a curve.

1. Double click on the right end of the straight line. Note that one of the node edit buttons says toCurve. Also take a moment to notice which buttons are available for use (in black type) and which are restricted to you (grayed type).

2. Click on the toCurve button or press the T key. When the dialog box disappears, the line will still be straight, but you will be able to see the control points (they will be right on the line, defining a straight curve).

Editing Nodes

Curve to Straight Line

You can also change a curve into a straight line.

1. With the shape tool selected, click on the top curve to select it.
2. Double click on the node at the right end of the curve. Now when the Node Edit dialog box appears, toLine is available and toCurve is grayed.
3. Click on toLine.

Note that when the dialog box disappears, the curve has become a straight line. Its control points were stripped away.

Other Node Editing Tools

You have probably noted that you have to double click on the terminating node to edit a line segment with the Node Edit toolbox. Try double clicking on the point of origin. The dialog box appears, but the only button available is Delete. Since you may not know which node is the terminating node, you can simply double click on the segment you want to edit. That will always select the terminating node and call up the Node Edit dialog box.

The tools in the Node Edit dialog box that haven't been discussed are Delete, Break, Cusp, Align, Add, Smooth, and Symmet. What would you use them for?

Delete
As you might suspect, selecting Delete causes the selected node to disappear. If it was the terminating node of a curve and the segment

along side was a line, the next segment is made a curve. If you delete one of the ends of a line with only two nodes, the line is deleted.

Break

Break is the opposite of Join, which you used earlier. Join connects two nodes, making segments into a single line. Break breaks the segments apart, making two lines out of one.

Align

If you want to place one node directly above or on exactly the same level as another node, Align is the button to use. To use this command, you will need to select two different nodes.

1. Hold down the Shift key and click on two different nodes on a line so they are both selected.
2. Double click on one of the nodes. You'll see the dialog box shown in Figure 2.16.

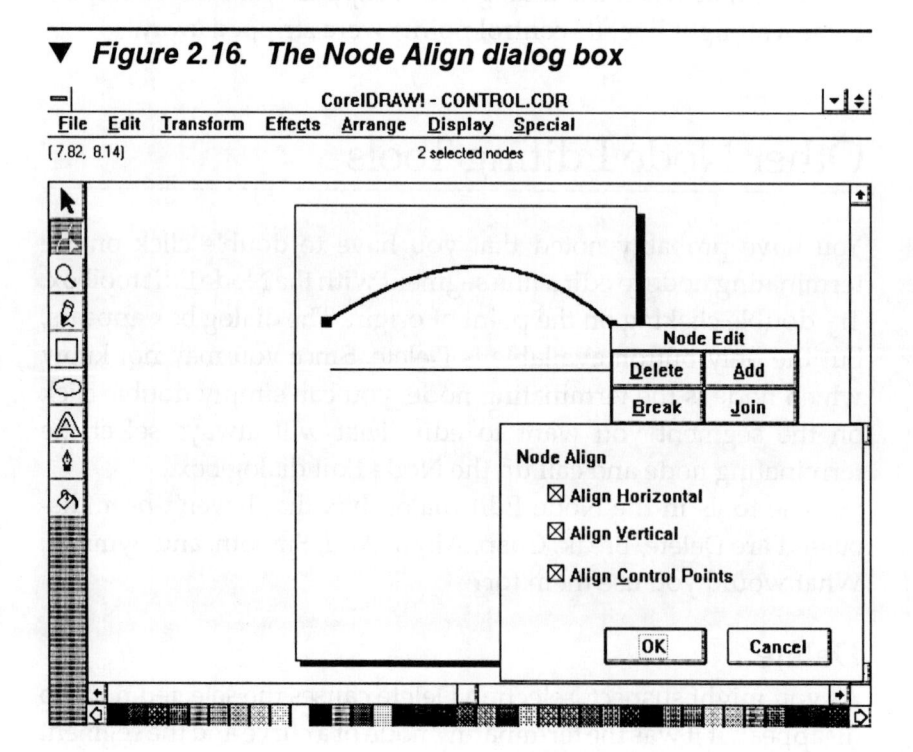

▼ *Figure 2.16. The Node Align dialog box*

Note that all the check boxes are selected. If you click on OK at this point, both of the selected nodes would be moved so they occupy the same place on the screen. If you leave Align Control Points selected, any curve in the line segment will be eliminated and a single line will emanate from the nodes. If you click on Align Control Points (turning it off), the curve in the line segment will remain. This is a little difficult to describe. In Figure 2.17, the top curve has been duplicated twice. In the middle example the nodes have been aligned with Align Control Points checked and in the bottom example, the nodes have been aligned with Align Control Points turned off.

Editing Nodes

▼ *Figure 2.17. Aligning control points (center) and leaving them unaligned (bottom)*

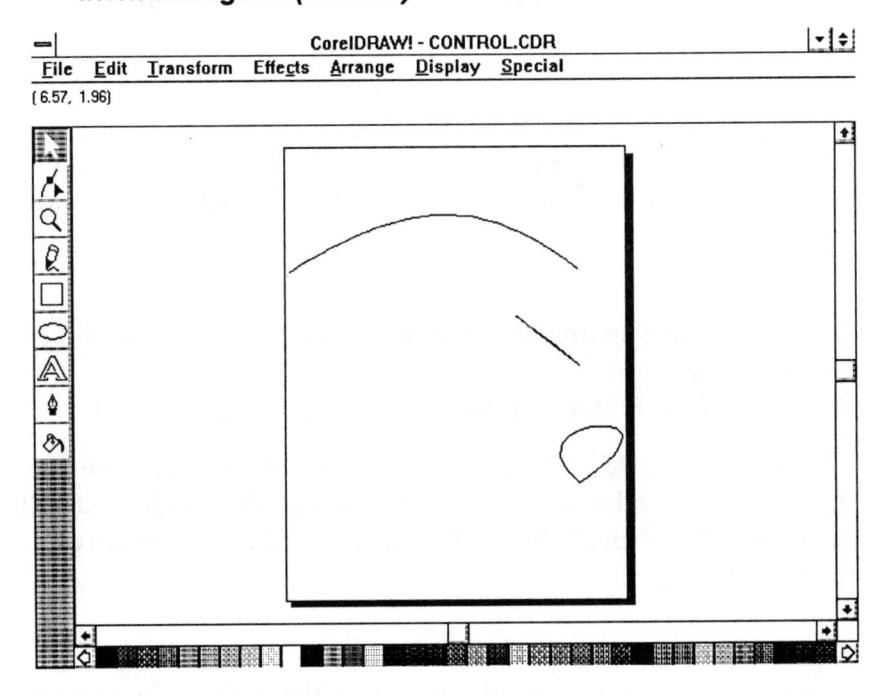

If you click on the Align Horizontal check box, it will no longer be selected and Align Control points will also be deselected. The nodes will be aligned so they are at the same distance from the bottom of the page area, but they may be at different distances from the left edge of the page area.

If you click on the Align Vertical check box, it will no longer be selected and Align Control points will also be deselected. The nodes will be aligned so they are at the same distance from the left edge of the page area, but they may be at different distances from the left edge of the page area.

Add

Sometimes you need to add control points to a line segment to increase the amount of control you have over it.

1. Clear the screen by selecting New and use the pencil tool to create a curve onscreen with only two nodes. If additional nodes appear, click on the shape tool and press Del until there are only two nodes left—one at either end of the curve.
2. If the shape tool isn't selected, click on it. Double click on the curve you just created.
3. When the Node Edit dialog box appears, click on Add.

When the Node Edit dialog box disappears, you will see a new node in the curve. Having additional nodes makes it possible to create jagged lines with curves. You can also add nodes to a straight line.

Now try this.

1. Double click on one of the selected nodes (all three should be selected).
2. In the Node Edit dialog box, click on Add again.

What happened? You should now have five nodes on the line. Do it again. Now there are nine. Each time you add a node, you will add nodes between all the existing nodes on the selected curve or line segment.

Smooth

Sometimes you want control points on either side of the node to function independently and sometimes you want them to act in concert. To understand this command, we will need to create a set of jagged curves.

1. Clear the page area by selecting New from the File menu.

Editing Nodes

2. Click on the pencil tool and draw a curve like a sine wave. If there are more than three nodes on the screen, eliminate all but the ones at the ends and one in the center.
3. Click on the center node to make the control points visible.
4. Place the mouse pointer on one of the control points attached to the center node and drag it up and down.

Note that although you can change the distance of the control point from the node so it is different from the distance of the control point on the other side of the node, the line formed by the handles going through the node is always straight. The reason for this is that this node is *smoothed*. Note that this is indicated in the center of the status line: "Selected node: Curve Smooth."

Cusp

Start with the same sine wave as before.

1. With the shape tool selected, double click on the center node to call up the Node Edit dialog box.
2. Select Cusp or press C.

When the dialog box disappears, the node doesn't look very different from before, but the status line now reads "Selected node: Curve Cusp."

3. Now try dragging one of the control points attached to the center node.

The control points are now completely independent. You can drag either control point in a 360-degree arc around the node without in any affecting the other control handle or the curve on the other side of the node.

Symmet

Finally, you can cause the line through the node to be straight and both control points to be an equal distance from the node by selecting Symmet (for symmetrical).

1. With the shape tool selected, double click on the center node of the sine wave.
2. When the Node Edit dialog box appears, click on the button marked Symmet.
3. Drag either of the control points up and down. Note that the other control point follows your motions exactly.

Cutting and Pasting

CorelDRAW! uses cut, copy, and paste like many other *Windows* programs. To see all your options, pull down the Edit menu.

Cut (Shift-Del) removes any selected objects from the screen and places them in a temporary storage area known as the Clipboard (when something is cut, you would say that it's "on the Clipboard"). If you cut something else, it replaces the contents of this temporary storage area. You lose whatever was on the Clipboard.

Copy (Ctrl-Ins) places a copy of any selected objects on the Clipboard. If you cut or copy something else, it replaces the contents of the Clipboard and whatever was there is lost. If you are trying to get an image from *CorelDRAW!* to some other *Windows* graphics program, this is the quickest and easiest way to do it:

1. Click on the pick tool.
2. Select the object or objects you want to copy to another program.
3. Select Copy from the Edit menu.
4. Minimize or close the *CorelDRAW!* window.
5. Start the other graphics program.
6. Pull down the Edit menu in the other graphics program.
7. Select Paste.

This procedure is a powerful way to import graphics into *CorelDRAW!* from programs like *Designer* and *Arts & Letters*.

Paste (Shift-Ins) places a copy of whatever is on the Clipboard on the page area.

Cutting and Pasting

Clear (Del) is similar to Cut, with one important difference. When you select Clear, it removes any selected objects from the screen, but it doesn't place them on the Clipboard. This is a handy way to get rid of unwanted objects when you don't want to disturb the contents of the Clipboard. It's also a very natural thing to press the Del key to get rid of unwanted objects. Remember, though, that the only way to return something removed with Clear is by selecting Undo from the Edit menu.

Duplicate (Ctrl-D) is a command you will use often. It has the same effect as selecting Copy and then Paste. Duplicate will cause a copy of any selected objects to be placed on the screen.

Copy Style From is a special kind of copy command. It doesn't copy an object but specific attributes of an object. Take a look at Figure 2.18.

If you want to make the circle look like the rectangle, you could guess what shade of red it is and how thick its outline is, or you could simply copy the attributes from the rectangle.

▼ **Figure 2.18.** *A rectangle and a circle with different styles and the Copy Style dialog box*

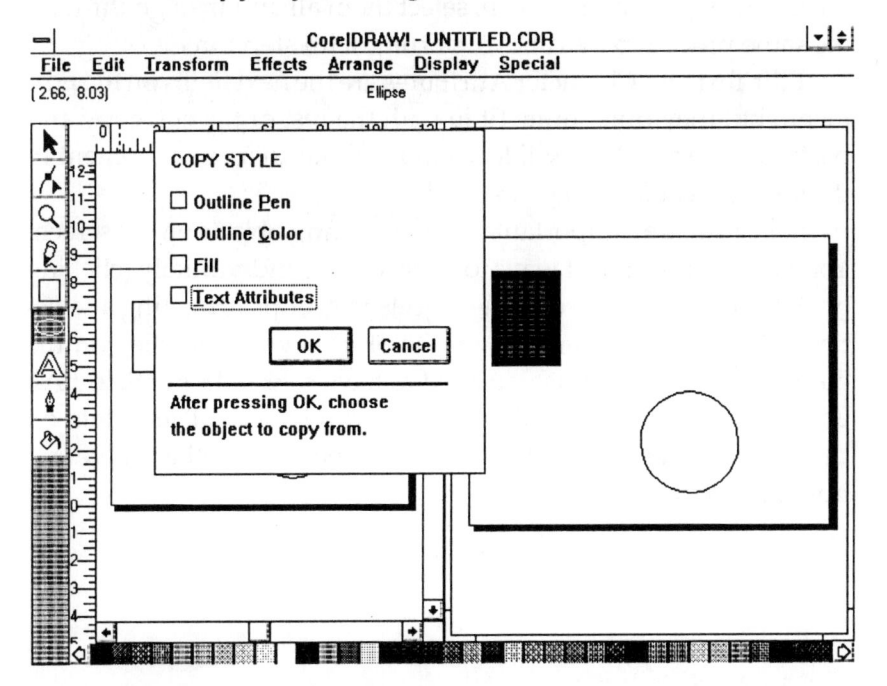

1. Create a rectangle and circle like the ones shown in the figure. Use any attributes you like, so long as the circle and the rectangle have radically different attributes.
2. Make sure the circle is selected.
3. Pull down the Edit menu and select Copy Style From. The Copy Style dialog box will appear, as shown in the figure.
4. Click on the attributes you want to communicate from one object to the other: Outline Pen, Outline Color, and Fill. Click on the OK button.

When you have clicked on the OK button, the dialog box will disappear and the mouse cursor will be changed to an arrow with the word "From?" written in it.

5. Click on the outline of the object whose attributes you want to copy: the rectangle. When you click on the rectangle, the circle will be redrawn so that it shares all the attributes of the rectangle.

This command doesn't just work from one object to another. If you have dozens of objects and you want them all to have the same fill as one object on the screen, select them all and then go through the same procedures as above, starting with step three.

Edit Text and Character Attributes are the next items on the Edit menu, but they don't quite fit in with the rest of the cut, copy and paste commands. You will learn more about them in a moment in the section called "Using Text."

Select All is an important way of selecting objects on the screen. You've seen a couple of ways to select objects individually (clicking on their outlines) and selecting objects in groups (dragging a selection rectangle or holding down the Shift key as you click on the outlines of all the objects you need to have selected). But Select All goes beyond these methods. It allows you to select every item on the screen at once, whether there is one or whether there are hundreds of objects.

TIP

If you want to select everything onscreen except for one or two items, it's very expeditious to use Select All to select everything on the screen, then hold down the Shift key and click on the objects you don't want selected. The more objects there are on the screen, the more efficient this method is.

Using Text

You've already seen some text used in *CorelDRAW!*. There are dozens of different typefaces included in the *CorelDRAW!* package, ranging from the ultra modern to the informal to the calligraphic to the classic. There are also symbol libraries like Musical_Symbols. You already know how to select a typeface, too:

1. Click on the text tool (the tool in the toolbox with a capital A on it).
2. Click on the page area where the text should appear. The Text dialog box will appear.
3. Type the text in the huge text box at the top of the dialog box.
4. Make any necessary settings in the dialog box.
5. Click on OK to place the text on the screen.

Editing Existing Text

Now that you have placed the text on the screen, you may discover that you have mistyped. How can you return to the Text dialog box and edit the text you have created? It's really very simple.

1. If the text isn't already selected, click on the pick tool in the tool box and click on the text to select it.
2. Pull down the Edit menu and select Edit Text.

The text box will open up and you can use the mouse cursor and editing keys to make any corrections.

Adjusting Text Spacing

There are a few specialized typographic tools in the Text dialog box. Begin with the Text Spacing dialog box.

1. To reach this box, the Text dialog box must already be open. Open the text dialog box either by using the Edit Text command or by clicking on the text tool and then clicking on the page area.
2. Click on the button marked Spacing. The Text Spacing dialog box shown in Figure 2.19 will open.

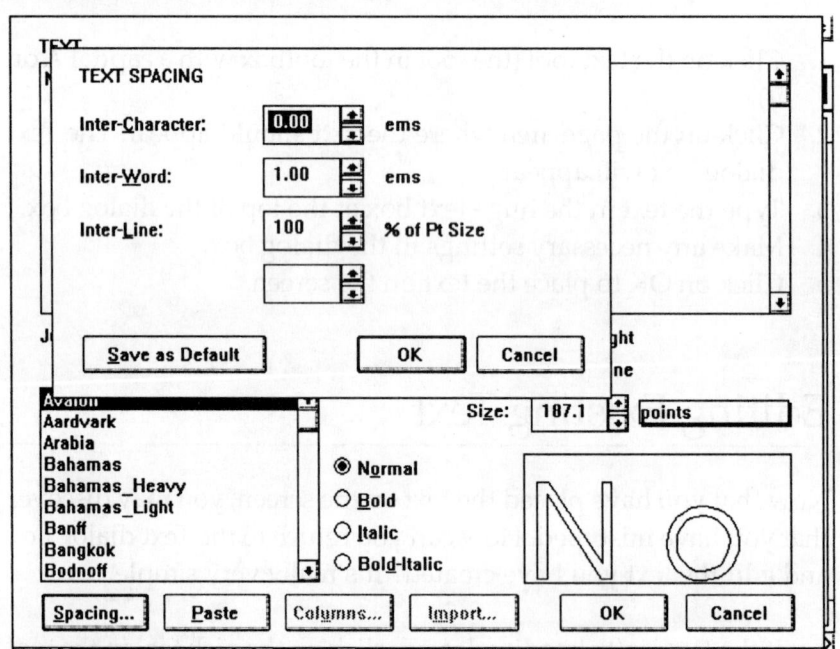

▼ *Figure 2.19. The Text Spacing dialog box*

The items in this box allow you to adjust the spacing between characters (intercharacter), between words (interword), between lines of text (interline), and between paragraphs (interparagraph).

Using Text

The first two (intercharacter and interword) are in ems, a spacing based on the width of the capital letter M in a given typeface. The second two (interline and interparagraph) are based on a percentage of the point size of the current typeface. A setting of 100 percent (the default) is adequate spacing to prevent letters from becoming enjambed between the lines, and yet lines are spaced closely enough to provide visual cues that allow your eye to see that one line is conceptually connected to the next. But you may not want to use these settings. Sometimes you want to place a warning label on your ad so that customers will have less basis to sue when your product explodes, melts, or runs away. You could create a statement like:

```
Warning: This product has been known to
burst into flames at random intervals and
for no known reason.
```

Naturally, you won't want that information to be as big and obvious as the headline of your ad or the picture of young adults enjoying your product at a fancy health spa. Therefore, you would use a tighter interline setting—perhaps 75 percent.

1. Return to the page area by selecting Cancel in the Text Spacing dialog box and the Text dialog box.
2. Click on the text tool in the toolbox.
3. Place your cursor near the bottom of the page area.
4. Press the left mouse button and drag a rectangle about two inches wide and two inches high. When you release the mouse button, the Text dialog box will reappear.
5. Enter the warning label as it appears (or make up your own).
6. Click on the button marked Spacing. Set the interline setting to 75 percent. Click on OK in the Text Spacing dialog box and the Text dialog box.

When you return to the page area, your warning will look something like Figure 2.20.

▼ **Figure 2.20. The warning label**

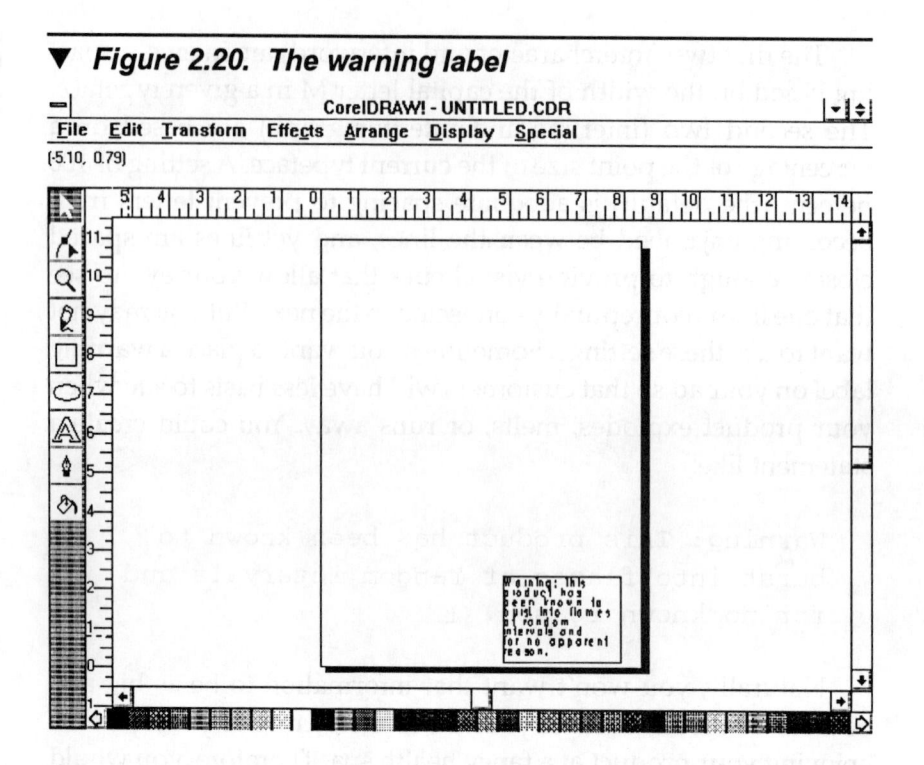

Making Your Text Fit in the Text Rectangle

You may discover that your text rectangle wasn't long enough to contain all the words. For this reason, you must proofread these text rectangles very carefully. Text that doesn't fit simply doesn't appear on the page area.

1. To lengthen the text rectangle, click on the outline of the rectangle. The eight familiar handles will appear.
2. Drag any of the handles to adjust the size of the rectangle to show all the text.

An alternate way of making all the text fit is to adjust the point size of the text (a point is approximately 1/72 inch, and it is the standard measurement for type size) or the interline space. You already know how to adjust the interline measurement.

1. To adjust the size of the text, select the text rectangle by clicking on its outline, then select Edit Text from the Edit menu.

Using Text

When the Text dialog box appears, note the Size: text box about midway down the right-hand side of the dialog box. You can change the form of measurement by clicking on the box to the right of the Size: box which normally says "points." You will cycle through measurements in inches, millimeters, and picas and points (a pica is roughly 1/6 inch or 12 points so 24 points translates into 2 picas, 0 points).

2. Either type in a smaller point size by dragging through the value in the Size: box or click on the downward-pointing arrow at the right of the text box to reduce the value in the box.

If you reduce the point size enough, you will be able to fit the text in the box. Be conscious of the legibility of the text in the box. Text that is smaller than seven or eight points will begin to strain eyes older than 35 years and smaller text may be completely illegible when printed on a 300 dpi laser printer because of the limited resolution of these machines.

You have now seen two ways of placing text on the page: You can click on the text tool and then click on the page area, or you can click on the text tool and drag a text rectangle. Using the first method puts the responsibility for aligning text on your shoulders. When you're typing a line of text in the Text dialog box, you have to watch your line length and press Enter when you think a line should "wrap" or return to the left margin. Using the second method makes the text wrap automatically to fit the box.

Text wrap brings up the whole issue of alignment. Text can be aligned in one of five different ways, each of which is provided in the Text dialog box. Call up the Text dialog box, if it is not already visible on the screen.

In the center of the box, beneath the text box in which you enter the words that should appear on the screen, are five radio buttons marked Left, Center, Right, Full (Left & Right), and None. Radio buttons act like the station-selecting buttons on an old-fashioned car radio. When you press any of the buttons, any button that is already selected will be deselected.

Left justification is the standard arrangement of text you would see on most typed documents: The left margin is smooth and the right margin is rough (this alignment is often called ragged-right justificaton). Center justification makes the text ragged on both margins. Each line is centered within the text box or relative to the place on the page where you clicked the mouse cursor. Right justification makes the right margin smooth and leaves the left margin ragged (sometimes called ragged-left justification).

Full justification is only available for text typed into a text rectangle. It causes *CorelDRAW!* to carefully insert space between letters and words in a line to make it fill the rectangle, left-to-right. In this way, both the right and left margins are made smooth. Although you might think this would be the most desirable alignment because having no ragged margins results in a very neat-looking paragraph, in fact full justification can lead to some headaches. Sometimes so much white space has to be pumped into a line that the line begins to look disconnected, like a collection of characters rather than words. Sometimes line after line has so much white space pumped in between the words that these white spaces form ugly channels of white space moving vertically through the text. These are particularly a problem when your lines are very short.

As long as you are aware that these problems can occur, and as long as you are alert to the potential problems, feel free to use full justification. If you find yourself falling prey to these problems, move to left or right justification. Perhaps some future version of *CorelDRAW!* will feature the ability to hyphenate text, which would largely eliminate this problem.

The None justification button would seem to be a mystery. How could there be no justification? Switching to None retains the justification that was set before, but it "disconnects" the individual characters on the screen, allowing you to position them individually.

Getting Text from the Clipboard

Now return to the Text dialog to see what else it has to offer. But first, you should create some text in the *Windows Write* word processor that was shipped with *Windows*.

1. Minimize *CorelDRAW!* by pulling down the system menu and selecting Minimize or by clicking on the minimize button (sec-

ond button from the right on the upper-right corner of the *CorelDRAW!* window.
2. Open the Accessories program group by clicking on it.
3. Double click on the *Write* icon.
4. Write a few words—your name perhaps or a bit of poetry: "Over one arm the lusty courser's rein/Under her other was the tender boy,/who blushed and pouted in a dull disdain."
5. Select the text by dragging the mouse through it. The text will be in reverse type, white for black. Pull down the Edit menu in *Write* and select Cut.
6. Double click on the close box in the upper left corner of the *Write* window. A dialog box will appear asking if you want to save your work. Click on the No button.
7. Restart *CorelDRAW!* by double clicking on its icon in the bottom left corner of the screen (if it's hidden by another window, close or minimize that window to make *CorelDRAW!* visible; if the window hiding the *CorelDRAW!* icon is the Program Manager, just minimize it—closing it will end your *Windows* session).
8. If the text on the screen isn't selected, click on the pick tool and select it.
9. Pull down the Edit menu and select Edit Text to open up the Text dialog box.

Using Text

Note that the word "Paste" appears on a button. This refers to the same cut and paste operation discussed in the previous section. *Windows* is a multitasking operating system shell that allows you to have several different applications going at the same time. The text you selected and cut in *Write* is still on the Clipboard.

1. Drag the mouse pointer through the text in the Text box that contains your warning. It should turn into reverse type—black-for-white.
2. Click on the Paste button. What happened?

If all went well, your warning text should have disappeared and in its place the text you created with the word processor should have appeared.

Getting Text from a File

1. Once again minimize *CorelDRAW!*.
2. Open the Accessories program group by clicking on it.
3. Double click on the *Write* icon.
4. Write a few words—perhaps the concluding words to the famous stanza from *Venus and Adonis:* "With leaden appetite, unapt to toy;/She red and hot as coals of glowing fire,/He red for shame, but frosty in desire."
5. Pull down the File menu and select Save. The save dialog box will appear.
6. Type in "VENUS" as the filename.
7. There are three check boxes in the dialog box marked Make Backup, Text Only, and Microsoft Word Format. Click on the button that says Text Only. This will prevent any formatting commands from being saved with the text—you don't want them.
8. Click on the OK button. *Write* automatically appends an extension, so the file will actually be saved under the name VENUS.WRI.
9. Double click on the close box in the upper left corner of the *Write* window.
10. Restart *CorelDRAW!* by double clicking on its icon in the bottom left corner of the screen.
11. If the text on the screen isn't selected, click on the pick tool and select it.
12. Pull down the Edit menu and select Edit Text to open up the Text dialog box.

Now you should be back at the familiar Text dialog box. The goal is to replace the first half of Shakespeare's stanza with the second half.

1. If there is no I-beam flashing in the text box, click at the end of the text to place the I-beam there (the I-beam indicates where your typing will appear).
2. Click on the button marked Import. This is the button you use to pull in text from a file.

Using Text

The Import Text dialog box will appear. Look at the Path box. It should read something like "C:*.TXT." That means it's going to look in the root directory for a file with the extension of TXT. That won't work. You need to enter a different path into this box. Your VENUS file was saved in the same directory that contained the *Write* program, which was probably your *Windows* directory (unless you've made radical changes in your *Windows* setup). Usually this is on the C: drive. If yours is elsewhere, you're on your own. I will assume that you saved VENUS.WRI in the WINDOWS directory directly under the root directory on your C: drive.

3. Drag the mouse pointer through the Path text box so that the type inside is highlighted.
4. Type C:\WINDOWS*.WRI and press Enter.

Your file, VENUS.WRI should appear in the Files list box.

5. Double click on VENUS.WRI.

You will be returned to the Text dialog box and the first part of the poem will be replaced with the second. Want to unite the two? If you have been following directions to the letter up until now, the text you placed on the Clipboard should still be there.

1. Click in the text box ahead of the first letter that appears there.
2. Click on the button marked "Paste."

The material on the clipboard will appear.

TIP

CorelDRAW! is not a desktop publishing program, though its output can be used in *Ventura Publisher* and other programs specifically developed for desktop publishing. There are severe limits on the amount of text that can be added at one time. If you have simply clicked on the screen with the text tool, you can only enter 250 characters. This is called a *text string*. If you have dragged a text rectangle, you can enter up to 4000 characters (around 600 words). This is called *paragraph text*. Although the individual strings and paragraphs are limited

in size, there is no practical limit on the number of strings or paragraphs you can place on the screen.

PRACTICE WHAT YOU'VE LEARNED

What You Should Do	How the Computer Responds
1 Create a text file with several pages of text in it. Drag a small text rectangle in the page area. Import the text you just created to *CorelDRAW!* via the Text dialog box.	1. The excess text simply doesn't appear in the text rectangle.
2. Create a narrow text rectangle (about two inches across) and type in some text with large words in it (you can simply type *typewriter* several times). Click on the Full (Left & Right) radio button in the Justification area of the dialog box and click on OK.	2. In justified text, particularly when the words are long and the column narrow, the spaces between letters and words can become excessive, ruining the appearance of the text. This is less of a problem with certain fonts and with text in extremely long lines, but if you can't solve the problem any other way, consider using left alignment for your text.

Changing the Appearance of a Block of Text

CorelDRAW! offers four standard type styles: Normal, Bold, Italic, and Bold-Italic. I'm sure you know what bold or italic text looks like. You can select these styles for an entire block.

Using Text

1. Click on the text tool in the toolbox and either click on the page area or drag a paragraph rectangle.

   When the Text dialog box appears, type in some text. Note the column of radio buttons at the center bottom of the Text dialog box marked with the four text styles.

2. Click on the various typefaces available.

   Note that when the Avalon typeface is selected, all four styles are available, but when you click on Aardvark, only bold is shown in black, indicating that it is the only available style. In the Arabia typeface, only Normal is available.

3. Select a typeface and a style and click on OK to return to the page area.

Changing the Appearance of Individual Characters

Say you have entered the text:

```
SALE: BLACK BEAUTY AND
THE BLACK STALLION
$14.95 EACH
```

in the text box. Good style requires that you italicize the names of the novels. This is easily accomplished.

1. Click on the text tool in the toolbox and click on the page area.
2. When the Text dialog box appears, type in the text written above.
3. Select a typeface that has both a normal and an italic style. I will use Casablanca (use the scroll bar at the right side of the typeface list box to scroll down to Casablanca). It is a very graceful typeface reminiscent of Caslon, one of the true classics

of the typesetting world. (Typesetters say, "When in doubt, use Caslon.")

4. Make sure the point size is 24, the style is Normal, and the alignment is Center.
5. Click on OK to return to the page area. You may need to drag the text to the center of the page. Make any necessary adjustments.

Now you need to set the two novel titles in italic.

1. Click on the shape tool.
2. Drag a selection rectangle that completely encloses BLACK BEAUTY. Pull down the Edit menu and select Character Attributes. You will see the dialog box in Figure 2.21.

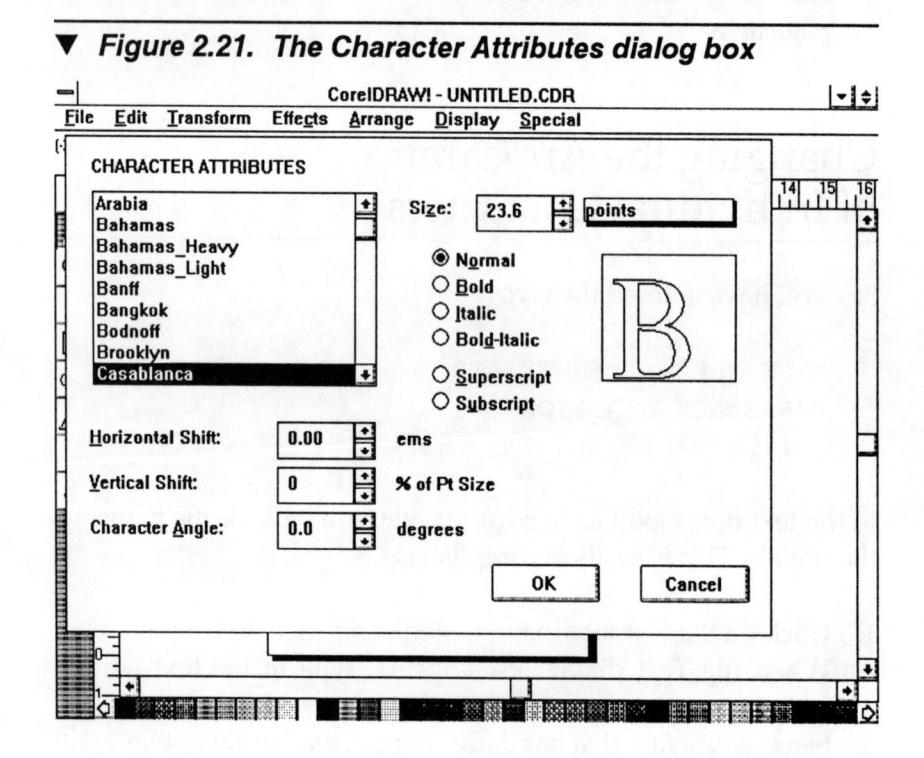

▼ *Figure 2.21. The Character Attributes dialog box*

This dialog box has an overwhelming collection of powerful commands. You can change the typeface, adjust the point size, change the style (including two additional options—superscript

Editing the Drawing ▲ 107

and subscript), and shift the selected text or characters in any direction or angle.

Using Text

3. Click on Italic. This is not the same as changing character angle because italic characters generally have a completely different appearance from roman characters of the same type family (compare lowercase e's and a's between Roman and italic types to see the sharpest contrast). While characters changed with character, angle simply rotates the characters without changing their appearance otherwise.
4. Perform the same task on *The Black Stallion*.

Using the Zoom Tool

Zoom in on the price for the next action.

1. Click on the zoom tool (third from the top) in the toolbox. You will see the zoom tool menu (Figure 2.22).

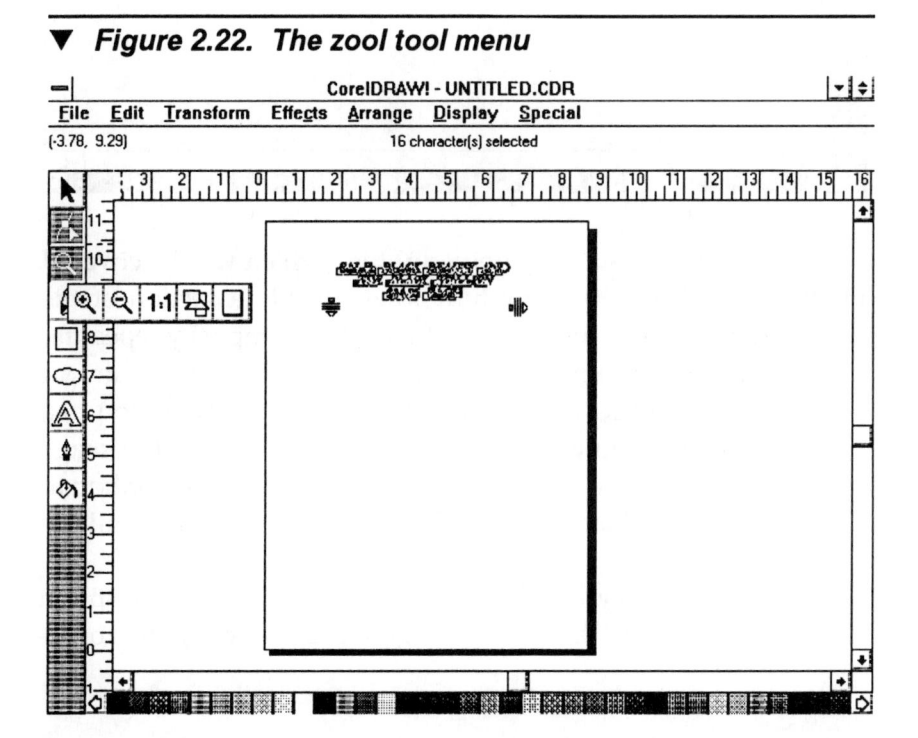

▼ *Figure 2.22. The zool tool menu*

2. Click on the zoom—in selection—the magnifying glass with the plus sign in it.
3. Drag a selection rectangle that includes the price—$14.95 EACH—in the page area. When you release the mouse button, you will see a screen similar to the one shown in Figure 2.23.

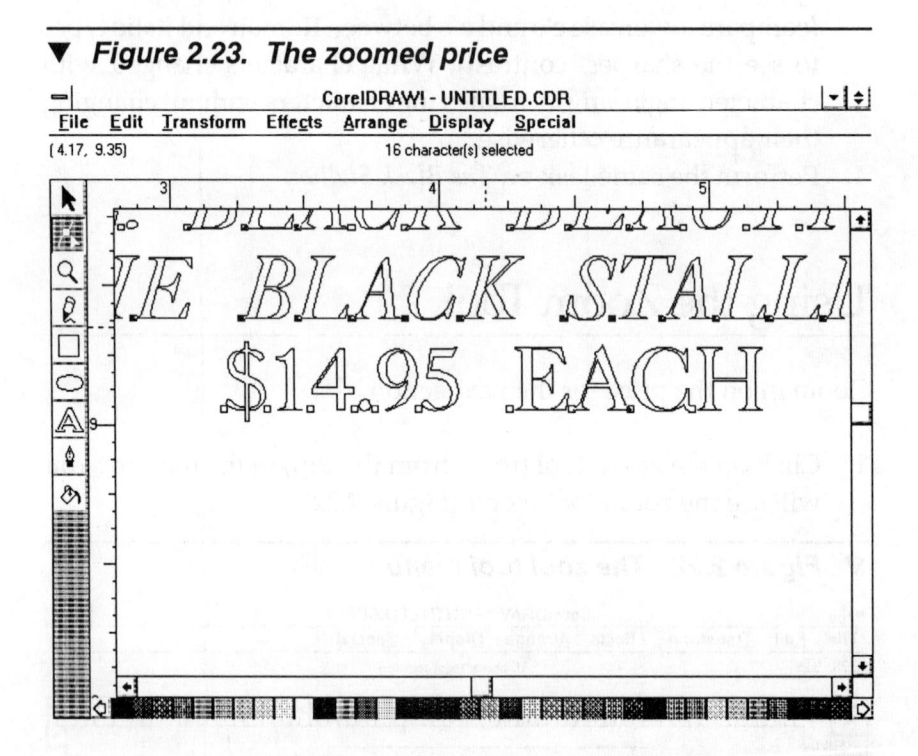

▼ **Figure 2.23. The zoomed price**

The zoom tool is a very powerful tool, which will be covered briefly here. You now know how to zoom into a section of the screen. You can zoom in far closer, if you want, simply by repeating the steps above. The other options on the zoom menu are zoom out (the magnifying glass with the minus sign), which takes you to a previous level of magnification. For example, if you have the image of Figure 2.23 on your screen, you could use the zoom-in option to zoom in on the dollar sign. The dollar sign would nearly fill the screen.

Selecting the zoom tool and clicking on the zoom-out option will take you back to the image in Figure 2.23. Selecting the zoom-out option again would take you back to the screen visible in Figure 2.22.

TIP

Using Text

When sizing an object, you can constrain the size to full multiples of the object's current size by holding down the Ctrl key while dragging a corner handle on the selection rectangle.

There are three other tricks having to do with sizing an object.

Hold the Ctrl key while dragging a side handle and the length (or height) of the object will change in multiples of the object's size. The Shift key in combination with dragging a handle will cause the opposite handle to move the same distance as the handle you are dragging, whether it is an end handle or a corner handle. Using the Shift and Ctrl keys together will cause the opposite handle to move in such a way that the object increased in full multiples of its current size. This may sound a little complicated, but give it a try and you will instantly catch on.

The 1:1 option on the zoom tool menu makes the image onscreen about the size it will appear when it is printed on paper. The next option looks like a conglomeration of shapes. It displays whatever objects are on the page so that they fill the screen. The last option returns to the standard view, with the entire page area visible in the *CorelDRAW!* window.

Next you will reduce the size of the .95 part of the price and turn it into a superscript (superscripts are elevated above the normal text line; subscripts are lowered below the normal text line).

It was not necessary to zoom in on the screen to perform this action, but it is easier to pick out a few characters of text when the screen is zoomed in on them.

1. Click on the shape tool and drag a selection rectangle around the .95 part of the price.
2. Select Character Attributes from the Edit menu.
3. Click on Superscript. There is no need to adjust the point size. *CorelDRAW!* will automatically scale the type so it is about half the size of normal 24-point type.

4. Click on the zoom tool and select the page option (the last option on the right) to return to the standard page view.
5. Pull down the Display menu and select Show Preview or press Shift-F9 to make the selection. The display should appear on the right half of the screen.
6. Pull down the Display menu and select Show Preview Toolbox. You will see the toolbox shown in Figure 2.24.

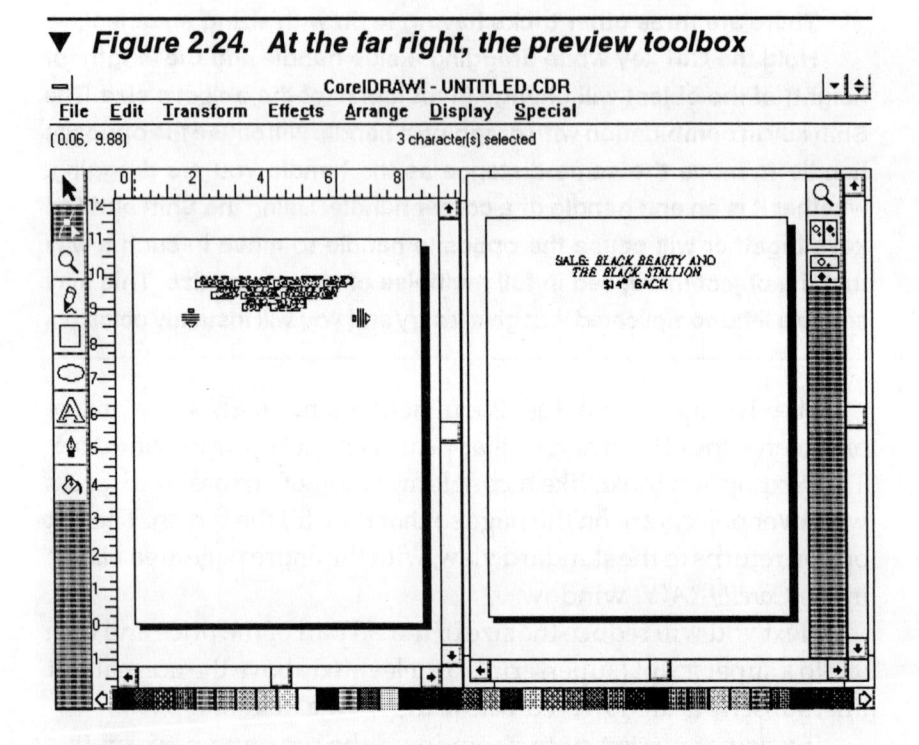

▼ **Figure 2.24. At the far right, the preview toolbox**

The three items in the preview toolbox have to do with zooming in on parts of the preview and with the position of the preview window relative to the page area.

1. Click on the zoom tool in the preview toolbox menu. You will see the familiar zoom-in, zoom-out, 1:1, objects, and page area options, just like the toolbox in the page area of the screen.
2. Select the zoom-in option and drag a selection rectangle around the price. Note that when you release the mouse button, the preview screen shows only the price, expanded to fill the preview screen.

Changing the Preview Arrangement

Using Text

The top tool in the preview toolbox is normally selected, causing the page area to appear to the left and the preview to appear to the right.

1. Click on the third and last item in the preview toolbox. You should see something like the screen in Figure 2.25.

▼ *Figure 2.25. The page area and preview in over-under arrangement*

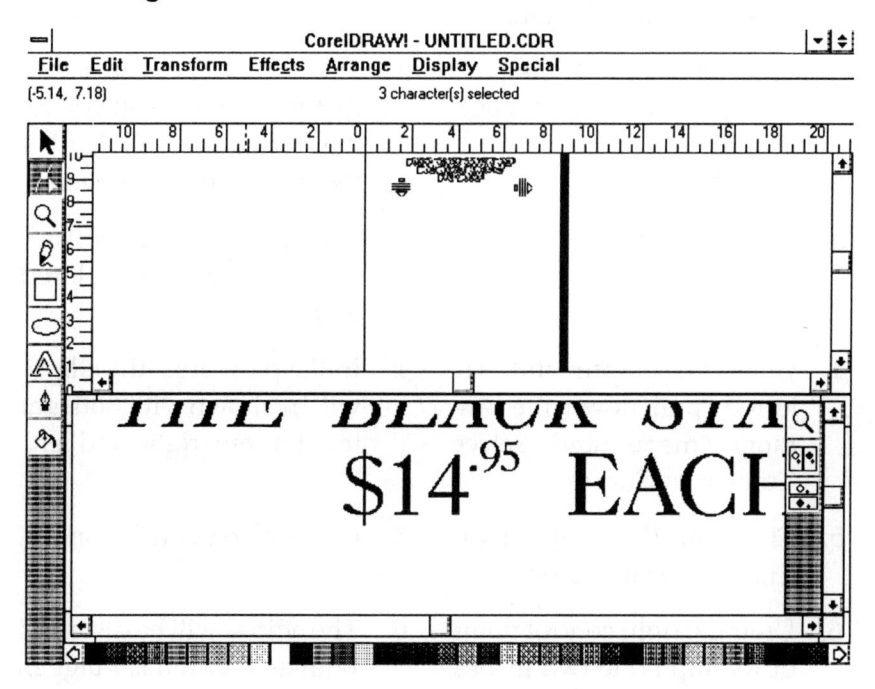

Note that the price is still zoomed and the preview toolbox is still visible. This arrangement is particularly useful if you are working with a page area that is wide rather than long.

Is that all there is to text? Believe it or not, over the past several pages you have barely scratched the surface. Chapter 9 is devoted to text.

Exercises

This exercise assumes that you have *CorelDRAW!* running and a new, blank page area visible. If you already have something on the screen, save it and select New from the File menu.

What You Should Do	How the Computer Responds
1. Click on the ellipse tool and drag your mouse diagonally on the page area. Release the mouse button.	1. An ellipse will be drawn in the page area.
2. Click on a color in the palette at the bottom of your screen.	2. The status line will show that you have an ellipse on the screen and will display the color you have selected.
3. Press Shift-F9.	3. The preview screen will appear, showing the colored ellipse.
4. With the ellipse still selected, pull down the Arrange menu and select Convert to Curves.	4. In the page area, the ellipse will be shown with nodes at top, bottom, right, and left.
5. Click on the shape tool. Click on the top node.	5. Control points will appear.
6. Drag the right control point of the top node two inches to the right.	6. The ellipse will be distorted with an enormous bulge in the top left and right quadrants. The node is symmetrical.

7. Double click on the bottom node and in the resulting dialog box, select Cusp. Drag the right control point of the bottom node two inches to the right.

8. Pull down the File menu and select Save.

9. Type the name DISTELLI in the box and click on the Save button.

10. Select New from the File menu.

7. This time only one quadrant of the ellipse is affected. The control points of the bottom node are in effect divorced from one another.

8. The Save Drawing dialog box will appear, with the cursor already in the File: text box.

9. Your ellipse will be saved to disk under the name DISTELLI.CDR.

10. The screen will be cleared and the word DISTELLI.CDR in the title bar will be replaced with UNTITLED.CDR.

Exercises

3 Printing

▲ Installing a New Printer
▲ Changing Printers
▲ Printing with *CorelDRAW!*
▲ Preparing Files for a Typesetter
▲ Merge Printing

You may have noticed that when you installed *CorelDRAW!*, you didn't have to specify what kind of printer or monitor or extended memory you had. Most programs need to know in detail what kinds of peripheral devices they will be working with but programs that run under *Windows* depend upon *Windows* to communicate with your monitor, your printer, and other peripheral devices. This chapter will get you set up to use *Windows* with your printer.

To start with, you may already be all set to work with your printer. When you installed *Windows*, you probably specified what kind of printer you are using. If not, it can be easily set (or changed) by using a program called the Control Panel.

1. Start *Windows*.
2. In the Program Manager window, locate the icon labeled "Main."
3. Double click on the Main icon.

This is the part of *Windows* that takes care of file management, printer spooling, shelling out to DOS, the Clipboard you've seen in use, and *Windows* setup. You might think that you need to run *Windows* Setup to set or change the printer, but this program only sets the display type, keyboard, mouse type, network settings, and location of the swap file.

You need to use the Control Panel to set or change your printer.

1. Double click on the Control Panel icon.

You'll see the program group shown in Figure 3.1. (Another way to get to the Control Panel is to select Control Panel from the File menu in *CorelDRAW!*. If you have a change to make in a hurry, that would be the preferable way.)

TIP

Control Panel is also an item on the File menu within *CorelDRAW!*. If you already have *CorelDRAW!* running, you could call the Control Panel this way and save a few steps.

▼ *Figure 3.1. The Control Panel program group*

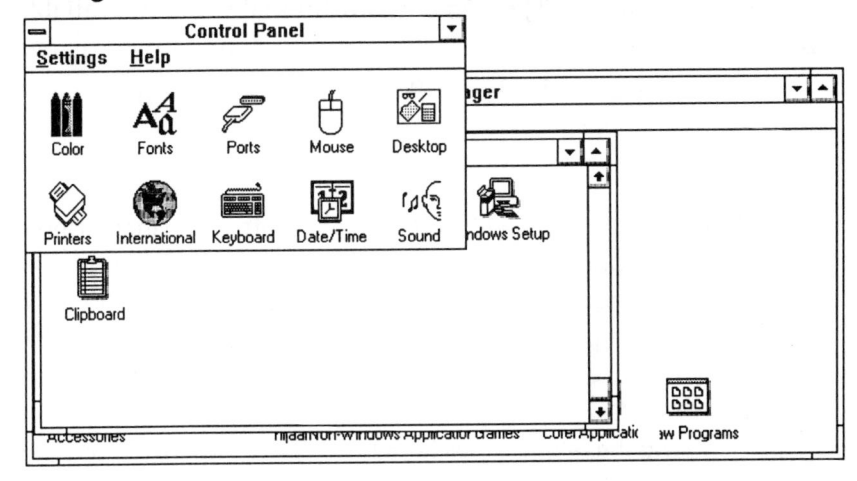

Printing

The options are Color, Fonts, Ports, Mouse, Desktop, Printers, International, Keyboard, Date/Time, and Sound.

2. Double click on Printers. You will see the dialog box shown in Figure 3.2.

▼ *Figure 3.2. The Printers dialog box*

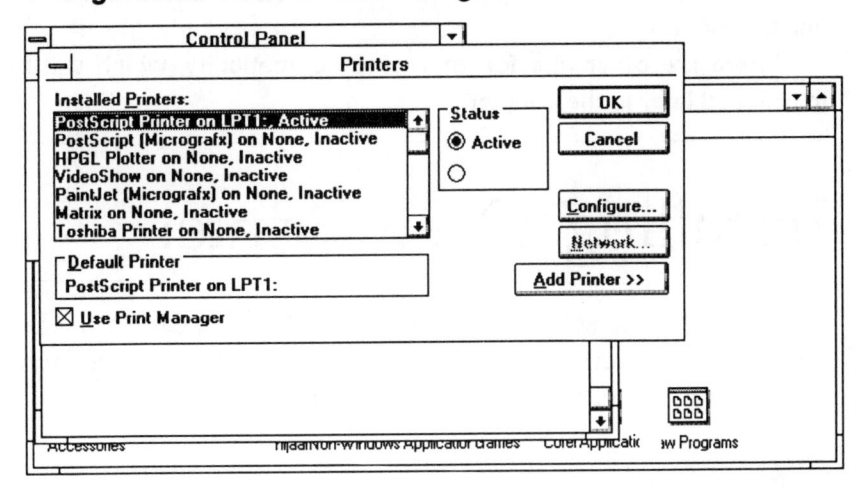

This is a pretty complex dialog box. In the Installed Printers list box, you can see the printers you installed when you set up *Win-*

dows. Just click on the printer name, if you want to change to one of the printers shown. There may be additional printers available. Just scroll through the list by clicking on the up- and down-arrows on the scroll bar at the right side of the list box.

TIP

As good as PostScript is, it isn't perfect. People often find their printers stalling because *CorelDRAW!* can create such complex graphics so simply. In fact, programs like *CorelDRAW!* are such a trial for PostScript printers that printer manufacturers have developed a standard list of actions to take with the Control Panel when you have problems printing to a PostScript printer.

First among these strategies is to turn off the Print Manager. It's a useful device that takes *Windows'* printer output and feeds it to the printer at the printer's speed while you are allowed to continue working (this is called "print spooling"). The advantage to turning off the Print Manager is that you avoid whatever incompatibilities may occur. Each time you add a link in a chain, you risk weakening it. In the same way, each time you add a program like the Print Manager to the stream of input/output, you add to the risk of incompatibilities. The disadvantage in turning off the Print Manager is that when you send information to the printer, your program is unavailable to you until the printer is finished printing.

There are other tips for improving compatibility, which will be introduced later in the chapter.

Installing a New Printer

You may want to select a printer that doesn't appear on the list. Click on the button marked "Add Printer." You'll be presented with a list of over 160 printers. Scroll through the list.

TIP

Your printer may not be listed. Refer to your printer's manual. It's likely that your printer is similar enough to one of the listed printers and this

Installing a New Printer

fact will be covered in your operator's manual. If it isn't, contact the manufacturer and ask for advice. The manufacturer will almost certainly have a suggestion for a compatible you can use or will provide you with a disk containing a driver you can use for your printer. *Windows* is like the proverbial 500-pound gorilla. It's too big to ignore and no hardware manufacturer would be so foolish as to introduce a device for the PC that can't work with *Windows*. The last item in the list of printers is Unlisted Printer. Click on this item and the Install button and you will see a dialog box to be used for installing the driver for your printer.

When you select a printer from the List of Printers and click on Install, you may be prompted to insert one of the *Windows* installation disks.

You can have several printers installed and I recommend that you take the time to install a PostScript printer (whether you own one or not), a PCL (Printer Control Language) printer (like the HP LaserJet), and an Epson compatible (like the Epson MX-80) in addition to whatever printer you are using. These will place about 90–95 percent of all printers within your control. Even if you don't own a PCL printer or one of the others, there is a simple way to "print to disk" so you can send a graphic on a disk for someone else to print. When you begin creating professional-quality graphics, you may want to proof on your dot matrix to get a general idea of the appearance of the drawing, then have those graphics printed on a typesetter or a laser printer.

It should be mentioned that there are many printers that can't print graphics. Most notably, daisywheel printers. If you have one of those, you will simply be unable to print your graphics unless you can borrow a graphics printer from someone.

Changing Printers

Many PostScript printers can be reconfigured to be PCL-compatible (which means that they will operate like a Hewlett-Packard LaserJet). If you have problems printing to your PostScript printer, an additional way of dealing with this is to change to a PCL printer and change your printer's page-description language (PDL) to PCL. This leaves the interpretation to *Windows* instead of your printer. Surprisingly, *Windows* is often more capable at this task than your PostScript printer. You can expect the printout to take far less time, but there is a trade-off. Many files won't print properly (or at all) on anything but a PostScript device. Also, you may see some degradation in the appearance of complex objects like letters in text.

Next you will learn how to change printers. This option will be useful in the event that your PostScript printer continuously stalls.

1. Call up the Printer dialog box from the Control Panel window.
2. Find the printer to which you want to change in the list of installed printers (or install it as described in the previous section and then select it).
3. Click on the Active button in the Status box.
4. Click on the Configure button. You will see the dialog box shown in Figure 3.3.

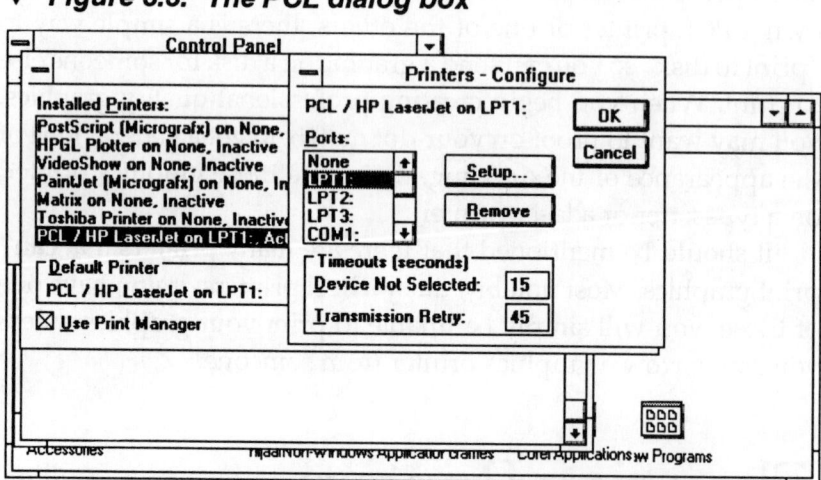

▼ *Figure 3.3. The PCL dialog box*

Configuring any printer will call up a similar box. You need to select the printer port to which the printer is connected (in this case, LPT1).

TIP

In the Printers-Configure dialog box, you have another setting that can help you deal with a recalcitrant PostScript printer. The Timeouts box at the bottom gives you settings for how long your printer can "timeout." A timeout is a period of time when the printer is signalling the computer that it's thinking or stalled for some kind of service. In the old days, dot-matrix printers didn't do a lot of thinking about the data they were fed, so a 45-second timeout was all that was necessary—that's about the amount of time it would take to change paper if you were printing a multiple page document on cut sheets.

By contrast, it isn't unusual for a PostScript printer to pause for half an hour to unravel a very complex set of PostScript instructions. Therefore, you should set the values in the Timeouts box to their maximums—999 seconds. Simply drag the mouse pointer through the values in the boxes and type 999.

You may still encounter problems with timeouts because, although 999 is the maximum setting, your printer may still need more time. Check a timed-out printer often. If you receive a dialog box with a message that *Windows* can't send any more information to the printer, click on the button marked "Retry" at least a few times to make sure the problem really is a stalled printer and not one that simply needs time to think. Faster RISC chips in laser printers may eliminate these kinds of problems in future printers.

The next step in changing printers is to click on the Setup button in the Printers-Configure dialog box.

1. Click on the Setup button.

This will call up the Setup dialog box shown in Figure 3.4. In this box, you can select the type of PCL printer that is installed.

2. Click on the downward-pointing arrow at the right of the Printer box. You will see a list of PCL printers.
3. Use the scroll bar to search through the list for the name that most closely matches your printer. Click on the printer name when you find it.

▼ **Figure 3.4. The Setup dialog box**

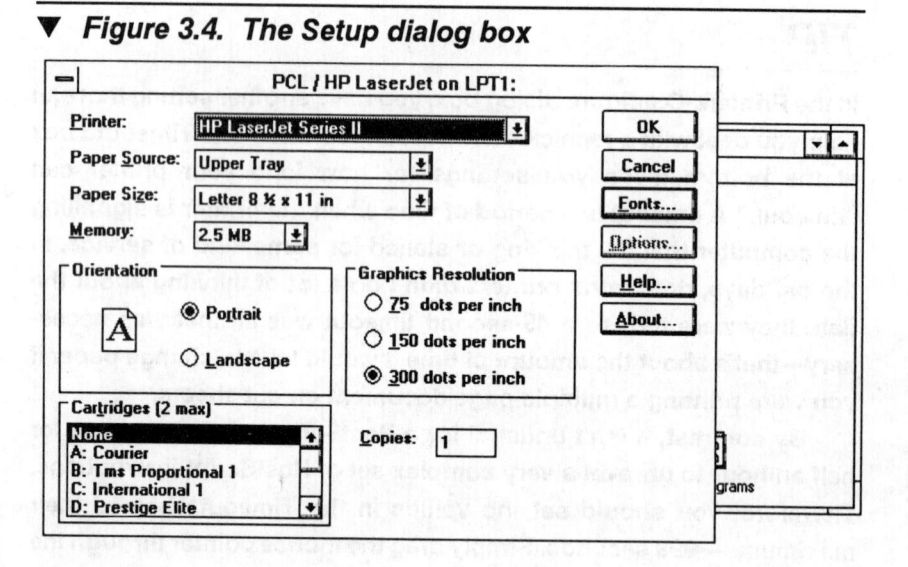

The settings in the other boxes with downward-pointing arrows at the right end can be made the same way.

4. Make sure the settings in the other boxes are correct.

Two settings that might give you pause are Orientation and Graphics Resolution. *Orientation* refers to the way the printing appears on the page, not the way the paper is fed through the printer. The paper will always go through the printer "tall" or in portrait orientation. If you want to change to "wide" printing—or landscape printing in *Windows* parlance—*Windows* will take care of rotating the print so that it appears rotated 90 degrees on the paper. You will have the option of making this setting in *CorelDRAW!*, so there is no need to change the setting here.

Your reaction to the question of resolution may be confusion. After all, your PCL printer may be capable of printing at 300 dpi, but the setting may be for some lower resolution. The reason is that printing at a low resolution will speed the printing process. A 75 dpi printout takes a mere fraction of the time it takes to print a 300 dpi graphic. But you will want to print final drafts of your graphics in 300 dpi mode.

Changing Printers

5. If you have cartridges installed in your PCL printer, make the appropriate selection in the Cartridges list box.
6. If you want to print multiple copies, you can make this setting in the *CorelDRAW!* Print dialog box. It's best to leave the Control Panel Copies setting at 1.

If you have soft fonts, proceed to install them by clicking on the button marked Fonts.

To exit from this chain of dialog boxes, click on the OK buttons that appear and then click on the close box of the Control Panel window and the Main program group.

TIP

If you will be using fonts from within Windows, you should invest in a font manager, such as *Adobe Type Manager* or *Bitstream Facelift*. Fonts can be quite a headache. The technology hasn't kept pace with users' expectations in this area. Another problem is that no standard has been established. Few of the available font systems and font managers are compatible with one another.

CHECK YOURSELF

1. What can you do when your PostScript printer refuses to print your *CorelDRAW!* drawing?

2. If you opt to print to a PCL printer at 75 dpi, what will the printout look like? Why would you want to print out like this?

ANSWERS

1. Turn off the print spooler.

2. The printout would look very blocky and coarse. You might use this setting if your printer won't accept any other setting, or so you can see a draft printout, just to get the idea of how objects in the drawing relate to one another.

Printing with CorelDRAW!

Now start up *CorelDRAW!* and take a look at the process of printing.

1. Start *CorelDRAW!* by double clicking on its icon in the Program Manager window.
2. Pull down the File menu and select Page Setup. You will see the dialog box in Figure 3.5.

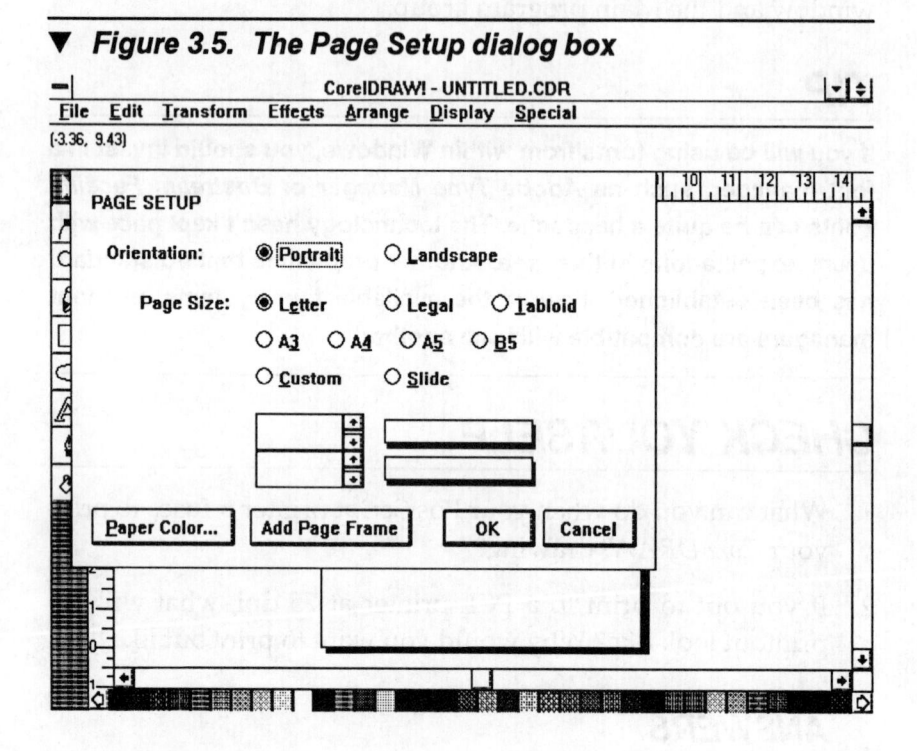

▼ **Figure 3.5. The Page Setup dialog box**

Note that you can change the page orientation and page size in this box. Up until now, you have seen the page in the portrait orientation, but just for experimentation, you should see it another way.

3. Click on Landscape and click on OK.

Printing with CorelDRAW!

Note that the page is now "sideways" in the *CorelDRAW!* window.

4. Return to the Page Setup dialog box and change the orientation back to Portrait. Click on OK.
5. Draw a rectangle on the page area. Click on one of the shades of blue in the palette at the bottom of the screen.
6. Pull down the File menu.

Note that you have the option of selecting the Control Panel. This will call up the Control Panel window you worked with earlier in this chapter.

7. Select Print. You will see the dialog box shown in Figure 3.6.

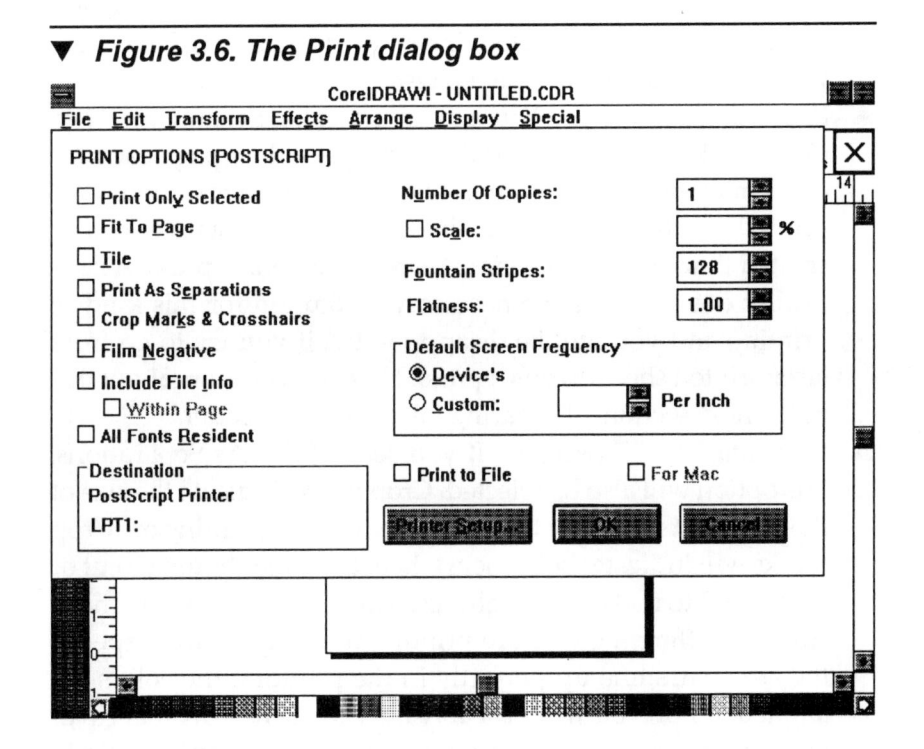

▼ *Figure 3.6. The Print dialog box*

Your first reaction may be similar to mine when I first saw the power the *CorelDRAW!* Print dialog box places in your hands—a rising panic. But don't fear. Most of the items are very easy to understand.

The print options apply only to PostScript devices and may be grayed and unavailable if you have another kind of printer. You should go through them quickly. Most apply to professional graphic design, so they may not be very useful to you now, but they're all interesting and well worth a look.

- ▲ Print Only Selected. This option will cause only selected objects to be printed.
- ▲ Fit to Page. This option causes whatever is on the page to be scaled to fill the page. If you place a small circle on the page area, it will be expanded to a circle as wide as the sheet of paper. Likewise, if your drawing is larger than the page, it will be scaled smaller to make it fit the page.
- ▲ Tile. Sometimes you will create a drawing larger than the page. If Tile is not selected, the portions that are off the page won't print at all. If Tile is selected, the portions that run off the page will be printed on additional pages.
- ▲ Print As Separations. You can create color separations with *CorelDRAW!*. A color separation will provide a page each for cyan, magenta, yellow, and black. These pages should be printed to a typesetting machine from which negatives can be created that can be turned into plates for an offset press. A laser printer doesn't have the necessary resolution for this kind of printing and you will be disapppointed if you try to go from laser printed sheets to offset press. There will be more about this in the next section, "Preparing Files for a Typesetter."
- ▲ Crop Marks & Crosshairs. If you select Print As Separations, this option will also be selected. Crop marks indicate the size of the page, if it is smaller than the sheet you are printing on. Crop marks will indicate the corners where the page should be cut or "cropped" to make it the right size. Crosshairs are used to make sure the different colors are printing properly on the paper. If the crosshairs line up perfectly in the printout, the colors are aligned. If not, you will probably have some narrow margin of acceptable error, and then if the crosshairs go beyond this limit, the printout won't be acceptable. You've probably seen this happen if your local newspaper prints color pictures: the cyan or yellow is printed half an inch away from where it should be.

Crosshairs will help prevent this from happening in your printouts.
▲ Film Negative. If you select Print As Separations, this options will also be selected. It simply prints black-for-white, like the negative of a black and white picture.
▲ Include File Info. This will print the name of the file being printed, the time, and the date on the extreme edge of the printed sheet of paper, outside the crop marks of a page that is smaller than the paper you are printing on. Unfortunately, you are usually printing a page that is exactly the size of the paper you are printing on. Therefore, you should click on Within Page if you want this information printed. This will place the information on the page. Generally, you should save this option for printouts routed through a Linotype or other typesetter to help keep track of your printing jobs.
▲ All Fonts Resident. This is a very advanced feature for people who have purchased Adobe fonts for use with their PostScript device. It indicates that instead of using *CorelDRAW!*'s fonts, your printer should substitute downloaded fonts.

Now take a look at the options on the right side of the Print dialog box.

▲ Number of Copies. This setting is fairly self explanatory. You can either drag the mouse pointer through the text box and type in the number of copies you want to make or you can click on the up-arrow until the number you want appears.
▲ Scale. The Scale option allows you to adjust the size of the printout by percentage.
▲ Fountain Stripes. Later in the book you will learn about a special kind of fill called a *fountain*. It is a gradual change from one color to another. On laser printers, there is no way to avoid visible stripes when printing with a laser printer because the resolution is simply too low to allow for a truly smooth change over an area. A low value in this box will speed your printout. A setting of 30 will print rapidly on a laser printer and will be virtually indistingushable from a setting of 128. If you are printing to a 1270 dpi typesetter, you should use the 128 setting. If you are printing to a 2540 dpi typesetter, run this value up to 200. On a

Printing with CorelDRAW!

typesetter, your fountains will be perfectly smooth. You won't be able to detect banding at all.

▲ Flatness. This sets the amount of jaggedness permissible in a curve. It might surprise you to know that even in PostScript a curve is made up of a large number of very short straight lines. A setting of 1 means that a straight line making up a curve may only be one dot long.

TIP

A flatness setting of 1—or a lower setting—may confound your printer or typesetter. PostScript is limited in the amount of complexity it can tolerate, as mentioned elsewhere. Therefore, if your printer "chokes" on a drawing, one of the things you can do to make it print is to increase its flatness. An increase to 2 may be sufficient and probably won't be noticeable on the printout. When the flatness increases beyond 3 or 4, it becomes increasingly obvious that curves are being broken up into short lines. The trade-off is not only the ability to print extremely complex graphics, but also a much faster printout. If you are only proofing and not preparing a final "camera-ready" graphic, raise the flatness to 10 or so to make sure everything is printing the way it should before investing the time to create a final image at a flatness of 1 or 2.

▲ Default Screen Frequency. This selection has nothing to do with your monitor's screen. A screen is the layout of dots on the page. Although the laser printer prints 300 dpi, it is only capable of producing a screen of around 60 lines. The reason for this is that in a screen, larger, more closely spaced dots are used to indicate a black or dark gray area and smaller, more spread out dots are used for light gray or white areas. These dots must be larger than the smallest possible dot because they are of variable size. In order to indicate varying degrees of grayness between black and white, these screen dots must be made up of clumps of printer dots and these clumps must be laid out at regular intervals. A screen of 60 lines means that each screen dot can be made up of from 0 to 25 dots, providing 25 shades of gray. You can use this default setting or click on Custom and change the number of lines. Increasing the number of lines won't improve the performance of a laser printer, unfortunately. You can decrease the number of lines below 60 to get some interesting effects, however.

Printing with CorelDRAW!

▲ Print to File. This option was mentioned early in the chapter. Perhaps by now it's clear why this is such a powerful option. Printing to file will send all the instructions that would normally be sent to the printer to a disk file instead. If you take this option, you will be prompted for a filename. The extension should be PRN to indicate a printer file. If you don't have a PostScript laser printer (or a PCL printer, for that matter), you can print your drawing to a file, save the file on a floppy disk, and take (or mail) the disk to someone who has a PostScript device (or a PCL printer, if the PRN file was created while a PCL printer was selected). Then that person can simply use the COPY command to send the information to the printer exactly as if *CorelDRAW!* were sending it directly to the printer. If your file was OORT.PRN, you can print it with the command

```
COPY OORT.PRN PRN
```

because DOS recognizes that PRN refers to the printer attached to the computer. This enables you to send a color-separated PostScript file on disk or over the telephone lines to a printing company that owns a typesetter and have the printer do the typesetting, then print a four-color version of your creation. When Print to File is selected, For Mac becomes available. This creates a PostScript file that a Macintosh will understand (they're slightly different from PC PostScript files).

▲ Printer Setup. Selecting the Printer Setup button calls up the dialog box shown in Figure 3.7.

This option allows you to select a different printer that uses the same basic driver. If you have an Apple LaserWriter selected but you want to create a file to be printed on a PostScript typesetter, you can select a typesetter in this box and create a PostScript file for it. It's simpler to use this option than to use the Control Panel.

You should try a couple of exercises to see what a couple of printing features do. You will print out a fountain fill at 60 lines and then at ten, so you will be able to see the difference. All of these

▼ **Figure 3.7. The Printer Setup dialog box**

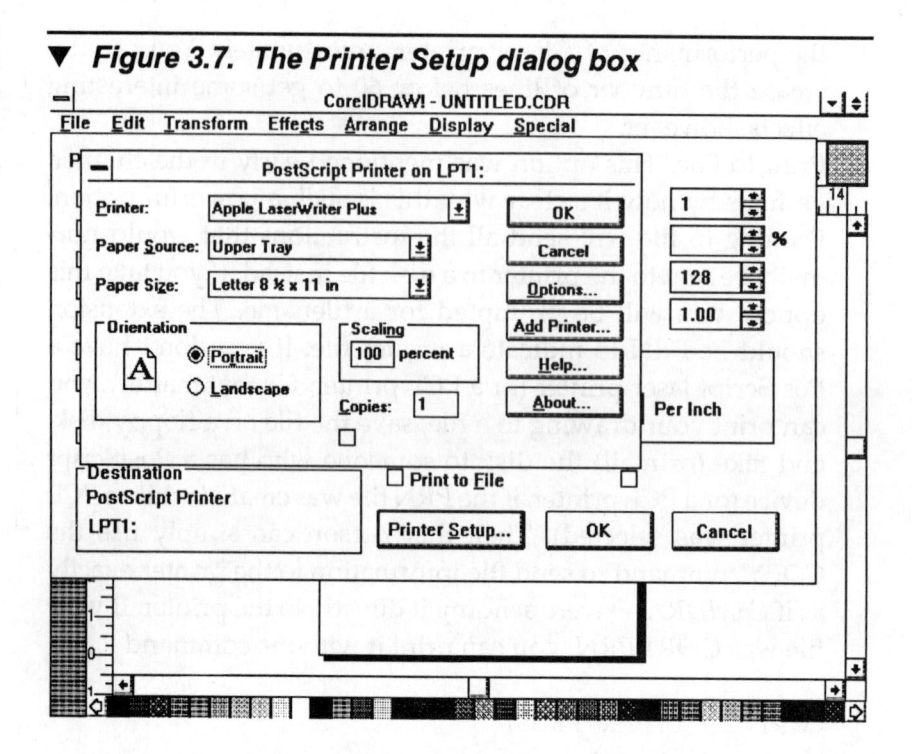

exercises assume that you have a PostScript printer at your disposal. If you don't, you might want to insert an additional step and print to a file. If you know someone who will let you use his or her PostScript printer, you will be able to see the effects yourself.

1. Start up *CorelDRAW!* or select New from the File menu to obtain a blank page area.
2. Pull down the File menu and select Page Setup.
3. In the Page Setup dialog box, click on Custom. Note that the Horizontal and Vertical boxes turn black so you can enter some custom measurements.
4. Enter 4 as the horizontal measurement and enter 5 as the vertical measurement (you can, if you wish, place the mouse pointer on the downward-pointing arrows at the right end of these text boxes and click until the value you want appears in the box). Click on OK to return to the page.
5. Make sure the rulers appear along the top and left edge of the screen as shown in Figure 3.6 (and most of the other figures in

Printing with CorelDRAW!

this book). If the rulers aren't visible, pull down the Display menu and select Show Rulers.

Note that the ruler shows the size of the page area. Although you will be printing on standard letter paper, the page area on that sheet of paper will be four inches by five inches. This is the difference between the paper setting in the printer setup and the page setup.

Now you will draw a circle on the page and fill it with a fountain fill (you'll learn all about fills in Chapter 7).

1. Click on the ellipse tool and press the Ctrl key. Drag diagonally on the page area, creating a circle about two inches in diameter.
2. Click on the fill tool in the tool box (the tool at the bottom). The fill tool menu appears.

Note that the second-to-last item in the top row of the menu looks like a starburst (it's between the double-headed diagonal arrow and the item marked "PS").

3. Click on the starburst. This is the fountain fill item. You will see the dialog box shown in Figure 3.8.

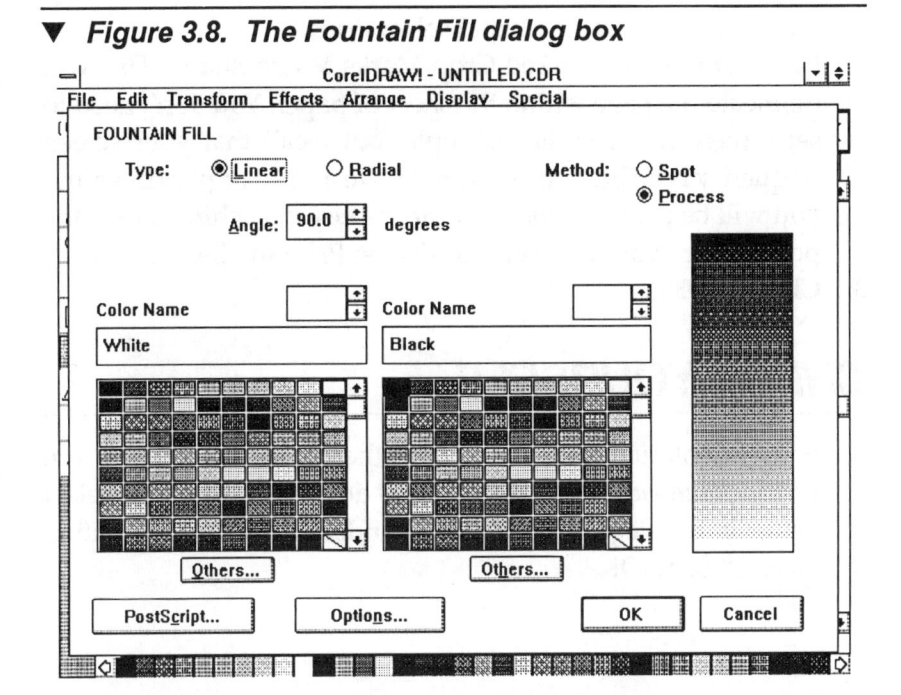

▼ *Figure 3.8. The Fountain Fill dialog box*

4. This dialog box is covered in detail in Chapter 7, but for now, click on the button at the top marked Radial and click on the button at the bottom marked OK.

When you return to the page area, note that the square at the right end of the status line shows a radial fountain fill that is light at the edges and dark at the center. When you print out the image, your circle will be gently shaded from light gray or white at the edge to black at the center.

TIP

You will probably notice that there are bands in the printout. If you reproduce the drawing with a photocopier, the banding will be even more noticeable. The problem is unavoidable with a 300 dpi laser printer. The banding will disappear and the fountains will be perfectly smooth if you print the drawing with a typesetter.

Now you will turn to printing the image. You should print it several times to illustrate the effect of changing the settings.

1. Pull down the File menu and select Print.
2. Click on the box marked Crop Marks & Crosshairs. This will delineate the page within the sheet of paper. You don't need to set screen lines for this example, but recall that your screen frequency is 60 lines. If you don't have a PostScript printer and you will be printing this on someone else's machine, this is the point where you will want to click on Print to File.
3. Click on OK.

CHECK YOURSELF

1. Four orientation terms you have heard in this chapter are *portrait, landscape, wide,* and *tall.* Pull down the File menu, select Letter in the Page Size area and Landscape in the Orientation area. Click on OK.

2. In this section, you learned another action to take when your PostScript printer fails to print your *CorelDRAW!* drawing. What was it?

Printing with CorelDRAW!

ANSWERS

1. Portrait=Tall and Landscape=Wide. The page should appear wider than it is tall.

2. Increase the flatness value in the Print dialog box to reduce the complexity of curves.

When the printout appears, it should look like Figure 3.9.

▼ *Figure 3.9. The printout at 60 lines with crop marks and crosshairs*

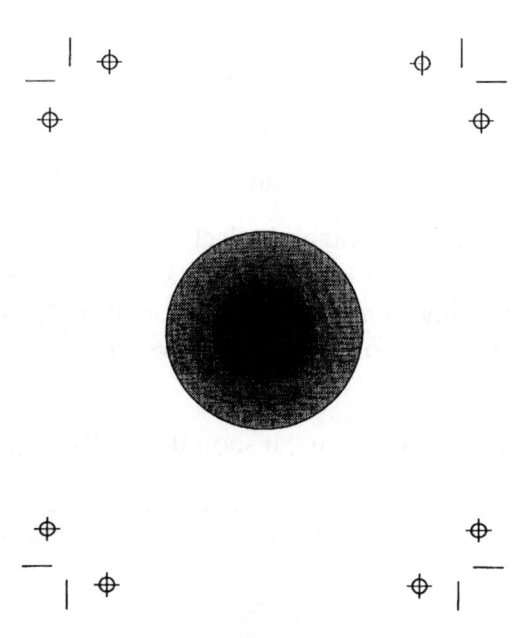

1. Pull down the File menu and select Print.
2. Click on Custom in the Default Screen Frequency. The value 60 appears in the Per Inch text box. Click on the downward-pointing arrow at the right end of this text box until the value in the box is 10.

3. Click on the box marked Crop Marks & Crosshairs. This will turn off the crop marks and crosshairs. If you don't have a PostScript printer and you will be printing this on someone else's machine, this is the point where you will want to click on Print to File.
4. Click on OK.

When the printout appears, it should look like Figure 3.10.

▼ **Figure 3.10. The printout at 10 lines**

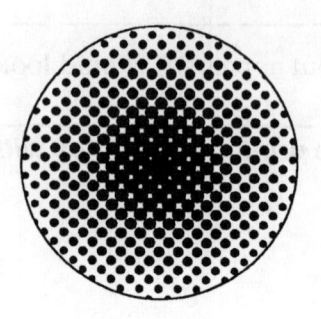

Finally, you will change the number of fountain stripes.

1. Pull down the File menu and select Print.
2. In the Default Screen Lines box, click on Device's, which will set the screen lines for the optimum for your printer.
3. Reduce the number of Fountain Stripes to 3.
4. Click on OK.

When the printout appears, it should look like Figure 3.11.

▼ **Figure 3.11. The printout with reduced fountain stripes**

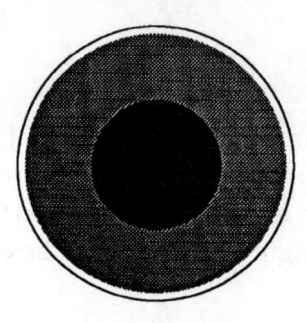

Preparing Files for a Typesetter

Preparing Files for a Typesetter

Typesetters and large printing companies can accept files on disk or over the telephone lines. These files need to be color separated. From these files, the printer will create photogaphic negatives from which plates can be created for an offset press. There are two different methods for printing colors: spot and process. Using spot colors, you would indicate an area on the page and specify a color to place in that area. This is useful if you are only printing one or only a few colors on a page. Process colors are best when the graphics might contain any color. Using this process, you would print the entire graphic three or four times with different colors that mix to create all the colors. The standard process colors are cyan, magenta, yellow, and black (known as CMYK). By varying the position of dots of these colors on the page, you can create any color.

Why would anyone prefer spot color with its limited use of color to process color, which lets you use all the colors of the rainbow (and some that aren't even in the rainbow)? Spot color provides a very solid color. For example, the yellow around the edge of the National Geographic cover or the red around the Time cover would be appropriate uses of spot colors. Creating the photograph within this border in spot color would be virtually impossible. Instead, process color is used.

How does process color work? It lays down a pattern of dots. You may not be able to see the dots in the National Geographic cover, but they are there. The screen fequency is so high that the dots are too small to see. Note the difference in screen frequency between Figures 3.12 and 3.13. The slight graininess in Figure 3.9 would be almost completely undetectable in a typeset graphic.

The first thing you should do when preparing files for a typesetter is to call the person who owns the typesetter and ask questions. Ask what format the typesetter wants. PostScript is the most common, but some may prefer a different format. You may also find typesetters who are unable to handle PC output and who have to use Macintosh files. In that case, you should consider creating the

Macintosh files (remember, that's one of the settings in the Print dialog box) and send them to the typesetter by modem. Find out how many dots-per-inch and screen lines the typesetting equipment can handle. You should also call up the printer and make sure the equipment needs photographic negatives with crop marks.

It will be assumed that your printer can handle four-color separated files in PC PostScript format.

1. Open the file.
2. Pull down the File menu and select Print.
3. In the Print dialog box, click on the box marked "Print As Separations." The boxes marked "Crop Marks & Crosshairs," "Film Negative," and "Include File Info" will automatically be selected.
4. Click on Print to File.
5. Make sure the screen frequency matches the maximum the typesetting machine can handle.
6. If the typesetter is a 1270 dpi machine, set the fountain stripes at 128. If it is a 2540 dpi machine, set the fountain stripes at 200.
7. Click on OK. You will see the dialog box shown in Figure 3.12.

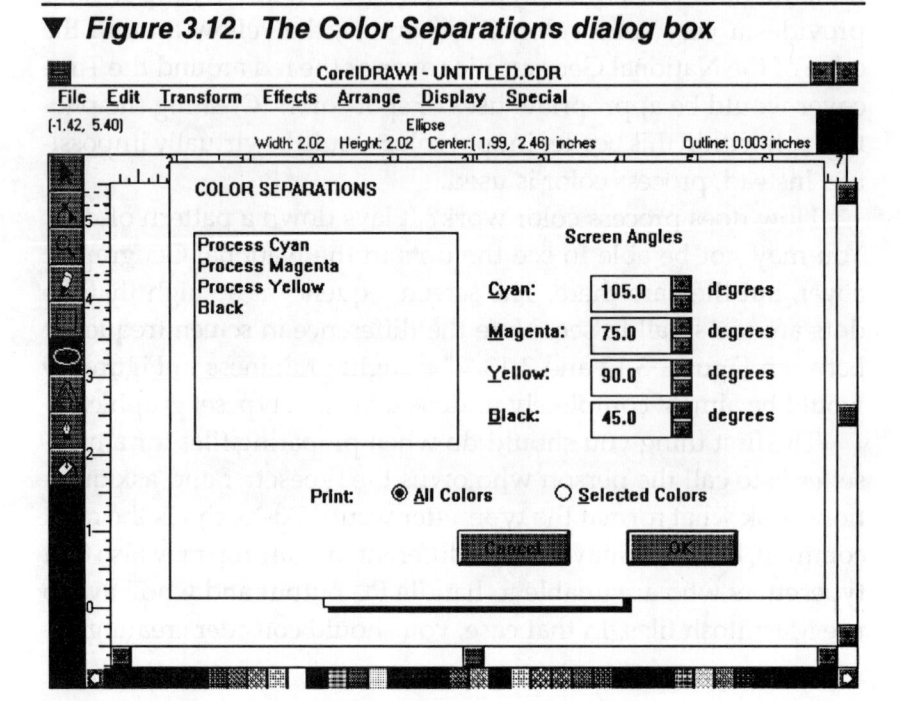

▼ *Figure 3.12. The Color Separations dialog box*

TIP

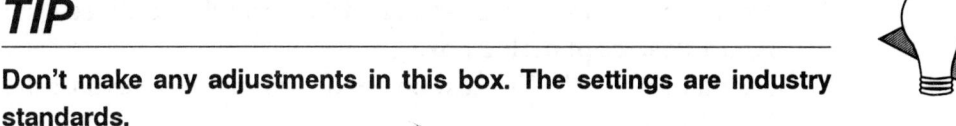

Don't make any adjustments in this box. The settings are industry standards.

8. Click on OK. You will see a printer setup box, which double-checks to make sure you have the proper settings.
9. When all the settings are correct, click on OK and *CorelDRAW!* will print your graphic to a file.

Your typesetter may prefer EPS (Encapsulated PostScript) files. These would be much more general than PRN files, which may contain information that applies only to a specific printer. In that case, you should not *print* the file but *export* it.

Exporting files will be covered in full at a later time, but you will walk through exporting an EPS file now. It's a very simple procedure.

1. Pull down the File menu and select Export. You will see the dialog box shown in Figure 3.13.

▼ *Figure 3.13. The Export dialog box with EPS highlighted*

2. Don't change any of the settings. Click on OK. You'll see the Export PostScript dialog box.
3. Enter a name in the File text box and click on OK to export the file in EPS format.

When the file is created in the format your typesetter wants, save it to a disk and send it to the typesetter. Unfortunately, printer files and EPS files can grow to staggering sizes, sometimes well over a megabyte. If the file is under 1.44Mb, you can save it on a high density 3 1/2-inch disk. If it's larger, you have little recourse but to send the file over the telephone lines with a modem.

Merge Printing

Merge printing is a fun feature of *CorelDRAW!*. It allows you to set up a data file containing text and use this text in printing out *CorelDRAW!* documents. You can create a certificate, for example, and leave the name on the certificate blank. Then, as the certificate is being printed, *CorelDRAW!* will automatically print the names you stored in the text file as it generates the certificates one-by-one.

1. You should begin by creating a certificate of graduation from a truck-driving school (Figure 3.14).

▼ *Figure 3.14. The Truck Driving Institute Diploma*

The Truck-Driving Institute

This is to certify that

Name

has completed the
course and is a truck driver
in good standing.

Signed,

Instructor

Merge Printing

2. Curving the text will be covered in a later chapter. For now, just enter the text and bear in mind that you can cause it to curve.
3. As a separate piece of text, type the body text, leaving a large blank area where you see "Name" and "Instructor" in Figure 3.14 by pressing the Enter key three or four times. Click on Center as the alignment and make the text 24-point type before leaving the Text dialog box.
4. As two separate pieces of text, enter "Name" and "Instructor" in the positions shown in Figure 3.14. Make these 30-point type.
5. If your certificate isn't perfectly centered, click on the pick tool, pull down the Edit menu and click on Select All. Pull down the Arrange menu and select Align. Click on the option to center the objects vertically.

Note the words "Name" and "Instructor" on the certificate. These are called *primary text strings*. When you merge the file, these words will be replaced by information from the text file. The merged text will be in exactly the same typeface, style, size, and alignment as the type you see used for "Name" and "Instructor."

Next, you need to create a text file. This has to be a pure ASCII file with no special formatting and it should look like the file being created in Notepad in Figure 3.15. Notepad is the preferred source for your text file for two reasons: First, it generates plain ASCII files and second, the files are automatically given the extension TXT when they are saved. These are two requirements for the text file for a *CorelDRAW!* merge print.

The file looks carefully formatted, and it is.

1. On the first line, enter a number representing the number of text strings in the certificate. You can have as many text strings as you want, but each is unique. For example, on the first certificate, wherever the word "Name" appears in the certificate, it will be replaced with "Billie Wilder."
2. On the second line, begin entering the primary text strings exactly as they appear in the certificate. At the beginning and end of each text string, you must enter a backslash. This is called a *delimiter*.
3. After you have entered all the primary text strings, you must enter the *secondary text strings*—the strings that will appear in

▼ *Figure 3.15. The text file being created*

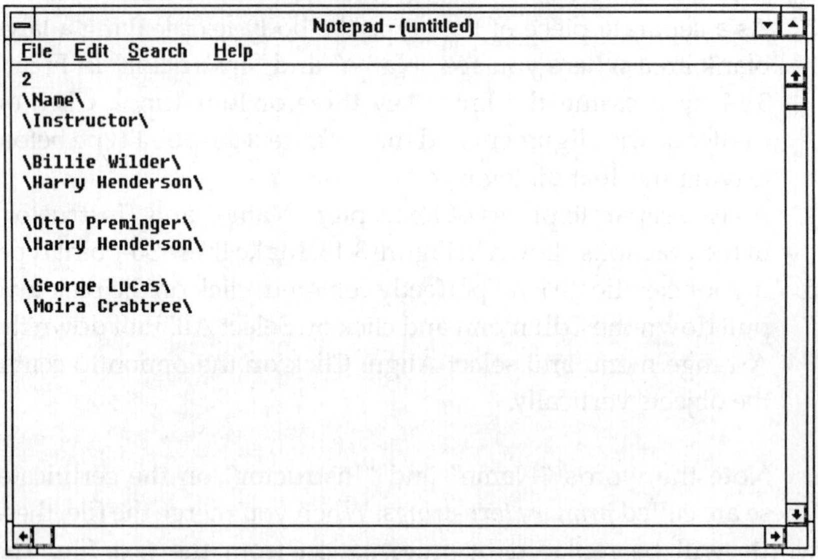

```
Notepad - (untitled)
File  Edit  Search  Help
2
\Name\
\Instructor\

\Billie Wilder\
\Harry Henderson\

\Otto Preminger\
\Harry Henderson\

\George Lucas\
\Moira Crabtree\
```

place of the primary text strings when the certificates are printed. These strings should be typed exactly as you want them to appear and should be delimited with backslashes before and after the secondary text string. These text strings should appear in the same order as the primary strings to which they correspond. The primary text strings appear with Name first and Instructor second. Likewise, in the secondary text strings, Billie Wilder will appear where Name is typed into the certificate and Harry Henderson will appear where Instructor is typed into the certificate.

Figure 3.16 shows an alternative arrangement of the text file. You can use either arrangement, but the setup in Figure 3.15 is preferable because it makes locating an individual piece of data easier.

1. Save the text file under the name MERGE.TXT by pulling down the File menu in Notepad and selecting Save.
2. Return to *CorelDRAW!* and select Merge Print from the File menu. You will see the dialog box shown in Figure 3.17.

Merge Printing

▼ *Figure 3.16. An alternative text file for CorelDRAW! merge*

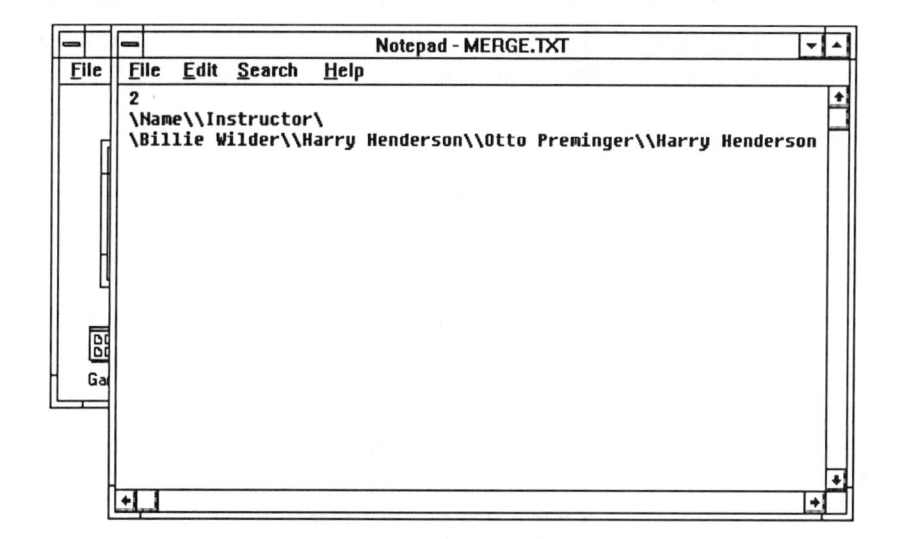

▼ *Figure 3.17. The Print Merge dialog box*

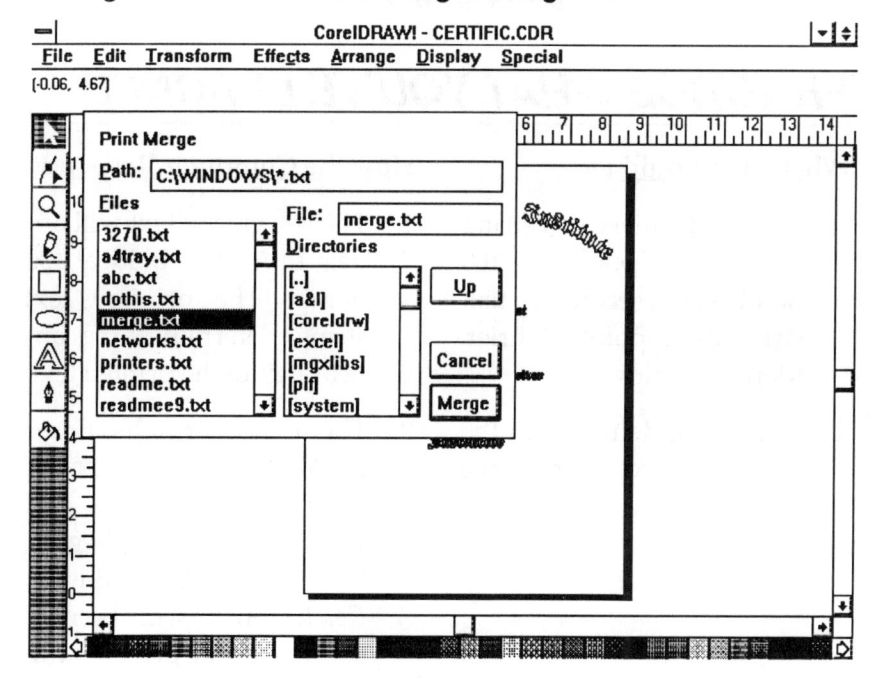

3. Double click on the filename of the file to merge: MERGE.TXT. The Print dialog box will appear. Make all the necessary settings in the Print dialog box, with which you should be well familiar by now, and click on the button marked OK to commence printing. Figure 3.18 shows the printed certificate.

▼ *Figure 3.18. The merged certificate*

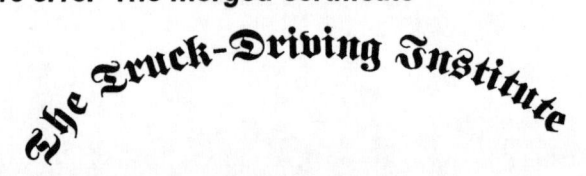

The Truck-Driving Institute

This is to certify that

Billie Wilder

has completed the course and is a truck driver in good standing.

Signed,

Harry Henderson

PRACTICE WHAT YOU'VE LEARNED

What You Should Do

1. Create a primary text string in Avalon, bold, at 100 points and a secondary text string in 12-point, Courier. Merge the files.

2. Take out a delimiter in the secondary text and remerge the text.

How the Computer Responds

1. The secondary text will appear in Avalon, bold, at 100 points. The primary text string determines the appearance of the printed text.

2. The delimiter tells *CorelDRAW!* where one piece of secondary text ends and where the next begins. Without the delimiter, *CorelDRAW!* will become confused and place text in inappropriate places.

Exercises

This exercise assumes that you have *CorelDRAW!* running and a new, blank page area is visible. If you already have something on the screen, save it and select New from the File menu. This exercise also assumes that you are using a PostScript printer. The exercise will work the same no matter what kind of printer you are using, but the name of your type of printer will appear where "PostScript" appears in this exercise.

What You Should Do

1. Draw a circle on the screen so you will have something to print. Pull down the File menu and select Control Panel.

2. Double click on Printers.

3. Click on the Configure button.

4. First, note the currently selected port. You will need to return to it in a moment. Scroll through the port selections until you arrive at FILE:. Click on FILE: and then click on OK in the Printers-Configure dialog box.

How the Computer Responds

1. The Control Panel will appear on your screen.

2. The Printers dialog box will open, giving you the option of adding a printer or configuring th current printer.

3. The Printers-Configure dialog box will open, giving you the options of selecting or removing a printer port or changing the setup.

4. The default printer selection will be PostScript Printer on FILE:.

5. Click on OK in the Printers dialog box and double click on the close box in the Control Panel.

6. Pull down the File menu and select Print. When the Print dialog box appears, make sure Print to File is not checked. Your selection in the Control Panel will take care of that automatically. Click on OK.

7. Type PRINTERF as the name of the file you want to print to and click on OK.

8. Start up your printer, if it isn't already running. Exit from *CorelDRAW!* and open the Main window. Double click on the DOS Prompt icon.

9. Type COPY PRINTERF PRN and press Enter.

10. Type EXIT to return to *Windows*. Start up *CorelDRAW!* again and repeat steps 1 through 5, only instead of selecting FILE: as the port, select the port that you had been using previously.

5. You will be returned to *CorelDRAW!*.

6. You will see the Print to File dialog box.

7. The disk drive will spin for a moment while your graphic is printed to a file.

8. You will find yourself at the DOS command line.

9. Your graphic will be printed.

10. Your system will be returned to normal.

4 Managing Files

- ▲ Backups
- ▲ Importing and Exporting Art
- ▲ Using Autotrace
- ▲ Using Clip Art
- ▲ Using Symbols
- ▲ Using Mosaic

The PC operates with files. A file is a collection of information laid out in traces of magnetism on a disk, whether that disk is a removable floppy disk or a fixed hard disk. Even the operating system of the PC is in the form of two files. Since its operation is so dependent on its ability to interact with disk drives, the PC was provided with an extremely fast and reliable disk operating system. This book is written with the assumption that you have at least a passing familiarity with the disk operating system and so there is no chapter covering details like how to insert a floppy disk or how information is laid out on the disk. However, some points can only benefit from frequent reiteration and some disk management tasks and techniques are unique to *CorelDRAW!*, so these need to be covered.

Backups

As has been mentioned, it is important to back up your *CorelDRAW!* installation disks and it is even more important that you save your drawings often while they are being prepared. You can save them under a single name on the hard disk, but this will cause DOS to destroy an old version of the file as it's creating a new version of the file.

Finally, once you have saved your file to disk, you must pause at the end of each day (or each week, or at some other regular interval) to save your work to floppies or on some other backup medium. You can accomplish this backup with DOS version 3.3 and newer versions by using the command

```
XCOPY \*.* A: /M /S
```

This command will locate all the files on the hard disk that have not been backed up and copy them selectively to the floppy disk in drive A. It will satisfy nearly all your backup needs. However, you should also consider setting up a real backup system, involving backup software like *Back It* or *FastBack* (there are about a dozen major dedicated backup packages on the market). Another option is to use the backup module in *PC Tools Deluxe* or some other integrated package or utility.

Importing and Exporting Art

Importing and Exporting Art

One of the most useful features of *CorelDRAW!* is its ability to pull in art created with other software packages (importing) and its ability to convert its art into other formats for use by other packages. As an example, you will import a graphic in TIF (tagged image file) format and you will export it back to TIF format.

Importing Art

Fortunately, Corel Systems has provided you with some pieces of graphic art to import. If you lack a scanner (TIF is the standard output format for scanning equipment), you can use one of the sample graphics included with *CorelDRAW!*. You might choose to import a PCX file or one of the other graphic formats *CorelDRAW!* supports.

1. Start up *CorelDRAW!* or clear the screen.
2. Pull down the File menu and select Import (it should be one of a very few selections available to you).
3. You will see the dialog box shown in Figure 4.1.
4. Click on the format you want to import (in this case, TIF) and click on the button marked OK. You will see the dialog box shown in Figure 4.2.

You probably remember from Chapter 1 the discussion of the difference between bitmap graphics and vector graphics. TIF and PCX files are bitmap files. Later in the chapter, you will see how to turn these files into vector files.

5. Use the Directories box to get to the CORELDRW subdirectory, if it isn't already the selected directory. Double click on the drive letter that contains the subdirectory. Click on the Up button until you reach the root directory of that drive, then follow the path to CORELDRW, which may appear as a subdirectory of

▼ *Figure 4.1. The Import dialog box*

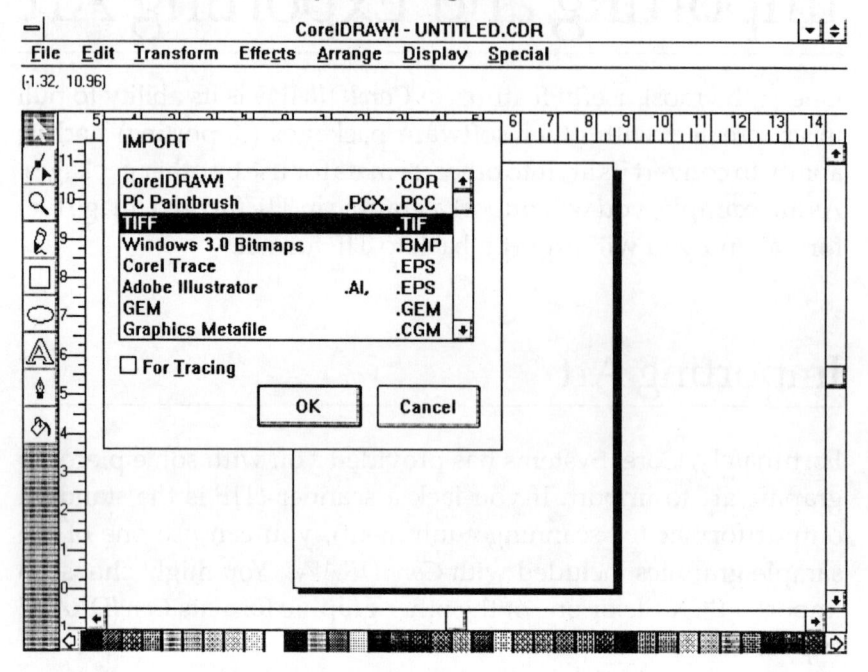

▼ *Figure 4.2. The Import Bitmap dialog box*

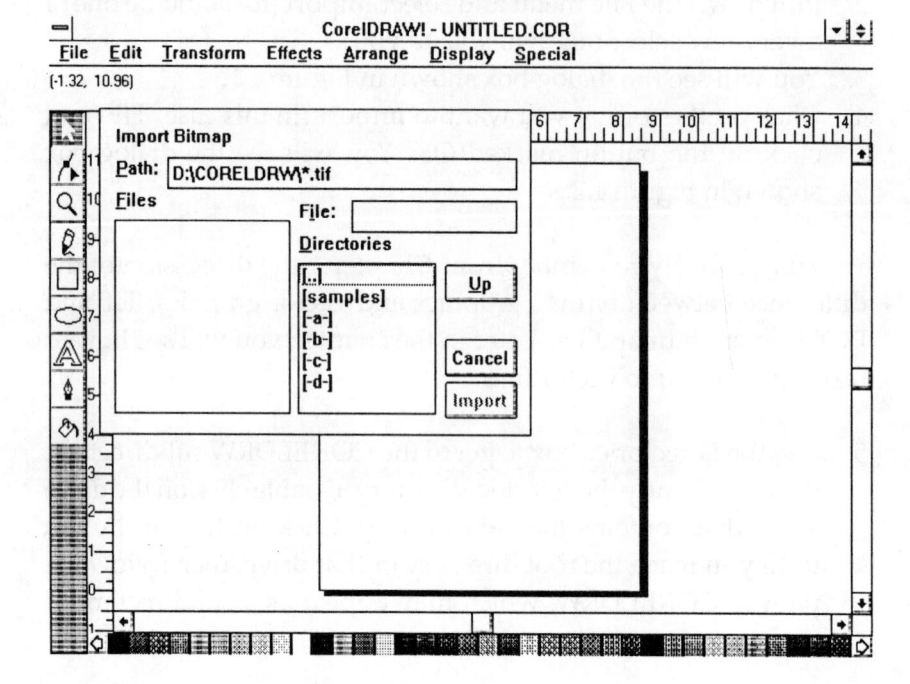

the root directory or of the WINDOWS subdirectory, depending on how you installed *CorelDRAW!*.
6. Click on the subdirectory marked [samples]. That will take you to a collection of sample art provided by Corel Systems.

Importing and Exporting Art

I scanned an image of my own creation to use for the sample, but feel free to import any of the TIF files (I recommend SHERMY.TIF).

7. Locate the file in the Files list box and double click on its name to import it (Figure 4.3).

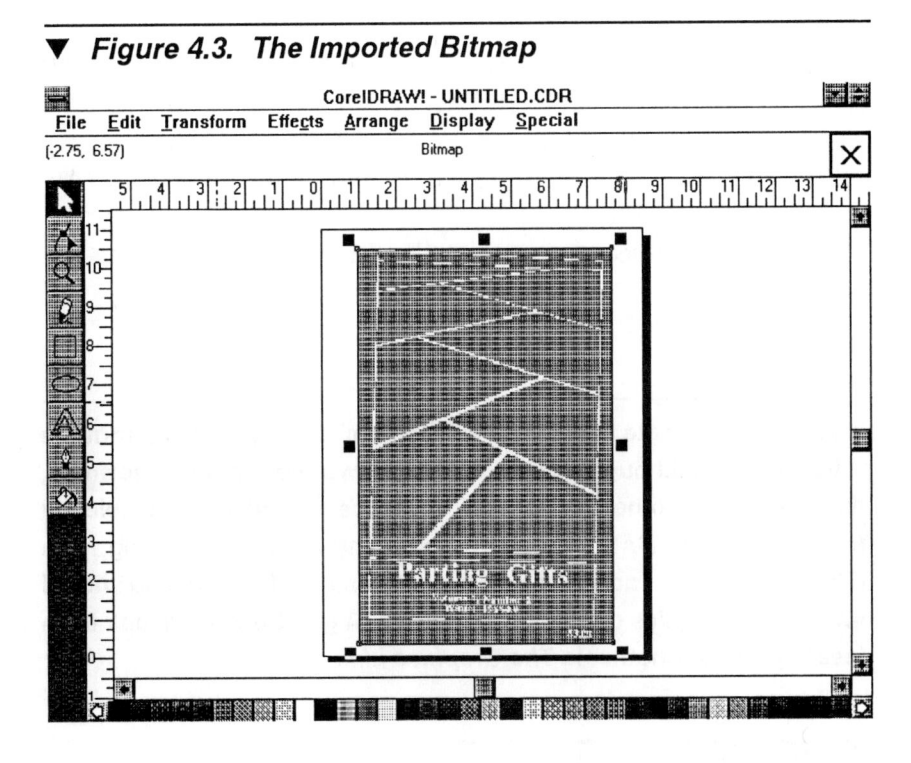

▼ *Figure 4.3. The Imported Bitmap*

You can rotate, flip, and perform other transformations on your imported bitmap, but some transformations will make it impossible for *CorelDRAW!* to show you the contents of the image. Therefore, if you are going to do any drawing based on the contents of the image, you should do those things before rotating or skewing the image (or do the rotating and skewing in your paint program before importing the image).

TIP

You can crop a bitmap very easily. If the bitmap drawing isn't centered, or contains things you want to leave out, here's how to crop it. With the bitmap selected on the screen, click on the shape tool. Cropping handles will appear at the periphery of the bitmap. Drag the cropping handle in the center of the side you want to crop toward the center of the bitmap. When you release the mouse button, the bitmap will be cropped.

You can import art in any of the following formats: CDR *(CorelDRAW!)*, PCX, PCC, TIF, BMP *(Windows Paintbrush)*, EPS, AI *(Adobe Illustrator)*, GEM, CGM, PCT (a Macintosh draw format), HPGL (the most commonly used plotter language), DXF *(AutoCAD)*, PIC, and PIF.

Shortly you'll learn about the "For Tracing" option in the Import dialog box.

TIP

It's important to note that *CorelDRAW!* is limited in the bitmap formats it will import. Although it will import the two most popular formats, there are many other formats in existence that will be completely foreign to *CorelDRAW!*. If you will be doing a lot of importing from different graphics packages, or different formats of clip art, you should invest in a graphics conversion program. A good one is *HiJaak* from Inset Systems. Another is *The Graphics Link*.

CHECK YOURSELF

1. Why would you want to use the import feature? Doesn't *CorelDRAW!* give you enough in a graphics package to make the rest of the programs irrelevant?

2. What are the advantages of backing up your disks frequently?

ANSWERS

1. Not really. You can't paint with *CorelDRAW!*, for example, and very little clip art is available in *CorelDRAW!*'s native CDR format.

2. You will be less likely to lose a file because of a hard disk failure.

Importing and Exporting Art

Exporting Art

For this task, you need to have a graphic on the page.

1. Click on the ellipse tool, hold down the Ctrl key and drag a circle about an inch in diameter.
2. Click on the Fill tool and select the fountain fill object (second from the right end). In the Fountain Fill dialog box, click on Radial (at the top) and OK.

That's the image you will export: a fountain-filled circle.

1. Pull down the File menu and select Export. You will see the dialog box shown in Figure 4.4.

   There are a number of export options that may confuse you (they aren't all available for all formats). An image header is available for EPS files. It's a bitmap of the EPS drawing that allows a program like a desktop publishing package to display the drawing in its onscreen representation. Without a header, the drawing might appear as a blank with an X through it. The All Fonts Resident option is for files being sent to a typesetter. It will cause the typesetter to substitute its own fonts for the fonts that appear in the drawing.
   You'll be exporting to TIF format.

2. Click on the word TIFF in the list box. Note that Resolution is highlighted. This will allow you to specify how coarse the exported drawing should be.

▼ **Figure 4.4. The Export dialog box**

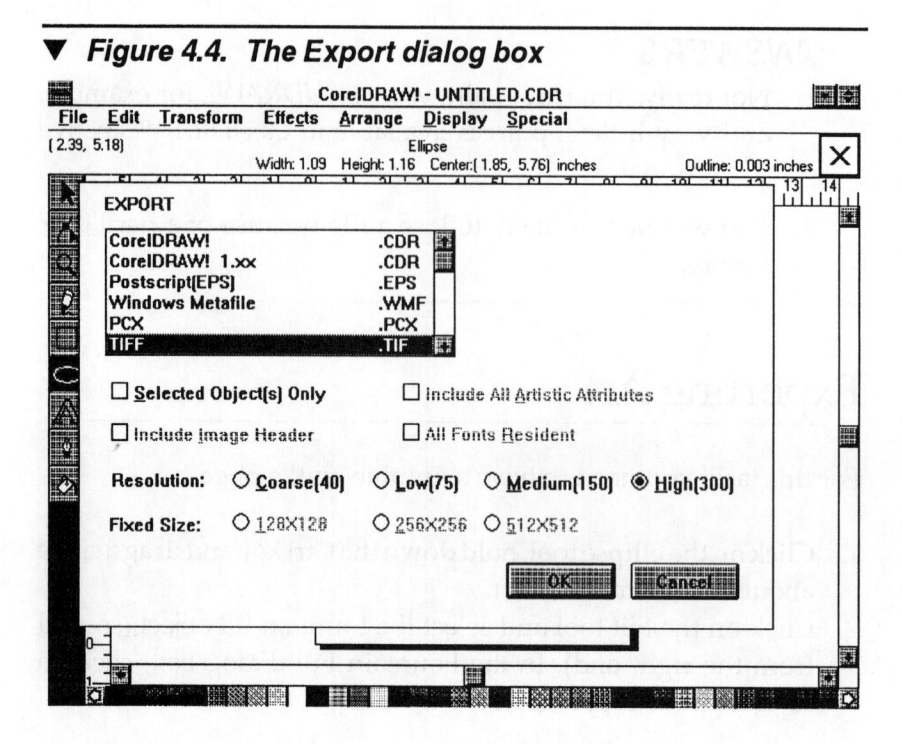

3. If you are using the drawing for any kind of presentation, click on High to obtain a 300 dpi bitmap, which will print at the maximum resolution of your laser printer (it also takes up the maximum disk space).
4. Click on OK. You'll see a dialog box asking for the name of the file that will contain the drawing. Enter a name in the File text box and click on Export.

You can export *CorelDRAW!* drawings to CDR format (2.*x* or 1.*x*), EPS, WMP (*Windows* metafile), PCX, TIF, WFN (a special *CorelDRAW!* format used for symbols and typefaces), CGM, GEM, WPG (for use with *WordPerfect*), SCODL (the most commonly used language for creating slides), PIC, HPGL, DXF, PIF, PCT, and AI.

Using Autotrace

Tracing is a method for creating a vector graphic from a bitmap graphic. Basically, a trace looks for the edge of a black area and plots a line along it. When the trace is finished, the line is converted into Bezier curves and straight lines with nodes that can then be edited with the node-editing shape tool. What is the value of a traced image? A traced image can be stretched and otherwise manipulated without the appearance of telltale jagged edges associated with bitmapped graphics that make the graphic look like a computer graphic.

There are two different ways to trace a drawing. You can run Corel Trace or use the autotrace option within *CorelDRAW!*. Corel Trace is covered in full in Chapter 8. Here, you'll work with autotrace.

Now you can import a graphic. You can import Shermy, if you like, from the SAMPLES subdirectory under *CorelDRAW!*. I'll use some text saved as a PCX file as my example (you have to use either a PCX file or a TIF file to autotrace).

Importing and Exporting Art

1. Import the graphic, making sure to click on the box For Tracing so that the check box is checked. (Note the words "For Tracing" at the right end of the status line.)
2. Make sure the bitmap is selected (you select a bitmap by clicking on the pick tool and then clicking on the rectangular outline that contains the bitmap). Click on the pencil tool in the toolbox. The mouse cursor turns into sort of a sideways dagger.
3. Place the long end of the mouse cursor (the right leg of the cross or the knife point of the dagger) on the line you want to trace. In this case, I will trace the outline of the letter *P*.

Experiment with the autotrace cursor. You'll discover that it traces the line slightly to the left of the dagger point. In Figure 4.5, the entire text was traced, letter by letter, and dragged to a location away from the bitmap. Note that you have to separately trace interiors of letters. The hole in the upper part of the *P* and the lower part of the lowercase *a* are known as a "bowls." Holes like these aren't automatically traced when you trace the exterior.

Next you should complete the autotrace by making the text look right in the preview screen.

1. Get rid of the bitmap by clicking on the rectangle outline and then pressing Del.

▼ **Figure 4.5. The autotraced text**

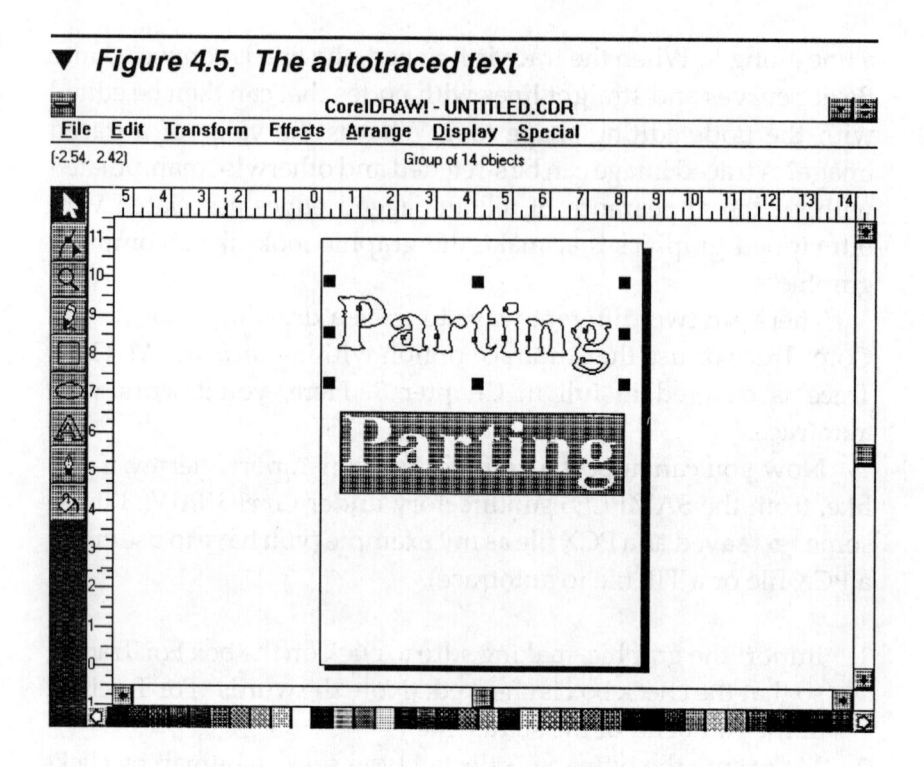

2. Pull down the Display menu and select Show Preview. The preview should show your graphic as outlines because you haven't specified an interior fill for the objects.

Although what I am going to do may not apply to the graphic on your screen, follow along. If you would like to place some text on your screen to follow along, this is easily done.

1. Write something on the page area using the text tool.
2. Export it to a TIF or PCX file.
3. Import it for tracing.
4. Select the bitmap and autotrace it using the steps mentioned earlier in this section.
5. Delete the bitmap.

Now you will fill the text.

1. Click on the Pick tool and drag a selection rectangle including all the autotraced text.

Managing Files ▲ 155

2. Click on the black square in the palette at the bottom of the screen. The previewed text is shown in Figure 4.6.

Importing and Exporting Art

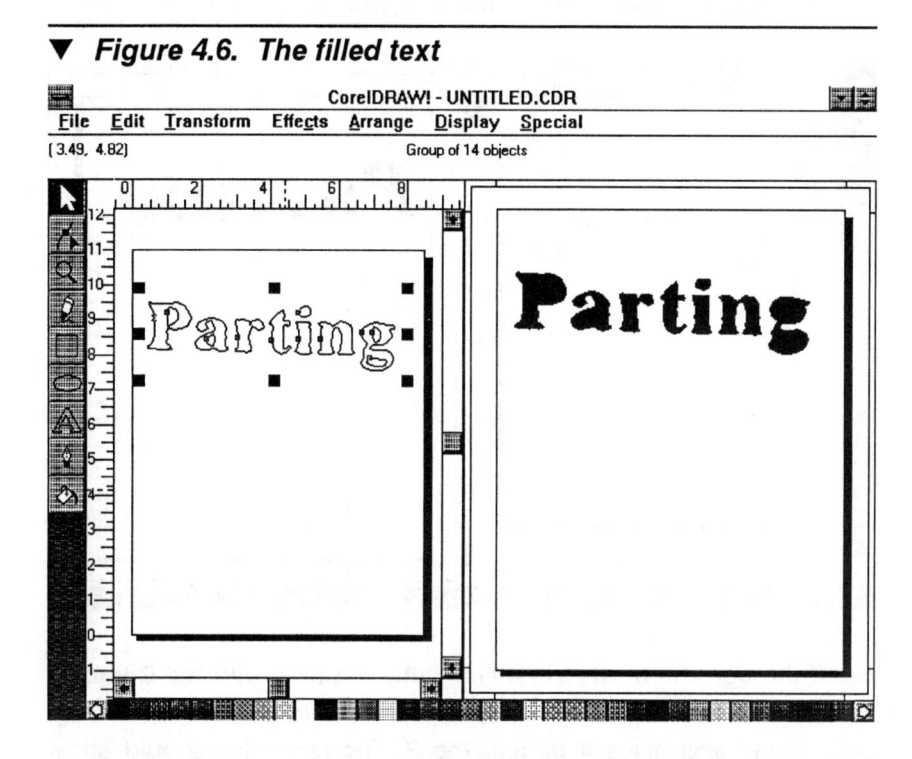

▼ **Figure 4.6. The filled text**

[Screenshot of CorelDRAW! - UNTITLED.CDR showing the word "Parting" in outline form on the left page and filled in black on the right page]

Note that some of the letters are missing parts—the bowls in the *P*, *a*, and *g*. This is because the bowls are also filled in black. You could make the bowls visible by selecting them, bringing them to the front with To Front from the Arrange menu, and filling them with white. But there is a better way.

1. Drag a selection rectangle that completely encloses the letter *P*.
2. Pull down the Arrange menu and select Combine. Do the same to the *a*, *i*, and *g*. Your preview screen should look like Figure 4.7.

TIP

Combining two graphics can be used to "cut a hole" in one of the objects. Combining is better than simply coloring the bowls white because if something appears behind the text, you ought to be able to

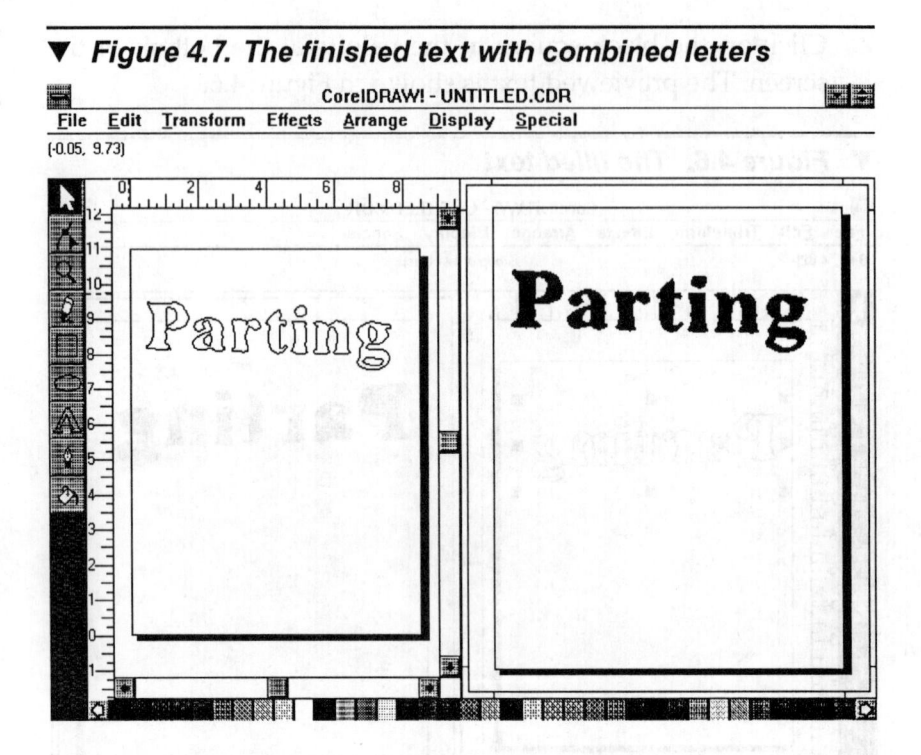

▼ **Figure 4.7. The finished text with combined letters**

see it through the bowls in letters. Cutting a hole with the Combine command makes the bowl transparent. To prove it, draw something, color it red and place it behind the *P*. The red color should show through the bowl of the *P*.

Now that the letters are in vector format, you can use the node editing tool to alter their shape, shrink, bend, or perform any kind of transformation and discover on printout that the lines are smooth. In Figure 4.8, I have reimported the text with For Tracing turned off (if you import for tracing, the imported graphic won't print or appear on the preview screen). I printed them to show how jagged the PCX file was (bottom) and how relatively smooth the vector graphic image is after tracing—and without any editing to make the outline smoother. This figure offers compelling evidence of the blockiness of bitmap graphics.

▼ **Figure 4.8. Bitmap image (bottom) and traced vector**

Importing and Exporting Art

CHECK YOURSELF

1. Draw a circle and then a square that completely encloses the circle. Select them both and select Combine from the Arrange menu. With the circle and square still selected, click on a color in the palette. If the preview isn't visible, press F9.

2. Import a CDR drawing. Based on what you have seen, do you think you could trace a CDR drawing?

ANSWERS

1. Combining objects causes them to cancel each other out where they overlap: Where the objects both have solid areas, the combined object will show a hole. The object you just created should look like a square with a bullet hole through it. Combining more than two objects makes this colorization scheme unpredictable.

2. The For Tracing option is not available when you import a CDR drawing. A CDR drawing is already in vector format and tracing it would be pointless.

Using Clip Art

CorelDRAW! is shipped with a full complement of clip art and symbols. This collection is so complete that it's entirely possible to cultivate a reputation for yourself as a computer artist without ever drawing a thing. You may be perfectly happy with the collection provided by Corel Systems, but the clip art libraries are actually samples of far more extensive art libraries available from other manufacturers. *Symbol and Clipart Libraries* is one of the many documents provided with *CorelDRAW!*. Take a moment to open the book and flip through it. Look at the first page (page 1) and note that each clip art image is accompanied by a description and a logo. The logo will direct you to the origin of the image. If you like the style of a particular image, note its manufacturer and turn to the back of the book to the section marked "Sources." This section is full of advertisements for the companies that created the clip art in the book. Many of the advertisements offer special deals to purchasers of *CorelDRAW!*.

Next you will import a piece of clip art—the charging bull at the upper left corner of page 1.

1. First, clear the screen by selecting New or Select All from the Edit menu and then press Del.
2. Note the name of the library at the top of the page: "Animals." Take out your *CorelDRAW!* installation disks and look through them until you find the one containing the Animals library. Its label probably reads "CLIPART LIBRARIES: Animals, Environment, Maps, Technology." Insert this disk into your disk drive.
3. Pull down the Special menu and select Preferences.
4. In the resulting dialog box, locate the check box marked "Use Mosaic." Click on the text or the check box so the box is checked. This supercharges your Open option on the File menu. Click on OK to close the Preferences dialog box.
5. Pull down the File menu and select Open. You will see the window shown in Figure 4.9.

▼ *Figure 4.9. The Mosaic window*

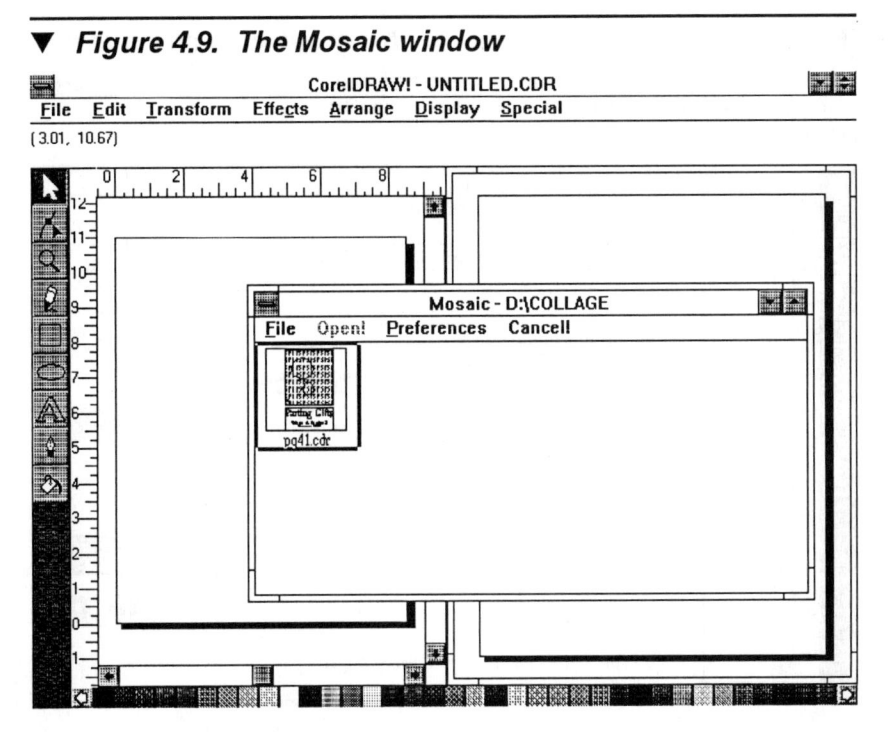

Using Clip Art

Note that selecting Open actually opens the Mosaic window. Along the top of this window, you have a new menu bar featuring menus marked File, Open, Preferences, and Cancel!

1. Pull down the File menu in the Mosaic window and select Change Dir. You will see the dialog box shown in Figure 4.10. Click on the button (at the bottom of the dialog box) marked "Library (CLB)" and click on the drive letter in the left list box that represents the drive where you have inserted the library disk. You will see the list of libraries shown in Figure 4.10.
2. Double click on the library named ANIMAL.CLB in the far right list box. The dialog box will disappear and you will see the Mosaic window containing the first 15 thumbnails from animals.clb.
3. Click on the image you want to use. If the image isn't visible, use the scroll bar at the right side of the window to scroll through the available images.
4. Click on Open! in the menu bar. This won't call up a menu but rather another dialog box with which you can tell Mosaic where

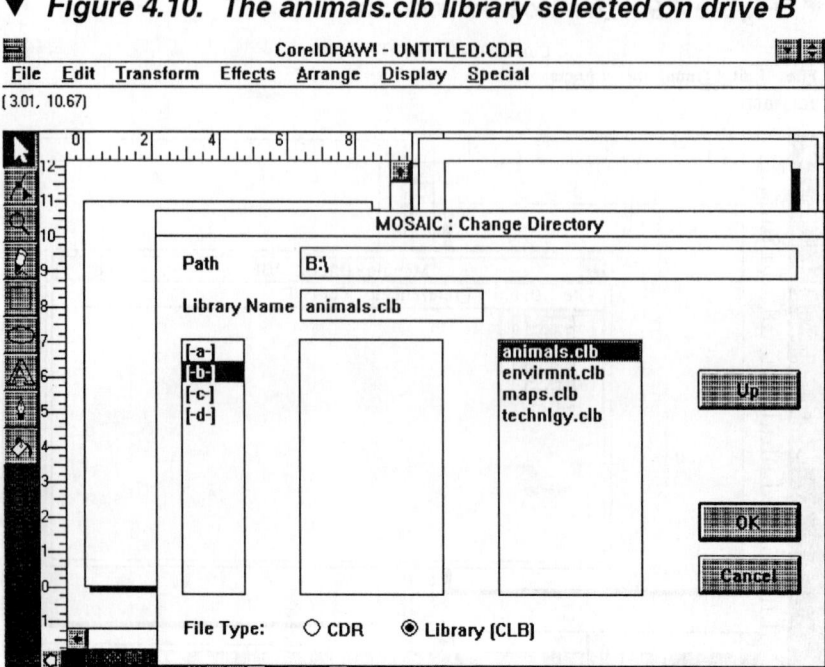

▼ **Figure 4.10. The animals.clb library selected on drive B**

to put the expanded image (all clip art images are stored in very compressed format that allows storage of a huge number of images on a single disk).

5. Click on the disk where you want the image placed. In my case it will be on my D drive, under the SAMPLES subdirectory under my CORELDRW directory. Note that when you click on a drive letter in the first list box, you are shown the directories on that drive. As you click on these directories in the second list box, you are taken to those directories and the files in these directories are displayed in the list box at the far right while subdirectories are displayed in the center list box.

6. When the Path box at the top of the Mosaic: Expand dialog box displays the directory where you want to place the bull, click on the OK button.

There won't be enough space on the library file disk to expand the file, so *Windows* will ask permission to look for another disk to use to expand the file. The program LHarc is used to compress the files. When the file is completely expanded, you will be returned to your page area with the clip art graphic in place (Figure 4.11).

Using Clip Art

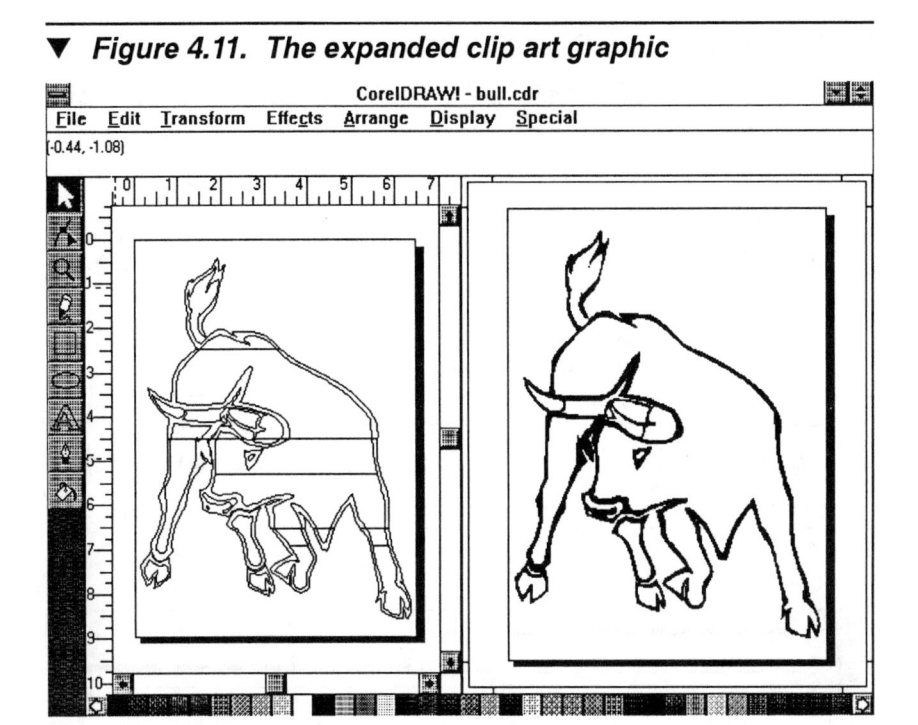

▼ *Figure 4.11. The expanded clip art graphic*

You might wonder about the horizontal lines through the bull. These are put in place to simplify the objects that make up the bull. You might recall from our discussion of printing graphics that PostScript has distinct limitations on the complexity of graphics it can print. By bringing together simpler objects, you create an image that can be very complex but won't exceed the bounds of PostScript.

Using Symbols

Symbols are very similar to characters in a special font. You use them much the same way you use text.

1. Click on the text tool in the tool box.

2. Hold down the Shift key and click the left mouse button. You will see the dialog box shown in Figure 4.12.

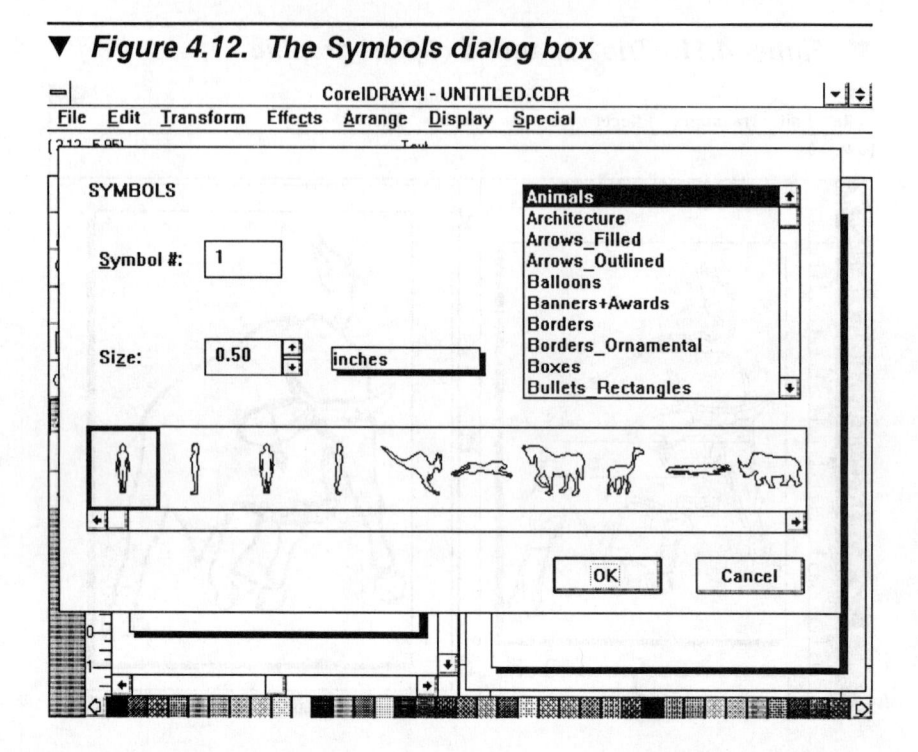

▼ **Figure 4.12. The Symbols dialog box**

Use the scroll bar to move through all the items in the current page of symbols. Note the list of libraries in the list box at the upper right corner of Figure 4.12. These libraries correspond to pages in the book Symbol and Clipart Libraries, (pages 41 through 86). Virtually every conceivable symbol has been included. You can do anything to these symbols that you would do to a text object. It will be obvious to you that these symbols are very simple, but they can really dress up a memo or a newsletter.

Using Mosaic

You've already seen Mosaic used to load clip art. It can also be used to load normal CDR files. As you create large amounts of art with *CorelDRAW!*, you will become hardpressed to come up with new, unique names to describe the art, particularly with the scant eight characters DOS allows you to use for your filenames. Mosaic turns your directories and disks of graphics into art galleries. You can select any piece of art according to its appearance rather than its name.

TIP

If you don't see any files in the Mosaic window, you are probably logged to the wrong directory or drive. Pull down the File menu within the Mosaic window and select a different drive and directory until you find the directory containing your files. If the files still don't appear, you may have the Library (CLB) button selected in the Mosaic Change Directory dialog box. Click on CDR to make your *CorelDRAW!* drawings appear in the window.

Figure 4.13 shows the SAMPLES subdirectory under the CORELDRW directory, with all the samples represented by tiny reproductions. To load any of these graphics, simply double click on it. (Note in Figure 4.13 the bull we added in the previous section.)

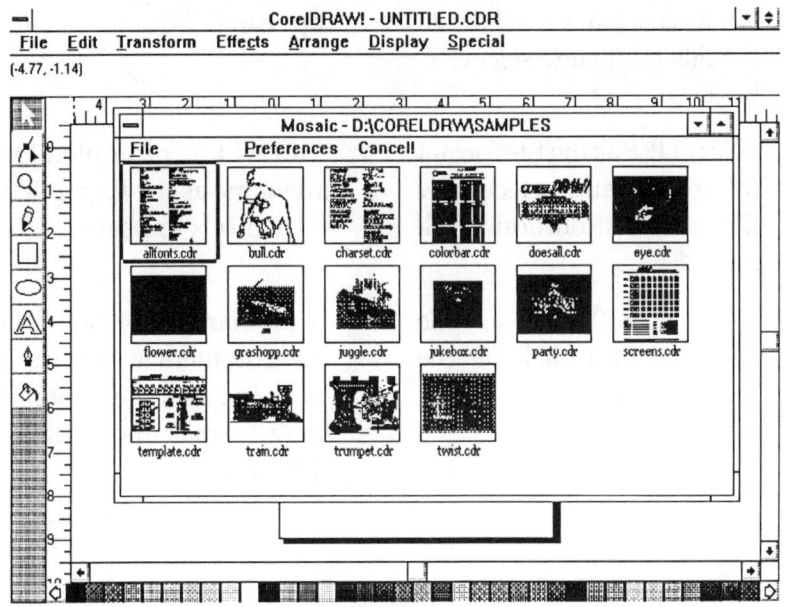

▼ *Figure 4.13. The Mosaic of the SAMPLES directory*

Using Mosaic

CHECK YOURSELF

1. Place a picture of a cornet on the screen.

ANSWER

1. Click on the font tool, hold down the Shift key and click on the page area. The Symbol dialog box will appear. Scroll through the libraries until Musical_Instruments appears in the list box. Click on it and scroll through the library until you locate a cornet (8th from the beginning is the most cornet-like instrument).

Exercises

This exercise assumes that you have *CorelDRAW!* running and a new, blank page area is visible. If you already have something on the screen, save it and select New from the File menu.

What You Should Do	How the Computer Responds
1. Draw a circle on the screen. Fill it with black. Pull down the File menu and select Export.	1. The Export dialog box will appear.
2. Select TIFF as the file format for export and select Low (75) as the resolution. Click on OK.	2. You will be prompted for a filename as the Export TIFF dialog box appears.
3. Type in CIRCLE as the filename and click on the Export button.	3. Your hard disk will labor for a moment as the graphic is being changed into the new format and sent to a TIFF file.

Managing Files ▲ 165

Exercises

4. Select New from the File menu and in the dialog box that prompts you to save your work, click on No. Pull down the File menu and select Import.

4. The Import dialog box will appear.

5. Click on TIFF as the file format to import. Make sure the For Tracing is checked. Click on OK.

5. The Import Bitmap dialog box will appear.

6. In the Files list box, double click on the name CIR-CLE.TIF.

6. The TIFF file will be imported and will appear, grayed, on the *CorelDRAW!* screen.

7. If the preview screen isn't visible, press Shift-F9 to make it visible. Click on the pencil tool. You are now ready for tracing. Move the right end of the tracing cross to a position near the imported circle. Click.

7. *CorelDRAW!* will trace the circle in a moment. It will appear in the preview screen as an unfilled wireframe circle. Because of the coarseness of the exported image and the vagaries of programming, the circle may be more or less perfect. Note that the imported circle doesn't appear on the preview screen. That is because it was only imported for tracing.

8. Press Del to eliminate the imported circle.

8. The bitmap imported for tracing will disappear.

9. Import the circle again, this time with For Tracing unchecked.

9. This time the imported circle will also appear on the preview screen. It should perfectly coincide with the traced circle, if you have followed directions to the letter.

10. With the imported bitmap selected, click on the shape tool. Place the mouse cursor on the lower left corner control handle of the bitmap selection rectangle. Depress the Ctrl key and move the mouse cursor to the center of the circle.

10. The image will be cropped, probably to a quarter section of the circle. The image in the preview screen will look like a pie graph.

5 Views

▲ Magnification
▲ Previews
▲ Grids and Snap
▲ Guidelines and Snap
▲ Rulers, Status Line, Color Palette

When you are working with your art, you will often want to take a closer look. This is the value of views. They give you additional control over your drawing. Grids and rulers are even more powerful. In this chapter, you will become an old hand at using these powerful tools to your best advantage.

Magnification

Magnification is the use of the zoom tool in the tool box to allow you to take a more careful look at your drawing. You can examine it so closely that it is like looking at a picture through a jeweler's loupe or you can make *CorelDRAW!* take a step back so that you are looking at your graphic as if you were standing across the room from it. The close examination is most useful when you are doing detail work and the more distant, disinterested view is useful if you are making sure the design works well as a unit.

TIP

There are many talented artists who have no trouble creating a pleasing drawing but are unable to compose, which is another word for designing a graphic. They become too close to their work. Before printing a graphic, you should take the time to zoom back to the page view to make sure that all the elements are working together, the graphic isn't excessively balanced or lopsided, and (if you are going to do a separation or a color print) the colors work together and are complementary.

Now you will draw something and examine it under each of the zoom levels.

Zoom In

1. With the normal page view displayed, clear the screen or select New from the File menu.

Magnification

2. Draw an ellipse and then draw a rectangle that completely encloses it. Try as hard as you can to make the top line of the rectangle *touch* the top of the ellipse, but not hide it.

   The purpose of this exercise is very realistic. When you think you have placed two lines next to each other, it's worth checking with the zoom tool to make sure that the relatively low resolution of the computer screen doesn't deceive you.

3. Click on the zoom tool. Take another look at the zoom tool menu (Figure 5.1).

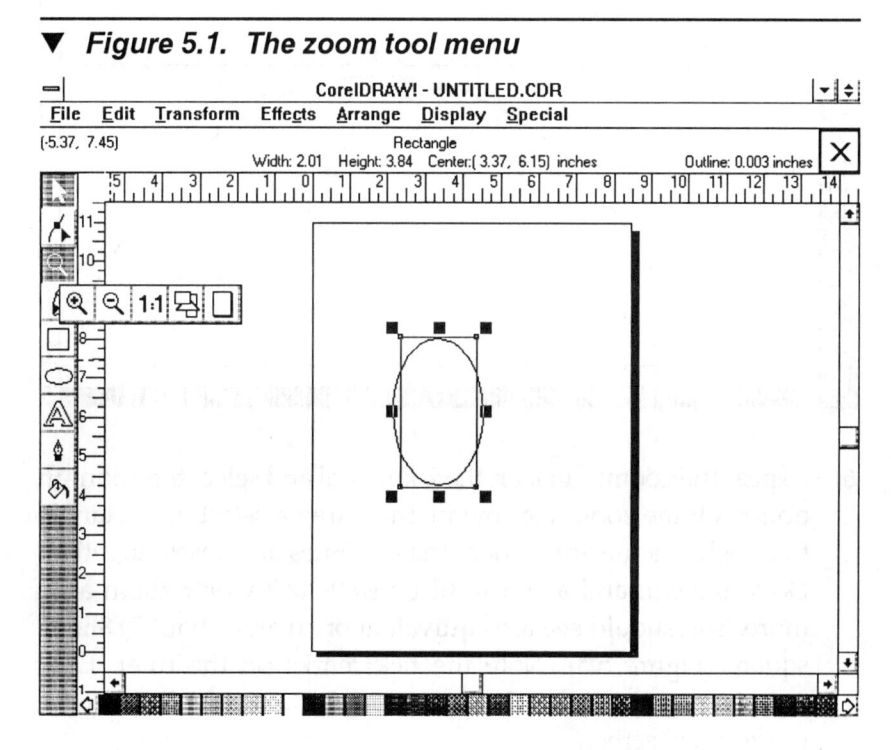

▼ **Figure 5.1. The zoom tool menu**

Note the slide bars that appear at the right edge and the bottom of the *CorelDRAW!* window.

4. Click on the first zoom tool—the zoom-in tool.
5. The mouse cursor turns into a little magnifying glass. With this glass, drag a selection rectangle about an inch on a side (refer to the ruler—if the ruler isn't visible, select Show Rulers from

the Display menu) containing the area where the top of the rectangle and the top of the ellipse come together. Don't be surprised if you see something like Figure 5.2.

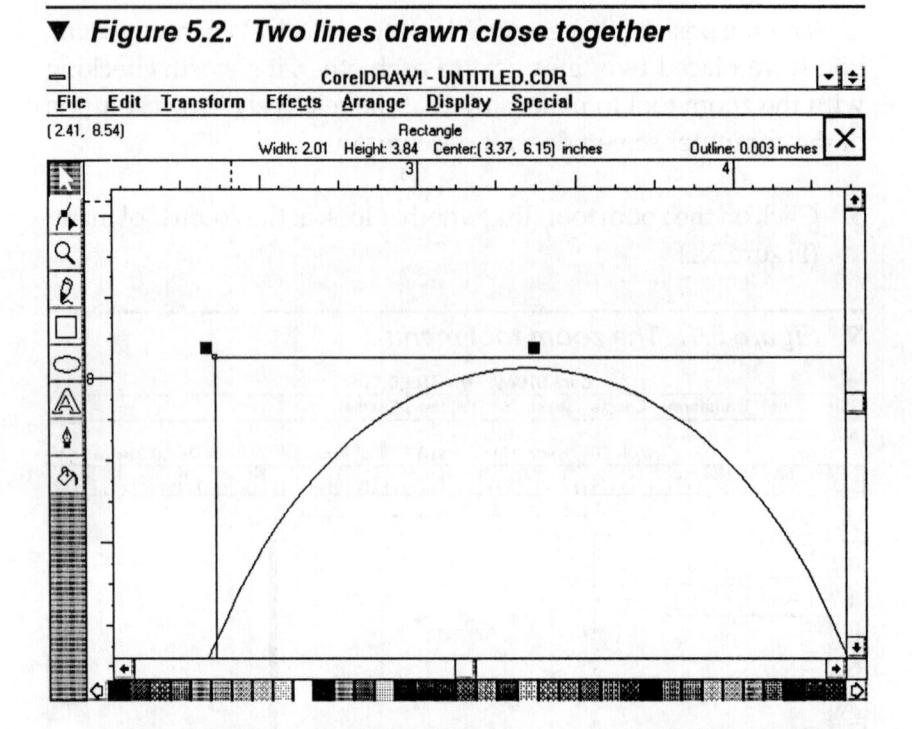

▼ **Figure 5.2. Two lines drawn close together**

6. Repeat the zoom: Click on the zoom tool and select the zoom-in option on the zoom tool menu, then drag a selection rectangle that includes the area where the two lines are closest together. Do this again and again until *CorelDRAW!* won't zoom anymore. You should see the equivalent of an area about 5/8 inch square (Figure 5.3). Note the tick marks on the ruler. Each represents 1/16 inch. Also note how far apart the lines are in the zoomed screen.

From the first zoom-in action, slide bars appeared at the bottom and the right edge of the *CorelDRAW!* window. If you want to zoom in on another part of the page, you don't have to return to the page view and then zoom in on that area. Rather, you can scroll the image on the screen so that the region of interest is visible.

▼ **Figure 5.3. The ultimate zoom**

Magnification

TIP

Naturally, if the picture is very complex or has large empty fields, you may prefer to zoom out and zoom back in again so you don't become lost in the image.

You can also access the zoom-in option by pressing F2 on the keyboard.

Zoom Out

The zoom out feature of *CorelDRAW!* is very interactive. *CorelDRAW!* remembers the steps you took zooming into the picture and it returns to previous levels of magnification.

1. With the magnified image on the screen, click on the zoom tool and click on the second item on the zoom menu—the magnifying glass with a minus sign.
2. Repeat step one until you return to the page view. Note that you don't return directly, but retrace the steps you took when you zoomed in.

You can also access the zoom-out option by pressing F3.

Actual Size (1:1)

This item, the third on the zoom tool menu, allows you to see the image on the screen in approximately the same size as it will appear when you print it on paper.

1. Click on the zoom tool and select 1:1, the third item on the zoom tool menu. You will see the view shown in Figure 5.4.

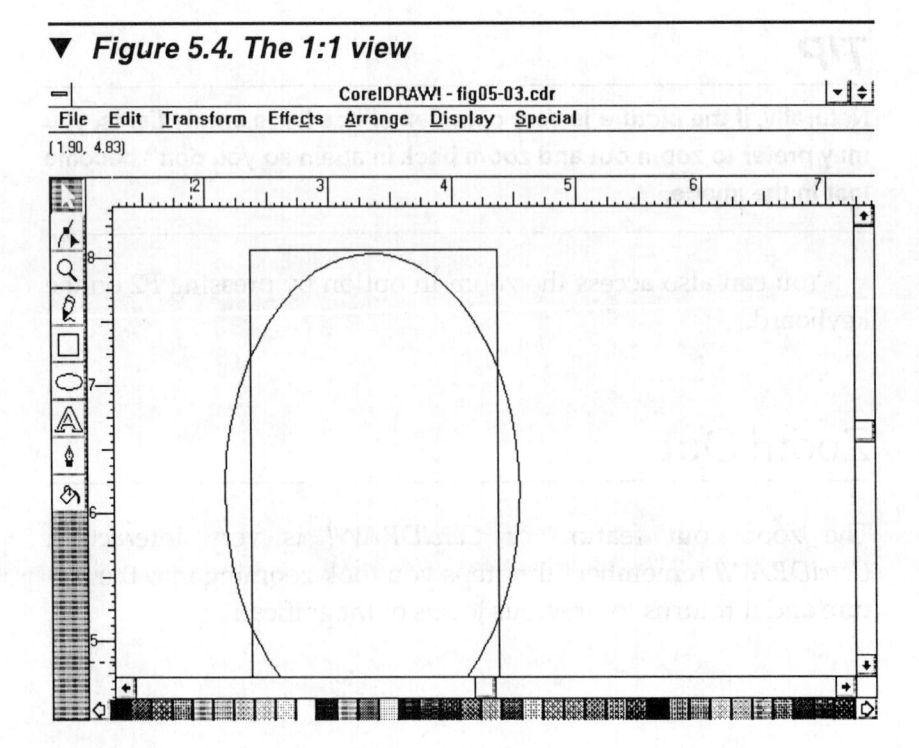

▼ *Figure 5.4. The 1:1 view*

Because of their design, some monitors slightly distort the image that appears on the screen; so the actual size view may not be exactly what you will see on paper.

Magnification

Fit in Window

Usually when you want to zoom into an object, you just want a good look at something small. If you are working on something that doesn't fill the page and you want to make it fill the *CorelDRAW!* window, click on the fourth item on the zoom tool menu—the fit-in-window option.

1. Click on the zoom tool. Select the fourth option on the zoom tool menu. You will see all the objects on the page magnified just enough to fill the *CorelDRAW!* window (Figure 5.5).

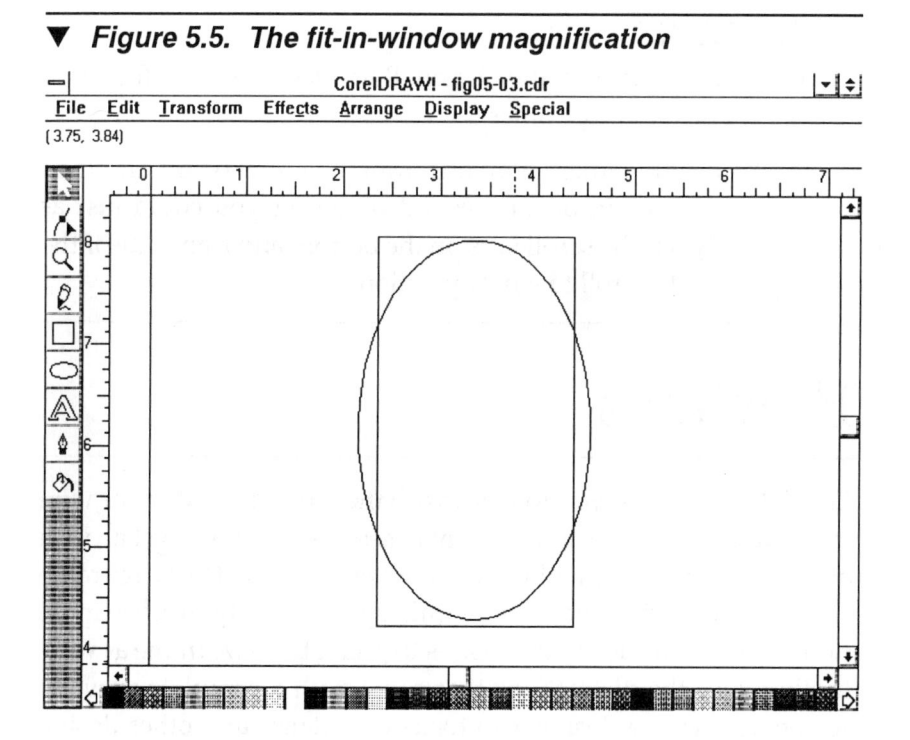

▼ *Figure 5.5. The fit-in-window magnification*

You can access the fit-in-window option from the keyboard by pressing F4.

Show Page

To return from any magnification to the page view, you can select the show page option, the last option at the right end of the zoom tool menu.

You can access the show page option directly from the keyboard by pressing Shift-F4.

CHECK YOURSELF

1. Zoom in three times and then zoom out three times.

2. Zoom in on an object at the right side of the page area. Now move to an equally tight zoom in on an object at the left side of the screen.

ANSWERS

1. You should see the screen that was visible before you zoomed in three times.

2. You could either zoom out from the initial object and then zoom back in on the second object, or you could just as easily use the scroll bars on the bottom and right side of the screen to scroll to a new position.

Previews

CorelDRAW! allows you to work with the wire frame alone or wire frame with preview. You will want to see the preview to get an idea of what the drawing will look like when printed. The wire frame alone allows you to work more quickly because it refreshes more rapidly. There are aesthetic reasons to prefer the wire frame as well. It eliminates the distractions that come with a complete preview screen, allowing a designer to focus on balance and other design considerations before turning to the issue of color.

Previews

However, you will want a preview sometimes. You should always preview the screen before printing a drawing, to save paper and extend the life of the forests (and incidentally extend the lives of graphic artists and other people who breathe oxygen). Also, if you are going to be doing color printing, you must have a preview screen visible to color things properly. Therefore, call up the preview screen.

1. Draw some images on the screen so you will have something to preview.
2. Pull down the Display menu and select Show Preview (see Figure 5.6). You've seen this screen, if you've been reading the book from the beginning. There are some elements of *CorelDRAW!* that can't be appreciated without it, so I succumbed to the temptation to use it in earlier examples.

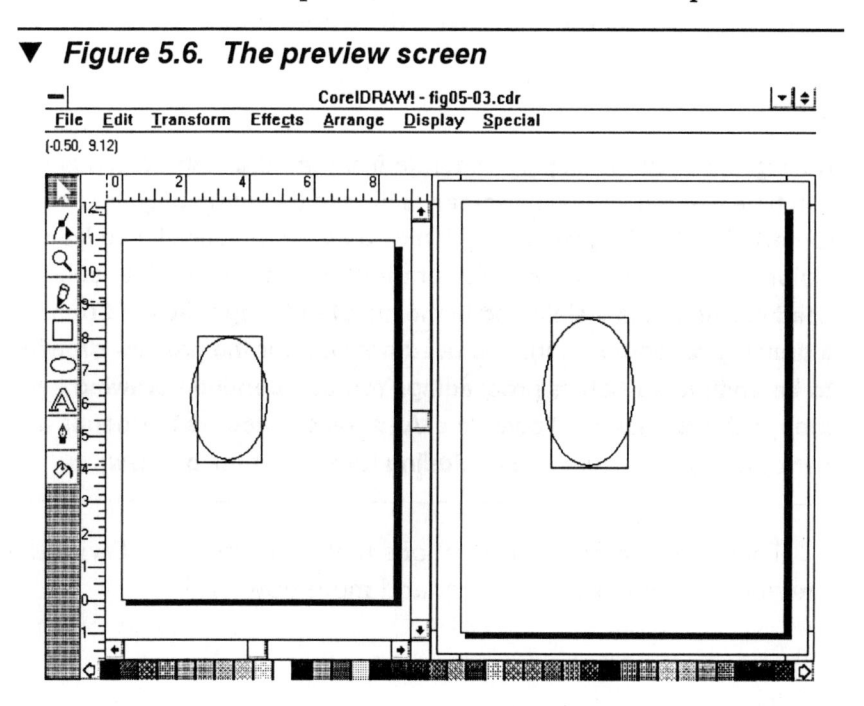

▼ *Figure 5.6. The preview screen*

It isn't much different from the wire frame view at this point. But click on one of the objects and click on a color in the palette at the bottom of the screen. The object in the left side of the screen will be unchanged but the object in the preview screen will be filled with the selected color (presuming that you have a color monitor).

TIP

Sometimes when you are working with the preview screen showing, you will "get ahead" of the preview routines. In other words, only part of the preview will appear, or small pieces of deleted or moved objects may appear. When this happens, click on the preview screen. This will cause the preview to refresh itself, clearing the screen and redrawing each of the objects in order of their precedence.

You can instantly display the preview screen from the keyboard by pressing Shift-F9.

Although colors and fountains will appear on the preview screen, you will not be able to see halftone screen effects (which won't be indicated on the preview) and PostScript texture fills (which are indicated by a fill with the letters *PS*).

TIP

Having the preview display separate from the drawing screen saves you time when the preview screen is hidden (when Display Preview is turned off in the Display menu). It may try your patience if you leave it visible all the time. You should turn it off when you don't absolutely need it. But, if it is visible and in the midst of being refreshed (having a drawing rendered on it), you need not wait for the preview drawing to be completed before proceeding. You can continue drawing even though the preview isn't complete. And you can access the menus and perform any other function (including turning off the preview).

There are several useful options that work in concert with the preview screen to make it faster and more powerful.

Full Screen Preview

You can quickly and easily blow up the preview screen by selecting Show Full Screen Preview. This allows you to see the preview screen in much more detail.

1. Pull down the Display menu.
2. Select Show Full Screen Preview. The preview image will fill the screen.
3. Press any key to return to the page view.

You can quickly go to the full screen preview by pressing F9.

Preview Toolbox

The preview toolbox is another item you've seen earlier, if you have followed the book sequentially from the beginning.

1. Pull down the Display menu.
2. Select the Show Preview Toolbox menu. You will see the toolbox shown at the right side of the preview screen shown in Figure 5.7.

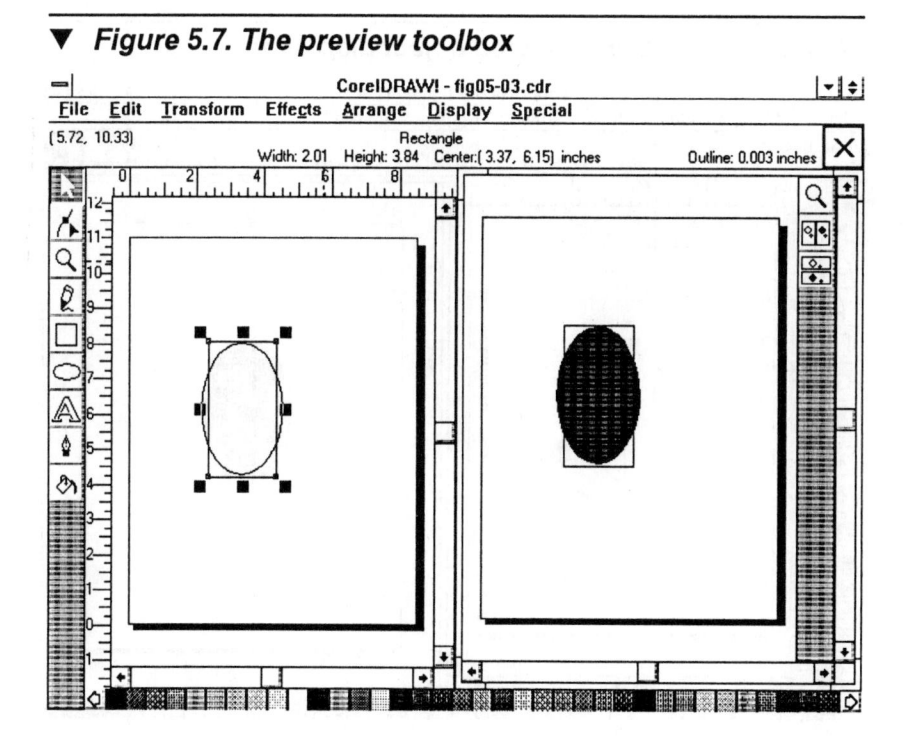

▼ *Figure 5.7. The preview toolbox*

The toolbox consists of the zoom tool, which is exactly analogous to the zoom tool covered in depth in the first part of this chapter, and two additional view options. The top view option is side-by-side, which is the view you have seen in the figures in this section of the chapter. The bottom view option is over-and-under, which places a short, wide preview underneath a short, wide version of the page area. The over-and-under view is best used for working with a landscape page orientation.

Preview Selected Only

You can cause the preview screen to display only the selected object.

1. Pull down the Display menu and select Preview Selected Only.
2. Click on one of the wire frames in the page area. You'll see something like Figure 5.8.

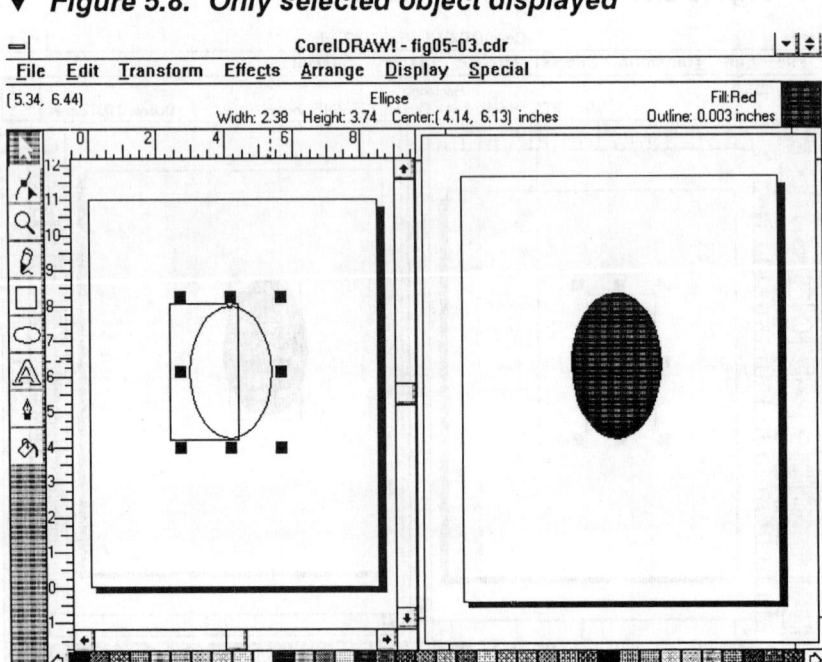

▼ *Figure 5.8. Only selected object displayed*

Previews

Naturally, this is a big time-saver in the preview, but it's also a powerful tool because, with other objects hidden, you can focus on something that normally appears in the background without the distraction of the objects that are in front of it.

CHECK YOURSELF

1. Press F9 to display a full screen preview. Now return to the normal screen.

   ANSWER
   1. Press F9 again.

Auto Update

Another tool that can save time is the Auto Update setting. It's normally turned on, so your preview screen will automatically refresh itself each time you change something on the page area. By turning this feature off, you can save an enormous amount of time because it will suppress updates until you specifically request them by clicking on the display screen.

Show Bitmaps and Refresh Wire Screen

Although these don't specifically apply to the preview screen, they do relate to the appearance of the limited preview you enjoy on the page area.

If you import a bitmap, it will normally be displayed on the page area and in the preview screen. This is because Show Bitmaps is normally turned on (if you pull down the Display menu, you will see a check mark next to the Show Bitmaps option in the menu). By clicking on this option, you will turn it off, preventing the bitmap from appearing on the page area, though it will still appear on the preview screen.

On the page area, the imported bitmap will appear as a rectangle which can be sized, skewed, or rotated.

TIP

With an imported bitmap selected on the screen, use the shape tool to crop it. You can move the individual sides of the bitmap, reducing the amount visible on the screen and limiting a bitmap to those areas that are interesting.

Refresh Wire Screen is an option that can be used when traces of "wire frame" are left behind on the page area as you make changes in the drawing. If you select this option, you will cause the page area to be refreshed, which means that it will be completely cleared and the wire frame will be completely redrawn.

You can access Refresh Wire Screen from the keyboard by pressing Ctrl-W.

Grids and Snap

Grids are a method for controlling the placement of objects on the screen. It's useful for two purposes, either placing objects at regular intervals or placing objects directly on top of one another. Now create a series of rectangles and place them at quarter-inch intervals. How did I arrive at this particular interval? Why didn't I say 1/10-inch intervals or 1/8-inch intervals? For a very good reason. The default grid is set at four positions per inch (in a moment you'll learn how to set this interval at any frequency you desire).

1. Draw four rectangles. It doesn't matter where they are on the page area, but they ought to be far enough apart to make them easy to manipulate. As an alternative, you could draw one rectangle and select Duplicate from the Edit menu three times.
2. Pull down the Display menu and select Snap to Grid (or press Ctrl-Y).

3. Drag the first rectangle by placing the mouse pointer on its upper left corner, pressing the left mouse button and moving the mouse. Note that as you move the rectangle, it seems to lurch ahead. This lurching is called *snap*. The rectangle is snapping to the grid. You can only move it in quarter-inch intervals. Place it anywhere on the screen.
4. Place the mouse pointer on the upper left corner of the second rectangle and drag the rectangle so its upper left corner is superimposed on top of the upper left corner of the first rectangle. Then move it one snap down and one snap to the right.
5. Perform a similar action on the third and fourth rectangles so that the rectangles are placed as shown in Figure 5.9. Not only do the rectangles look as if they are placed at regular intervals, but you can be assured that they are exactly 1/4 inch apart.

Grids and Snap

▼ *Figure 5.9. The rectangles snapped to a 1/4-inch grid*

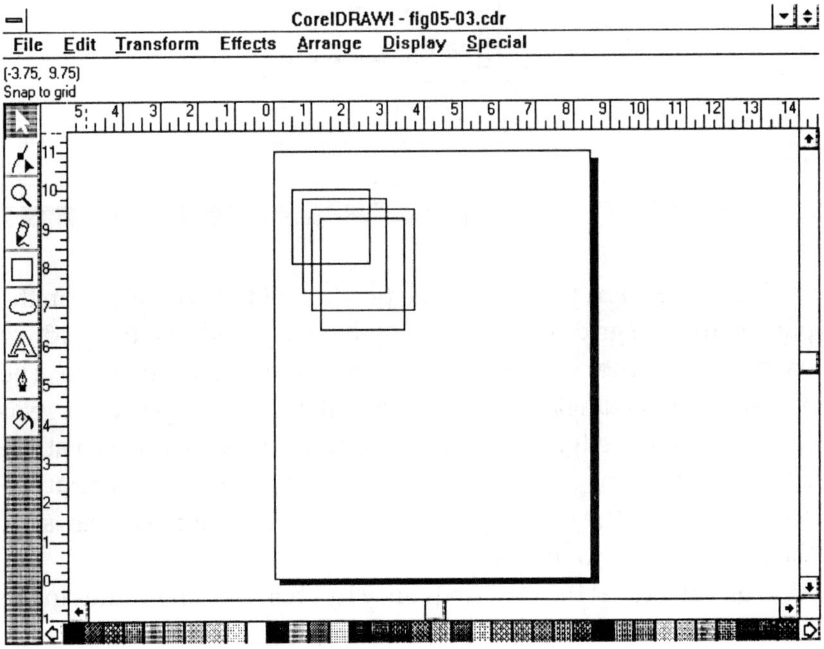

Now adjust the grid and use our adjusted grid to place the lower right corners of the rectangles.

1. Pull down the Display menu and select Grid Setup. You'll see the dialog box shown in Figure 5.10. Another way to obtain the Grid Parameters dialog box is to double click on the ruler.

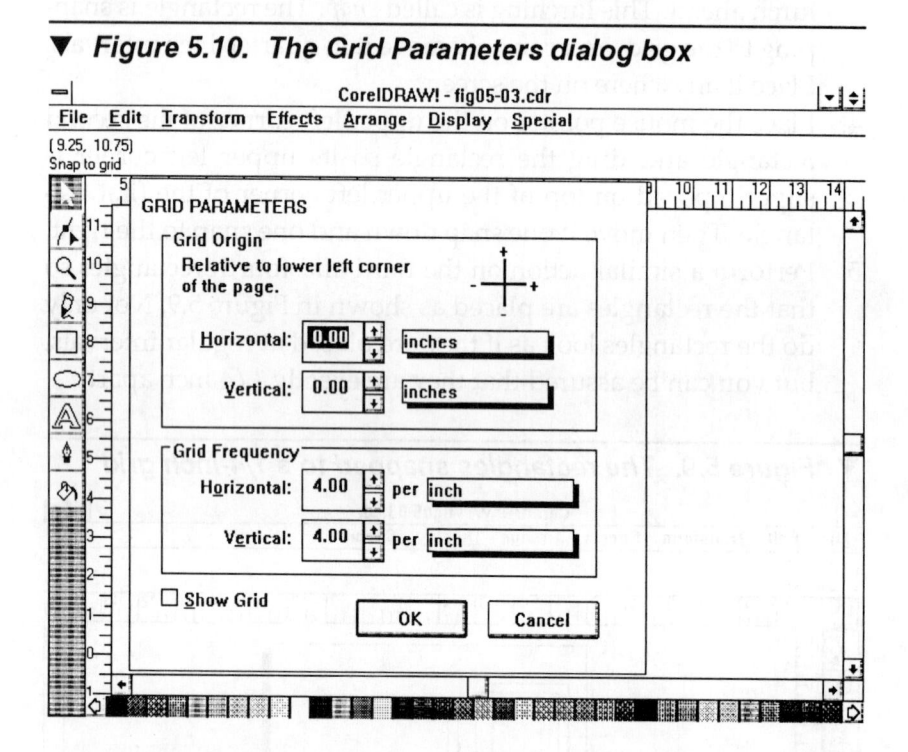

▼ **Figure 5.10. The Grid Parameters dialog box**

Using this box, you can set the position of the grid origin on the page using the grid origin. You may have noticed that the grid we used in the earlier example was exactly oriented to the page. The edges of the rectangles were placed at the 1/4-inch positions relative to the page edge. The horizontal ruler began with zero at the left edge of the page and the vertical ruler began with zero at the bottom edge of the page. By changing the grid origin, you can shift the ruler relative to the page.

You can adjust the grid frequency by changing the values in the text boxes in the lower half of the dialog box.

TIP

Try clicking on the small boxes that contain the word "inch". What happens? They should cycle through the measurements of millimeter,

pica, point, and back to inch. Printers and typographers speak in terms of picas and points, an ancient measurement unique to the printing field. A pica is 12 points, or about 1/6 inch. A point is about 1/72 inch. If you have an object that is 100 points from the edge of the page, a printer might say that it's 1 pica, 28 points or 1,28 from the edge of the page.

Grids and Snap

By clicking on the up- and down-arrows at the right of the text box containing the measurement, you can adjust the frequency by half intervals—4, 4.5, 5, and so on. Double click on the text box containing the measurement to highlight the entire value and type in the value you want. This is the method you'll use to set the value.

1. Double click on the Horizontal text box and type 3.
2. Double click on the Vertical text box and type 3.
3. Click on Show Grid.
4. Click on OK.

Take a look at the rulers. What happened? The only evident change is the appearance of dots at one-inch intervals. These are the visible grid, showing the unit of measurement. Now you're going to place the lower right corners of the rectangles.

1. Click on the outline of the first rectangle. Place the mouse pointer on the handle on the center of the right side and drag it to a new location. Notice that the snap is coarser than before because it's snapping 1/4 less frequently. Do the same with the handle on the bottom of the rectangle.
2. Perform the same task on the other three rectangles, placing each side and bottom one snap beyond the side and bottom of the previous rectangle. You'll end up with a drawing like Figure 5.11.

Now here's a question: Why not simply drag the handles in the lower right corners of the rectangles? The reason is that the rectangles are of irregular sizes. Dragging the lower right corner (or any corner handle) would adjust the size of the rectangle *proportionately*. Since it's unlikely that both the right and the bottom sides would

▼ **Figure 5.11. Finished drawing**

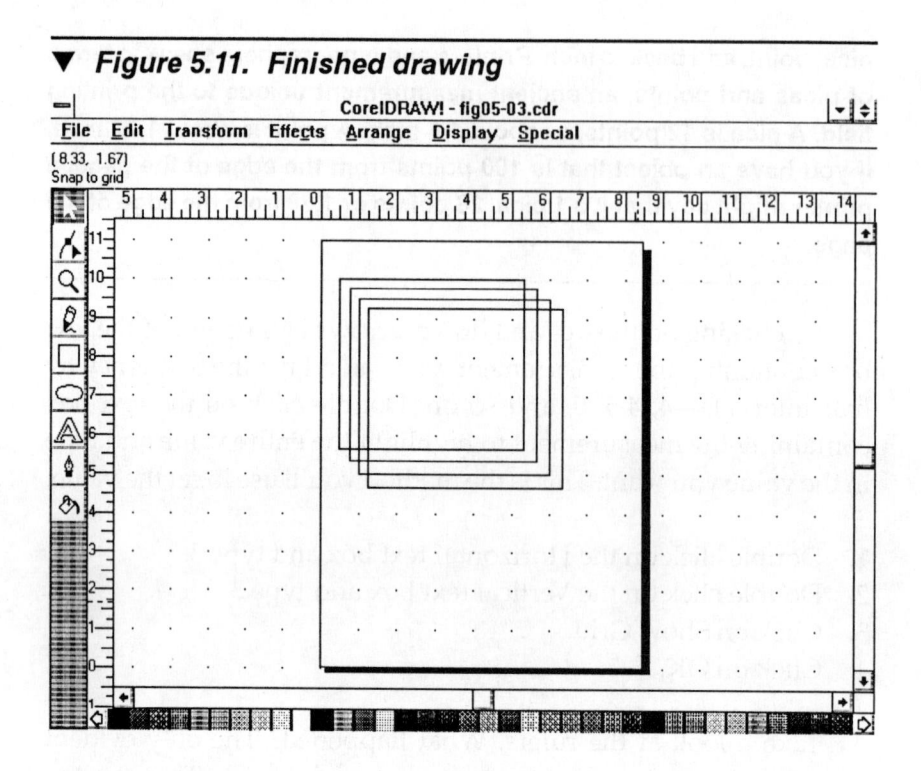

end up snapping to the same grid mark, you could end up with irregular placements of the sides. Therefore, you have to adjust the sides independently.

Before leaving this section, return the settings in the Grid Parameters dialog box to their previous settings:

1. Double click on the ruler at the top of the screen. The Grid Parameters dialog box will appear.
2. Double click on the Grid Frequency Horizontal text box and type 4.
3. Double click on the Grid Frequency Vertical text box and type 4.
4. Click on the Show Grid box to uncheck it.
5. Click on OK.

The grid settings are saved with the drawing. If you save the drawing with the settings at 1/3-inch intervals, you will find the grid set at that interval whenever you load the picture. The grid settings are also saved when you exit *CorelDRAW!*, along with all the other dialog box settings you make. It's best to stick with the default settings unless you have some strong reason not to, because otherwise you will find that you won't know what to expect when you start up *CorelDRAW!*. It will always reflect the requirements that you met for your last drawing.

Grids and Snap

Guidelines and Snap

Now that you are familiar with the concept of snap and the grid, you should know that there is another powerful way to use snap. You can create a guideline that establishes a placement of objects on the screen.

1. To begin to learn about guidelines, clear the screen by selecting New from the File menu.
2. Make sure Snap to Grid is turned off. Pull down the Display menu and see if there is a check mark next to the Snap to Grid option. If there is, select it. Selecting an option with a check mark turns it off.
3. Draw something on the screen. For the purposes of this demonstration, we will create a series of irregular ellipses whose vertical diameter will be identical, so start with an ellipse.
4. Place the mouse pointer on the ruler at the top of the screen, press the left mouse button and drag the mouse downward. Note that a broken line follows your mouse downward. This is a guideline. Drag the guideline so it coincides with the top of the ellipse you just created.
5. Repeat step four, only this time drag the guideline down until it coincides with the bottom of the ellipse. Your drawing should look something like Figure 5.12.
6. Now pull down the Display menu and select Snap to Guidelines. Now whenever you move something close to one of the guidelines (within about five pixels), it will snap to the guideline.
7. Draw a new ellipse. This time, before beginning to draw, place the mouse pointer close to the guideline. Drag the mouse as far horizontally as you please, but vertically only as far as the other guideline. If you miss the guideline, the ellipse will still snap to it.

▼ **Figure 5.12. The ellipse and the guidelines**

[Screenshot of CorelDRAW! window showing an ellipse positioned between two horizontal dashed guidelines on the page.]

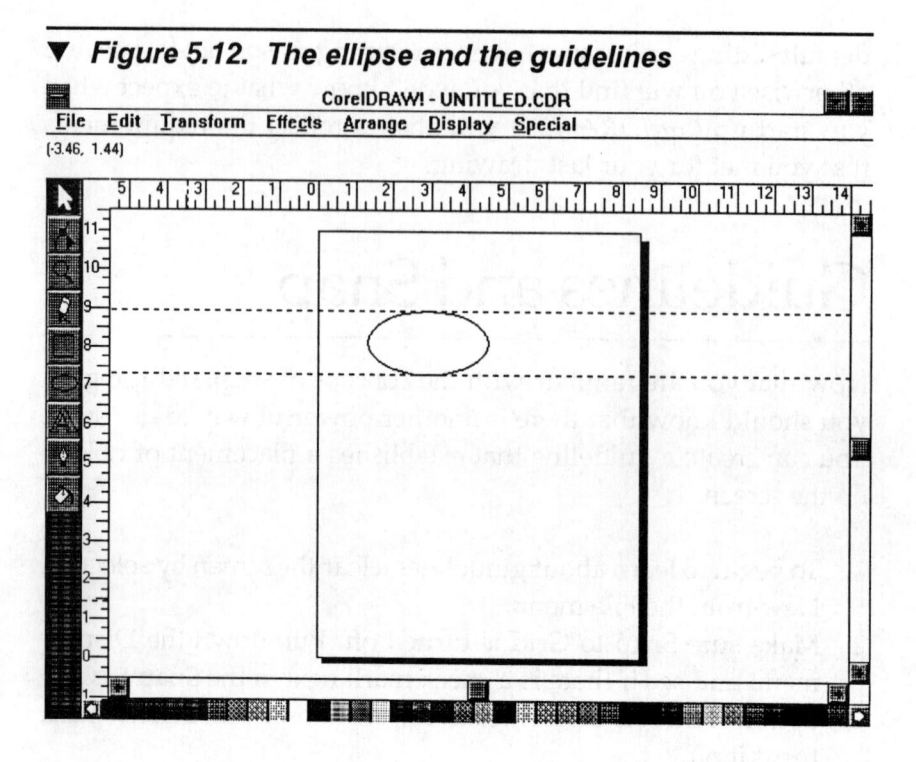

8. Pull two guidelines out of the ruler at the left edge of the screen. Draw ellipses that fit these guidelines as well.

   You can create as many guidelines as you please.

TIP

If you have Snap to Grid on, your guidelines will snap to the grid, so there isn't much point in using them. The guidelines are useful when you want to guide off of an object that is already on the screen.

Now use the guidelines to align a letterhead.

1. Start fresh by selecting New from the File menu.
2. Pull down three guidelines. The first two will be about 1/4 inch apart and the second and third should be about 3/4 inch apart. Use the rulers to place the guidelines if you like, but as you have

probably guessed, the exact placement doesn't matter very much. Your screen should look like Figure 5.13.

Guidelines and Snap

▼ *Figure 5.13. The guidelines in place for the letterhead*

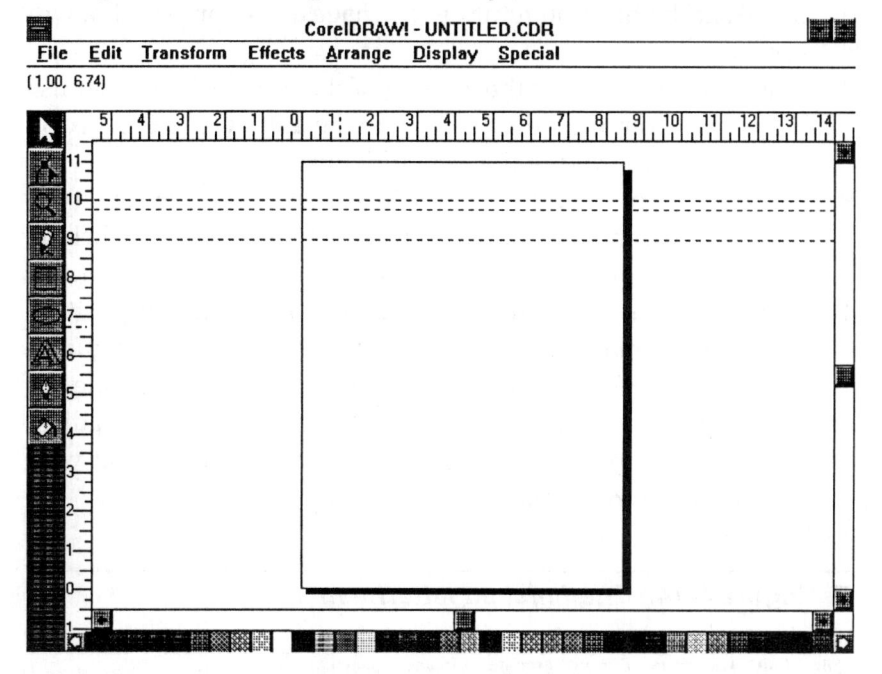

3. Click on the text tool and on the page area. In the text dialog box, type "Bonzai and Dimbulb." Use the PalmSprings font (it's Corel's version of Palatino). Click on OK to return to the page area. Use the pick tool to size the text so it is about 3/4 the width of the page area.
4. Drag the text until its baseline (the bottoms of the letters) is on the top guideline.
5. Click on the text tool and the page area again. Type "Attorneys at Law" in the Text dialog box and once again select Palm-Springs. Click on OK.
6. Drag the new text so its baseline is on the bottom guideline.
7. With the text tool still selected, press the Shift key and click on the page area. That will call up the Symbols dialog box. In the list box at the right, click on Sports+Hobbies option (you'll need to use the scroll bar to scroll through the options). In the symbols box, you will see a line of symbols. Use the scroll bar

to move horizontally through this collection of sports symbols. Select one that accurately represents your opinion of the legal profession as it relates to sports (note that an eight ball is available) and click on it. I have selected the basketball. Click on OK and when you return to the page area, your symbol will appear.

8. Place the basketball at the left end of the top guideline and use Duplicate from the Edit menu to make a copy. Place the copy on the opposite end of the top guideline.
9. Click on the page and when the Text dialog box appears, type "Specializing in sports law and contract negotiation." Click on OK and place this text on the middle line of the letterhead.
10. Now adjust the position of the guidelines to specify the position of the items on the page. Note that when you place the guidelines, you don't move the items that are on the guideline. To make the items snap to the guideline again, you have to adjust it with the mouse. Figure 5.14 shows the final letterhead with the preview screen visible.

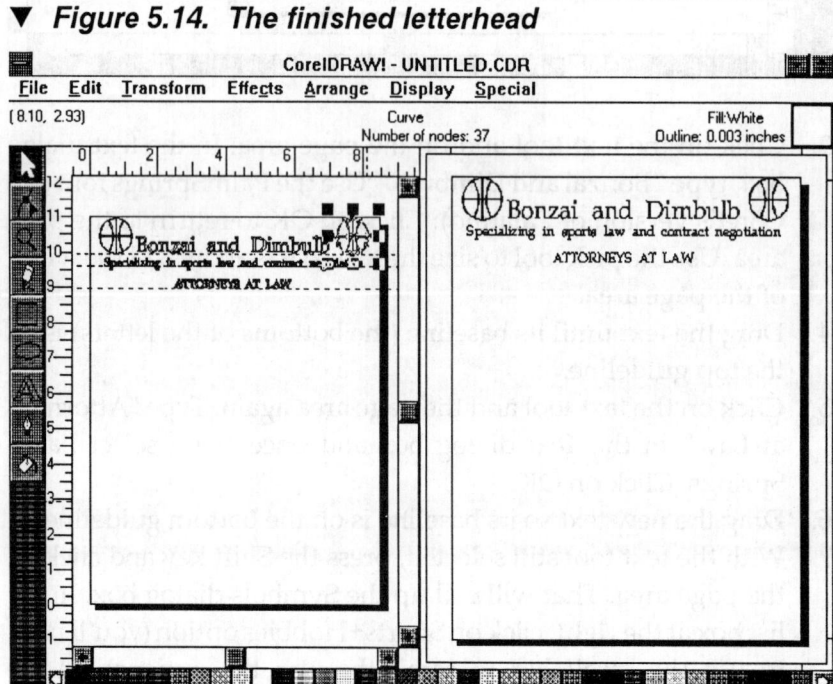

▼ **Figure 5.14. The finished letterhead**

You may want to place guidelines at a particular position on the screen.

Guidelines and Snap

1. To set a guideline at a particular position, select Guidelines Setup or pull a guideline out of the ruler and double click on it. You will see the dialog box in Figure 5.15.

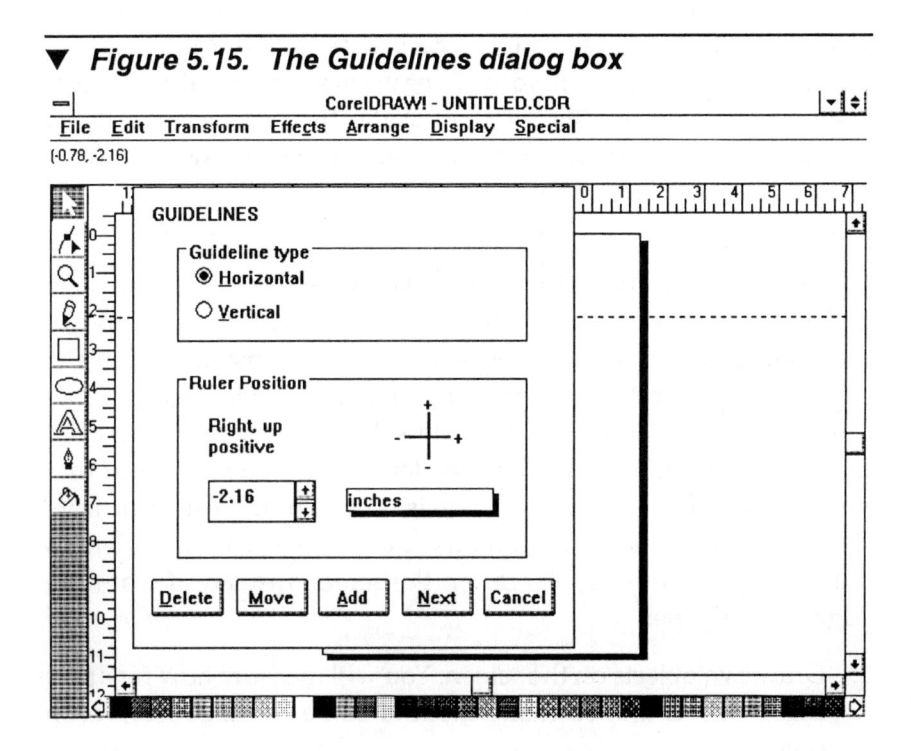

▼ *Figure 5.15. The Guidelines dialog box*

2. Select whether you want a vertical or a horizontal guideline in the top section of the dialog box. Enter the exact position of the guideline in the text box at the bottom.

Rulers, Status Line, Palette

You have probably noticed that certain items are always on the screen—the rulers, status line, and the palette. The first two provide a wealth of information about the drawing and the third is a great convenience for coloring objects on the screen. But some people may not want them visible, either because they are working with wire frames alone so the palette is useless to them, or because they restrict the screen somewhat. With all of these assists turned off, much more of the drawing can be seen on the screen.

TIP

To turn off the rulers, status line, and palette, pull down the Display menu. About halfway down, you will see the menu items: Show Rulers, Show Status Line, and Show Color Palette. They should have check marks beside them, meaning that they are turned on. By clicking on these items, you can turn them off.

The ruler is useful in that it helps you to see the size of the page and estimate the positions of things on the page, not just relative to each other, but in absolute terms reflecting its distance from the edge of the paper. You can place the mouse pointer next to something and see dotted lines in the rulers that indicate the distance of that point from the bottom and the left side of the paper. But that may not be sufficient for you. Here is how to pull those indicators right out of the rulers to the mouse pointer and use the rulers to measure distance from objects on the screen instead of from the edges of the paper.

1. Draw two objects on the screen. You will measure how far apart these objects are, so make them at some distance from each other.
2. Place the mouse pointer on the place where the rulers come together at the upper left corner of the *CorelDRAW!* window.
3. Press the left mouse button and drag onto the screen. Crosshairs will follow the mouse pointer, which you can use to measure distances on the screen. Move the mouse pointer so it is next to an object on the screen.
4. Release the mouse button. Note what happened to the rulers. The zero point on the rulers is placed where you released the mouse pointer. Now by moving your mouse pointer to another object on the screen you can use the indicators on the rulers to see how far apart the two objects are. Note that the values on

the left end of the status line also reflect distances from the new zero points on the rulers.

Rulers, Status Line, Palette

Now that you have the rulers in this position, how would you go about returning it to its previous orientation—with zero at the left and bottom edges of the page?

1. Pull down the Display menu and select Grid Setup or double click on the ruler.
2. In the top area of the resulting Grid Parameters dialog box, you will see your new settings in the Grid Origins section of the dialog box. Double click on the text box corresponding to the Horizonal grid origin and type 0. Double click on the text box corresponding to the Vertical grid origin and type 0.
3. Click on OK. The rulers should be back to normal.

CHECK YOURSELF

1. Turn on Snap to Grid and Snap to Guidelines. Call up Grid Setup and select Show Grid to make the grid visible. Pull a guideline out of the ruler and place it between grid marks (note that the guideline also snaps to the grid). Create a rectangle and drag it around the screen.

ANSWER

1. The guidelines take precedence over the grid, but the rectangle should snap to both grid and guideline.

Exercises

This exercise assumes that you have *CorelDRAW!* running and a new, blank page area visible. If you already have something on the screen, save it and select New from the File menu.

What You Should Do	How the Computer Responds
1. Pull down the Display menu and if Snap to Grid is not turned on, turn it on now.	1. Snap to Grid will appear at the left end of the status line.
2. Pull down the Display menu again and click on Grid Setup. In the Grid Parameters dialog box, make sure the Show Grid check box is checked. Click on the button marked OK.	2. The grid will appear on the page area; in fact, it will fill the whole *CorelDRAW!* window.
3. If it is not already turned on, turn on the preview screen by selecting it in the Display menu or by pressing Shift-F9. Click on the zoom tool in the toolbox. Select zoom-in, the magnifying glass with the plus sign in it. Move the mouse pointer back to the page area.	3. The mouse pointer will now be a magnifying glass.
4. Drag a rectangle about one inch on each side and release the mouse button.	4. When you release the mouse button, you will see the page area fill with grid marks. If you haven't altered the defaults, these grid marks should be 1/8-inch apart. If they are inconveniently far apart, pull down the Display menu and select Grid Setup and change the Grid Frequency settings to eight per inch.

5. Click on the rectangle tool in the toolbox and drag a rectangle 1/8-inch on a side. Try to start and finish at a distance from the grid mark.

5. The rectangle will snap to the nearest grid mark, resulting in a perfect rectangle. If the rectangle doesn't snap to the correct grid mark, click on the Pick tool and use the control handles to adjust it to 1/8-inch on a side.

6. Click on the ellipse tool and create an ellipse with the point of origin at the first grid mark above and to the left of the rectangle, and the terminating point at the first grid mark below and to the right of the rectangle.

6. A perfect circle will be formed. The rectangle will be centered in the circle.

7. Click on the pick tool and drag a selection rectangle that includes both the circle and the rectangle.

7. Both objects will be selected, as indicated at the center of the status line (2 objects selected).

8. Click on the outline of one of the selected shapes.

8. The rotate and skew handles will appear.

9. Drag the top skew handle (the straight arrow in the center of the top of the selection rectangle) slightly to the right. Try to end with the corners of the skewed rectangle between grid marks.

9. Note that you can rotate and skew without snapping to the grid.

10. Click on the zoom tool in the toolbox and select full-page view from the zoom menu.

10. Note how small the object is that you have been working on.

Exercises

6 Node Editing

- ▲ Delete Nodes
- ▲ Control Points
- ▲ Smooth Curves Through Nodes
- ▲ Break Nodes
- ▲ Turn Curves into Lines
- ▲ Cusp Nodes
- ▲ Add Nodes
- ▲ Attach Nodes
- ▲ Turn Lines into Curves
- ▲ Make Nodes Symmetrical
- ▲ More Node Editing Features

I remember the first time I saw node editing. My reaction was "So what?" or something equally glib. I couldn't see any purpose in moving little pieces of lines around. It was only when I sat down to use the nodes that I realized how valuable they were. As steady as my hands are and as powerful as my scanning equipment and tracing programs are, the art on the page never seems to be exactly the way I want it. I'm not a perfectionist, but I like to have control over the art I create. If the artist doesn't exercise some control, the "art" becomes simply another product of the machine.

If your rulers aren't turned on, pull down the Display menu and select Show Rulers.

Start with some scanned art, which we will trace and then node edit. For the purposes of this trace, I will lend a common object, seen in Figure 6.1.

Ordinarily, it's difficult to scan three-dimensional objects, but the Chinon DS-3000 scanner is a flat-bed scanner that looks more like an overhead projector than a Xerox copier. Since its scanning hardware looks down on a flat plate rather than looking up through a piece of glass, this particular scanner makes it possible to scan three-dimensional assemblages.

If you don't have an image to scan, or if you don't have a scanner, use one of the TIF or PCX files in the SAMPLES subdirectory under your CORELDRW directory.

1. Start up *CorelDRAW!* or select New from the File menu to start with a clean slate.
2. Use the Import command on the File menu to import a PCX or TIF graphic. Make sure For Tracing is checked in the Import dialog box. Figure 6.1 shows the imported bitmap graphic.
3. Make sure that the imported bitmap is selected and click on the pencil tool. Trace the bitmap by placing the "point of the dagger" slightly to the right of the edge to be traced and clicking. If you accidentally trace the same edge a second time, remember to press the Del key immediately to eliminate the unnecessary object.
4. When all the edges have been traced, click on the rectangle that defines the bitmap and press the Del key to eliminate the bitmap. My trace resulted in the image shown in Figure 6.2.

Node Editing ▲ 197

▼ *Figure 6.1. The imported bitmap graphic*

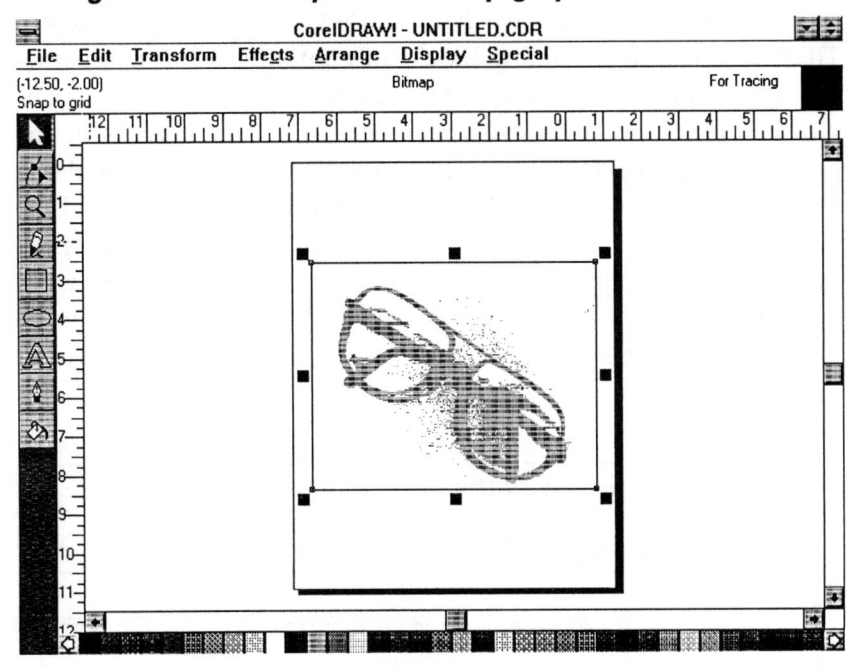

Node Editing

▼ *Figure 6.2. The trace*

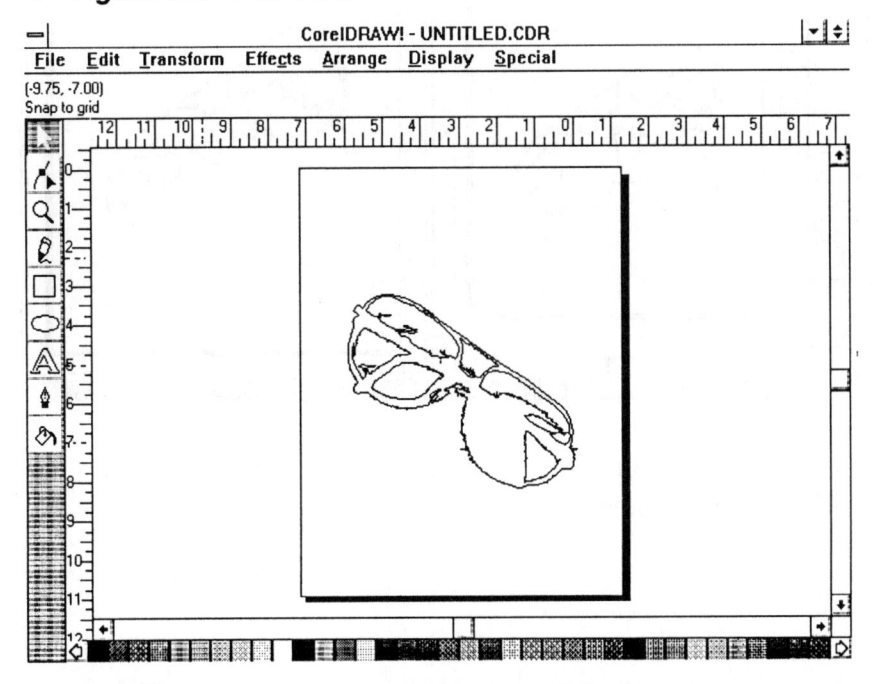

I don't know about you, but to my eye this image looks like a pair of glasses only if I know in advance that it is a pair of glasses. That's one of the stumbling blocks of computer art. It can sometimes be extremely abstract, and since you know what the image is, it's difficult for you to tell when there are enough clues in the graphic. Figure 6.3 is the same image as Figure 6.2 with the pieces of the graphic selected and then combined, using the Combine command from the Arrange menu. I've colored the image dark gray and turned on the preview screen by selecting Show Preview from the Display menu. I did all of this to emphasize how abstract the graphic is. You're seeing it in the best possible light in its current state.

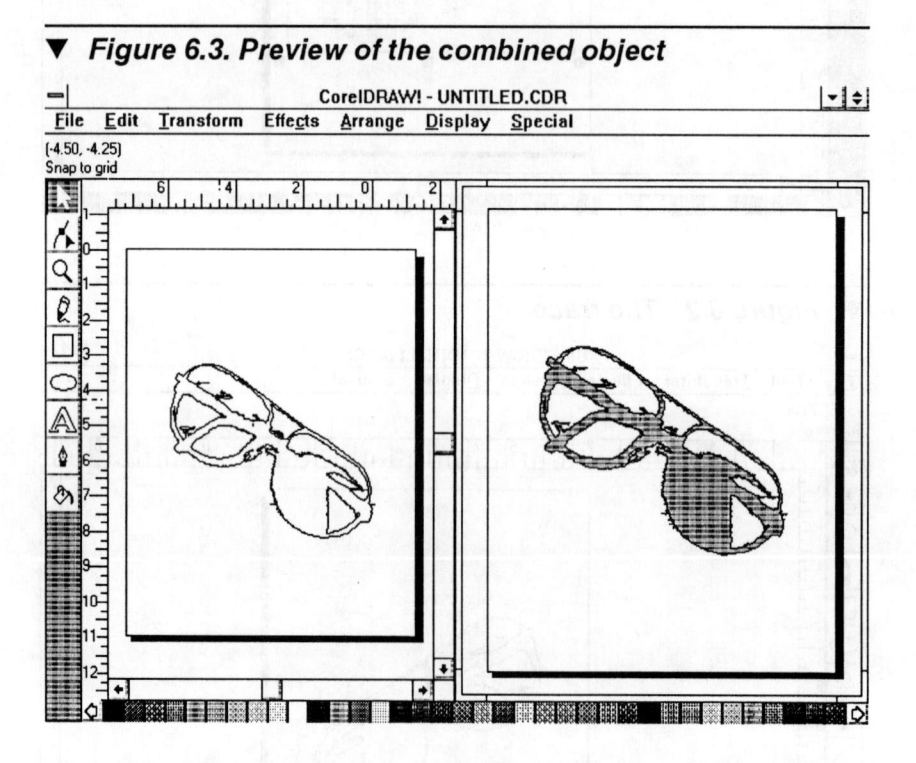

▼ *Figure 6.3. Preview of the combined object*

How will you clarify this object? If you guessed, "By node editing," give yourself a star.

Delete Nodes

First of all, many of the nodes in this image are unnecessary.

1. Click on the zoom tool and select the zoom-in option.
2. Select a section of the bitmap that appears somewhat irregular. You should end up with an image like Figure 6.4.

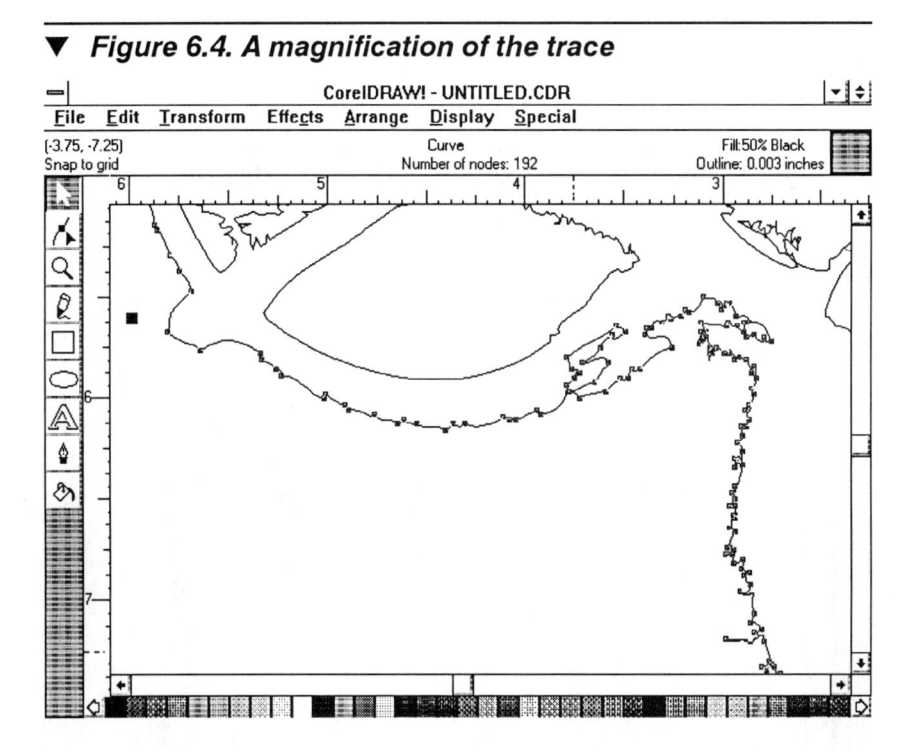

▼ *Figure 6.4. A magnification of the trace*

One of the reasons for the jagged appearance of this trace is the fact that the bitmap was very jagged. You will begin by going around the image and deleting nodes. This has the effect of smoothing the image.

1. Click on the shape tool.
2. Click on the line whose nodes you want to edit.

The next step is to determine which nodes should stay and which should go. Generally, you will want to keep a node at the beginning of a curve, at the end of a curve, and at the middle of a curve. This means that in the large curve shown in Figure 6.5, you want to eliminate all but three of the nodes.

3. Drag a selection rectangle to select several nodes between one of the ends of the curve and the middle of the curve. Don't worry about selecting too many because you can always replace nodes.
4. Press Del. Don't worry if the curve looks weird—in fact, it almost certainly will (Figure 6.5.)

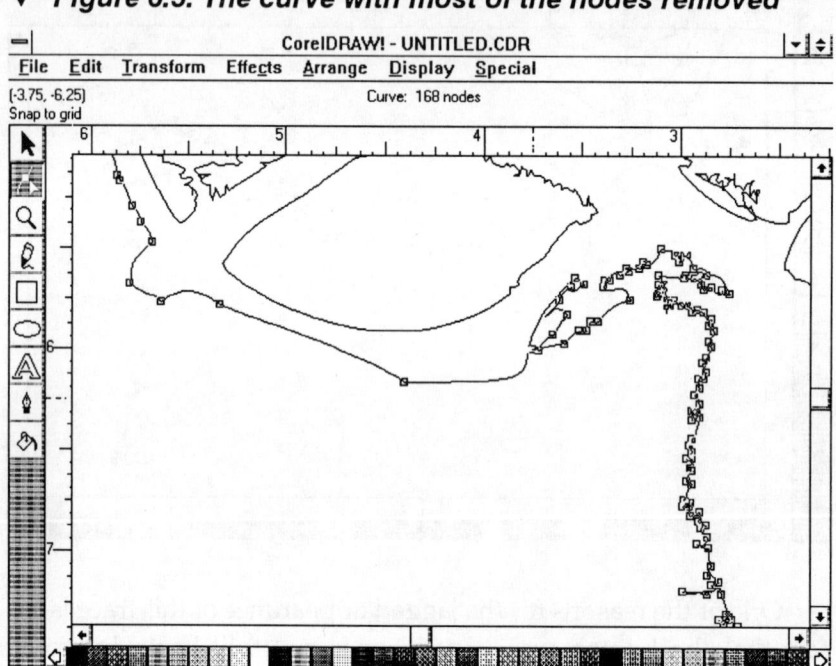

▼ **Figure 6.5. The curve with most of the nodes removed**

Now that you have seen nodes deleted wholesale, delete a node individually.

1. Locate another unnecessary node, either in the curve or in some other part of the trace.

2. Double click on the node. You will see the Node Editing dialog box shown in Figure 6.6.

Delete Nodes

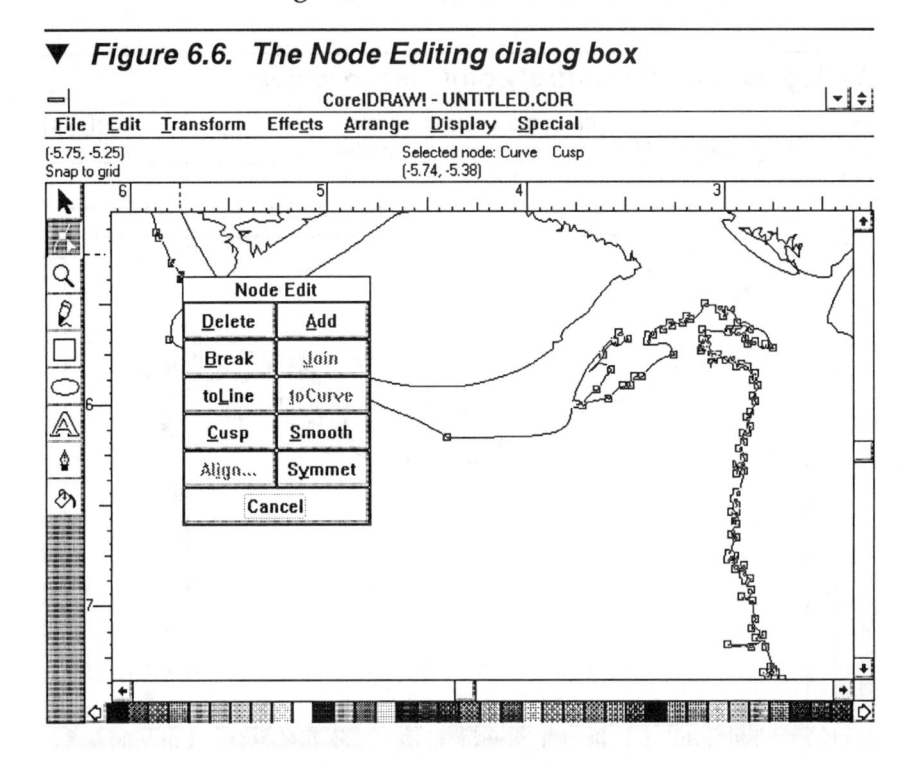

▼ *Figure 6.6. The Node Editing dialog box*

3. Click on Delete or press D.

There is no advantage in one deletion scheme over the other. One stresses the mouse and the other stresses the keyboard. You can delete large numbers of nodes with the Node Editing dialog box. Simply drag a selection rectangle including a number of nodes and double click on any of them. When you click on the Delete button, all the selected nodes will be eliminated.

Control Points

Now make your curve look more like a curve by using control points.

1. Click on one of the nodes at the end of the irregular curve. Its control points will appear (Figure 6.7).

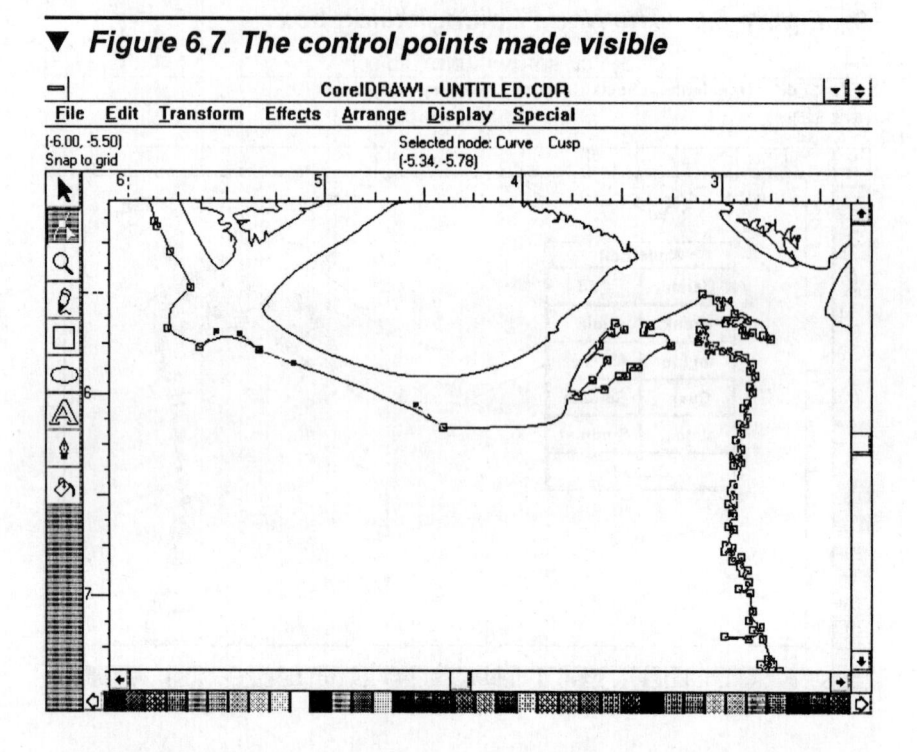

▼ *Figure 6.7. The control points made visible*

2. Adjust the control points so that the curve is more natural looking.

You can move the middle control point closer to the curve of the interior of the lens by simply placing the mouse pointer on it and dragging it. The result can be seen in Figure 6.8.

TIP

If the handles seem to jump around uncontrollably while you adjust them, the reason may be that you have left Snap to Grid turned on in the Display menu.

▼ Figure 6.8. The adjusted curve

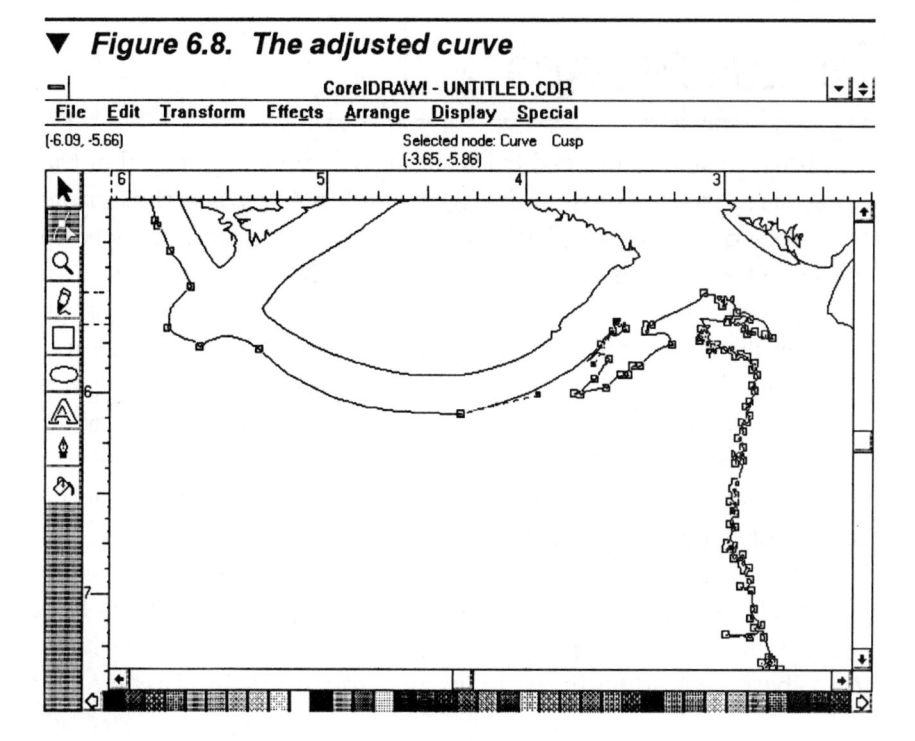

Control Points

Smooth Curves Through Nodes

The curve through the central node of our curve ought to be smooth. Although the line curves away gently on either side of this node, it goes straight through the node itself. There is no cusp or hairpin turn here. Therefore, you should take this opportunity to smooth the curve through the node.

1. Double click on the central node.
2. When the Node Edit dialog box appears, select Smooth or press S.

    Smooth makes the curve absolutely smooth through the node.

Break Nodes

You have probably noticed the temple, which has appeared at the upper left corner of most of the figures so far. As a trace, the temple is a piece of the lenses. This happened because the glasses were folded when the scan occurred. In fact, glasses with the temples attached to the lenses would be practically useless. It's one of the items in the graphic that will confuse a viewer. Therefore, it would be a good idea to separate the two images. In this way, the ring that holds the lenses can be colored light gray and the temple can be colored dark gray so that it can be seen as a separate piece. To do this, you will need to break nodes and attach them (which is the subject of the next section).

1. Double click on the node that marks the place where the lens holder and the temple come together.
2. When the Node Editing dialog box appears, select Break.

Although the broken node looks much the same, it is actually two nodes. In Figure 6.9, one of the nodes has been moved slightly apart from the other.

The node should be adjusted so that it completely crosses the lens holder and breaks the node on the other side of the temple, as shown in Figure 6.10.

CHECK YOURSELF

1. Create a rectangle in a paint program and import it into *CorelDRAW!* Trace it, and then simplify the traced line.

ANSWER

1. The fastest way is to select and delete nodes wholesale. Be careful to leave nodes in the middle of curves and at corners to retain the general shape. Then adjust the remaining nodes to make the shape correct again.

▼ *Figure 6.9. The broken node*

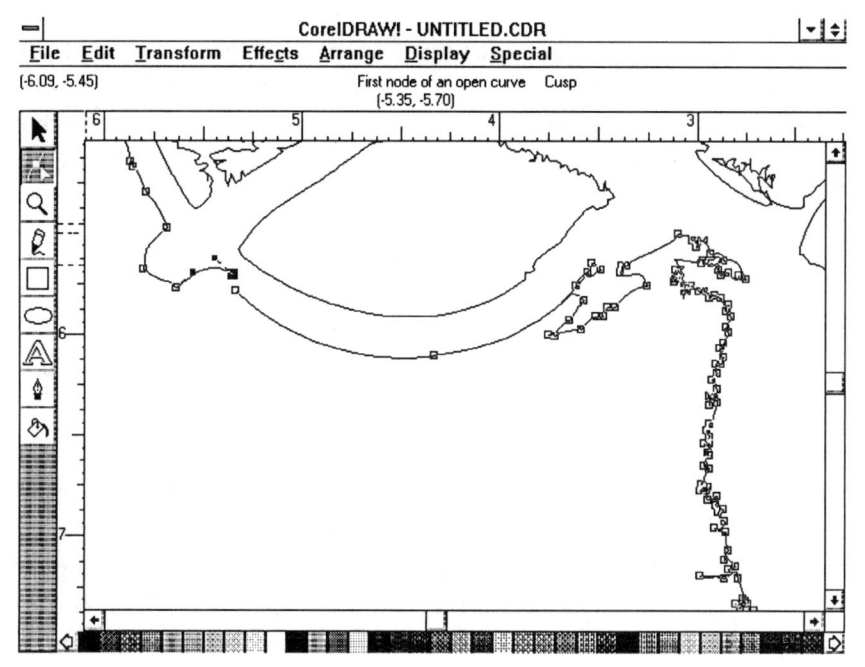

Break Nodes

▼ *Figure 6.10. The second broken node*

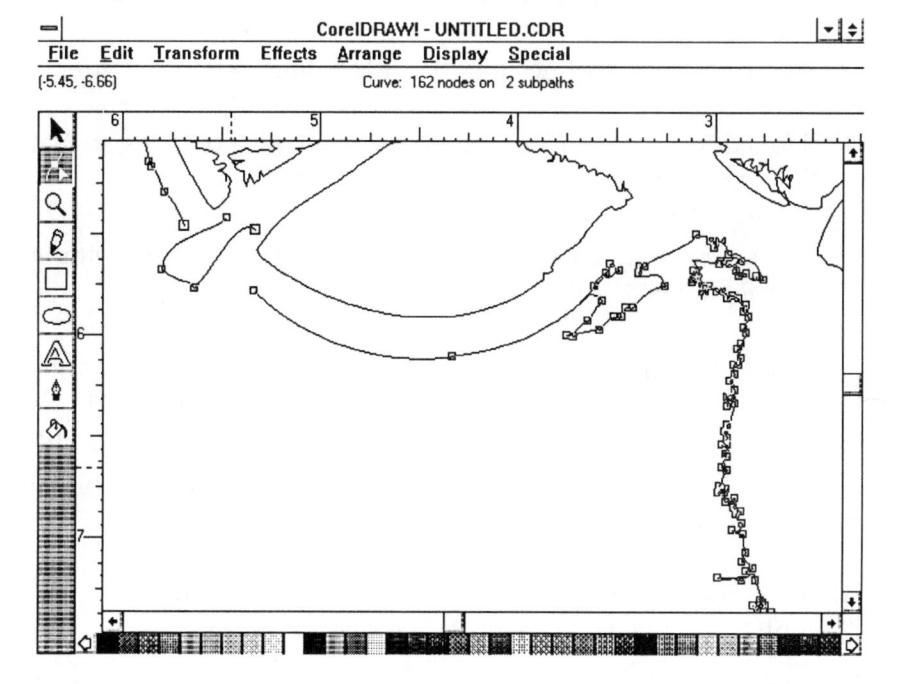

TIP

To reduce the number of nodes that appear when you autotrace, you can adjust the sensitivity of the trace. Pull down the Special menu and select Preferences. Click on the Lines & Curves button and note that in the resulting dialog box there is a setting for Autotrace Tracking. This can be set from one to ten. The lower the number, the higher the sensitivity of the trace and consequently, the more nodes that are generated.

Attach Nodes

There are two ways to attach nodes. If two nodes are the end nodes of the same object, simply use the shape tool to drag a selection rectangle that selects the end nodes of an open object (or hold down the Shift key and click on both ends); then double click on one of them and when the Node Edit dialog box appears, select Join. If two nodes are the end nodes of separate objects, you need to select both objects with the pick tool and select Combine from the Arrange menu. Then perform the same action as with the end nodes of the same object.

You'll start by reconnecting the ends of the open lens holder.

1. Hold down the Shift key and click on the two end nodes, so that both are selected.
2. Double click on one of the nodes.
3. In the resulting dialog box, select Join. You will see something like Figure 6.11.

Oddly enough, even though you have disconnected the temple from the lens holder, they are still part of the same object. This is because although they are completely disconnected, they are still *combined*. Therefore, you will want to break them apart so they can be individually manipulated.

1. Make sure the temple and the lens holder are selected.
2. Pull down the Arrange menu and select Break Apart.

▼ **Figure 6.11. The joined ends**

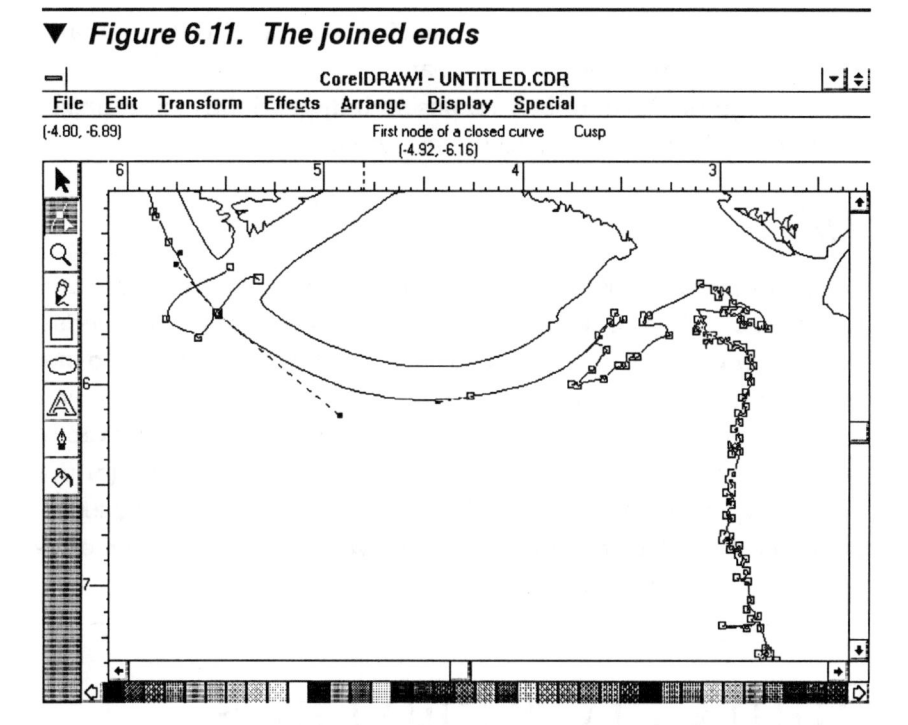

Attach Nodes

Next, adjust the ends of the temple so they are in line with the temple that crosses the lens. Connect the ends with a line to make the temple object a closed object. This involves the use of the Combine command on the Arrange menu.

1. With the temple object selected, click on the pencil tool.
2. Place the pencil tool on one of the nodes of the temple and press the mouse button.
3. Drag the pencil tool to the other end of the temple object. When you release the mouse button, the line necessary to close the object will be in place.
4. Click on the pick tool.
5. Click on the new line to select it, if it isn't already selected.
6. Hold down the Shift key and click on the temple object to select it.
7. Pull down the Arrange menu and select Combine.
8. Click on the shape tool and drag a selection rectangle that contains only the node at the end of the new line and the

endpoint of the temple. Double click on one of them to make the Node Edit dialog box appear.
9. Select Join. The temple becomes an independent, closed object that can be placed behind the lens holder.

TIP

You may discover that the Join option on the dialog box is grayed and not available. This could be because there are more than two nodes selected or because only one node is selected. You might want to use the zoom-in option again to take an even closer look at the nodes you are connecting. It's very easy to end up with two nodes almost exactly on top of one another. In that case, use the delete command (or the delete key) in combination with the shape tool to eliminate any extraneous nodes. Also watch out for areas where three lines come together. You can't join more than two nodes.

Turn Curves into Lines

In another part of the drawing, there is a section of the temple that was traced as a curve but should have been a line. It's shown near the center of Figure 6.12. A curve is a powerful thing, but it's difficult to keep straight when you want it to be straight, and what looks straight on the screen may not be straight on the page. Therefore, you will have to convert it into a line.

1. Double click on the endpoint of the line. Sometimes it's difficult to tell which is the correct node for the curve. If the wrong curve segment becomes highlighted, click on the Cancel button on the Node Editing dialog box and double click on the node at the other end of the curve. Or you might prefer simply to double click on the line or curve segment itself. That always selects the correct node.
2. When the Node Edit dialog box appears, click on the button marked toLine (or press L).

▼ **Figure 6.12.** *The curve that should be a line*

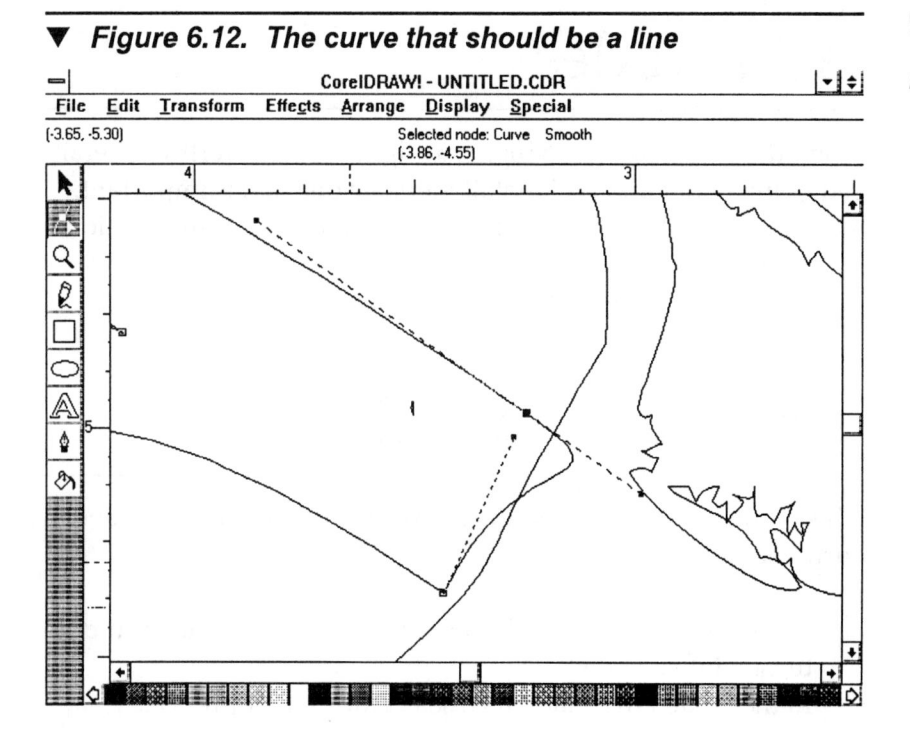

Turn Curves into Lines

Cusp Nodes

In the very same line, you may run into trouble with the next curve segment because it won't bend. The control point won't budge from a straight line with the line segment just created. What does that mean? It means that during the trace operation, *CorelDRAW!*, in its infinite wisdom, made this a smoothed node. In order to get a smoothed node to bend independently, it's necessary to turn it into a cusp.

1. Double click on the node again.
2. When the Node Edit dialog box appears, click on Cusp.

   This will give you complete control over the control point.

Add Nodes

In another part of the drawing, you might become overly exuberant removing nodes and accidentally remove one that is important.
1. Simply double click on the segment that needs an additional node.
2. Select Add from the Node Edit dialog box.

Turn Lines into Curves

This editing job did not require it, but frequently, you may have to turn lines into curves.

1. Double click on the end node of the segment that should be turned into a node.
2. In the Node Edit dialog box, select toCurve or press C.

Make Nodes Symmetrical

A symmetrical node not only has a smooth curve running through it, but it also has control points at equal distances from it. Once again, it was not required for this editing job, but if you need to make a node symmetrical:

1. Double click on the node.
2. When the Node Edit dialog box appears, select Symmet or press Y.

TIP

Symmetrical nodes are useful for regular, flowing curves. The nodes of a circle or an ellipse are symmetrical. If you make the "side" nodes of an ellipse unsymmetrical, you will create an oval.

More Node Editing Features

One of the more interesting ways to edit nodes is to edit them in groups. To edit more than one node at a time, hold down the Shift key as you click on the nodes to be edited. There is no reason to select nodes in a single line or several nodes in a row (though you can do this by dragging a selection rectangle). Although you probably *will* edit nodes in groups only when they are close together, you can select any group of nodes. Then you can drag all the nodes by dragging one node, or make them all symmetrical, and so on.

Crop Bitmaps

The same tool that you have been using for node editing can be used to crop bitmaps. Select the bitmap to be cropped and click on the shape tool in the toolbox. Special handles will appear around the edges of the bitmap. Simply drag the handles toward the center of the bitmap and the bitmap will be cropped, eliminating from view the portions you hid by moving the sides.

Exercises

This exercise assumes that you have *CorelDRAW!* running and a new, blank page area is visible. If you already have something on the screen, save it and select New from the File menu.

What You Should Do	**How the computer Responds**
1. Pull down the File menu, and select Import. In the Import dialog box, select TIFF as the format and make sure the For Tracing check box is checked. In the Import Bitmap dialog box, go to the SAMPLES directory under your CORELDRW directory and locate a file called OUT_HOUS.TIF (it isn't what you might think). Double click on this filename.	1. The haunted house graphic will be loaded into *CorelDRAW!* for tracing.
2. Trace the house (don't bother with the bats). You'll also have to trace the moon. Sorry. When the house and moon are traced, make sure the bitmap is selected and press Del.	2. The bitmap will be deleted.
3. Use the zoom tool to zoom in on the point where the top of the moon encounters the parapet. Click on the outline tool. Click on the node that appears where the moon meets the parapet. (Sounds a little like a song lyric, doesn't it?) Double click on the same node.	3. The Node Edit dialog box appears, with all its buttons.

4. Click on Break to break the node (and line) in two. Use the mouse pointer to drag the nodes slightly apart, (this makes it easier to see what you're doing). Repeat this procedure with the other node that joins the moon to the parapet (there is an inside and an outside line for this moon). Use the same procedure to separate the moon from the lower part of the house.

5. Click on the pick tool. Click on the inside line of the moon (the one that's closer to the house), pull down the Arrange menu, and select Break Apart. Do the same thing with the line that makes up the outer part of the moon.

6. Click on the outer moon line. Hold down the Shift key and click on the inner moon line. Press Del.

7. Click on the house outside of the place where the moon once joined it; then hold down the Shift key and click on the part of the house that once lay between the two ends of the inner moon line.

8. Pull down the Arrange menu and select Combine.

4. The moon is completely separated from the house. But the lines that make it up are still combined with the house lines.

5. The moon and the house are now four completely separate lines.

6. The moon disappears.

7. Both parts of the house are now selected.

8. The house is now all one piece. But it isn't a closed object yet.

Exercises

9. Click on the outline tool and drag a rectangle that encloses the end nodes of both parts of the house where the moon was joined to it lower down on the roof. Double click on one of the two selected nodes. In the resulting dialog box, select Join. Repeat this procedure with the two nodes where the moon met the parapet.

9. The house is now a closed object that may be colored as you please.

10. Use the control handles of the resulting joined nodes to make the roofs smooth again (or as smooth as a haunted house can be).

10. The outline of the house is now smooth and complete. It doesn't look as scary without the moon, but there is more you can do with it.

7 Lines and Fills

- ▲ Vector and Raster Patterns
- ▲ Fountain Fills
- ▲ PostScript Patterns
- ▲ Pen Points
- ▲ Putting Fills to Work
- ▲ Brush Colors
- ▲ Color and Shape Blends
- ▲ Mixing Colors
- ▲ How and Why to Use Pantone Colors

This chapter covers all the options on the fill menu, one of the most interesting and involved menus in *CorelDRAW!*. Start up *CorelDRAW!*, if it isn't already running. If your rulers aren't on the screen, select Show Rulers from the Display menu.

Vector and Raster Patterns

CorelDRAW! has a wide array of fill options, and we will cover all of them in some depth in this chapter. The vector and raster fills are the simplest, so they will be covered first.

TIP

A fill pattern in a draw program behaves differently from a fill pattern in a paint program. The pattern in a draw program always maintains its orientation regardless of the trasformation of the outline of the drawing, while the fill and outline of a painted object will both be affected by transformations.

Vector Fills

You've already learned about the differences between vector and raster graphics. It might surprise you to know that *CorelDRAW!* can provide either kind of fill—either a raster fill that is made up of points in a set pattern or a vector fill that uses a formula to determine the positioning of points.

The easiest way to see how vector fills work is to use one. Now create an ellipse and fill it with a vector pattern.

1. Click on the ellipse tool and drag the mouse on the page area. Make your ellipse narrower than it is tall.
2. Click on the fill tool. You will see the fill tool menu shown in Figure 7.1.

Lines and Fills ▲ 217

▼ *Figure 7.1. The fill tool menu*

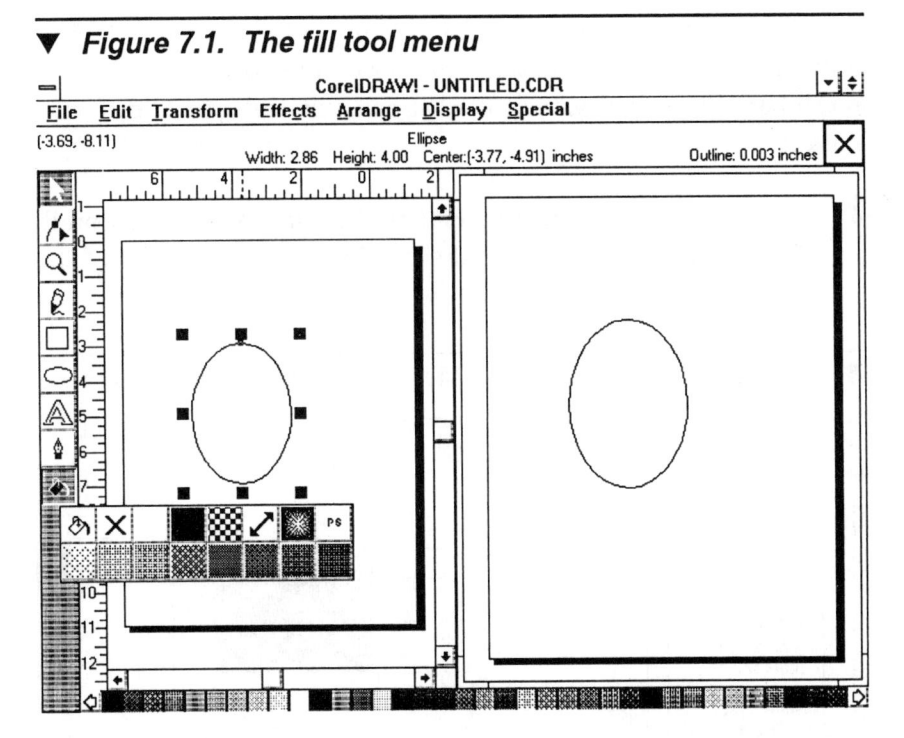

Vector and Raster Patterns

Along the bottom of the fill tool menu is an eight-gray-scale palette, a hold over from old versions of *CorelDRAW!* that didn't display the onscreen palette. Each of the items along the top of the fill tool menu refer to types of fills, some of which call up special dialog boxes so you can set values. Clicking on the first item, the bucket of paint, gives you access to a special color-mixing dialog box that gives you access to literally millions of colors for filling objects. The second item removes all fill from the selected object. Look at the right end of the Status line in Figure 7.1 (your screen probably looks the same). Note the rectangle there with the X through it, it indicates that the selected object has no fill.

The next two items are simply all-white fill and all-black fill (two more palette colors). The next item is the raster fill, which will be covered shortly.

3. Click on the fill tool menu item that has a two-headed arrow in it. This is the vector fill item. You will see the dialog box shown in Figure 7.2.

Note that you have a long list of items in the list box, which is only visible through the C's. If you click on the down-arrow on the scroll bar at the right side of the list box, you will see 37 different patterns.

4. Scroll to the item WEAVE2.PAT in the list box and click on it. The pattern will appear in the display box at the right of the Load Vector Pattern dialog box (Figure 7.2).

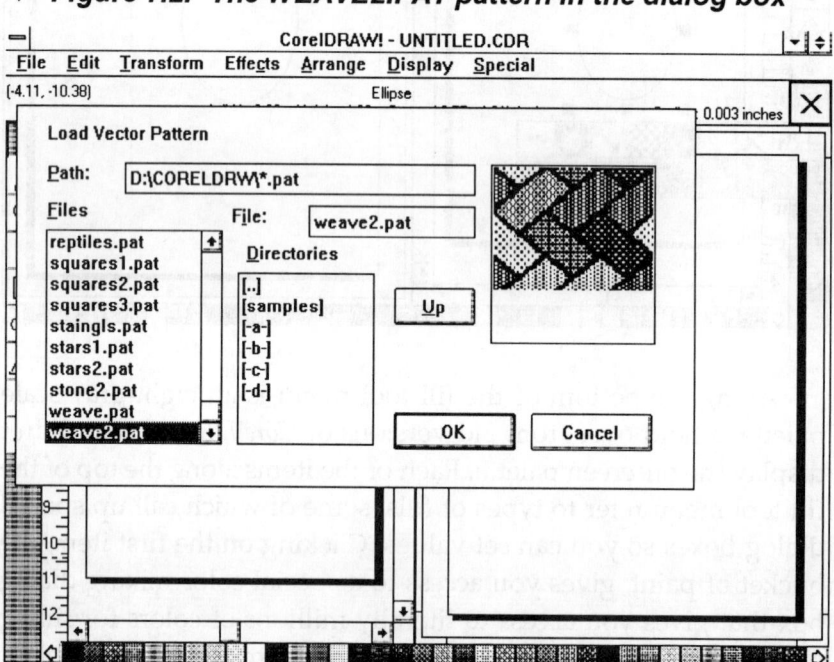

▼ *Figure 7.2. The WEAVE2.PAT pattern in the dialog box*

Notice how ornate this pattern is.

5. Click on the OK button. You will see the Vector Fill Pattern dialog box shown in Figure 7.3.

When the patterns appear in the object, it is in the form of tiles. Often these tiles are discrete from one another—that is, there will be a small space between the tiles. That doesn't matter much when the pattern is open and the tiles need not be connected, such as the COREL.PAT, which is simply the Corel Systems logo. A weave, by

Lines and Fills ▲ 219

▼ *Figure 7.3. The Vector Fill Pattern dialog box*

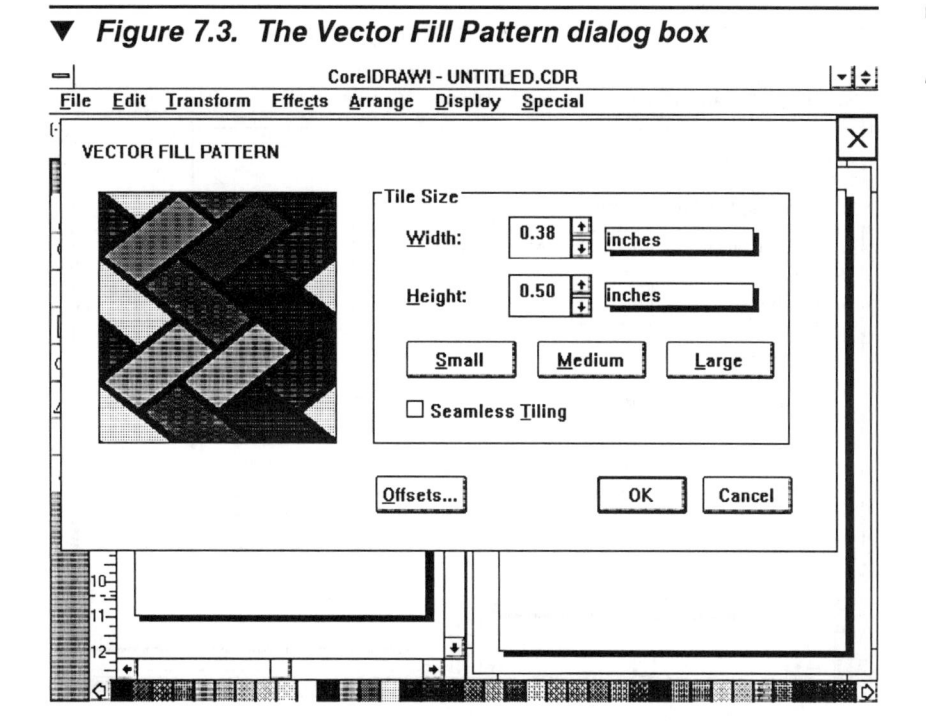

Vector and Raster Patterns

its very nature, needs to be connected, however, and so you should click on the Seamless Tiling check box.

You can make certain adjustments in the existing pattern. By using the text boxes in the Tile Size box at the right side of the Vector Fill Pattern dialog box, you can adjust the size of the pattern as it appears in the filled object. These adjustments are for fine adjustment. You can make the pattern tiles up to three inches square. In addition, because these are vector fills, you can size them without affecting their appearance.

If the exact size isn't of importance, which is most of the time, you can make gross adjustments by clicking on the Small, Medium, or Large buttons. If, when you look at your filled object, you discover that the fill patterns needs to be shifted slightly, use the Tile Offsets dialog box shown in Figure 7.4. It is accessed by clicking on the Offsets button in the Vector Fill Pattern dialog box.

You can go much farther than that for changing a pattern, though. The patterns you see in the Load Vector Pattern dialog box are actually *CorelDRAW!* drawings. The only difference is that they

▼ *Figure 7.4. The Tile Offsets dialog box*

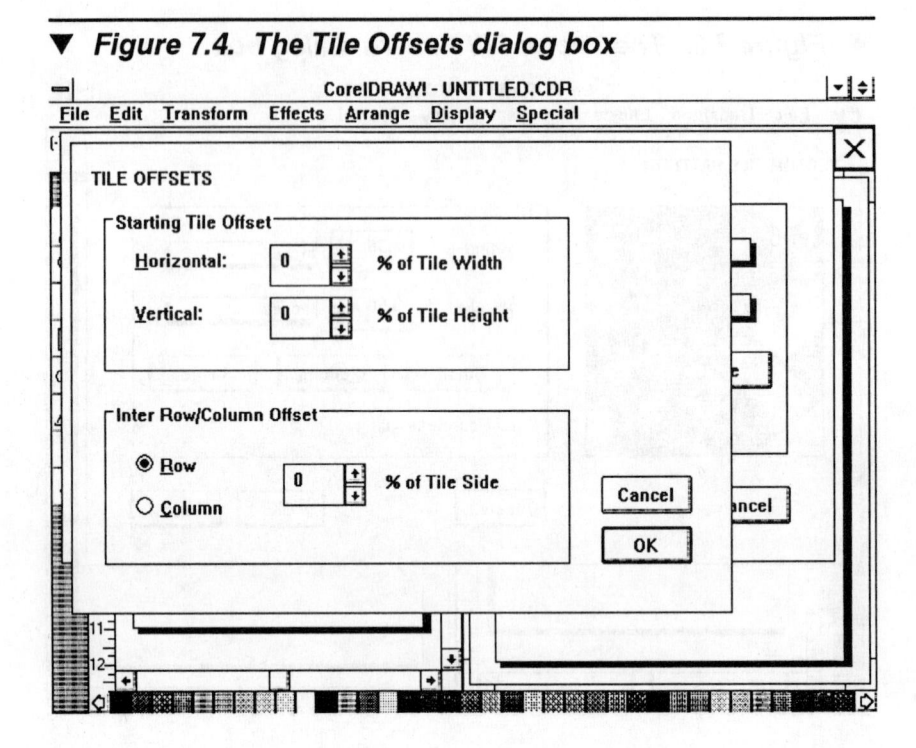

have been given the extension PAT. Now load a pattern and alter it. When you are through, you'll save the pattern as a new pattern.

Start by making sure Mosaic is turned off.

1. Pull down the Special menu and select Preferences.
2. Make sure the check box that says Use Mosaic isn't checked. If it is checked, click on it to turn it off or press the U key.

You could use Mosaic for this purpose, but turning it off will eliminate the necessity for two sets of instructions—one for people with Mosaic and one for people who have turned it off.

Now load a pattern into the page area.

1. Pull down the File menu. Select Open.
2. Make whatever adjustments are necessary to change directories to the directory containing your *CorelDRAW!* files.
3. In the Path text box, drag the mouse pointer through the CDR extension and type PAT, the extension used for patterns, and press Enter.

4. Turn on Display Preview in the Display menu. Double click on the file you want to edit. I have chosen WEAVE2.PAT, the last pattern in the dialog box. It is shown onscreen in Figure 7.5.

Vector and Raster Patterns

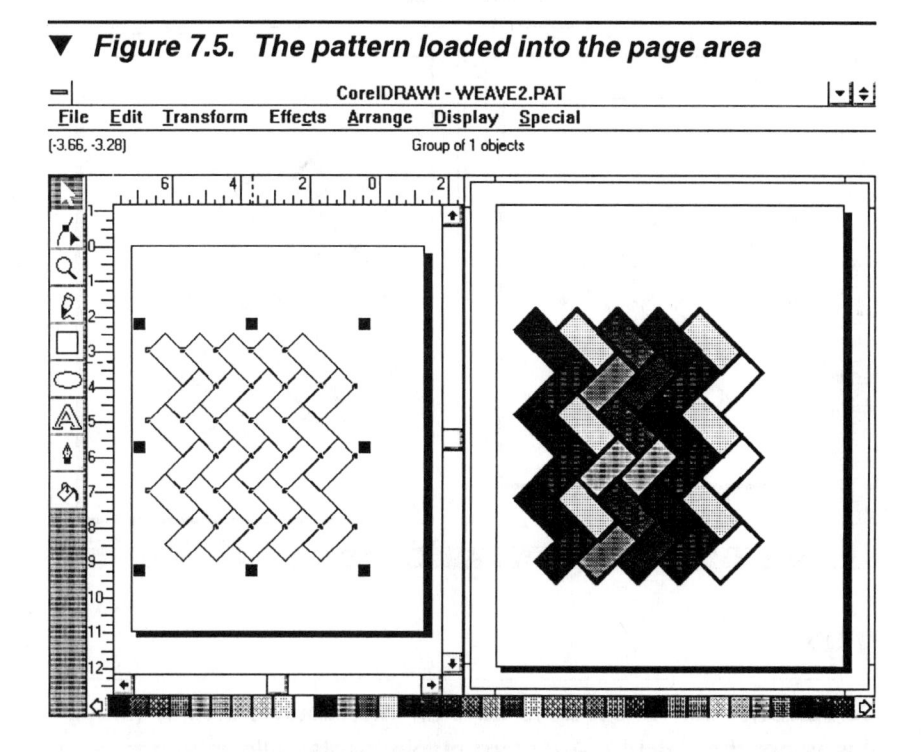

▼ *Figure 7.5. The pattern loaded into the page area*

This pattern is a grouped object, so in order to edit its elements, you will need to ungroup it.

5. If the pattern isn't selected, click on it.
6. Pull down the Arrange menu and select Ungroup.
7. Make any changes you want in the individual elements of the pattern. For my pattern, I will simply change the fill of all the elements to white. If you want to do the same, you don't even need to ungroup the pattern, simply select it and click on the white color in the palette at the bottom of the *CorelDRAW!* screen (Figure 7.6).

▼ **Figure 7.6. The pattern, all colored white**

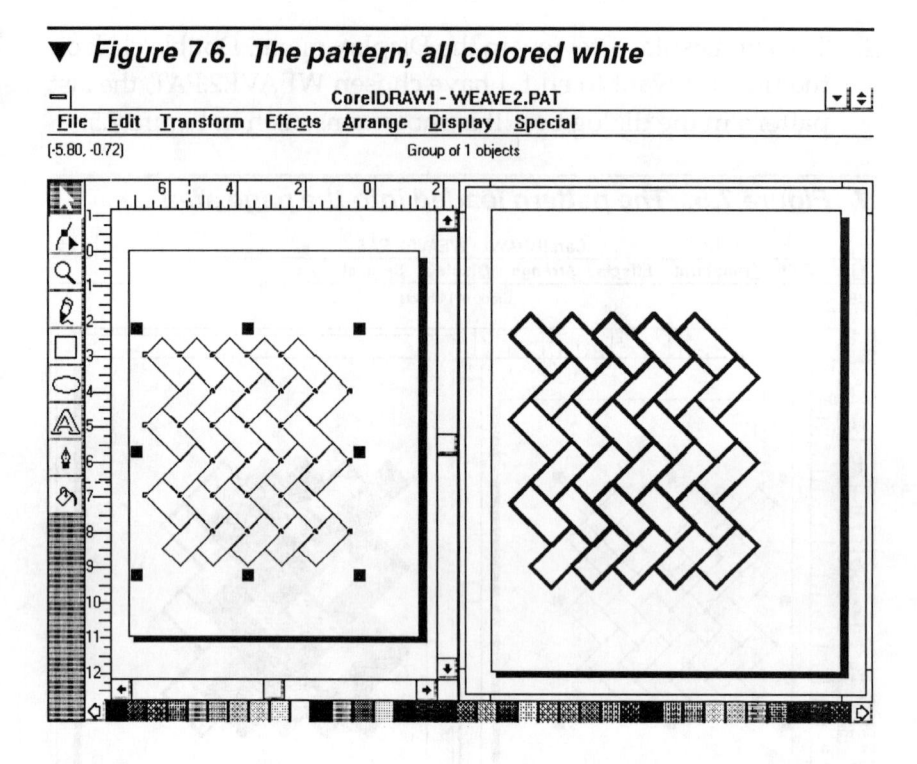

TIP

CorelDRAW! can be set up to have an interruptable display (though this is not the default). An interruptable display allows you to draw without waiting for the screen to be refreshed, which translates into saved time when your drawing is very complex. When your screen is being refreshed, you can click on a tool, or pull down a menu, or use the keyboard. The process of drawing objects on the screen will be paused until you finish your action. To make your display interruptable, pull down the Special menu and select Preferences (or press Ctrl-J). In the Preferences dialog box, about halfway down, are four check boxes titled Cross Hair Cursor, Show Page Border, Interruptable Display, and Use Mosaic. Click on the Interruptable Display, if the check box isn't already checked.

Next you need to save the pattern so it will be yours to use.

Vector and Raster Patterns

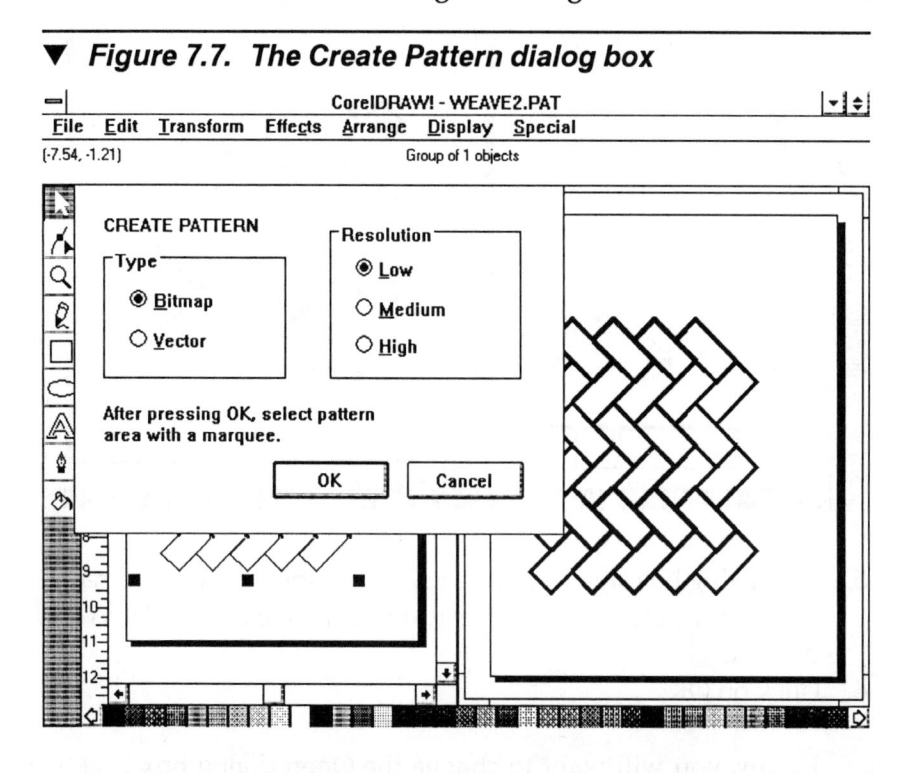

1. Click on the pick tool and drag a selection rectangle that includes the entire pattern. Pull down the Arrange menu and select Group.
2. Pull down the Special menu and select Create Pattern. You'll see the Create Pattern dialog box in Figure 7.7.

▼ *Figure 7.7. The Create Pattern dialog box*

You have the choice of saving the pattern as a bitmap or a vector pattern. If you were saving a bitmap pattern, you could specify whether you wanted to save it as a low-, medium-, or high-resolution bitmap.

3. Click on the radio button marked Vector and then click on OK. Your mouse pointer will turn into a crosshairs (Figure 7.8).
4. Drag a selection rectangle to include the part of the pattern you want to turn into a pattern used by *CorelDRAW!*. When you release the mouse button, you will see a small dialog box asking whether you want to create a pattern using the selected area. Click on OK if the selection rectangle contains the pattern you want to create.

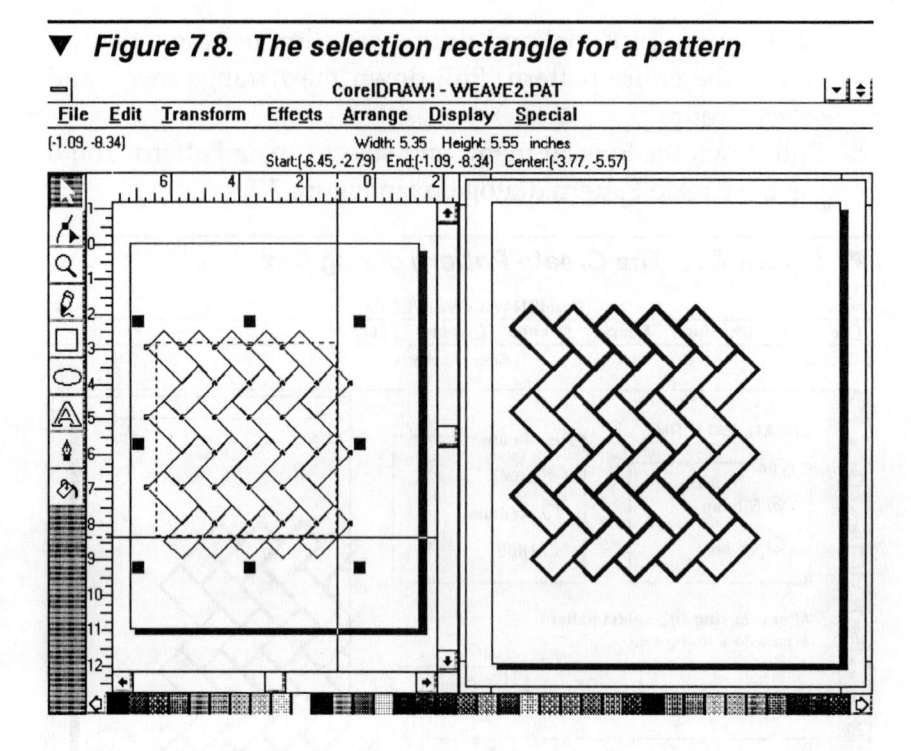

▼ **Figure 7.8. The selection rectangle for a pattern**

5. The dialog box shown in Figure 7.9 will appear. Type the name of the new pattern in the File: text box. I have typed MYPAT in the box.
6. Click on OK.

Finally, you will want to change the Open dialog box back to opening CDR files instead of patterns.

1. Pull down the File menu and select Open. You will be prompted with an alert dialog box telling you that WEAVE2.PAT has changed and asking whether you want to save it. Click on No. The Open Drawing dialog box will appear.
2. In the Path: text box, drag the mouse pointer through letters PAT. Type CDR in its place and press Enter. To make this change permanent, you will need to load a CDR drawing. Double click on the Samples subdirectory (which appears in the Directories: list box) and double click on any CDR drawing. This drawing will load into the page area and CDR will be made a permanent part of the Open Drawing dialog box.

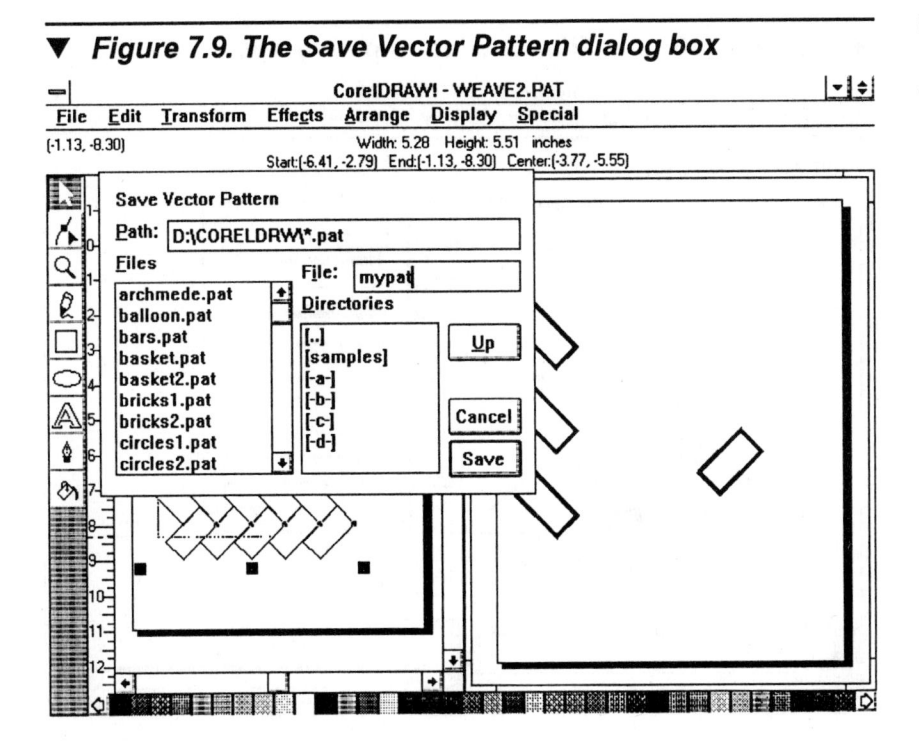

Vector and Raster Patterns

▼ *Figure 7.9. The Save Vector Pattern dialog box*

Raster Fills

Raster fills can be as ornate and complex as vector fills. They have the advantages of being easier to edit and faster to print, and the disadvantages of coarser grain and a greater tendency to be distorted when sized.

Fill an object with a raster fill.

1. If your page area isn't blank, select New from the File menu.
2. Draw an object to fill. I have drawn another oval, like the one that appeared in Figure 7.1.
3. Click on the fill tool. Click on the checkerboard option on the fill tool menu. This is the raster fill option. You will see the dialog box shown in Figure 7.10.

This dialog box is significantly different from the dialog box you saw earlier.

▼ **Figure 7.10. The Bitmap Pattern dialog box**

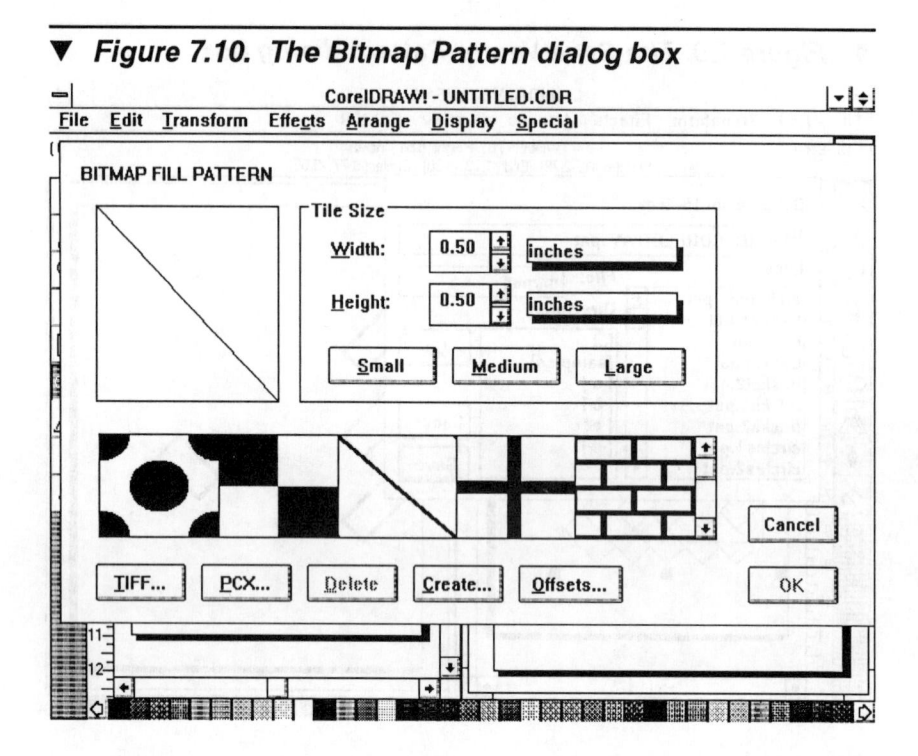

4. Select a pattern by clicking on it. If you don't like any of the patterns shown, click on the arrow at the bottom of the scroll bar at the right end of the displayed patterns to scroll downward through the available patterns.

There are 49 available and a number of unoccupied slots. These slots weren't left unoccupied because the *CorelDRAW!* programmers are lazy, but so that you can create and save your own patterns. Now create your own pattern. If you read the section on Vector patterns, you saw that it was possible to create a pattern by saving it. You can also load any PCX or TIF file as a pattern. But there is another way, and I think it's more fun.

1. Click on Create... at the bottom of the Bitmap Fill Pattern dialog box. You will see the dialog box shown in Figure 7.11. It fills nearly the entire screen.
2. Click with the left mouse button on any square you want black and click with the right mouse button on any square you want to change from black to white.

▼ **Figure 7.11. The Bitmap Pattern Editor**

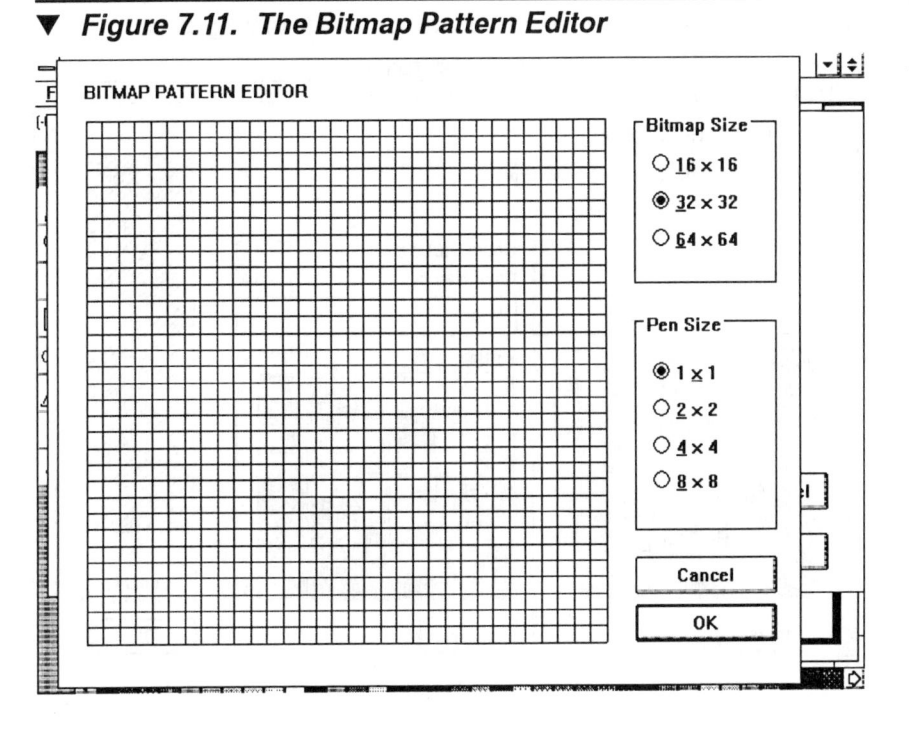

Vector and Raster Patterns

You can create a pattern as fine as 64 by 64 dots. The pen size setting can save you a lot of time by allowing you to fill an area quickly with a large (eight by eight) pen.

3. Click on OK when you are through.

Move forward and place the pattern in your object.

1. Whether you create a bitmap pattern, select one of the existing patterns, or load a TIF or PCX graphic as a pattern, the next step is to click on the pattern in the Bitmap Pattern dialog box. When you do so, you will go to the Bitmap Pattern Color dialog box shown in Figure 7.12.
2. Use this box to change the color of the foreground (the areas that appeared in black in the Bitmap Pattern dialog box) and the background (the areas that appeared in white in the Bitmap Pattern dialog box).

▼ **Figure 7.12.** *The Bitmap Pattern Color dialog box*

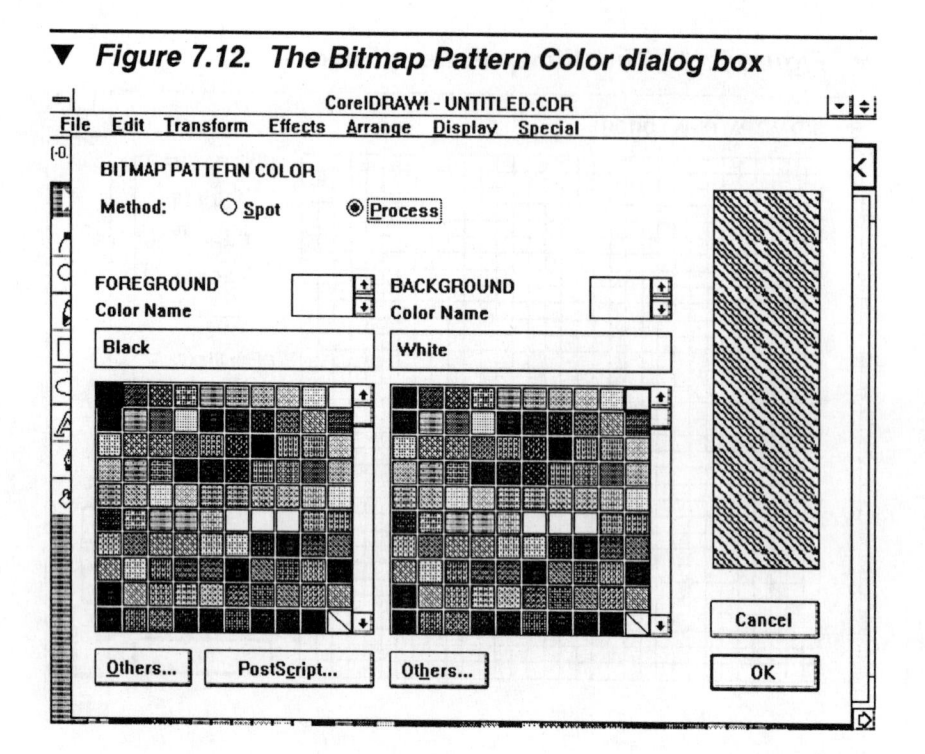

If you don't like any of the colors, click on the buttons marked Others.

3. We will get into the differences between spot and process colors later in the chapter, but for now, click on Spot, which changes the colors available and makes the PostScript dialog box usable. Click on the button marked PostScript. You will see the PostScript Controls dialog box. This dialog box will be covered in detail later in the chapter, but it's important enough to take a glance at now. Using this box, you can adjust the way shades of gray are shown in the printout. The default is to use a dithering pattern. You can change this to dots, lines, or one of several different schemes.

4. Click on OK to escape the PostScript Controls dialog box. Click on OK in the Bitmap Pattern Color dialog box. The object will be filled with the pattern. Note that the checkerboard appears at the right end of the status line, indicating that the selected object has a bitmap fill.

TIP

Early releases of *CorelDRAW!* exhibited a bug when printing bitmap fills to a PostScript printer. If your bitmap fill escapes from the object, printing elsewhere on the page (typically in rectangular sections), either arrange to get an updated version of the product or print your graphic on a PCL printer. Many PostScript printers are also able to emulate the HP LaserJet PCL printer.

CHECK YOURSELF

1. Fill an object with a continuous bitmap pattern and turn Seamless Tiling off.

ANSWER

1. When you are using a fill pattern that should be continuous, some patterns display slight discontinuities between tiles.

Fountain Fills

As you have seen, you can fill an area with a raster or a vector pattern. You can also fill an area with a solid color (this was covered in Chapter 2). But that's not all there is to say about fills. This section will cover fountain fills and the next will cover the use of PostScript textures.

A fountain is a gradation of color or gray over an area. Using fountains, you can approximate the shading of a rounded object.

Try to make a circle look like a sphere. To see this function in action, begin by drawing a circle on the screen.

1. Begin by clearing the screen. Select New from the File menu.
2. Click on the ellipse tool in the toolbox at the left of the *CorelDRAW!* screen.
3. Place your mouse pointer in the drawing area. Press the left mouse button and hold it down while dragging the mouse diagonally. A circle will appear on the screen and will follow

your pointer. (To create a true circle, rather than an ellipse, hold down the Ctrl key.) When the circle is large enough to suit you, release the mouse button and the circle will become solid. A single node will be visible at the top of the circle, indicating that the circle is currently selected. (This is visible in Figure 7.13).
4. Click on the fill icon in the toolbox (it's at the bottom of the toolbox; it looks like a can of paint at the point of spilling). You will see the menu shown in Figure 7.13.

▼ **Figure 7.13. The Fill Tool menu; the Fountain Fill item is second from right**

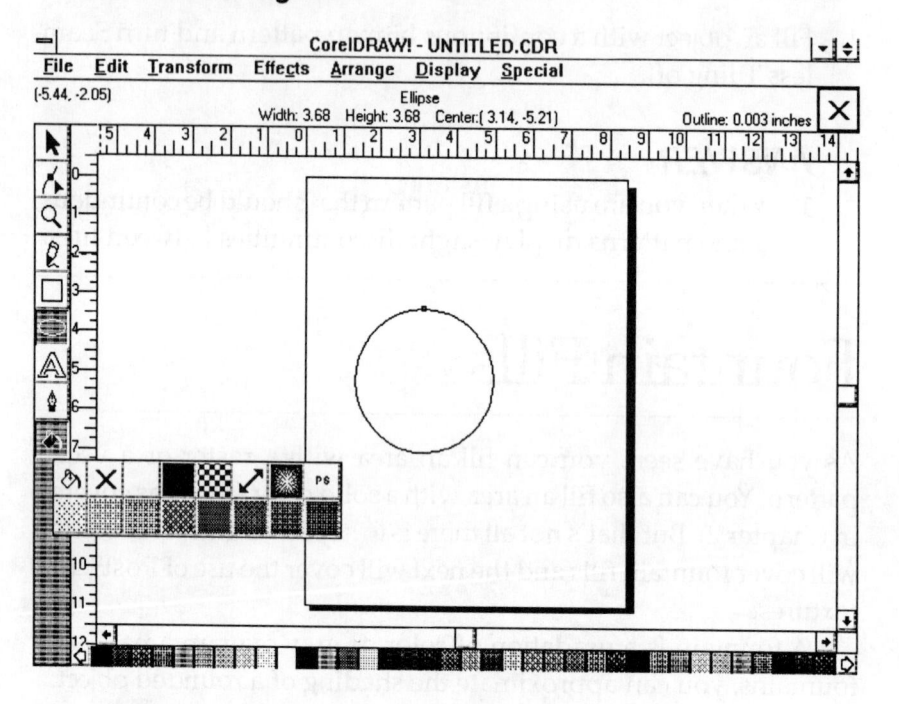

5. Click on the item next to the end of the menu. This is the fountain fill item. You will see the dialog box shown in Figure 7.14.

Here you have a broad range of options. The default option is to use a linear gradation between white and black at a 90-degree angle.

6. Click on OK to select the default gradient.

Lines and Fills ▲ 231

▼ *Figure 7.14. The Fountain Fill dialog box*

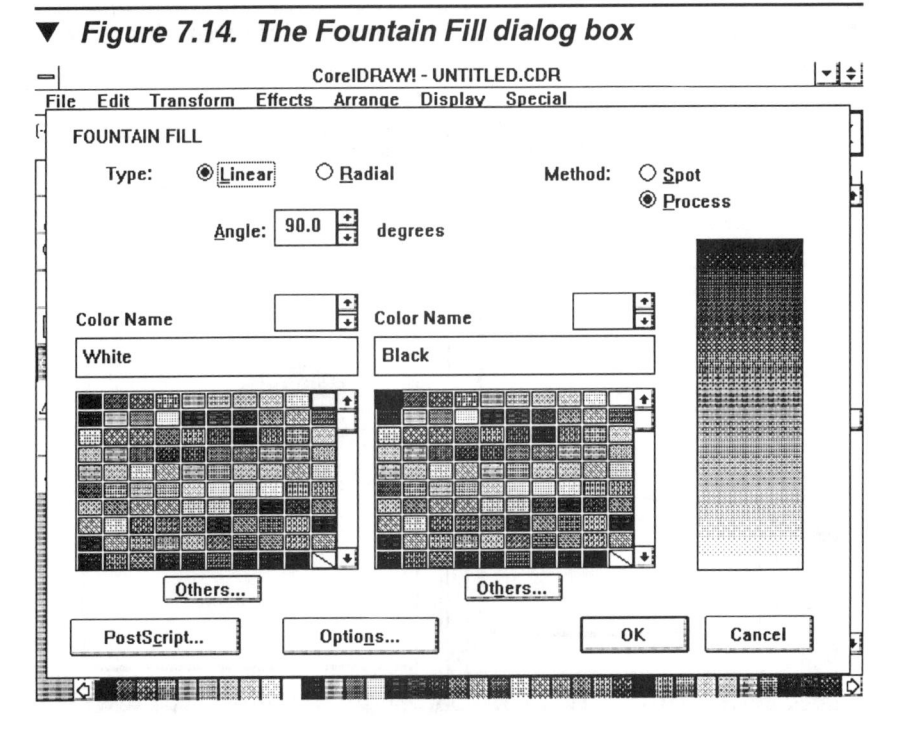

Fountain Fills

[Screenshot of the Fountain Fill dialog box in CorelDRAW!, showing Type options (Linear selected, Radial), Angle 90.0 degrees, Method options (Spot, Process selected), Color Name fields set to White and Black, color palettes, and buttons for PostScript..., Options..., OK, and Cancel.]

7. When you return to the main *CorelDRAW!* screen, pull down the Display menu and select Show Preview. You will see the screen shown in Figure 7.15.

This sort of gradient would be fine for many purposes, but it doesn't make the circle look like a sphere.

1. Return to the Fountain Fill dialog box (Figure 7.14) and select the Radial fill option (it's at the top of the dialog box, next to Linear). Click on OK and you will see the graphic in Figure 7.16.

Clearly it is closer to what we want. Two things need to be done. The black area needs to be swapped for the white area to provide the sphere-like highlight, and the highlight needs to be moved off center, to a top-right or top-left area, to look more realistic.

1. Return to the Fountain Fill dialog box. Make sure Spot color is selected in the Method area in the upper right corner of the Fountain Fill dialog box (if Process is selected, click on Spot).

▼ *Figure 7.15. The 90-degree linear fountain from black to white*

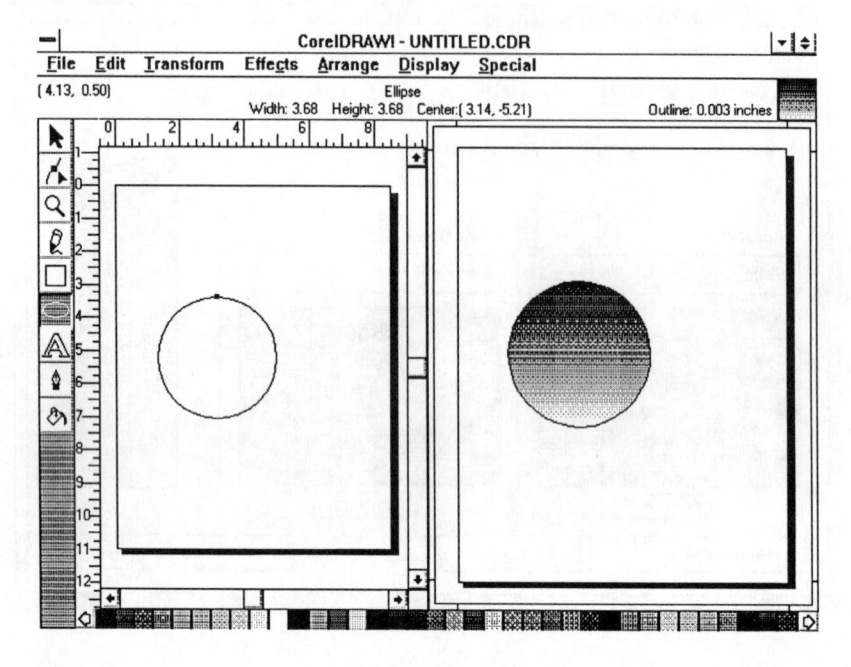

▼ *Figure 7.16. Closer to a sphere*

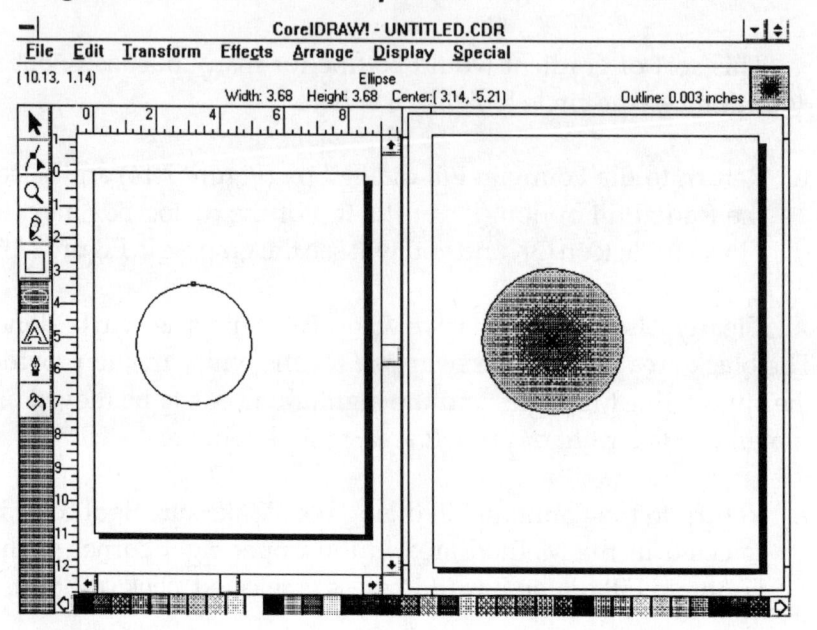

Fountain Fills

2. Make sure the left %tint box reads 100. If it doesn't, drag through it with the mouse pointer and type 100.
3. Make sure the right %tint box reads 0. If it doesn't, drag through it with the mouse pointer and type 0.
4. Click on OK.

The next step is to draw the highlighting away from the center of the circle.

1. Click on the pencil tool in the toolbox.
2. Place the mouse pointer well off to the upper left of the circle and draw a short line (shown in the upper left corner of Figure 7.17).
3. Either pull down the Edit menu and select Select All or use the pick tool (the top tool on the toolbox) to drag a rectangle that encompasses both the circle and the little line you just drew. Handles should appear as shown in the left half of Figure 7.17.
4. Pull down the Arrange menu and select Combine.
5. Click on the outline tool (it looks like a pen nib) on the toolbox and select the large X to eliminate the outlines and to prevent the added line from appearing in the preview or printout.

The fountain fill area shifts as a result of combining the new line with the circle. The fountain will always be centered within the selection rectangle of an object and by combining the line and the circle, you have slightly distorted the selection box, resulting in the spherical fill shown in Figure 7.17.

That's how you had to do it when you created this sort of fountain fill with *CorelDRAW!* prior to version 2. Now there's a better way.

1. Get rid of the extra line we drew. Click on the combined objects, pull down the Arrange menu and select Break Apart.
2. Click away from the objects to deselect both.
3. Click on the line and press Del. This will eliminate the line.
4. Click on the circle again to select it and click on the fill tool. Select the fountain fill option.
5. When the Fountain Fill dialog box appears, select Options. You will see the dialog box shown in Figure 7.18.

234 ▲ **CorelDRAW! 2**

▼ *Figure 7.17. The completed sphere*

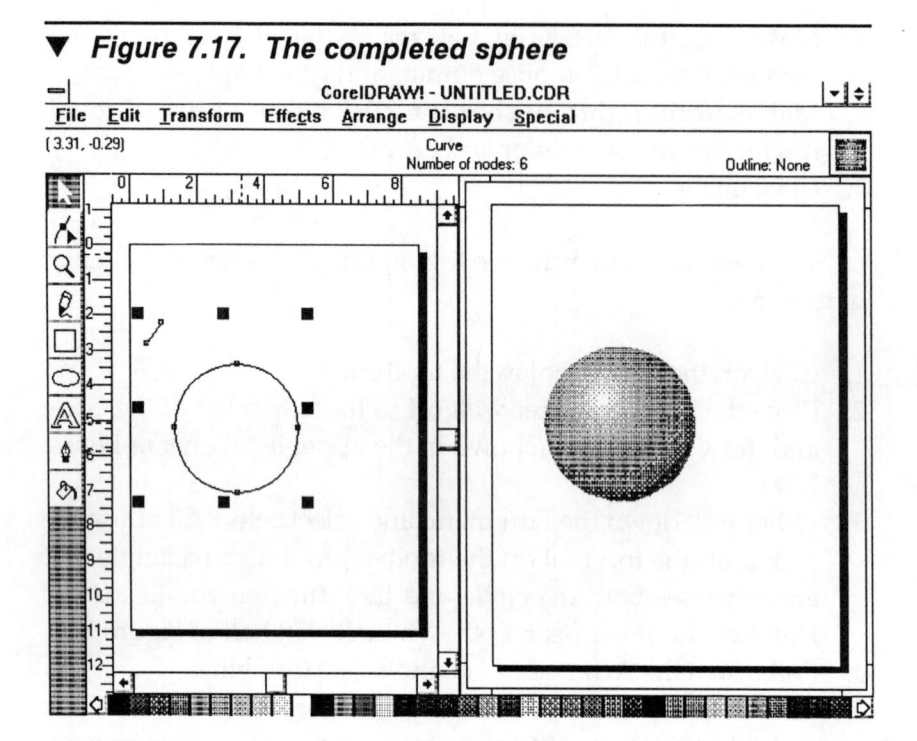

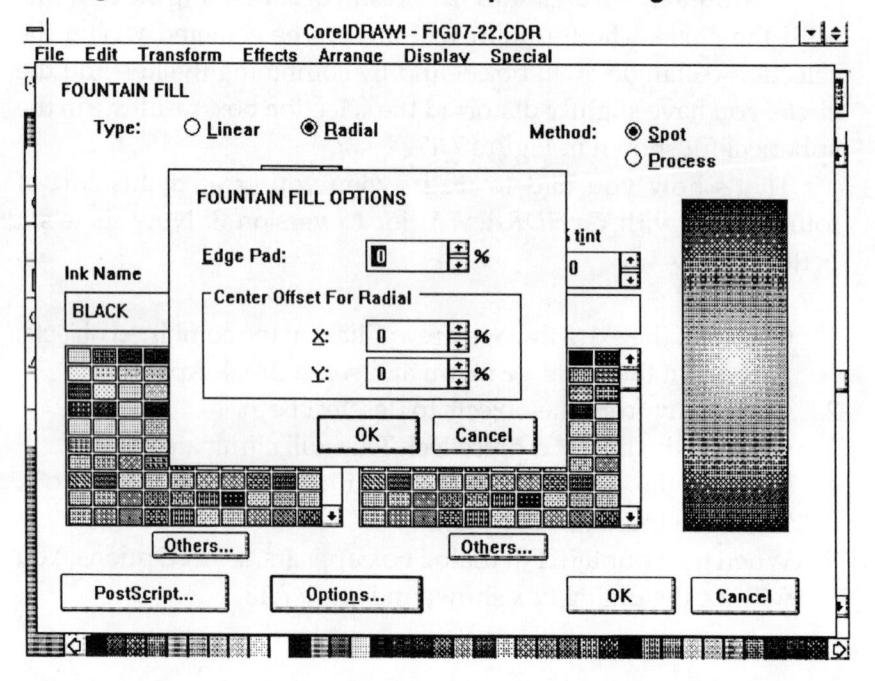

▼ *Figure 7.18. The Fountain Fill Options dialog box*

Fountain Fills

Now we'll spend some time on edge padding. Sometimes irregular objects have very large selection boxes, which causes much of the fountain fill to be distant from the actual object—that is to say, that it's invisible. By padding the edge, you can narrow the part of the selection rectangle that contains the actual fountain.

That's not a concern with a regular object like a circle, though. To approximate the coloration of the sphere shown in Figure 7.17, enter the values –25 for the x offset and 25 for the y offset. This moves the center of the fountain 25 percent of the width of the selection rectangle to the right and 25 percent of the height up from the center. The result is shown in Figure 7.19. Note how much cleaner this version is.

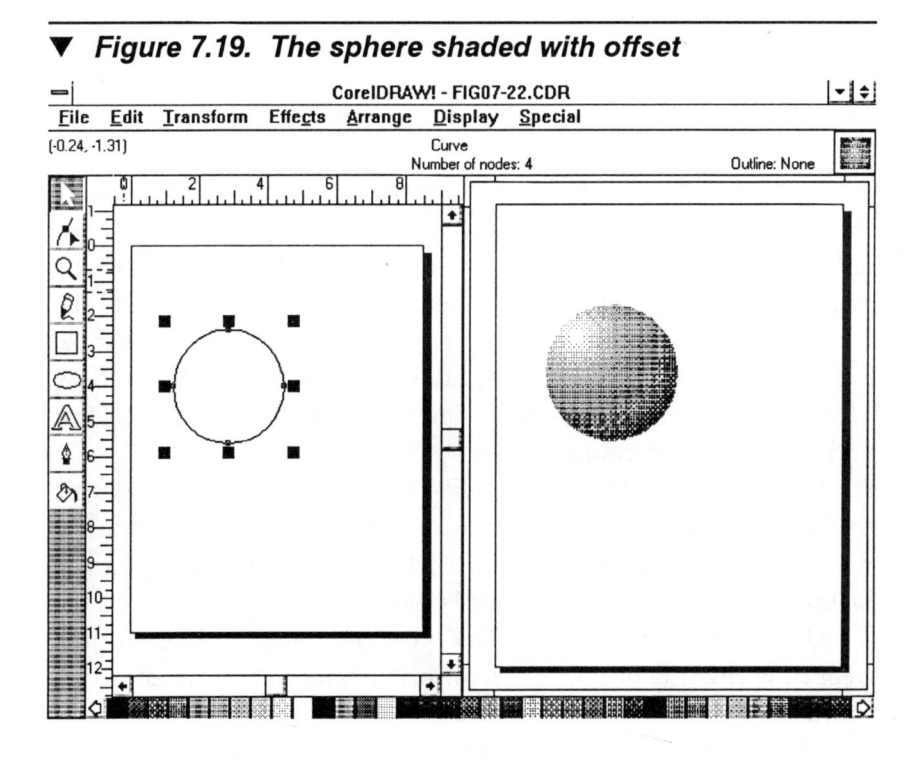

▼ **Figure 7.19. The sphere shaded with offset**

You probably noticed many settings within the Fountain Fill dialog box that weren't mentioned. Here is an explanation of these settings.

Beginning at the top of the dialog box, you can select linear and radial fountains, which you have already seen. The default setting for a linear fountain is 90 degrees, but you can drag through this value and enter any value between −360 and 360 degrees. The crosshairs at the right side of the top of the Fountain Fill dialog box tell you which way the linear fountain will flow. A 90-degree linear fill will proceed from the bottom to the top.

The prepositions "from" and "to" in the previous sentence are significant because they help you to visualize how the fountain will use the colors in the second half of the dialog.

Spot Color

You have seen how to use the %tint settings to change the intensity of the colors in the boxes from one extreme to the other, but you haven't seen how to use the Color setting. Click on a color other than black to change the color settings. You will see a value in the Ink Name box.

These numbers represent specific standard color mixes known as the *Pantone colors*. They can be used to specify colors when talking to a printer at a remote location. You will each have a book containing the standard colors. These books have been carefully inspected to ensure that when you are talking about color number 3935, you are both talking about the same exact shade of yellow. This will be discussed at greater length under the headline "How and Why to Use Pantone Colors."

You can specify the method used to display gradients if you are using spot color. The button is at the bottom of the Fountain Fill dialog box, marked PostScript... Click on this button and you will be taken to the PostScript Controls dialog box (Figure 7.20).

Using the settings in this box, you can take complete control over how fine the dots or lines (or other screen) that make up the fountain. Take a look at Figure 7.21.

Clockwise from the upper left circle, the circles are shaded with the Default, Dot, Line, and Diamond screens. (In addition to these screens, you can select patterns known as Dot2, Grid, Lines, Microwaves, Outcircleblk, Outcirclewhi, and Stars.) The difference wouldn't ordinarily be evident on a printout from a 300 dpi laser printer, particularly when the graphic has been reproduced at least once in order to be placed in this book, and in the process was

▼ *Figure 7.20. The PostScript Controls dialog box*

Fountain Fills

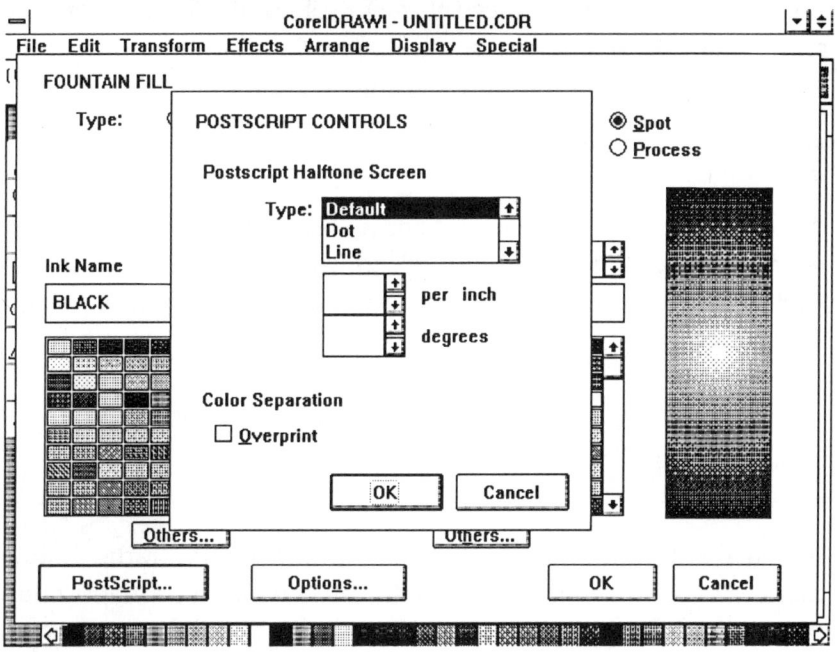

▼ *Figure 7.21. Four fountain-filled circles*

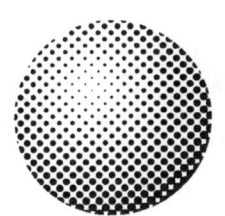

probably reduced in size, thus losing even more resolution. I cheated a little and produced these graphics at a 10 line-per-inch resolution, the minimum possible. The default setting can't be adjusted to change the lines per inch.

TIP

If you intend to use color separations (if this term is unfamiliar to you, review Chapter 3) and you are working with spot colors, you should limit your fountains. They should only be between two tints of a single Pantone color.

Process Color

If you want to mix your own colors, click on the radio button marked Process and then click on the button marked Other underneath the existing palette colors. You will see the dialog box shown in Figure 7.22.

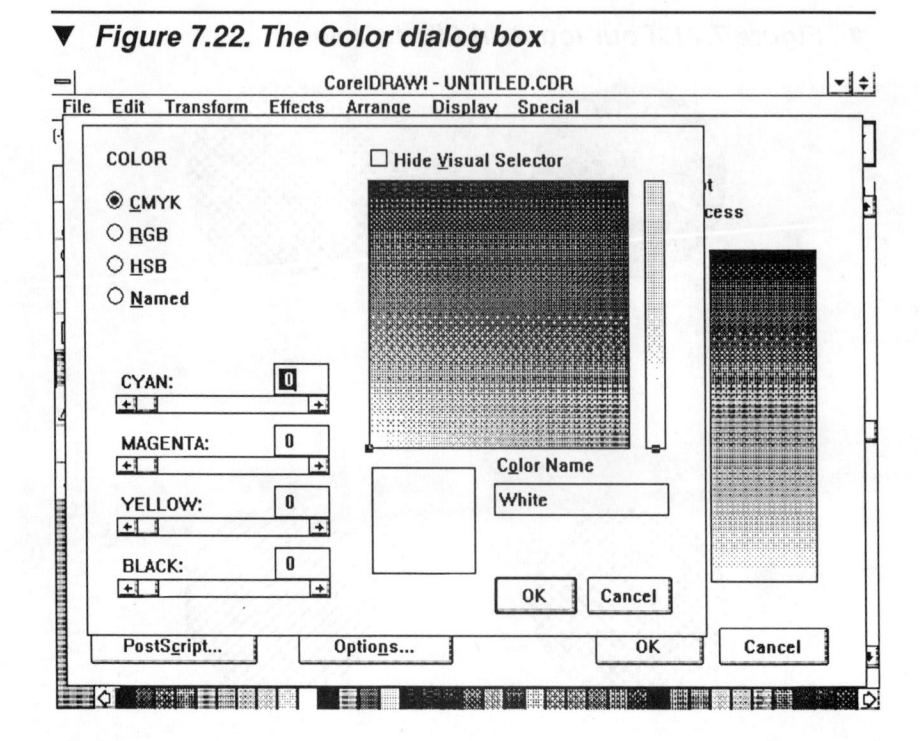

▼ *Figure 7.22. The Color dialog box*

Fountain Fills

This dialog box has several ways for you to mix colors. You'll cover color mixing shortly, and at that time you'll learn the differences between CMYK, RGB, HSB, and Named.

Note that you can enter values in the text boxes at the right of the slide bars or use the slide bars themselves to adjust the colors. But there is a more interesting way. Place the mouse pointer in the large colored box at the upper right of the Color dialog box and press the mouse button. Note that you can select any color in this area and each time you release the mouse button the settings will automatically be set in the text boxes and slide bars at the left of the dialog box. When the color you want appears in the box at center bottom, you can click on OK and the color will be set in the fountain fill dialog box.

Here is something else that's interesting: place the mouse pointer on the tall, narrow box at the extreme right of the dialog box, press the mouse button and drag the mouse pointer to a new location. When you release the button, the colors in the large box will be changed. This tall, narrow box adjusts the amount of yellow in the mix while the larger box determines the amount of cyan, magenta, and black in the mix.

Take a moment to click on RGB. The dialog box doesn't change much. The Cyan, Magenta, Yellow, and Black slide bars are replaced by Red, Green, and Blue slide bars. Its action is very similar to the CMYK box.

Click on the HSB option. You will see a color wheel on the screen. With this box you adjust the Hue, Saturation, and Brightness to specify a color—a slightly more abstract and less useful way to set colors.

Finally, click on the Named button. You will be provided with a list box containing the names of dozens of colors available to you. As you click on the names, the color appears in a box at center bottom.

When you mix a color that you like, you can name it by typing a name in the Color Name text box.

PRACTICE WHAT YOU'VE LEARNED

What You Should Do	How the Computer Responds
1. Create an object and fill it with a linear fountain. Click on the pick tool and click on the object again to make the arrow handles visible. Rotate the object.	1. The fill is rotated, too.
2. Create a long, narrow object and give it a fountain fill.	2. The fountain fill will be attenuated by the object's odd shape. Use padding.

PostScript Patterns

The authors of *CorelDRAW!* provided an added option to users with PostScript printers. *CorelDRAW!* features a series of fills that can only be used in PostScript output (whether from a laser printer or a typesetter). These fill patterns include many eye-catching and beautiful options ranging from the simple geometrical patterns like Triangle, StarOfDavid, and StarShapes to the sinuous Spirals, Spokes, and DNA to the enigmatic Grass, Leaves, and Honeycomb.

In all, there are 49 different designs available, each of which can be adjusted almost infinitely. The complete set of designs can be seen in Appendix B. Four favorites can be seen in their default state in Figure 7.23.

1. Create or select an object you want to fill. Its handles will appear at the four corners and sides.
2. Click on the fill tool. The fill tool menu will appear.
3. Click on the last item on the right end: the letters PS (PostScript). You will see the dialog box shown in Figure 7.24.

PostScript Patterns

▼ *Figure 7.23. Four favorite PostScript fill patterns with default settings: Grass, Honeycomb, Impact, and Reptiles*

Grass

Honeycomb

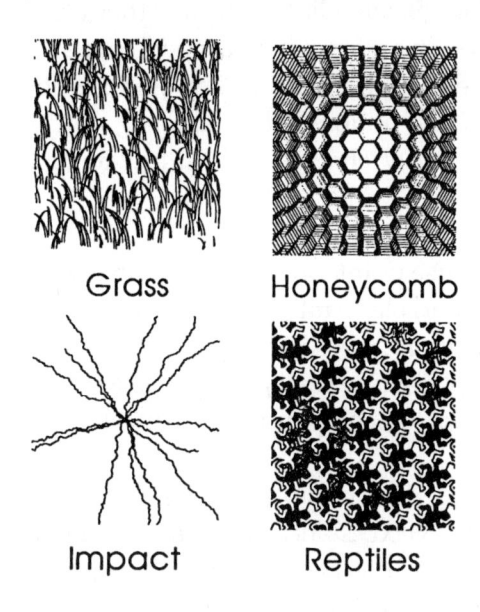

Impact

Reptiles

▼ *Figure 7.24. The PostScript Texture dialog box with Reptiles selected*

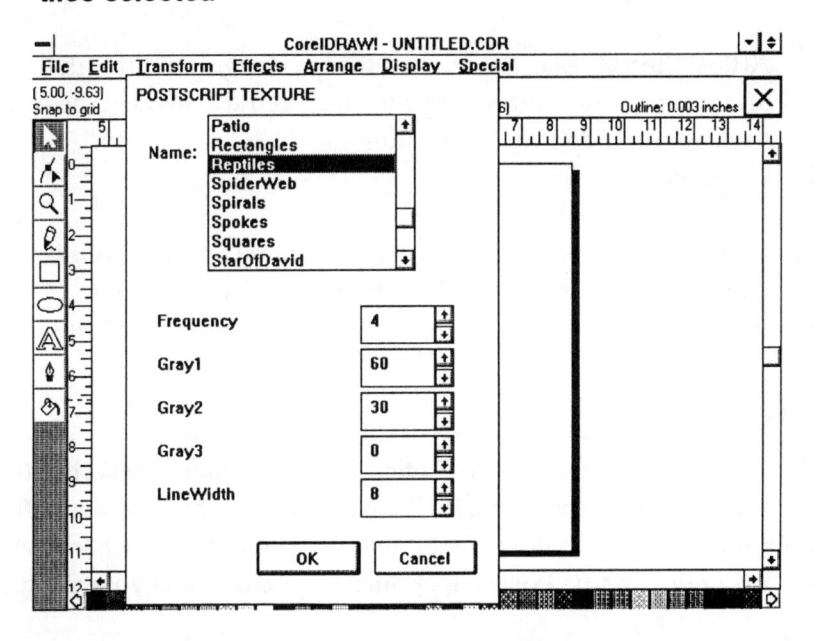

Reptiles was selected for the purposes of this figure. If you wanted to change the pattern, you could scroll through the options in the Name: list box and click on some other texture.

Note that you can alter certain aspects of the drawing. You will see many different options as you click on different patterns. In the case of Reptiles, the options are Frequency, Gray1, Gray2, Gray3, and LineWidth. Now change the pattern to TreeRings, another option.

4. Place the mouse pointer on the lower arrow of the scroll bar of the text box and click until TreeRings is visible.
5. Click on the word TreeRings. You will see the specifications in the PostScript Texture dialog change to MaxDistance, MinDistance, LineWidth, BackgroundGray, and RandomSeed.

These options determine the distribution of rings in the fill (MinDistance and MaxDistance), the width of the lines (LineWidth), the level of gray in the background (BackgroundGray, where 0 represents white and 100 represents black) and RandomSeed. RandomSeed affects the series of random numbers generated to create the fill. If you use the same random seed, you will always generate the same series of random numbers. That sounds self-contradictory, but it's true.

6. Adjust the values in the boxes either by dragging through them and typing new values or by clicking on the arrows at the right to increase or decrease the value.
7. Click on OK.

When you click on OK, the new fill will be applied. You won't be able to see it either on the normal *CorelDRAW!* screen or the Preview screen. It will only appear on the PostScript printout.

TIP

Of all the features *CorelDRAW!* offers, fountains and PostScript fills are the most problematic to a PostScript device. Some PostScript fills print with no trouble on any PostScript-compatible printer, while others will only print on true PostScript printers. Be aware that your printout

will take a very long time under most circumstances, and read Chapter 3 for suggestions on making your drawings more palatable to your printer.

PostScript Patterns

By adjusting the settings in the text boxes in the PostScript Texture dialog box, you can radically alter the appearance of the resulting fill pattern. The TreeRing pattern is used in both text sets in the lower part of Figure 7.25, but different values were specified in the dialog box.

▼ *Figure 7.25. Two versions of TreeRings and the changed panel*

Pen Points

Like Rapidograph, *CorelDRAW!* provides a number of pen widths for your use. Unlike Rapidograph, Corel Systems doesn't charge extra for the points. They come free with the basic package.

A range of pen points is important because you will use them for a range of applications. If all you want to do is pick a thicker point, selecting pen points is as simple as selecting a fill.

1. Click on the outline tool (the pen nib) in the toolbox. The pen point menu opens (Figure 7.26).

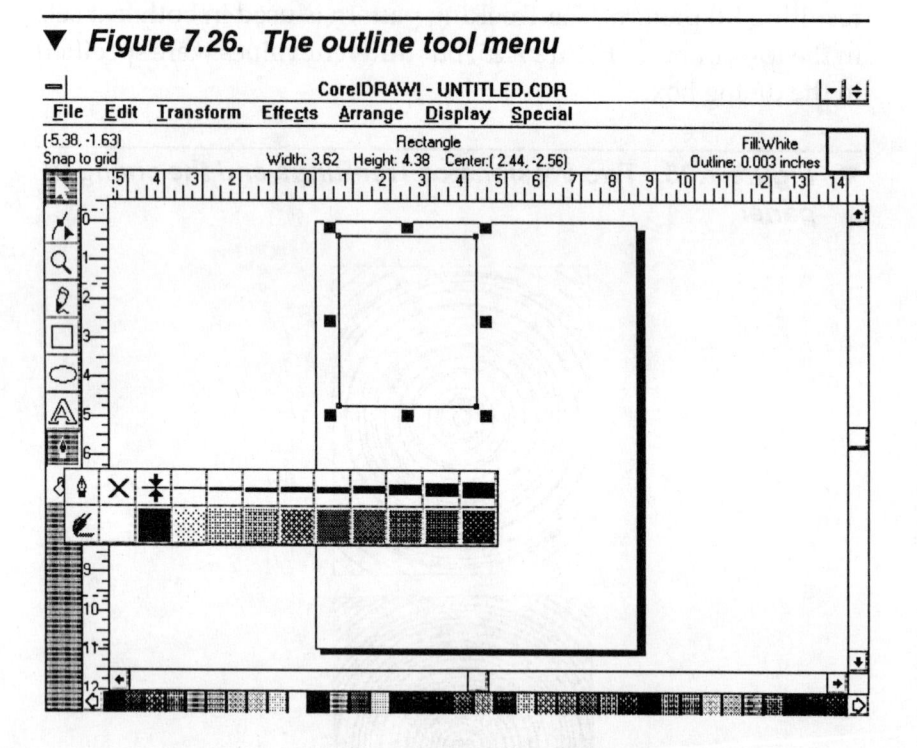

▼ *Figure 7.26. The outline tool menu*

The top part of the menu is pen thicknesses and the options are outline pen (which calls up a dialog box covered in a moment), none (X), hairline (the default), and nine additional thicknesses, each slightly thicker than the last. In the lower half of the menu, you are given the brush options, which are simply shades of gray for the pen. The options from left to right are outline brush (which calls up a color mixing dialog box like the one in Figure 7.22); and the colors white, black, and then nine shades of gray from light to dark, each slightly darker than its neighbor to the left.

What could be simpler?

But that isn't all there is to a pen point, and shades of gray aren't the only colors available.

Pen Points

In order to take the next step, you will need to have something drawn on the screen.

1. Select the pencil tool and draw a squiggle, or write a name (the name we will work with is Leon, but you might prefer to work with your own name).
2. Click on the pen nib in the toolbox. The pen point menu will open. Click on the pen nib in the menu. You will see the dialog box shown in Figure 7.27.

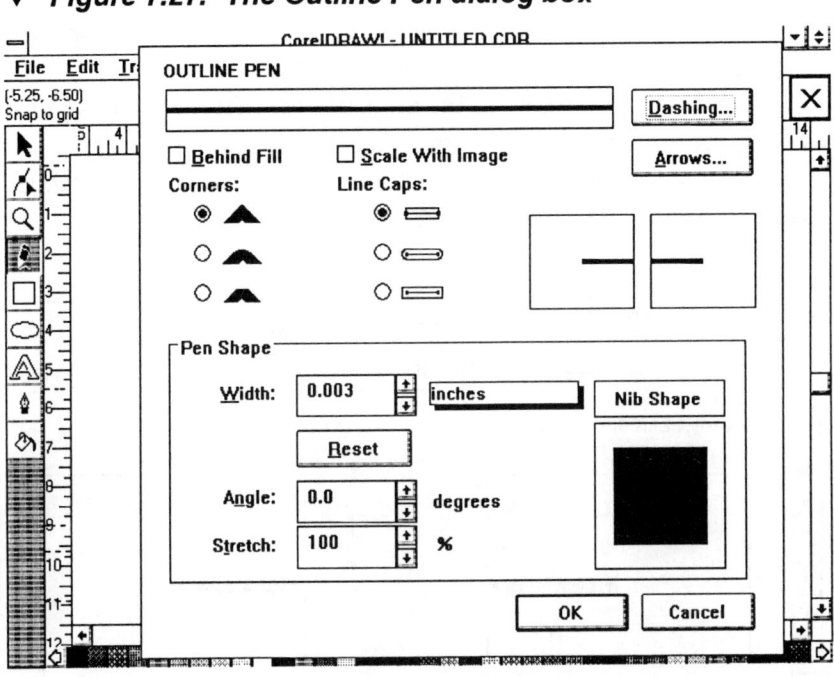

▼ *Figure 7.27. The Outline Pen dialog box*

The contents of this dialog box are all related to the shape of the pen. Starting from the top:

Type. The pen type represents the kind of line drawn by the pen. You can opt to have no line (None), a solid line, a dashed line, or a dotted line. (Click on the button marked Dashing to select a different type of line.)

Behind Fill. You can opt to have the line Behind Fill, which means that the pattern that makes up the inside of a closed object will cover half of the pen line. If you are drawing a thick line, which occasionally loops very close to itself, this might be your best choice to prevent parts of the shape from looking as if they were pinched off.

Scale With Image. Not so much when you are drawing but frequently when you are composing (putting drawings together into a page), you may find yourself continually changing the size of images. If you don't select Scale With Image, the lines will remain at the thickness you have set for them, possibly resulting in grossly thick lines on tiny images or very thin lines on larger images. This setting allows you to retain a proportional relationship between the thickness of the line and the size of the object.

Corners. You have three well illustrated options for cusps and corners on your drawings: pointed, rounded, and beveled.

Line Caps. This refers to the ends of lines. The caps are square-at-end, round, and square-beyond-end.

Arrows. When you click on the Arrows button, you'll see the dialog box shown in Figure 7.28.

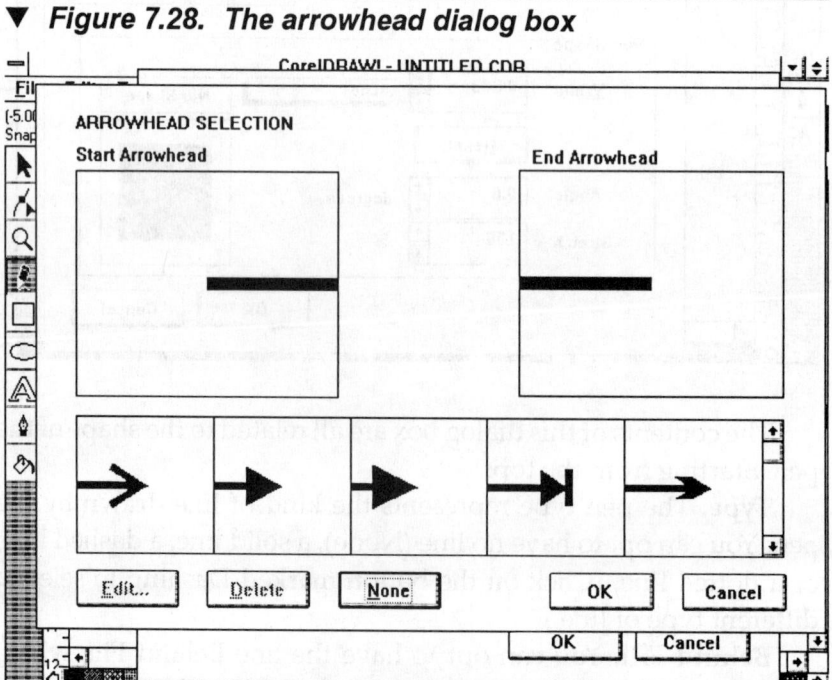

▼ *Figure 7.28. The arrowhead dialog box*

Pen Points

The selection of arrowheads is quite extensive. To place an arrowhead at the start of the line, click the left mouse button on an arrowhead in the selection box. To place an arrowhead on the terminal end of the line, click the right mouse button on an arrowhead. Of course, not all the selections are actually arrowheads. Some are circles, squares, and the feather-end of the arrow. To see the complete selection, use the scroll bar at the right end of the selection box.

Pen Shape. Most of this section of the box is related to calligraphy, which will be covered in Chapter 10. Briefly, you can custom set the width of the pen or adjust the shape of the pen. Angle refers to degrees from the vertical and Stretch refers to the proportion between height and width. Try adjusting these. A stretch of 150 is very wide and a stretch of 50 is narrow. By adjusting the stretch to some value remote from 100 percent and clicking on the up-and-down arrow next to the Angle text box, you can see the pen nib rotate in the Nib Shape box at right. To return to the default pen shape and angle, click on the button marked Reset.

One of the interesting things you can do with pens is superimpose one line on another, which you can do now.

1. Adjust the pen width to .5 inches either by clicking on the upward pointing arrow next to Width in the Pen Shape area of the Outline Pen dialog box until the value in the box is 0.50 or by dragging the mouse pointer through the default value in the box (0.00) and typing .5 as your new thickness.
2. Click on OK and you will return to the *CorelDRAW!* screen.
3. At this point, you will want to see the preview because pen thicknesses are not shown on the normal drawing screen. Therefore, select Show Preview in the Display menu. The current line is shown in Figure 7.29.
6. Duplicate the line. With the line selected, pull down the Edit menu and select Duplicate. A second image of the line will appear on the screen.
7. To superimpose one line over the other, click on the pick tool (the top tool in the toolbox) and drag a selection rectangle that includes both lines. Then pull down the Arrange menu and select Align. Select center vertically and center horizontally and click on OK.

▼ **Figure 7.29. The .5-inch line**

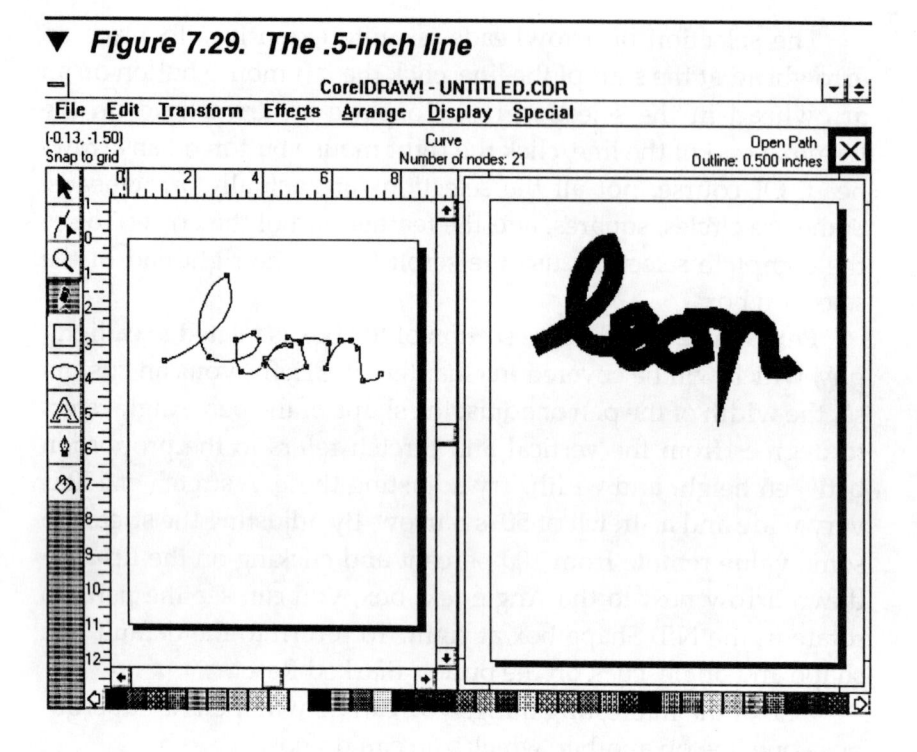

8. Click away from the lines to deselect them, then click on the line again, which should select the line that is on top.

> **TIP**
>
> **Once you have selected the top object in a pile of objects, you can select objects lower down by pressing the Tab key.**

9. Click on the outline tool in the toolbox and click on the white box in the lower half of the menu to change the current line to white. If the lines aren't perfectly aligned (which isn't crucial for this project), you may see an interesting three-dimensional representation of your line.
10. Once again click on the outline tool in the toolbox. This time click on the pen nib in the menu that appears. In the resulting Outline Pen dialog box (shown in Figure 7.27), adjust the pen width to about .1 inch either by clicking on the downward-pointing arrow next to the Width text box until the value 0.10

appears in the box or by dragging the mouse pointer through the box and typing .1 as the pen width. If you are in a mood to experiment, adjust the stretch and angle of the pen. Click on OK. You will see the preview shown in Figure 7.30.

Pen Points

▼ *Figure 7.30. The resulting graphic*

There's a lot more you can do with open paths like this, but that will be saved for more advanced chapters.

CHECK YOURSELF

1. Fill an object with a PostScript pattern. Print it on a PCL printer.
2. Draw a line on the screen and click on the outline tool in the toolbox. Click on the penpoint and in the dialog box that appears, click on Arrows. Place an arrowhead on both ends of the line.

ANSWERS

1. The object will have no fill at all. These patterns will only print on PostScript printers.

2. Select the arrowhead for the origin of the line with the left mouse button and the arrowhead for the end of the line with the right mouse button.

Putting Fills to Work

Now create a bowl of fruit. You'll use a variety of fills and line styles and create a pear and an orange. Make sure Show Preview has been selected so you can see your progress.

1. Clear the screen by selecting New. Create a circle by selecting the ellipse tool on the tool box and holding down the Ctrl key while dragging.
2. Give the circle a .25-inch thick line and select Behind Fill and Scale With Image.
3. Fill the circle with a radial fill. Select Spot color. Click on the same orange color for both the right and left selections. Make the left selection 100 percent and the right selection 50 percent tint.
4. Finally, click on Options and adjust the x offset to -20 and the y offset to 20. The result can be seen in Figure 7.31. This is an orange.
5. Create another ellipse. This time it doesn't matter whether it is perfectly circular.
6. Change it into a free-form object by pulling down the Arrange menu and selecting Convert to Curves. At this point, your ellipse should have four nodes.
7. Use the node editing skills you gained in Chapter 2 to alter the ellipse into a pear shape (which will be covered in the next few steps).
8. Click on the shape tool (second from the top in the toolbox). Click on the node at the left side of the ellipse. You will see the control points.

▼ Figure 7.31. *The orange for our still life*

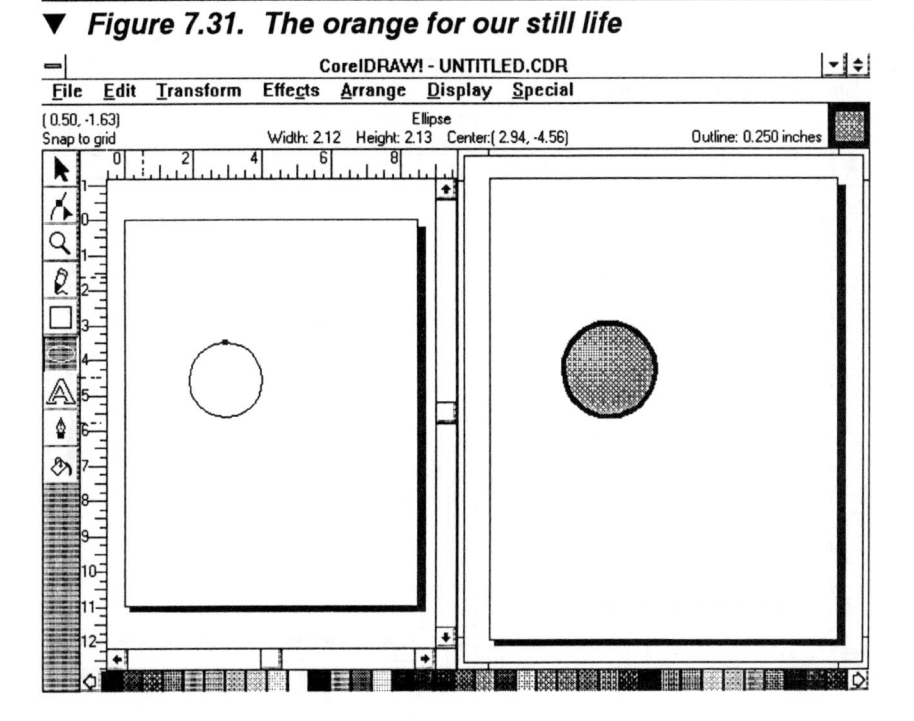

Putting Fills to Work

9. Drag the top control point of the left node slightly to the right.
10. Perform a similar action on the node at the right of the ellipse, dragging the top control point slightly to the left. The pear-like shape can be seen in Figure 7.32.
11. Use the pen point tools to give this drawing a .33 inch thick line. Once again, select Scale With Image and Behind Fill. Call up the fountain fill dialog box and select Spot color and Radial and select the same greenish tint for both palettes. Enter 100 percent for the left %tint box and 0 percent for the right %tint box. Because of the odd shape of the pear, similar to a shape often seen among career Navy men, there is no need to take special pains to move the highlight off center. The pear can be seen in Figure 7.33.
12. Finally, you will create a bowl to contain this fruit. Draw another ellipse. Draw it very wide.
13. Duplicate the ellipse and position the copy on top of the original.

252 ▲ *CorelDRAW! 2*

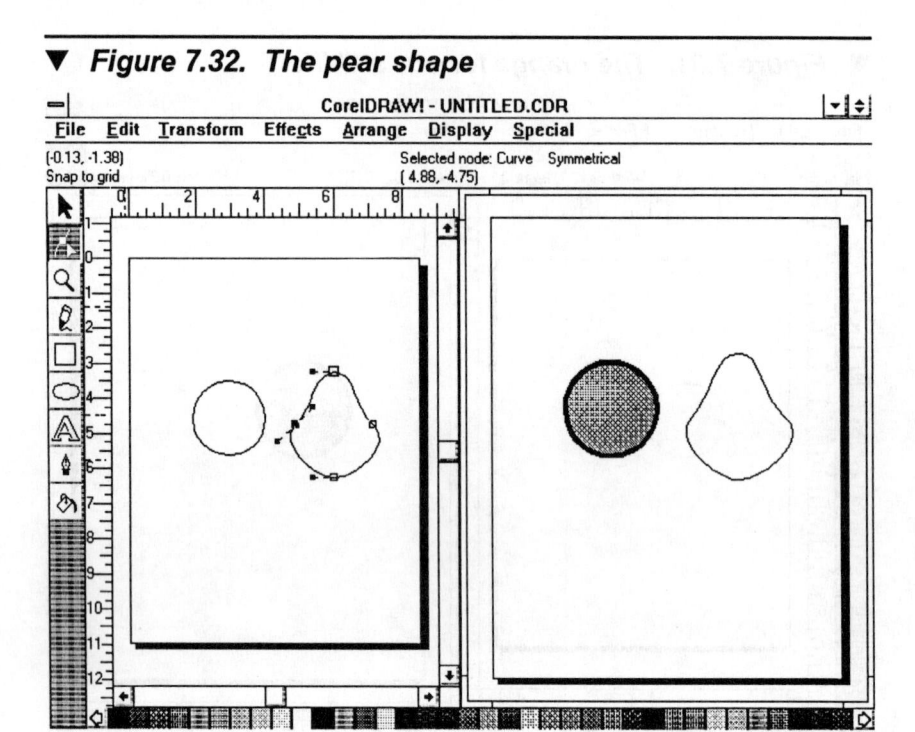

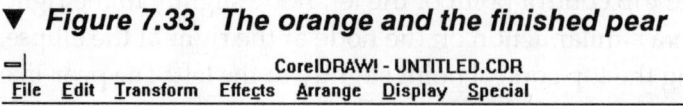

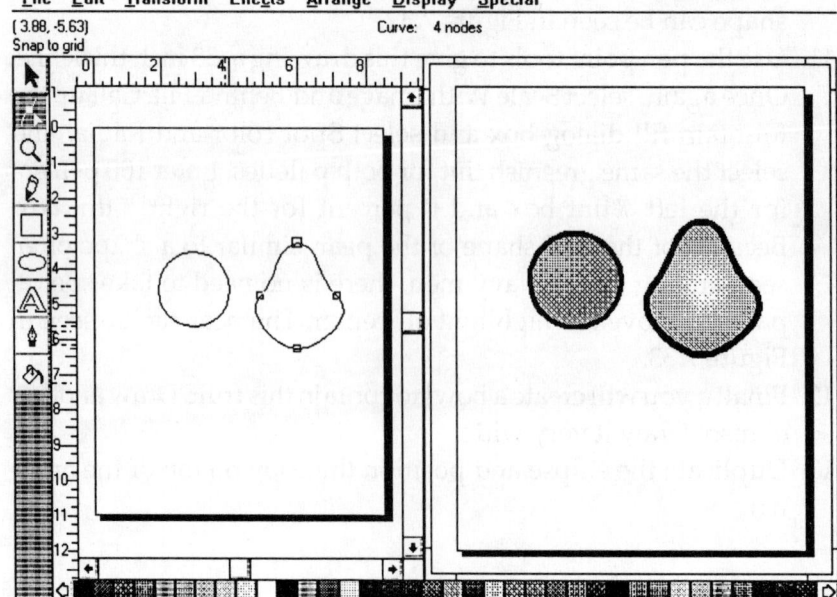

▼ *Figure 7.32. The pear shape*

▼ *Figure 7.33. The orange and the finished pear*

Putting Fills to Work

14. Pull down the Arrange menu and select Convert to Curves. Click on the node-editing tool (second from the top in the toolbox).
15. Double click on the node at the left side of the new ellipse. This is advanced node editing, which was covered in Chapter 6. You will see the Node Edit menu. Click on Cusp.
16. Move the top control handle of the left node until it lies at about a 45-degree angle to the right of the bottom control handle.
17. Perform a similar adjustment on the node at the right side of the bowl. Then drag the top node downward so it is a short distance from the bottom node. This will create the shape of a wide, shallow bowl (Figure 7.34).

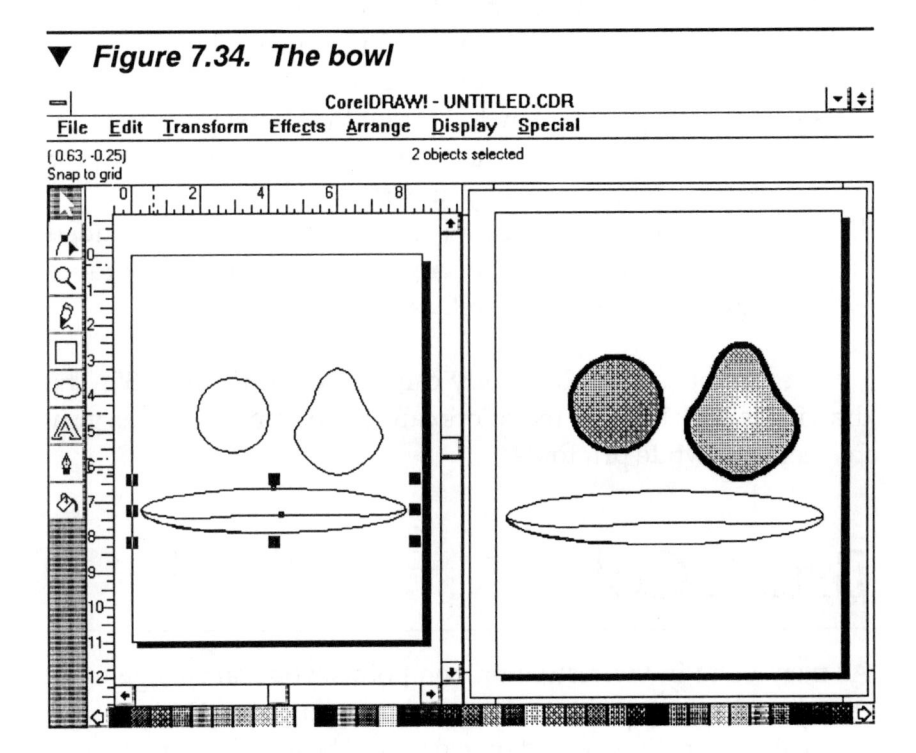

▼ *Figure 7.34. The bowl*

18. Click on the pick tool and drag a selection rectangle around both parts of the bowl so they'll both be selected.
19. Call up the outline tool dialog box and make the line .1 inch thick and click on Behind Fill and Scale With Image.

Now you will make the bowl terra cotta.

1. Use the Fountain Fill dialog box to give the outside of the bowl (the part we adjusted) a 180-degree linear fill. Select a brownish Pantone color for both palettes. Make the left %tint 100 percent and the right %tint 50 percent.
2. Use the Duplicate command on the Edit menu to create several fruits of different sizes. Double click on a couple of the pears and drag a corner handle to tip the pears slightly (they rarely stand at attention). Arrange the fruits in the bowl. What happened? Since you drew the fruits first, they have a lower precedence than the bowl, so they appear to be behind the bowl. It's all right for the front of the bowl to be in front of the fruit, but the back of the bowl (or the interior) should appear behind it. Step three shows how to solve the problem.
3. Click on the original ellipse you drew to make the fruit bowl. Pull down the Arrange menu and select To Back. This will automatically give the bowl's interior the lowest precedence in the drawing, so all the fruit and the front of the bowl will appear in front of it, which is what you want.
4. Pull down the File menu and save your work. As an added challenge, you might want to create a few bananas and grapes to balance the creation, as well as stems for the pears.

The completed still life study can be seen in Figure 7.35. The drawing is dark because the colors can only be represented as gray in black-and-white printouts.

Brush Color

As mentioned in the section on pen points, you can change more than just the shape and thickness of the pen point. You can also adjust the color. The color adjustments will be familiar to you if you have read the section on fountain fills or the section in Chapter 2 on solid fills. In fact, virtually the same dialog box is used. The dialog box is shown in Figure 7.36.

Lines and Fills ▲ 255

▼ *Figure 7.35. The still life study*

Brush Color

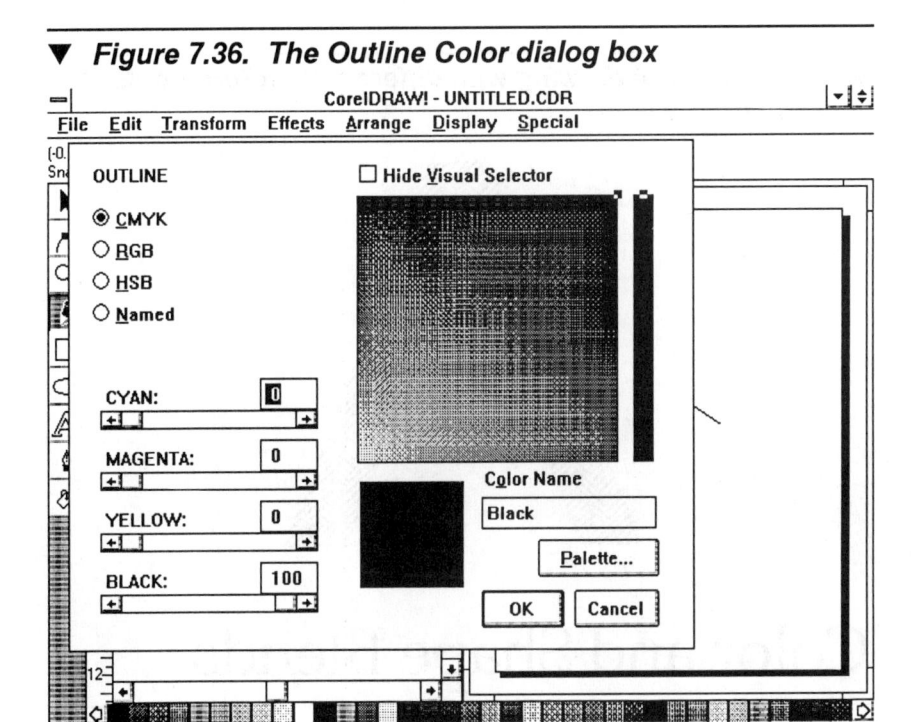

▼ *Figure 7.36. The Outline Color dialog box*

TIP

You can establish a new default pen thickness, pen color, or a new default fill simply by making sure that nothing is selected before clicking on the outline or fill tool in the toolbox. You will be shown a dialog box asking you to confirm the kind of default you are establishing. Then, when you have chosen the pen thickness, color, or fill, each object drawn thereafter will have that attribute.

Color will be covered in full in the upcoming sections "Mixing Colors" and "How and Why to Use Pantone Colors." If you would prefer to select colors from a palette rather than mix the colors for yourself, click on the button marked Palette.

The PostScript button calls up the PostScript Controls dialog box shown in Figure 7.20. By providing an object with different PostScript halftone for the interior and the outline, you can create some very striking drawings (Figure 7.37).

▼ **Figure 7.37. A drawing with different PostScript outline and fill**

Color and Shape Blends

One of the most exciting aspects of the new *CorelDRAW!* is its ability to create blends. Blends were unknown before in *CorelDRAW!*, so even if you are passingly familiar with *CorelDRAW!*, this may be new to you.

The best way to explain a blend is to create one.

1. Create two shapes on the *CorelDRAW!* page area: a circle and a square.

2. Click on the pick tool and drag a selection rectangle that contains both shapes (alternately, you could hold down the Shift key and click on both shapes).
3. Pull down the Effects menu—a real treasure-trove of powerful and fun effects. Click on Blend. You'll see the dialog box in Figure 7.38.

Color and Shape Blends

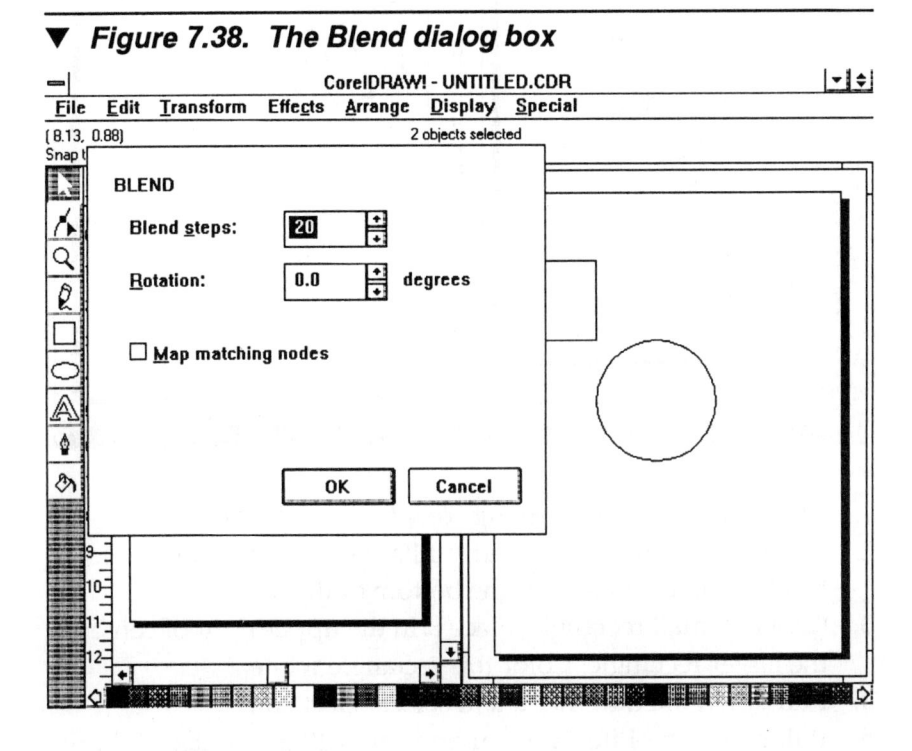

▼ *Figure 7.38. The Blend dialog box*

It's easier to see the blend in action if you select a lower number for Blend steps than 20.

4. Double click on the Blend steps text box and type 4.
5. Click on OK. You'll see something like the graphic in Figure 7.39.

Note how each of the four intermediate shapes moving from the square to the circle is slightly less like a square and slightly more like a circle. That's only a small part of what blend can do. Next, you'll blend colors.

▼ **Figure 7.39. The square blended into a circle**

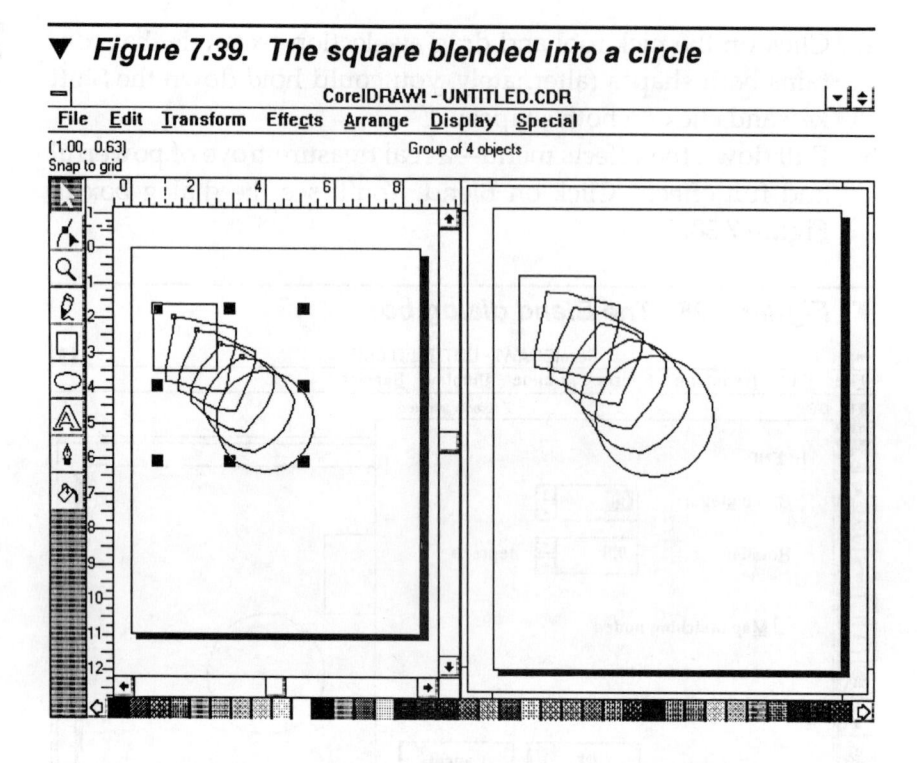

1. Clear the screen by selecting New from the File menu.
2. Create a rectangle that nearly fills the page area and color it black using the palette at the bottom of the screen.
3. Create a small rectangle. Place it in the upper right of center of the larger rectangle. Color this rectangle white.
4. Pull down the Edit menu and select Select All.
5. Pull down the Effects menu and select Blend. Enter 10 in the Blend steps box. Click on OK. The result is shown in Figure 7.40.

You can blend any two colors or shapes together this way, or blend both color and shape at once. The Blend dialog box also allows you to specify which nodes of each object should be considered equivalent (Map matching nodes). By selecting opposite corners of rectangles, for example, you can cause the rectangles to flip as they blend and the Rotation text box allows you to enter a number of degrees to rotate the shapes as they blend. I will leave these to your experimentation.

▼ **Figure 7.40. The blended colors**

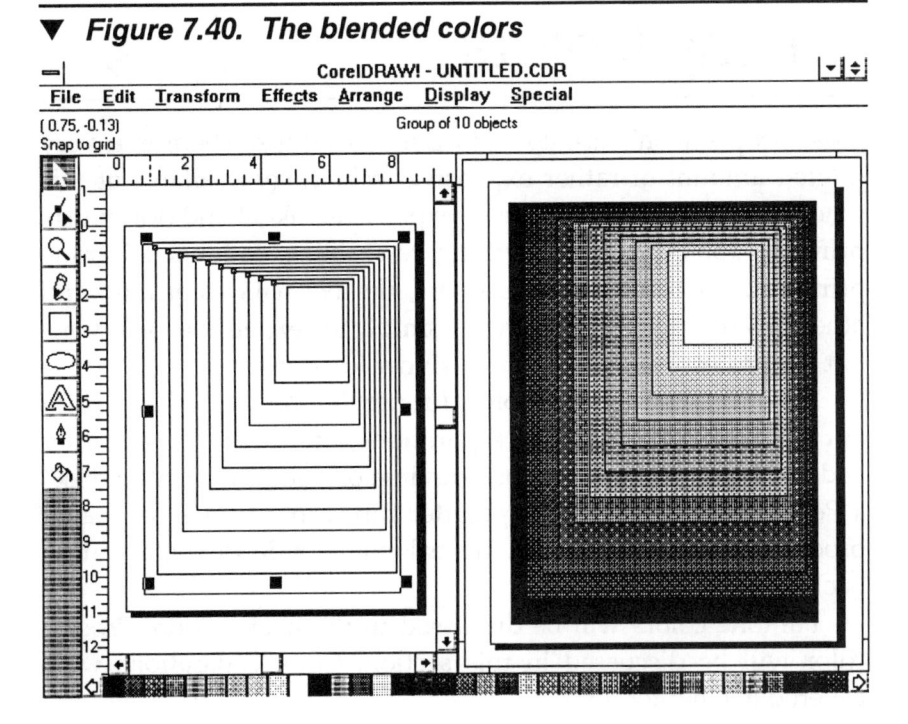

Color and Shape Blends

TIP

Blending closed shapes to open shapes and blending objects made up of many shapes, such as text, into a single shape, such as a rectangle, will result in some or all of the intermediate shapes being left open. This can result in some interesting effects.

TIP

You should note that the intermediate shapes are a single, combined object. Oddly, you can't break up this combined object to manipulate the intermediate shapes as you can with *Arts & Letters*. Also, the intermediate shapes will be selected at the end of the blend, but the starting and ending shapes will not. Therefore, if you manipulate the blend without holding down the Shift key and clicking on the starting and ending objects, you will only manipulate the intermediate shapes.

Mixing Colors

Most people won't use color in their printouts. There is a very limited amount of rather expensive technology available at this time for color printing. The least expensive, ink-jet and dot-matrix printers, don't provide anything resembling commercial-grade printouts. The better quality printers, like thermal wax printers and other new desktop technology, are simply too expensive for anyone but the professional printer or designer to afford.

However, you can mix colors (or use Pantone colors) and print out color separations. These separations can be taken to a printer and used as proofs for photoengraving, or you can "print to disk" a PostScript file, which a typesetter can turn into real separated proofs for publication. This is the real intent for desktop illustration packages like *CorelDRAW!*.

Pantone colors will be discussed in the next section. Process color will be discussed in this section. Color separations were covered in Chapter 3.

Process colors are a bit of a risk. If you are creating something professionally, you would be wiser to stick with the Pantone colors. The reason for the risk is that it's difficult to estimate the real printed color from the color that appears on the screen. If you have ever read a review of computer monitors that shows the displays of several monitors on the same page, you have probably been struck by the wide variation in the appearance of the screens. Some seem to have a green cast, some blue. Even manufacturers of so-called paper-white monitors seem to take this seemingly absolute standard liberally.

However, if you want complete control of your printout, you will want to use process color. There are hundreds of spot colors in the standard—enough for most applications, but there are millions of process colors.

There are four primary colors in the process color universe: Cyan, Magenta, Yellow, and Black. The color mixing dialog boxes of *CorelDRAW!* provide a potential of 104,060,401 different colors: percentages of saturation from zero to 100 of the four primaries. Naturally, the differences between two colors one percentage apart

Mixing Colors

is invisible to the human eye and could not be displayed on even the best PC monitor, though this is approximated by dithering, which ends up close to the color, but will never match it exactly. (Actually, the number of potential colors is even higher than 104 million because the text boxes allow you to enter decimal values.)

You will want to mix your own colors, so we won't provide a long list of percentages to achieve colors here. However, it might be useful for you to know that:

Blue	=	100% Magenta	+	100% Cyan
Green	=	100% Cyan	+	100% Yellow
Red	=	100% Magenta	+	100% Yellow
Black	=	100% Black	+	anything
Black	=	100% Magenta	+	100% Cyan + 100% Yellow
Gray	=	equal proportions of Cyan, Magenta, and Yellow		

How and Why to Use Pantone Colors

The question of why to use Pantone colors is similar to the question of why people use language or value systems to communicate with each other. If you and I were speaking over the telephone, we would have no trouble agreeing on the meaning of the word "No" or "Crime." Unfortunately, we might both think we know what the other means when the word "Red" is used, but a quick glance down the aisle of the local supermarket will convince you that "Red" is a very flexible color. Red appears in thousands of variations from pink to purple to orange.

Colors appear in ranges, some of which will complement other colors, and some of which will not. If you specify red and blue and the printout comes back reddish orange and a blue bordering on chartreuse, you will probably be disappointed in the appearance of the product.

With the emergence of color as an important medium of design and communication, the printing industry needed a standard that could be used to communicate color information exactly from one place (usually the publisher or designer) to another (the printer) so that unpleasant surprises wouldn't happen.

There is a trade-off, though, for the power of spot color: You can only use a few colors; you shouldn't create fountains from one spot color to another, if you are planning to do color separation; and spot colors are anything but flexible. Therefore, the decision to use spot colors should be based on the number of colors in the art (you can use multiple tints of the same Pantone color without penalty, however), the importance that the colors be exact, and whether there are fountains in the artwork.

Exercises

This exercise assumes that you have *CorelDRAW!* running and a new, blank page area is visible. If you already have something on the screen, save it and select New from the File menu. You're simply going to try different kinds of fills.

What You Should Do

1. Draw a series of six rectangles on the screen. Or draw one rectangle and duplicate it five times. If the preview screen isn't visible, pull down the Display menu and select Show Preview or press Shift-F9 to make the preview screen visible. Click on the first rectangle and click on a red color in the palette at the bottom of the screen. If a red color isn't available scroll through the palette until one appears.

How the Computer Responds

1. The rectangle in the preview screen will be colored red.

2. Click on the second rectangle. Click on the fill tool and click on the can of paint.

3. Click on the Open button.

4. Click on DITHERED.PAL and click on the Load button (the default palette is the CORELDRW.PAL), so you can return to it when you're through with this exercise.

5. Click on the third rectangle. Hold down the Shift key and click on the fourth rectangle, so both are selected. Click on the Fill tool and select the fountain fill option. Select a radial fill, process color from red to green, and click on OK.

2. You are at the main Uniform Fill palette. It has more capabilities than the palette at the bottom of the screen. From here, you can mix colors, load a different palette, or use the PostScript button to specify a special screen, as was done earlier in the chapter for fountain fills.

3. The Open Palette dialog box lists a series of palettes available for your use.

4. The new palette will appear in the Uniform Fill dialog box. Click on a dark violet color and click on OK to return to the *CorelDRAW!* screen.

5. Each will fill in turn, with one color at its center and the other color at its periphery.

Exercises

6. Now pull down the Arrange menu and select Combine.

7. Click on the fifth rectangle. Click on the fill tool and select vector fill from the fill tool menu (it's the one with the double-headed arrow in it).

8. Select CUBES.PAT as your pattern and click on OK. Next the VECTOR FILL PATTERN dialog box will appear. Select Small and make sure the Seamless Tiling check box is checked. Click on OK.

9. Click on the sixth box. Click on the fill tool in the toolbox and click on the raster fill option (it looks like a checkerboard). In the resulting BITMAP FILL PATTERN dialog box, click on a brick pattern and click on OK.

10. Select a dark red color for the background and gray for the foreground. Click on OK.

6. The rectangles will be redrawn and refilled. This time, the color at the center of the radial fill will be halfway between the two rectangles and the other color will appear at the edges of the rectangles that are farthest apart.

7. The Load Vector Pattern dialog box appears.

8. The box will fill with a tiny cube pattern.

9. The BITMAP PATTERN COLOR dialog box will appear, allowing you to select a foreground and a background color.

10. Your last box should be filled with a fairly realistic brick pattern.

8 Corel Trace

▲ Starting *Corel Trace*
▲ Create Color and Grayscale Tracings
▲ The Batch Feature

What is Corel Trace? It's an extremely advanced way to turn raster graphics into vector graphics. It intelligently traces TIF or PCX images while you watch. Why would you need such a tool when *CorelDRAW!* has an autotrace built right into it?

If you went through the exercise of tracing an object, you probably discovered that doing it yourself can be a terrific inducement never to do it again. It's so difficult to trace exactly the area you want traced that you will almost certainly come away from the experience thinking, there has got to be a better way. Then your boss hands you a sheaf of papers about fifty pages thick, with orders to scan them and trace them so the images on the papers can be used in *CorelDRAW!*. Wait! Don't quit your job. There *is* a better way to trace bitmap images—a much better way.

I first caught sight of Corel Trace in action in the 1990 Summer PC Expo in New York City and it took my breath away. They had loaded a very complex drawing and Corel Trace was quickly and efficiently tracing it from top to bottom, turning it into a vector graphic that could be converted for use with *CorelDRAW!*. That's right—it doesn't trace directly into CDR format. It traces into EPS format, a format you could send directly to your printer or convert for use with another vector graphics program.

To use this chapter, you will need a ready source of traceable art. Fortunately, there is such a supply provided with *CorelDRAW!* in the SAMPLE subdirectory that should be underneath the CORELDRW directory. You are welcome to use these or any clip art you have available, or for the sake of an exercise, you could do a *CorelDRAW!* drawing and export it as a PCX or TIF file for tracing. Of course, you would never do this in real life.

Starting *Corel Trace*

The installation program you ran to set up *CorelDRAW!* should have created a program group known as Corel Applications. To get to this program, follow these steps:

1. Start *Windows*.

2. Pull down the Window menu in the Program Manager window and select Corel Applications.
3. When the Corel Applications window opens, the Corel Trace icon will look like a lightbulb with a sheet of paper above it and a pencil above that. Double click on this icon and you will see the window shown in Figure 8.1.

Starting Corel Trace

▼ *Figure 8.1. The Corel Trace window*

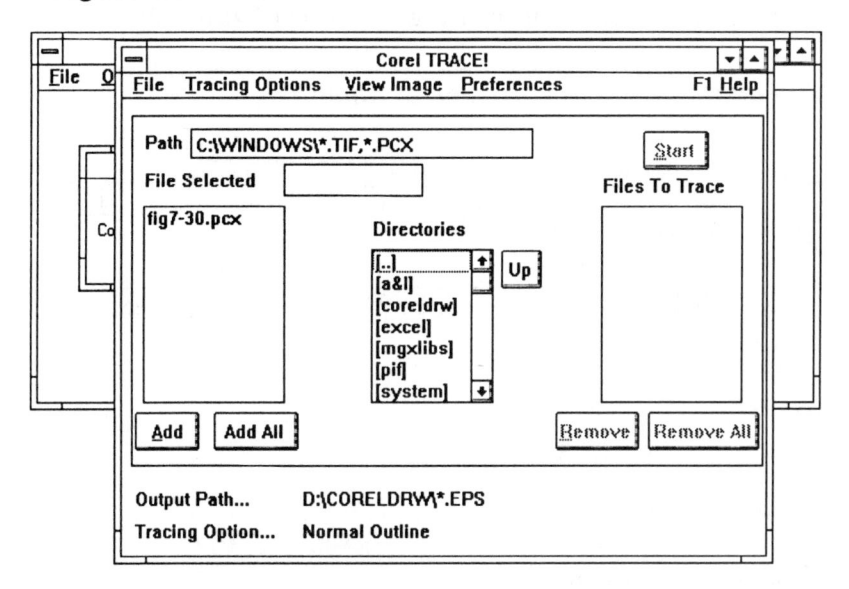

First and foremost, you must use the various controls in the window to locate your raster image file. This shouldn't be difficult, if you know where your CORELDRW directory is and if you are going to use the files in the SAMPLES directory.

Now you will load up a file and trace it. When you locate the directory with your traceable files in it, the filenames should appear in the list box at the middle left of the window.

1. Double click on the filename of the file you want to trace. The filename will be entered into the list box at the right side of the window.
2. For fun, pull down the View Image menu and select Display Image. The picture in the raster graphic file should appear onscreen.

3. To start tracing, you need to click on the Start button at the upper-right corner of the Corel Trace window. You might need to adjust the position of the display window and the Corel Trace window by dragging them by their move bars. Remember that the move bar is the bar that contains the name of the window—either Corel Trace or the name of the file you are tracing. When you click on the Start button, the image will disappear from the preview screen and a bar will appear at the lower-right corner to show you how far the trace has gone (Figure 8.2).

▼ *Figure 8.2. In the process of tracing*

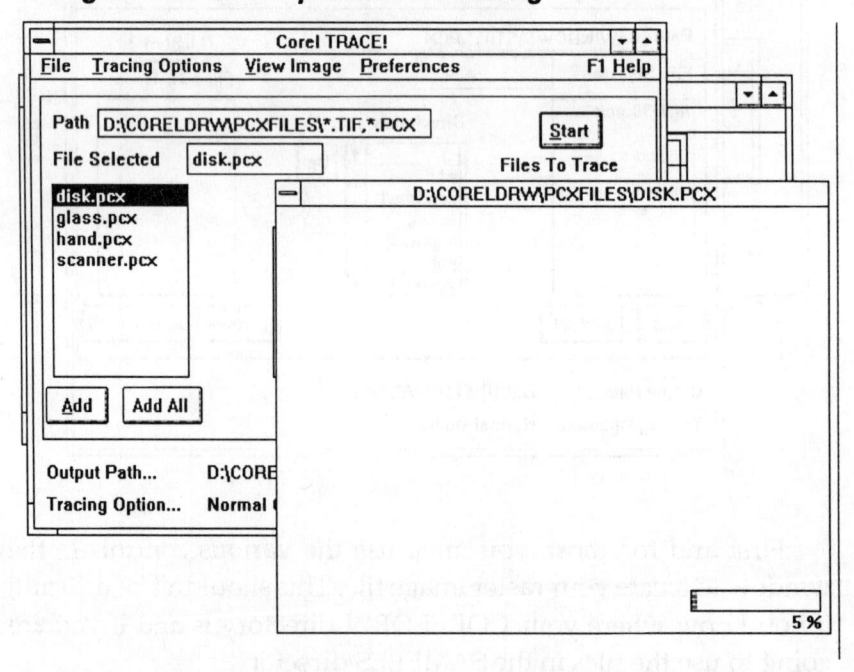

When the trace is completed, you will see the complete trace on the screen. This trace is already saved to disk in a format that you could send directly to your PostScript laser printer (though due to the limitations on PostScript, it's possible that it will be unable to print it). When the trace is completed, you will see the traced object in the window, as shown in Figure 8.3.

The next step is to load the trace into *CorelDRAW!*.

▼ Figure 8.3. The trace completed

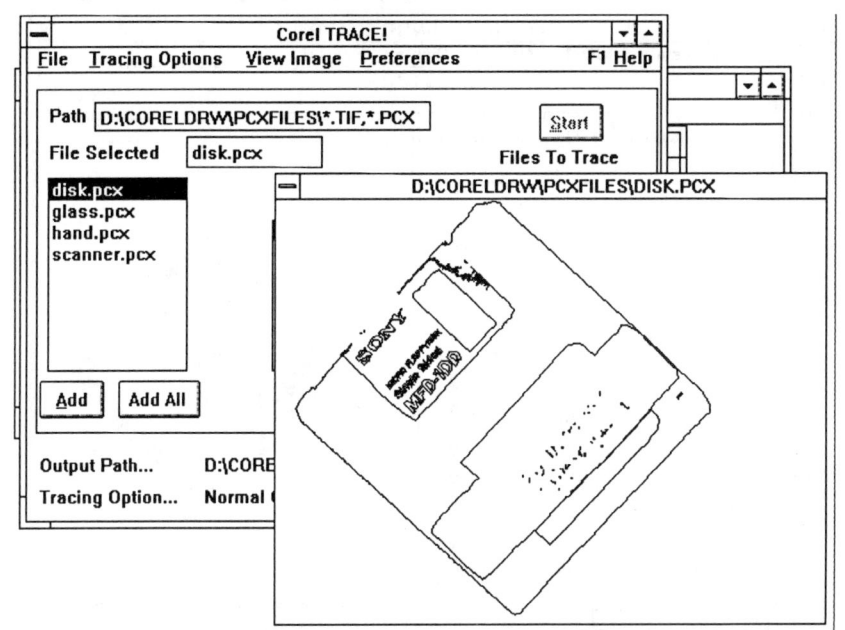

Starting Corel Trace

1. Click on the minimize box or double click on the close box of the Corel Trace utility and start up *CorelDRAW!*.
2. Pull down the File menu in *CorelDRAW!* and select Import.
3. In the list box of the Import dialog box, you will see two different EPS formats: *Adobe Illustrator* and Corel Trace. Double click on Corel Trace and you will see the Import Corel Trace dialog box, which will list all the EPS files available for importing in the current directory. You may have to change directories to get to the place where the EPS file is placed, but unless you have changed some settings, it should have been placed in the same subdirectory as your Corel Trace program and the *CorelDRAW!* program. The filename of the traced file will be the same as the filename of the EPS file you traced, so you should have no trouble identifying it.
4. Double click on the filename and the file will be imported. In Figure 8.4, you can see the traced image and the preview screen showing what the final printout should look like.

▼ **Figure 8.4. The traced and imported graphic**

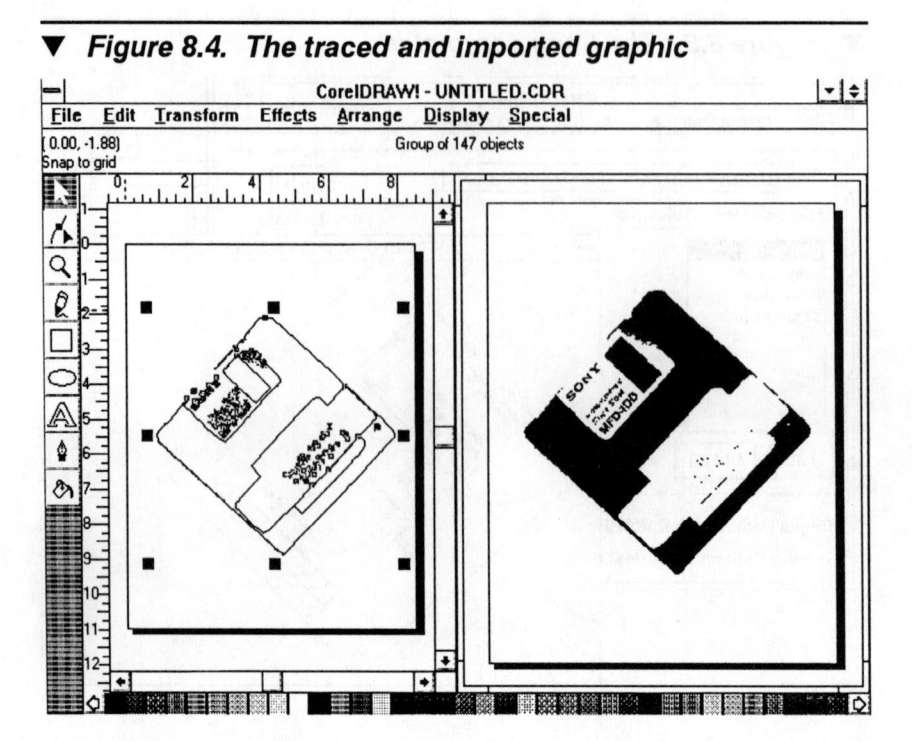

In all, there are 147 objects in the trace. How would you like to trace *that* by hand?

As I mentioned, the graphic might be (and, in fact, *is*) too complex to print on a PostScript printer. But after simplifying it with the techniques described in Chapter 6, you can make this unprintable image simple enough even for Adobe PostScript. The printed version of this graphic is shown in Figure 8.5.

But there are ways of simplifying the drawing even before it's traced. Taking steps ahead of time will save time later.

Close *CorelDRAW!* and start up Corel Trace again. Pull down the Tracing Options menu. The options are Edit Option, Normal Outline, Normal Centerline, and a series of ellipses (. . .). Click on an ellipsis and you will see the dialog box shown in Figure 8.6.

Use this box to specify how closely the tracing program should trace the bitmap file. You will want to experiment with the settings to get them the way you want, but the settings you see in Figure 8.6 are the settings used for the trace of the computer disk.

Corel Trace ▲ 271

▼ **Figure 8.5.** *The simplified, printed disk image*

Starting Corel Trace

▼ **Figure 8.6.** *The Tracing Options dialog box*

Here are some settings that will make the trace less complex and more workable (or at least more printable).
- ▲ Select lines in the Convert Long Lines box.
- ▲ Select very Loose in the Fit Curve box.
- ▲ Enter 20 or more in the Remove Noise text box.
- ▲ Select smooth in the Edge Filtering box.
- ▲ Select coarse in the Sample Rate dialog box

When you have the settings the way you want them, double click on the text box in the Option Name dialog box and type a name like COARSE. When you pull down the Tracing Options menu, this option will appear in the menu, so you can select it from the menu without having to make the settings each time. By setting up a series of personalized tracing schemes, you can have a special kind of trace ready to use for any task. If you ever want to edit (change) the contents of your Tracing Options dialog box, click on its name in the Tracing Options menu and click on the Edit Options option.

TIP

You probably noticed the selections Normal Outline and Normal Centerline in the Tracing Options menu and similar options in the upper-left corner of the Tracing Options dialog box. For solid objects and grayscale objects, you should use Normal Outline, which traces the edges and fills so that the resulting trace resembles the bitmap image. The Normal Centerline trace is intended for tracing text or other bitmaps that consist of thin lines that should be traced in the form of lines and not solid objects.

Create Color and Grayscale Tracings

What you saw in the previous section was a trace of a monochrome PCX file into an EPS graphic. If all you want to work with is black and white images with no shades of gray, you needn't read any further. However, most real-world images are not made up of areas of black and white, but images with many colors and many shades of gray.

Fortunately, Corel Trace makes tracing grayscale and color images very easy. You need to remember, though, that as complex as a monochrome drawing can be, a color or grayscale drawing represents a multiple of this complexity.

Pull down the Preferences menu and select Color Reduction. In the resulting dialog box, you can make several selections that will simplify graphics made complex by a large number of colors or grayscales. Click on the downward pointing arrow at the right of Reduce Colors To... You can reduce the numbers of colors to 8, 16, 64, or 256 colors just by clicking on the value in the resulting list box.

Click away from Reduce Colors To list box to close it and click on the downward-pointing arrow next to Reduce Greys To.... In this box, you have the option of reducing greys to 4, 8, 16, 64, or 256 greyscales.

Reduction of colors or greyscales can result in a graphic with a very high contrast color scheme known as posterization.

The function of the Convert to Mono check box is obvious: It will reduce any drawing—color or greyscale—to black and white.

Also on the Preferences menu are selections that will allow you to Trace Partial Area (you are provided with a selection box within the tracing window). There are also three selections that change the onscreen information you see during the trace: Show Progress Rate, Show Tracing Info, and View Dithered Colors.

Create Color and Grayscale Tracings

The Batch Feature

If you have a number of bitmaps to trace, simply load them all into the Files to Trace list box. Set them up to trace overnight and your computer will not only do the tracing work for you, but will do the file-management work as well.

9 Text

▲ Creating and Displaying Text
▲ Fitting Text to Path
▲ Interactive Kerning
▲ Editing Character Outlines

Text was discussed to some degree earlier in this book. It was necessary to provide a foundation in the use of text in *CorelDRAW!* early so you could learn to use the other tools. However, I have waited until now to go into text in detail. Text is a powerful design feature. Not only does it communicate immediately ("text" is just another word for "words," after all), but the face itself tells you something important about the information being conveyed. *CorelDRAW!* has been shipped with a very generous collection of fonts that range from the whimsical to the formal. Although it is too advanced to cover in a getting started book, *CorelDRAW!* even has the ability to create new fonts that can be downloaded to your PostScript printer and used in documents printed with your word processor or other *Windows* software.

Creating and Displaying Text

You've already seen text created in *CorelDRAW!*, but to recap, there are two basic methods for creating text. You can:

1. Click on the text tool in the toolbox.
2. Click on the page area.
3. Enter the text in the Text dialog box, make any other settings, and return to the page area where the text will be displayed.

Or you can:

1. Click on the text tool in the toolbox.
2. Drag a rectangle to contain the text on the page area.
3. Enter the text in the Text dialog box, make any other settings, and return to the page area where the text will be displayed.

You also learned about the ability to paste text into *CorelDRAW!* from the clipboard, allowing you to enter the text with a tool more suited to text entry (a word processor or text editor), cut or copy it to the clipboard, switch to *CorelDRAW!*, and paste it into the Text dialog box. A related procedure would be to create text with the Notepad utility provided with *Windows* and import it. Getting text to appear on the *CorelDRAW!* screen is not a problem. The creators of *CorelDRAW!* recognize the design value of text and they have made it as easy as possible to use it.

Since you are already familiar with the rudiments of text, we can plunge directly into altering text to make it more interesting and pleasing to the eye.

Creating and Displaying Text

Fitting Text to Path

There are several terms that you should know when dealing with text. A handful of them will be covered here, but there is a special language used by typographers and type afficionados that couldn't possibly be covered here. If you are interested in type and type design, you should seek out books on the topic in your library. The language used to desribe type is both technical and poetic. Listening to true lovers of type describe various typefaces, you might think they were describing fine wines.

The important terms for you to know now are baseline, ascender, descender, and x-height. If these terms are already familiar to you, just skip ahead to the end of this section.

Baseline: The baseline is the bottom of letters like b, c, d and all uppercase letters. The baseline is the line on which the type appears to rest.

x-Height: The x-height is exactly what it sounds like—the height of the letter x of a given font. Note that this height almost always equals the height of lowercase letters a, c, e, i, m, n, o, r, s, u, v, w, and z. Since this height represents another invisible line in a line of type, it's an important way to describe type.

Ascender: An ascender is any part of a letter that pokes up above the x-height. Generally, the ascender is exactly the same height as the cap-height of a font—the height of the capital letters. The term "ascender" refers to the aerial parts of lowercase letters b, d, f, h, k, l, and t.

Descender: A descender is the part of the letter that digs down below the baseline. Most descenders are of approximately the same depth. Letters with descenders are g, j, p, q, and y.

For a graphical representation of these terms, refer to Figure 9.1.

▼ *Figure 9.1. Elemental type*

Axilary — ascender, x-height, descender, baseline

TIP

This short list of terms is only a basic introduction to type. There are many excellent books on type and desktop publishing, which you should consult for the complete story on text. Generally, the advice they provide boils down to keeping your text simple, avoiding elaborate fonts for long stretches of text, using only one or two fonts in a given page, and choosing those fonts with an eye to harmony. Remember that fonts too similar (like Bangkok and Brooklyn, for example) can clash as disturbingly as fonts too different (Paradise and Homeward_Bound, for example). Use fancy faces for accents and major heads. Don't be afraid of being too plain. A conservative look is usually preferable to an overly flamboyant one.

Altering the Baseline

Sometimes design requires that you alter the baseline. There are many ways you can do this, but the most interesting involves making a curving baseline. If you wanted to work with a curving text baseline, you could break up the text and use the pick tool to manually reposition text (in fact, you often may prefer this method). But *CorelDRAW!* comes equipped with an automatic routine that binds text to any baseline. However, you can't do this with paragraph text. Here is how to bind text to an ellipse:

Fitting Text to Path

1. Draw an ellipse on the screen.
2. Click on the text tool and click on the page area. Type some text in the Text dialog box and click on OK to place it on the page area.
3. Click on the pick tool and drag a selection rectangle that includes both the ellipse and the text (or use one of the other options to select both).
4. Pull down the Arrange menu and select Fit Text to Path (or press Ctrl-F).

The results of binding text to a path can be seen in Figure 9.2.

▼ *Figure 9.2. Text bound to an ellipse*

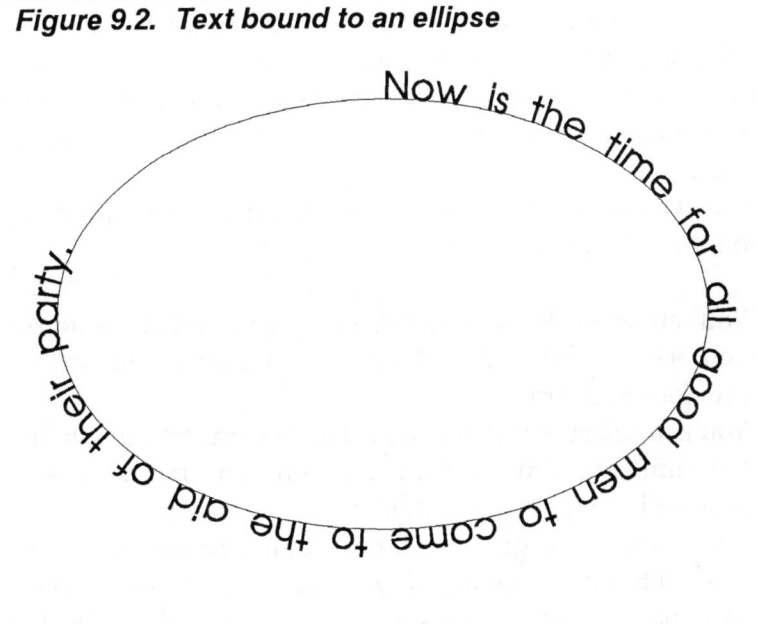

Letting *CorelDRAW!* take care of the details results in the placement of each letter in its proper position. But, just as many drummers dislike drum machines because they eliminate the human feeling from the beat, many graphic artists prefer to place letters themselves. This will be covered a little later.

With an ellipse it's difficult to see, but this text begins at the beginning node of the curve and continues until the routine runs out of running text. In the case of an ellipse, it would be very simple to make the text "bite its own tail" by sizing the ellipse smaller before the Fit Text to Path operation.

TIP

Watch out for concave curves. You may have to take great pains to keep letters from being placed atop one another at a bend in the line. In the next section, you will learn how to move individual letters closer together and farther apart ("Interactive Kerning"). You can use interactive kerning to make text look more attractive when it is fitted to a path.

The reason the text begins at the start/end node of the ellipse is that the text was originally created as left justified. This phenomenon will also occur if the text is created with no justification (None box checked in the justification area of the Text dialog box). Centered text will be centered between the start/end points. Right-justified text will appear with the last letter of the text up against the end node.

If you want to "unfit" text to a path, there are three options open to you. In order of preference:

▲ You can select Undo (if you haven't performed any action since you selected Fit Text to Path). This returns your text to its previous appearance.

▲ You can select Straighten Text. This returns text to a baseline, but eliminates any interactive kerning you might have done (this will be covered shortly).

▲ You can select Align to Baseline. This has an almost humorous effect, literally dropping all your text to the lowest common baseline, with all rotation and spacing still in effect. The letters sometimes look as if they were dumped out of a sack.

CHECK YOURSELF

1. Enter some text on the screen—several words. Draw a very short curve, shorter than the text. Select both and click on the Fit Text to Path option in the Arrange menu.

2. Remove the path once the text has been fitted to it.

ANSWERS

1. The text will appear on the line, continuing to the end and then starting again at the beginning of the line.

2. Simply click on the path and press the Del key The text and the path are completely independent objects.

Interactive Kerning

Interactive kerning is a very powerful capability. It puts you in charge of the complete appearance of the text on the page. You can manipulate the individual letters with the mouse pointer and the shape tool, or use a special capability known as nudge that employs the cursor keys to make fine, even adjustments in spacing and positioning.

You will start by placing some text on the *CorelDRAW!* screen.

1. Click on the text tool in the toolbox and click on the page area.
2. In the Text dialog box, type "AVIONIX."
3. Enter 100 in the Size: text box.
4. Click on OK and the text will appear on your screen as shown in Figure 9.3.

Note that each letter has a tiny box associated with it. The box is like a little handle that will allow you to use the shape tool to grasp the letter and move it around on the screen. Now move some of the letters around.

▼ **Figure 9.3. The starting text**

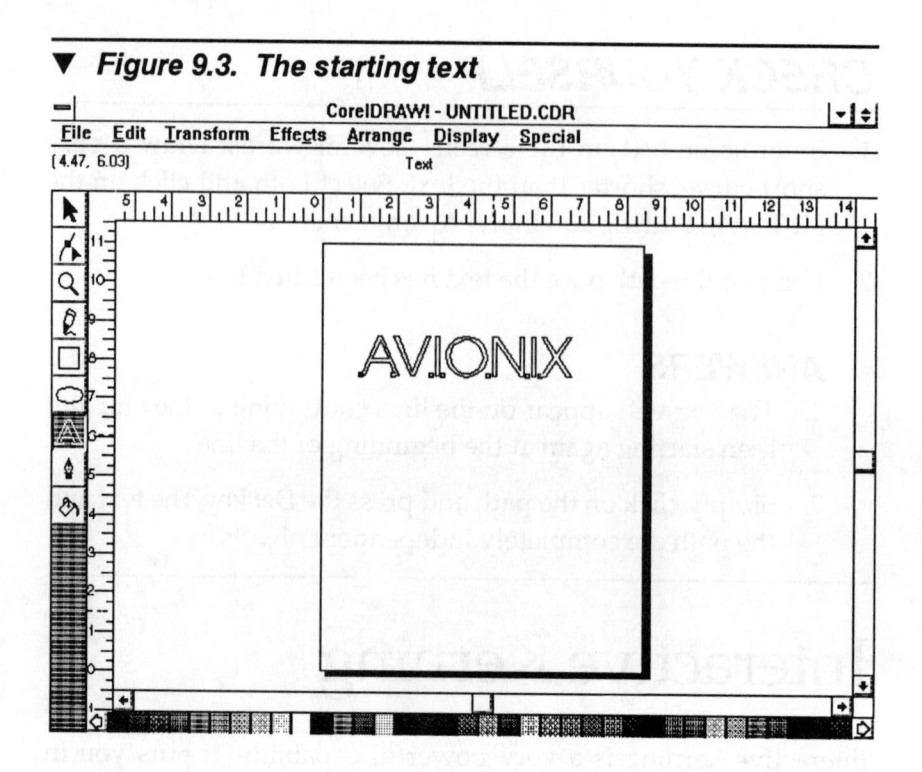

[Screenshot of CorelDRAW! window showing "AVIONIX" text on the page]

1. Click on the shape tool. Your page area should look something like Figure 9.4.

   Note that you have two additional tools on the screen. They appear at the lower-right and lower-left corners of the text and they look like little springs. These are called the *spacing control handles*.

2. Click on the box to the left of the first I. It will turn black, indicating that it is selected.

   You now have complete control over the I. You can move it to any position on the screen simply by placing the mouse pointer on its handle and dragging. To return it to its proper position, select Straighten Text from the Arrange menu. Unfortunately, this has the effect of straightening all the letters, undoing all your interactive kerning.

   A few paragraphs ago, I spoke of nudging text. Here's how it's done:

▼ **Figure 9.4. The text selected with the shape tool**

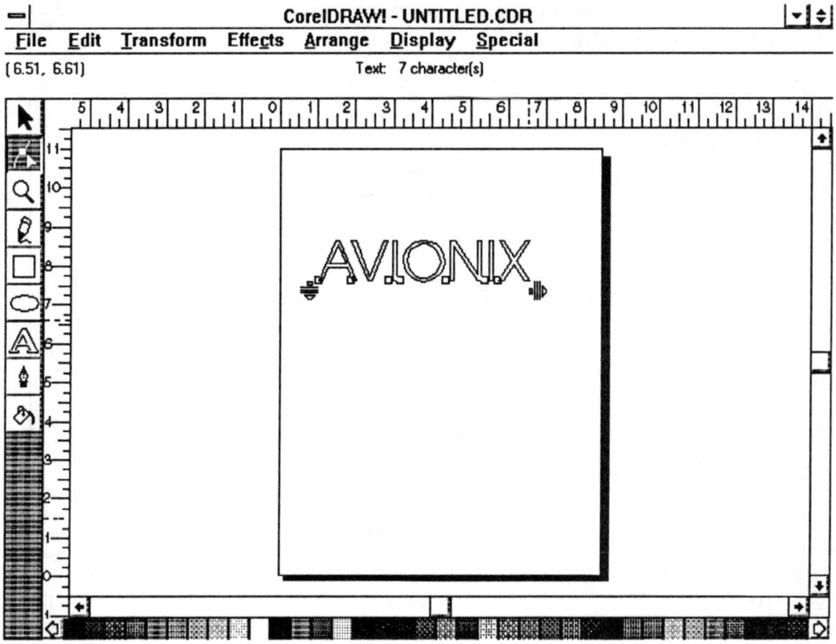

Interactive Kerning

1. With the I still selected, press a cursor key.

Note that the letter moves a certain distance. Each time you press the cursor key, the letter will move the same set distance in the direction of the arrow on the cursor key. What if you want to change the distance moved by the letter? This is very simple.

1. Pull down the Special menu.
2. Select Preferences. You will see the dialog box shown in Figure 9.5.

Note that in the Nudge: text box, the value entered is .1 inches. As with all measurements in *CorelDRAW!*, you can change inches to millimeters, picas, or points.

3. To change the amount of nudge for each press of the cursor key, enter a different value in the text box and click on OK.

Now take a look at the spacing control handles.

▼ **Figure 9.5. The Preferences dialog box**

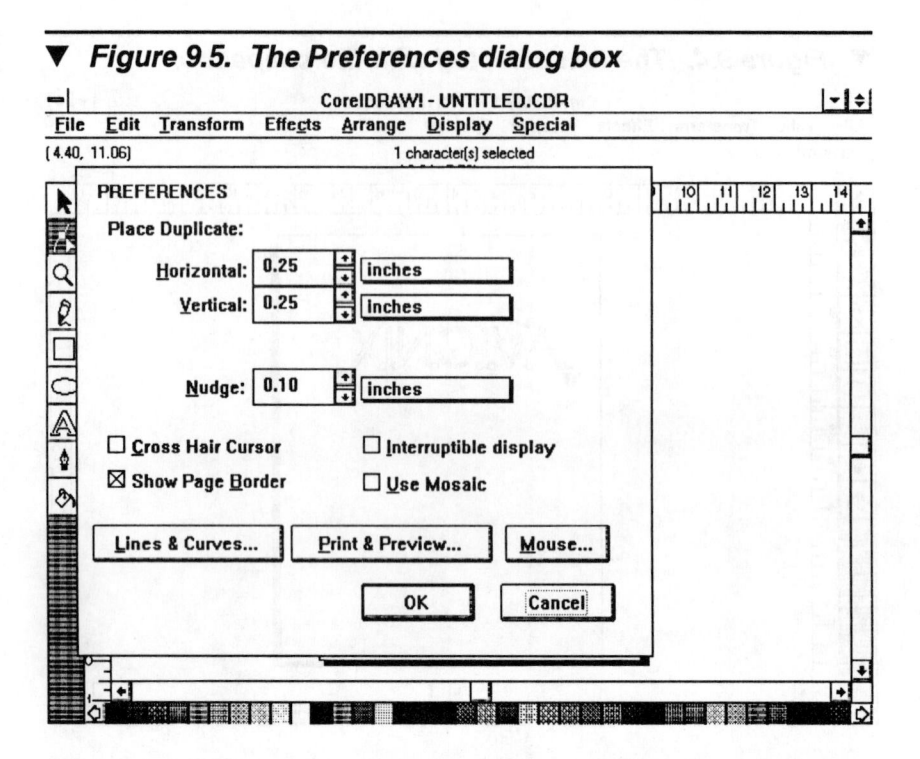

The vertical spacing control handle, which appears under the lower-left corner of a block or line of text affects the interline spacing of multiline text. If you move a letter beneath the baseline of a single line of text with the nudge or the mouse pointer, the vertical spacing control handle will follow the letter down so that it defines the lower extent of the text. If you have multiple lines of text on the screen and you drag this handle downward, the text will "open up," increasing the leading or the spacing between baselines.

The horizontal spacing control handle appears under the lower-right corner of the text. It is used to affect the intercharacter or interword spacing of text.

1. Clear the screen by selecting New from the File menu.
2. Use the text tool to enter the following text on the page area:

```
Getting Started
with Corel Draw
```

You can break text into two lines simply by pressing Enter after finishing the first line. This text should be centered and in large enough type to be easily seen without overrunning the limits of the page area. A 60-point size should be adequate.

Interactive Kerning

3. Click on the shape tool.
4. Place the mouse pointer on the horizontal spacing control handle at the lower-right corner of the text and drag this handle to the right. When you release the mouse button, the spaces between the letters should be increased. The text will remain centered, however, in accordance with its alignment as set in the Text dialog box (Figure 9.6).

▼ **Figure 9.6. The text with intercharacter spacing increased**

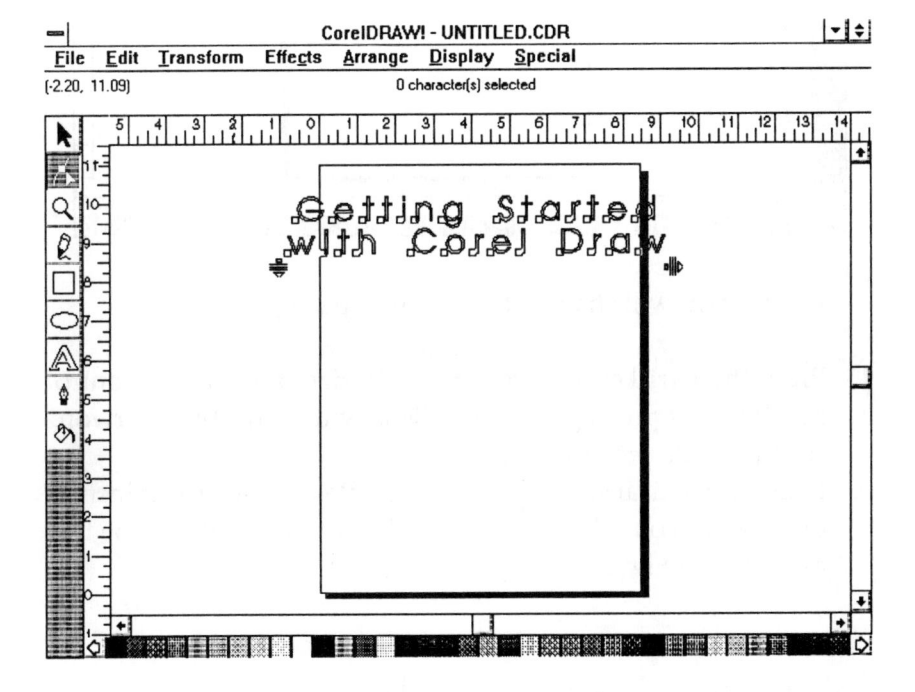

Now change the interword spacing of the text.

1. Return the horizontal spacing control handle to approximately its previous position.

2. Hold down the Ctrl key and drag the horizontal spacing control handle. When you release the mouse button, the text should look like Figure 9.7.

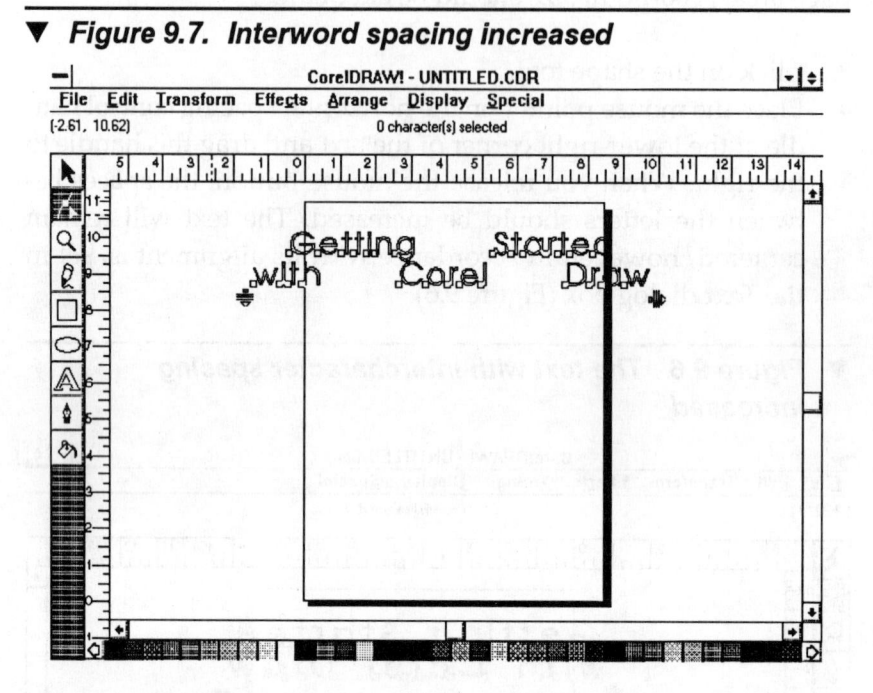

▼ **Figure 9.7. Interword spacing increased**

Finally, you will change the interline spacing.

1. Press the Ctrl key and return the horizontal spacing control handle to its previous position. This will return the interword spacing to its previous setting.
2. Drag the vertical spacing control handle downward an inch or two. When you release the mouse button, you will see the text as shown in Figure 9.8.

Interactive Kerning with Multiple Characters

You may recall that you can use the shape tool to select multiple handles by dragging a selection rectangle containing more than one

▼ **Figure 9.8.** *The interline spacing increased*

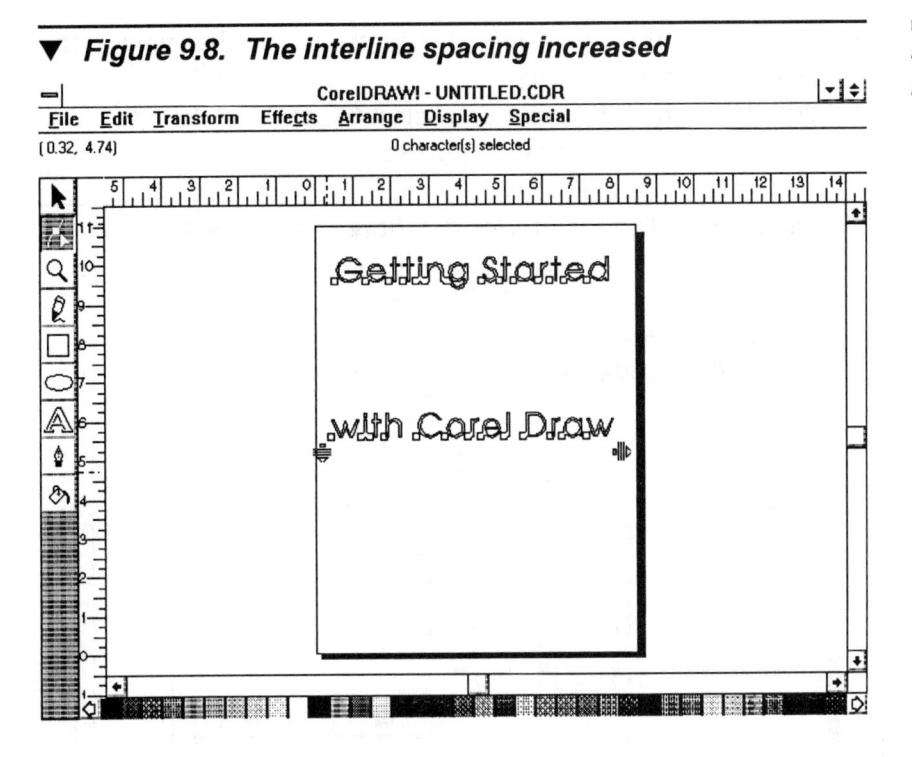

Interactive Kerning

control handle or by holding down the Shift key and clicking on multiple handles. This is also true when interactively kerning text. You can use either of these techniques to select several letters at once for manual alteration.

Changing the Character Attributes

The interactive kerning mode is closely related to the many settings in the Character Attributes dialog box. You will use it with the *Getting Started with Corel Draw* text to make it more interesting.

You can't type text in different fonts and sizes using the tools in the Text dialog box. But you can use the Character Attributes dialog box to alter text once it is entered. Now reduce the size of the first three words of *Getting Started with Corel Draw*.

1. Drag a selection rectangle that selects all the handles in the first line.

2. Hold down the Shift key and click on the handles next to the letters of the word *with*.
3. Pull down the Edit menu and select Character Attributes. You will see the dialog box in Figure 9.9.

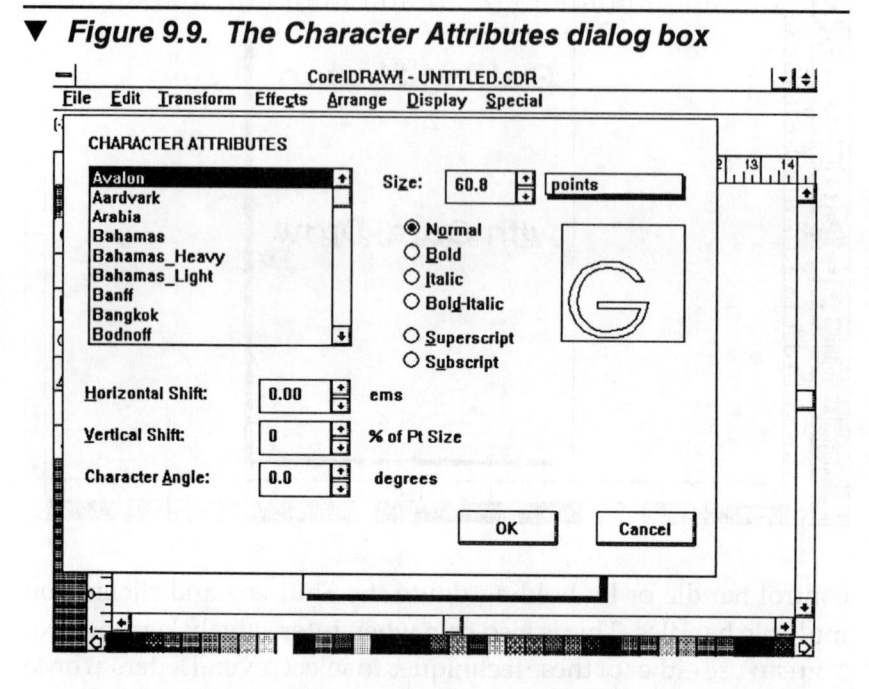

▼ *Figure 9.9. The Character Attributes dialog box*

Note that by using the individual settings in this box, you can adjust the size, face, angle, and style of the individual characters, as well as their relationship to the baseline. Other settings will be left to your experimentation (you'll certainly want to try rotation) and simply reduce the size of the selected text to 30 points.

TIP

Adjusting the angle of a font does not make it italic. An italic font is generally distinct from its base font (this is particularly evident in the appearance of the lowercase *e* and *a*. If you want to see a good example of this, call up the Text dialog box and select PalmSprings. Type *eaeaea* in the text box and click on the Normal and Italic radio buttons at the center-bottom of the dialog box. Note the change in the appearance of the letters in the example box at the bottom-right of the Text dialog box.

4. Double click in the Size: text box and type 30.
5. Click on OK. When you return to the page area, you will see the results shown in Figure 9.10.

Interactive Kerning

▼ **Figure 9.10. The results of editing the character attributes**

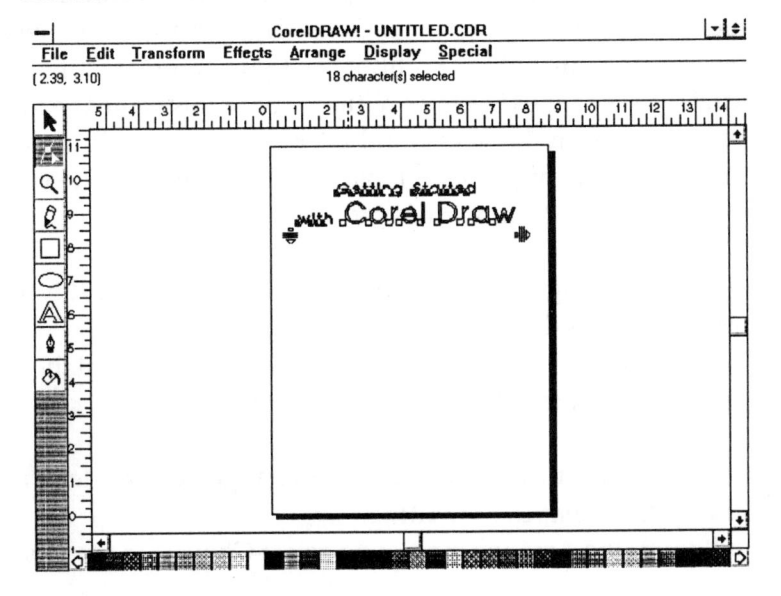

CHECK YOURSELF

1. Place some text on the screen with center alignment. Click on the shape tool and click on one of the letters to select it. Use the nudge feature to move the letter far beyond the right end of the text.

2. Enter a trademarked name (like *Kleenex*) and type *TM* after the text. Make this text small and elevated above the baseline.

ANSWERS

1. As you nudge the letter, the text slowly creeps to the left to maintain the center-alignment. Similar effects can be caused with left- and right-alignment.

2. Use the tools in the Character Attributes box.

Editing Character Outlines

Editing the simple position of text is only the beginning. You can use the shape tool to affect the overall shape of the letters. One of the interesting things about text is that it is composed of individual graphics. Each letter is a graphic. Generally, these tiny, elemental graphics are not amenable to editing, but you can make them so, and edit them as shapes in very exciting ways. Now write the name of a guitar player on the screen and alter the letters in his name to look the way they might have looked on a poster pasted on the Fillmore West in the Summer of Love.

1. Begin by clicking on the text tool and the page area and typing JIMI in the Text dialog box.
2. Click on the pick tool and drag the control handles until the text is large enough to fill the page from left to right.

Now it's time to alter the text, to change it from text into something else—shapes for editing.

3. Pull down the Arrange menu and select Convert to Curves.

After converting the text to curves, you will be unable to convert it back to text again. That means that the Convert to Curves option is a one-way ticket. You are stuck with the text as graphic from that point on.

TIP
Whenever any shape is converted to curves, including ellipses and rectangles, it cannot be converted back again.

Although the text is now converted to curves, it is still combined, which means that although the letters look to be separate and discrete entities to *you*, *CorelDRAW!* considers them to be parts of a single object.

4. Click on the shape tool and drag a selection rectangle that encompasses all the control points in the lower half of the text.
5. Place the mouse pointer on one of the selected handles and drag them all down and to the left (Figure 9.11).

Editing Character Outlines

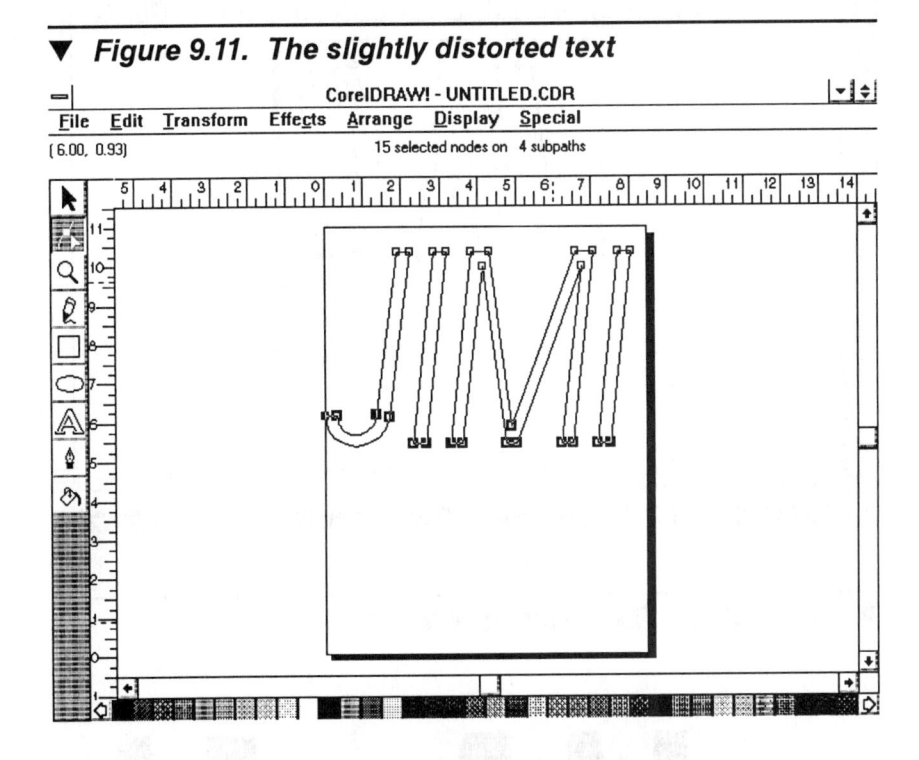

▼ *Figure 9.11. The slightly distorted text*

This makes the text look slightly like italic text.

6. Click away from the text to deselect all handles. Now click on the right handle of all handle pairs at the bottoms of the letters as shown in Figure 9.12.
7. Now drag one of these handles to the right. They will all follow, resulting in the graphic shown in Figure 9.13. The alternating black and white areas are caused by the fact that the objects in the text are combined.

Note that the name is difficult to read. Although generally good design should stress legibility, this is not always the case. It was particularly not the case with poster art from the late 1960s and

292 ▲ *CoreIDRAW! 2*

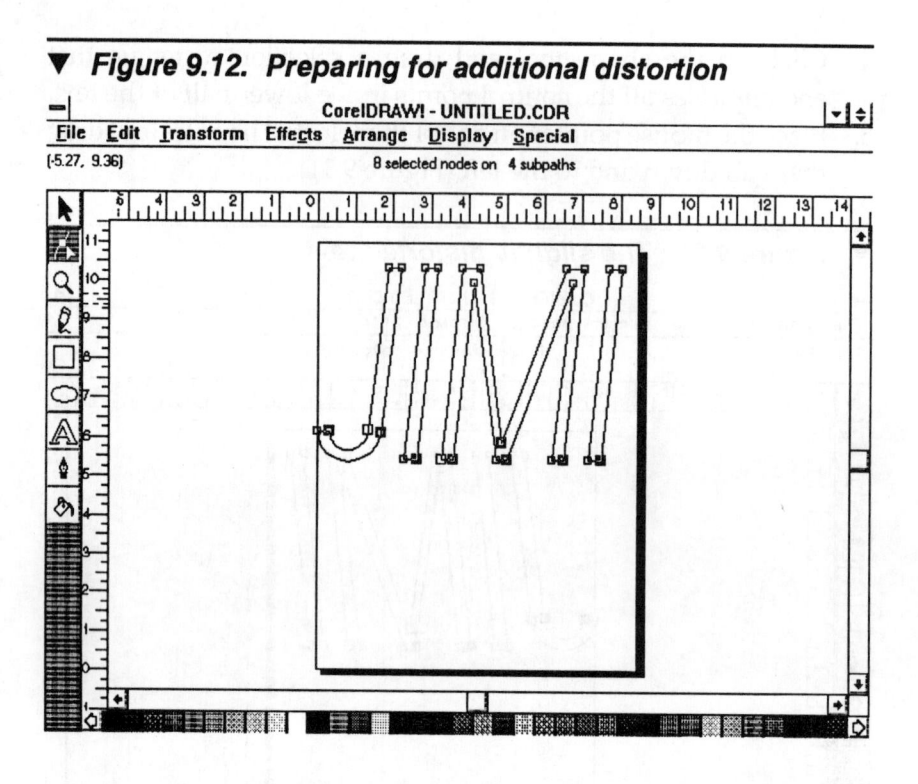

▼ *Figure 9.12. Preparing for additional distortion*

▼ *Figure 9.13. The resulting text*

early 1970s. The more difficult a poster was to read, the more attractive it was considered to be.

Now go all the way with this one, and add Jimi's trademark Fender Stratocaster guitar. You should retrieve it from the symbol libraries.

1. Click on the text tool.
2. Hold down the Shift key and click on the page area. You will see the symbol libraries dialog box.
3. Scroll downward through the names of the symbol libraries until you find Musical_Instruments.
4. Scroll horizontally though this library until you locate guitars at the extreme right end of the library. There are three: a Gibson-style guitar (machine heads at either side of the head), a Fender-style guitar (machine heads on one side the the head), and an acoustic guitar.
5. Click on the Fender-style guitar and click on OK to return to the page area.
6. Enlarge and rotate the symbol—remember that Jimi played a right-handed guitar left handed. You might want to convert it to curves and correct certain anomalies (it seems to be a five-string guitar, for example). But if not, your image might look like Figure 9.14.

▼ *Figure 9.14. The completed poster*

Editing Character Outlines

Exercises

This exercise assumes that you have *CorelDRAW!* running and a new, blank page area is visible. If you already have something on the screen, save it and select New from the File menu.

What You Should Do	How the Computer Responds
1. Click on the text tool in the tool box and click the mouse pointer about halfway across the page area. Type NATIONAL in all uppercase letters in the Text dialog box. Select Left as alignment, Fujiyama as the font, 100 as the point size, then click on OK.	1. NATIONAL will appear on the *CorelDRAW!* page area. It should be legible. Use the pick tool to size the text until it fills the page area left to right.
2. Click on the pencil tool. Draw a curvy line along the bottom of the word. Hold down the Shift key and click on the word. Then pull down the Arrange menu and select Fit Text to Path.	2. The word will be fitted to the path. Depending on how curvy the line is, it may not even be legible anymore.
3. Click away from the text so nothing is selected, then click on the text again. Pull down the Arrange menu and select Straighten Text.	3. The text will return to its original appearance again.

Exercises

4. Click on the curving line and press the Del key to delete it. Click on the shape tool and drag the node at the lower left of the letter I until it is centered on the O. Drag a selection rectangle with the shape tool that encompasses all the nodes of the first three letters of the word. Drag the node of the T until the T is next to the O.

4. All three of the first three letters move at the same time to close up the word.

5. Click away from the text and then double click on the node of the N.

5. The Character Attributes dialog box appears.

6. Increase the size of the N by about 20 points and select Fujiyama_ExtraBold as the font. Click on OK.

6. The N appears larger and "fatter" than the other letters.

7. Click on the text tool again and this time hold down the Shift key when clicking on the page area.

7. The SYMBOLS dialog box appears.

8. Select Household_Items as the symbol library and click on the track light with three lights on it (fifth from the extreme-left end of the library). Click on OK.

8. The track lights appear in the page area, very tiny.

9. Click on the pick tool and size the track lights so they are about half the size of the text. Move the track lights so they are tight against the underside of the text. Size it further so that it runs from the right leg of the left A to the left leg of the right A.

10. If the preview screen isn't visible, make it visible now by selecting Show Preview from the Display menu or by pressing Shift-F9. Make sure the track lights are selected and click on black in the palette at the bottom of your *CorelDRAW!* window.

9. The result should look a little like a business logo.

10. Note what parts of the lights are colored and what parts are not colored.

10 Advanced Topics

▲ Blends
▲ Manipulating Envelopes
▲ Perspective
▲ Extruding
▲ Programming the Right Mouse Button
▲ Repeat

There are many powerful options that you will certainly go on to explore on your own, but here are a few that really make *CorelDRAW!* stand out from the competition.

Blends

Blends were discussed briefly in Chapter 7. Here are some more ideas about how to use this feature. What if you want to make several copies of an object in a row? How would you accomplish that? For me, this most often comes up when I want to provide lines to fill in on a sign-up sheet or graph-like setup. Here's how to accomplish it.

1. Click on the pencil tool.
2. Click on the page area where the left and top margins would come together. Move the pencil tool to the right side of the page area, make sure your line is perfectly horizontal, and click where the right margin should be.
3. Click on the pick tool and select the line, if it isn't already selected.
4. Pull down the Edit menu and select Duplicate. Drag the duplicate line so it is at the bottom end of the area you want filled with lines.
5. Select both lines, pull down the Arrange menu, and either align the lines at their centers, or their right or left ends. Since the lines are of identical lengths, their alignment doesn't matter.
6. Pull down the Effects menu and select Blend, or press Ctrl-B. You will see the dialog box shown in Figure 10.1.
7. Double click in the Blend steps: text box and enter the number of lines you want *between* the two you have just created. Click on OK and *CorelDRAW!* will place the intervening lines for you almost instantly. Figure 10.2 shows the result.

The blend consists of the lines between the two original lines. Remember that! If you want to include the two original lines, click on them with the Shift key depressed. It would be a good idea to pull down the Arrange menu and select Group so that you will be

Advanced Topics ▲ 299

▼ *Figure 10.1. The Blend dialog box*

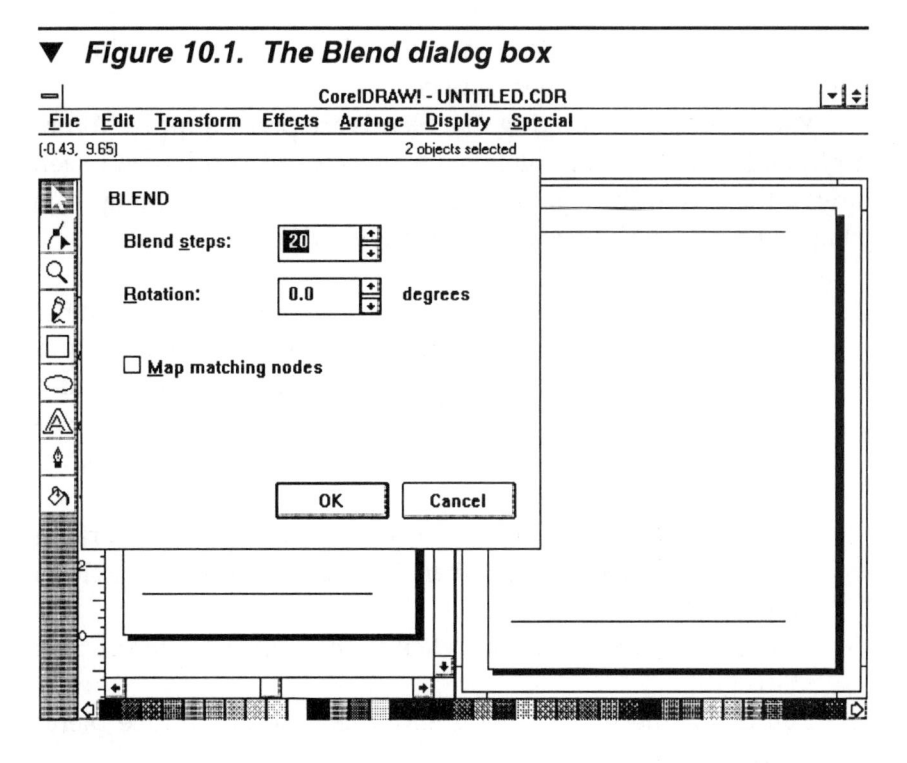

Blends

▼ *Figure 10.2. The completed blend*

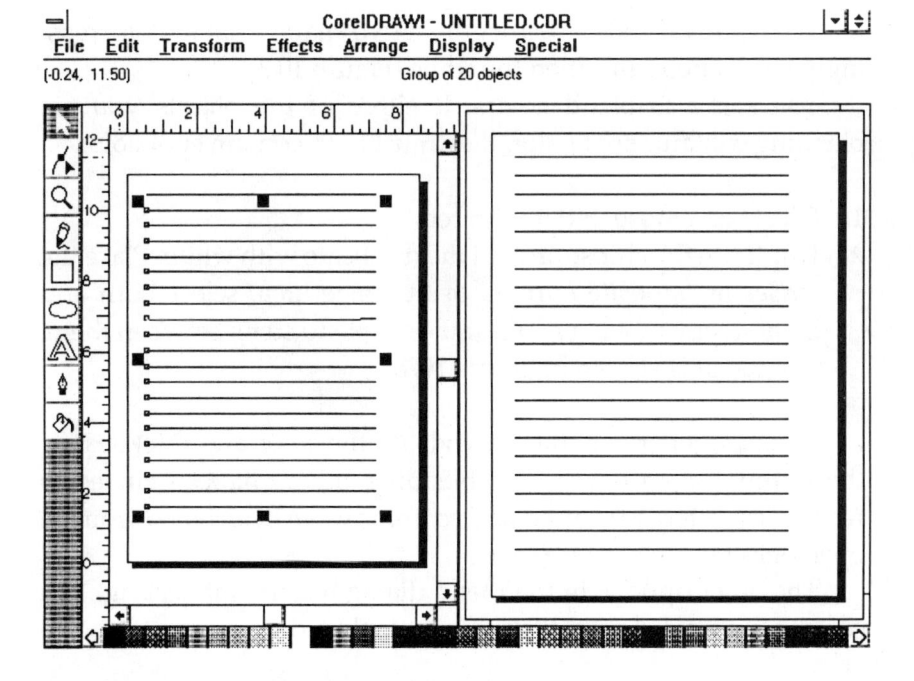

sure to move or otherwise manipulate all of the blend, including the beginning and end lines, at once.

You're probably thinking that blends are pretty simple. You're right and you're wrong. Blends are simple, but you haven't seen any of the possibilities yet. Blends can be created that change one shape to another. Now you will change a guitar into a circle.

1. Click on the text tool, hold down the Shift key, and click on the page area. Open the Musical_Instruments symbol library and scroll to the far-right end of the images. Click on a guitar and click on the OK button. Enlarge it so it's large enough to see easily. With the guitar still selected, pull down the Arrange menu and select Break Apart.
2. Click on the Ellipse tool, hold down the Ctrl key, and drag a perfect circle next to the guitar. Click away from the circle to deselect it.
3. Hold down the Shift key and click on the ellipse and the outline of the guitar.
4. Pull down the Effects menu and select Blend. Reduce Blend steps to two.
5. Click on OK.

What you are left with is a guitar, two shapes that look increasingly like a circle, and then the circle (Figure 10.3).

You can also blend colors. If either of the objects you are blending contains spot color, they must both contain spot color.

1. Create an ellipse. Fill it with red.
2. Duplicate the ellipse and fill the duplicate with white. Place the circles at opposite corners of the page area, select both and blend them, making any number of blend steps between them. The result is shown in Figure 10.4.

You can perform similar blends on the color and thickness of the outline of an object. Try blending other shapes—circles to rectangles, letters to shapes, and so on. You can even blend from an open object to a closed object.

The other options in the Blend dialog box are interesting. You can specify a rotation, which causes the blend steps to rotate. You

Advanced Topics ▲ 301

Blends

▼ *Figure 10.3. The guitar-to-circle blend*

▼ *Figure 10.4. Blended colors*

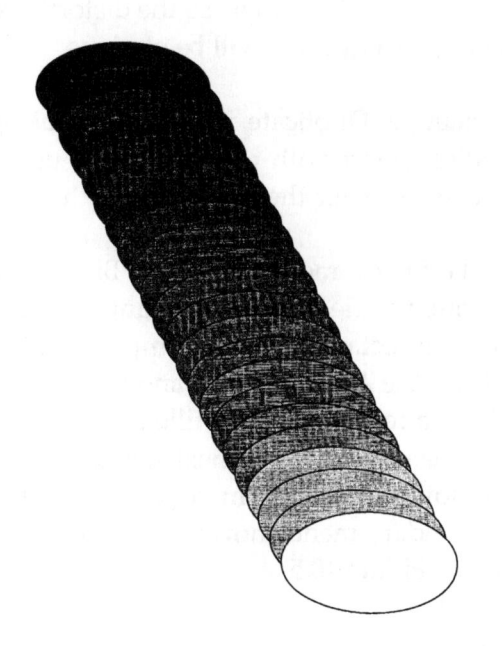

can also specify which nodes in the two objects should match. This means that the node you specify in the first object will be the same as the node you specify in the second object.

TIP

Another interesting effect can be achieved by clicking again on the objects selected for the blend. This will place them in their skew and rotate condition. Note that at the center of the selection rectangle there is a bulls-eye. This is the center of rotation, but it is also used in blends. Drag it away from the center and the blend will not be a straight line from one object to the other, but a curve that moves through the position of the center of rotation. The amount of deflection will be determined by the value entered in the Rotation text box—the larger the value, the larger the amount of deflection.

Manipulating Envelopes

What is an envelope? It is approximately the same as a selection rectangle, but it's much more flexible. You will create a blend from a large rectangle to a small rectangle so the distortions imposed on it by manipulating the envelope will be obvious.

1. Create a rectangle. Duplicate it and size it using one of the corner handles. Select both rectangles and use Align on the Arrange menu to center the rectangles both horizontally and vertically.
2. Pull down the Effects menu and select Blend. Make 20 blend steps, no rotation angle, and no matching nodes.
3. Drag a selection rectangle that encompasses all of the rectangles. Pull down the Arrange menu and select Group.

Now you have a rectangle that is filled with additional rectangles like Russian nesting dolls. The next step is to distort this set of rectangles. Pull down the Effects menu and select Edit Envelope. You'll see the secondary menu shown off to the side of the Effects menu, as shown in Figure 10.5.

▼ **Figure 10.5. The Edit Envelope menu**

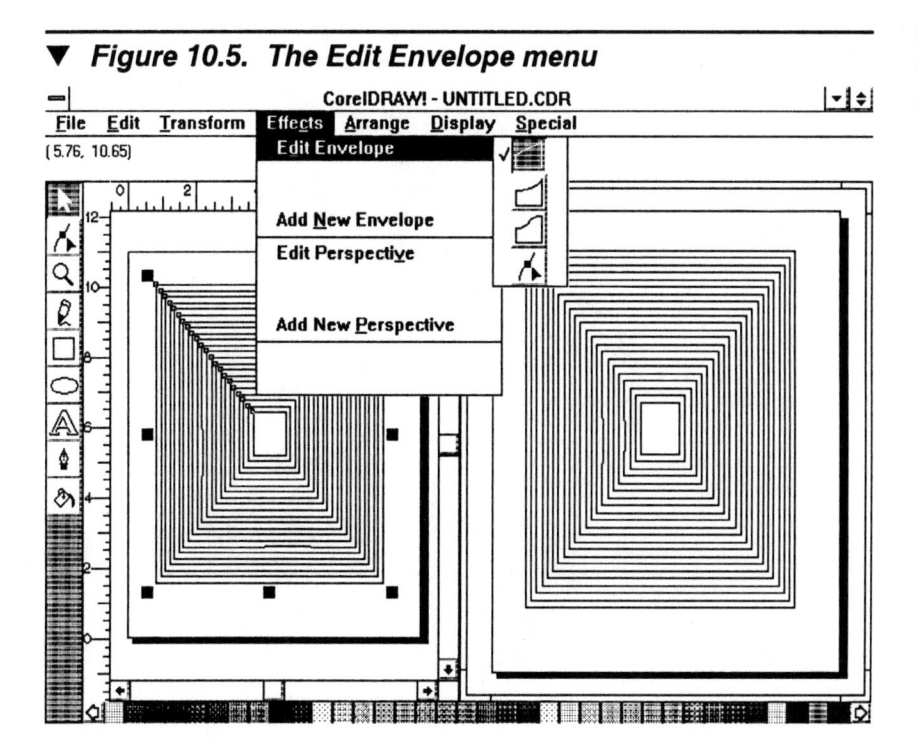

Manipulating Envelopes

This menu gives you the choice of making angular changes in the envelope, single-direction curves, dual-direction curves, or node-editing changes. The only way you can get a good picture of what these options will do for you is to try them all. Figure 10.6 shows how the first three options operate. Node-editing would be difficult to illustrate because it's completely free-form. The envelope looks like a selection rectangle. You manipulate it by dragging its handles. In node-editing mode, you are also provided with control points with which you can change the curvature of the envelope.

Now take some text and use the node-editing, free-form option to fit the text in a circle.

1. Draw a circle (hold down the Ctrl key while dragging an ellipse).
2. Place the name MARY on the screen in the font of your choice. Place the text inside the circle and enlarge the text so it fills the circle as nearly as possible.

▼ **Figure 10.6. Examples of envelope editing options**

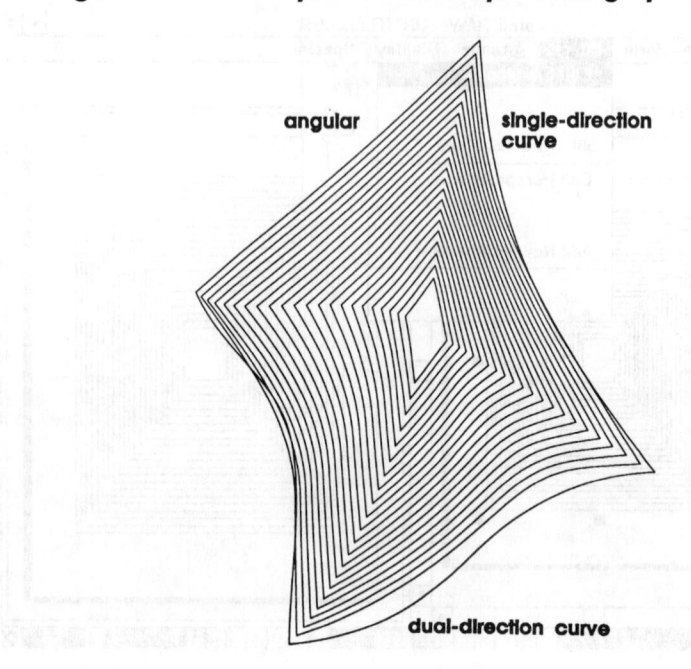

angular

single-direction curve

dual-direction curve

3. With the text selected, pull down the Effects menu and select Edit Envelope. Select node-editing. Place the handles of the envelope on the perimeter of the circle and adjust the control points associated with the handles until the envelope is as close to a circle as possible.
4. Click on the circle and press the Del key to eliminate it.

You'll see the screen shown in Figure 10.7.

There are three interesting constraint features involved with the edit envelope command, if you are using one of the constrained editing options (angular, single-, or double-curve). Holding the Shift key down while dragging one of the envelope handles will cause the handle on the opposite side to move in the opposite direction. Holding the Ctrl key down will cause the handle on the opposite side of the envelope to move in the same direction as the one you are moving. Holding both the Shift and Ctrl keys down and dragging a corner node will cause all the corner nodes to mirror each other. Dragging a side node with the Shift and Ctrl keys held down will cause all four side nodes to mirror each other.

Advanced Topics ▲ 305

Manipulating Envelopes

▼ *Figure 10.7. The resulting text*

Clear Envlope, the second option on the Effects menu, clears the last change you made to the envelope.

TIP

If you are editing the envelope of an object that has been converted to curves, and then you want to edit its nodes with the shape tool, you will discover that the shape tool returns you to envelope editing. You must select Convert to Curves again from the Arrange menu in order to edit the nodes of the object.

Copy Envelope From is another interesting option, which you will take a closer look at now.

1. Place the name BOB on the screen next to MARY.
2. With BOB selected, pull down the Effects menu and select Copy Envelope From.

3. Click the mouse cursor on MARY. BOB will instantly change to resemble MARY's shape (Figure 10.8).

▼ *Figure 10.8. BOB's envelope copied from MARY's*

If you have edited a shape's envelope and you want to start with a fresh, rectangular envelope, select Add New Envelope.

CHECK YOURSELF

1. Draw a line on the page area with the pencil tool and duplicate it. Place the two lines next to each other. Pull down the Effects menu and select Blend. Enter 100 for the blend steps and 360 for the rotation. When you click on OK, the blend starts.

ANSWER
1. The blend should look a little like a spoked cartwheel.

Perspective

CorelDRAW! now allows you to create images as if they were on a plane and then change the position of that plane relative to the apparent plane of the screen. Use MARY again to see how this works.

Perspective

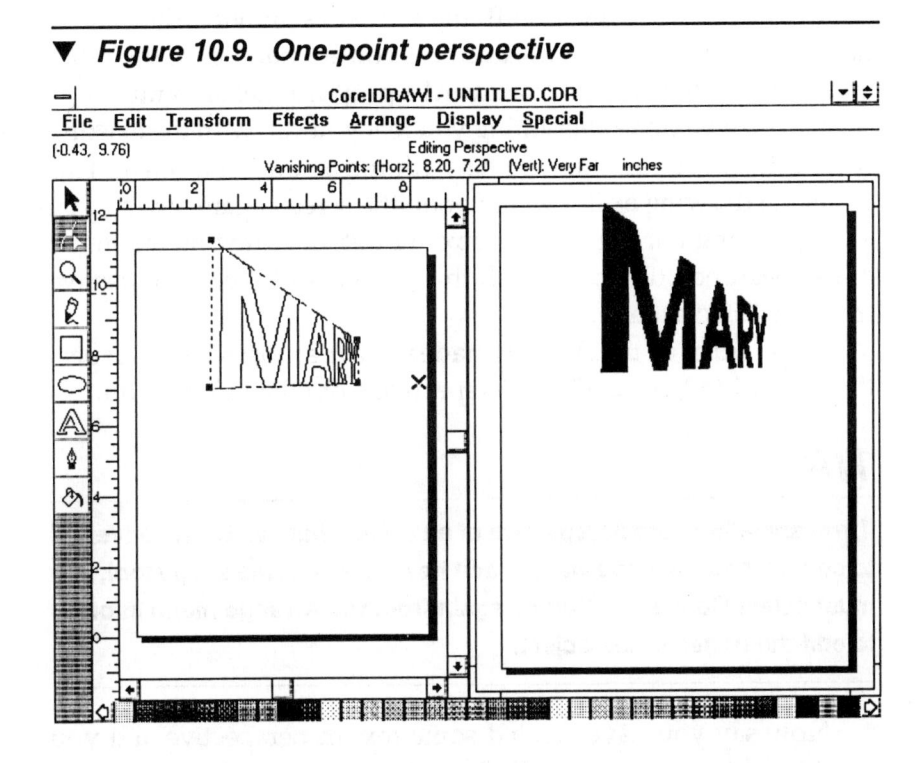

1. Enter the text MARY on the screen.
2. Pull down the Effects menu and select Edit Perpective. A rectangle will appear around the text very similar to the envelope edited in the previous section, except this envelope only has four handles, situated at the corners of the envelope.
3. Place the mouse pointer on the handle in the upper-left corner and drag it upward. Note that you are able to move the handle not just vertically, but horizontally as well. To constrain the horizontal movement of the handle, press the Ctrl key. Note the tiny X that appears at the right of the text. This is the vanishing point. The result is shown in Figure 10.9.

▼ *Figure 10.9. One-point perspective*

This form of perspective is called one-point perspective because it only has one vanishing point.

To add some complexity to the drawing, you can do two-point perspective. Drag the lower-left corner to the right until a second tiny X appears on the screen. This is the second vanishing point. The X's need not appear on the screen. If you use perspective, the X may not be visible, but there is always a vanishing point.

You can reposition the vanishing point (if it's visible).

> **TIP**
>
> **Moving a control handle toward the center of a drawing causes the drawing to appear to move away from you. Moving a control handle away from the center makes the drawing appear to be coming closer to you.**

You can constrain the drawing to a single vanishing point by holding down the Ctrl key when you move the control handles.

If you hold down the Shift and Ctrl keys, moving the control handle up on one side will cause the control handle on the other end of that side to move downward a proportional amount.

If you have done everything you feel you can with the existing perspective, you can start again by adding a new perspective. This treats the drawing as if it were flat on the screen again, giving you a new, rectangular perspective box, though the drawing retains its old appearance. To accomplish this, select Add New Perspective from the Effects menu.

To get rid of all the changes made since the most recent perspective was added, select Clear Perspective from the Effect menu.

> **TIP**
>
> **If you are editing the perspective of an object that has been converted to curves, and then you want to edit its nodes with the shape tool, you must select Convert to Curves again from the Arrange menu in order to edit the nodes of the object.**

Now say you have created some text in perspective and you want to add more text to it. Will you have to spend hours fiddling with the text and Perspective, trying to get it to appear on the same plane as the original? No way! You can use Copy Perspective From. In Figure 10.10, there is some text already in perspective and some new text added with no evident perspective.

▼ **Figure 10.10. The problem: add perspective to BOB**

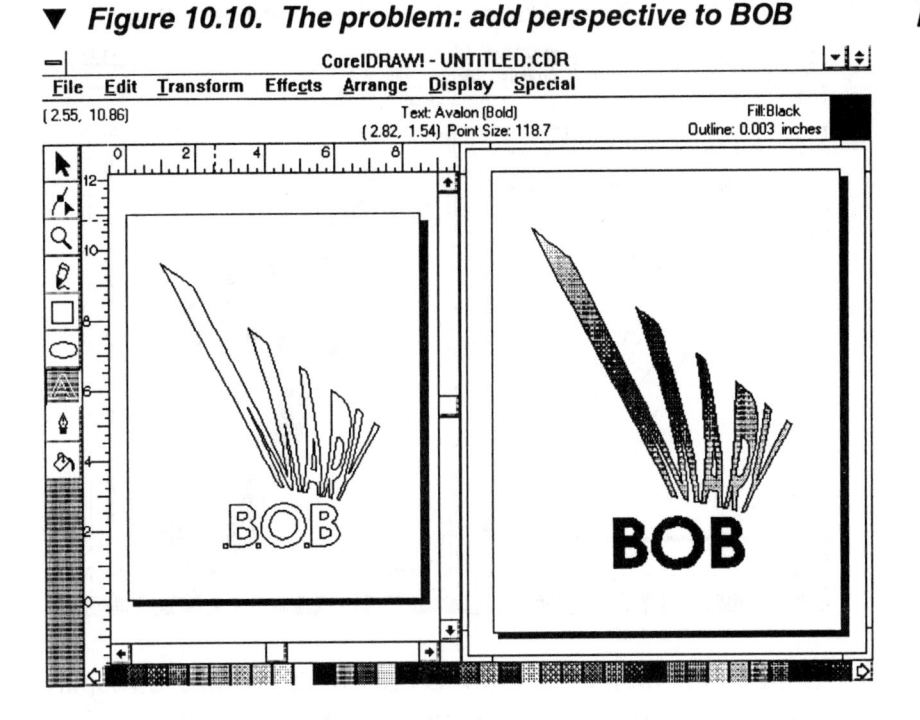

Perspective

1. Select BOB.
2. Pull down the Effects menu.
3. Select the option Copy Perspective From.
4. Click the mouse cursor on the object from which you want to copy the perspective (MARY). Instantly, BOB will take on MARY's perspective (Figure 10.11).

Well, even now, they're not perfect. They have the same perspective, but they look as if they belong in the same spot rather than next to each other. Why is that? It's because they each have the same vanishing points relative to themselves, but different vanishing points from each other. How are you going to resolve this problem? You will have to find a way to make the vanishing points coincide.

1. Begin by clicking on the object you want to leave alone. Pull down the Effects menu and select Edit Perspective. This will display the vanishing point (if it doesn't, try reducing the size of the entire drawing).

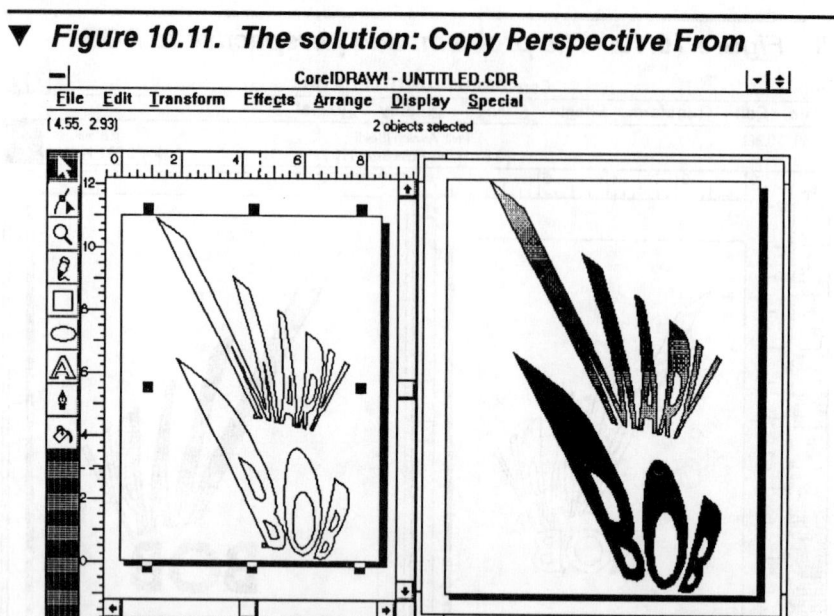

▼ **Figure 10.11.** *The solution: Copy Perspective From*

2. If the rulers aren't visible, select Show Rulers in the Display menu. Place the mouse pointer on the top ruler and drag downward. A guideline will come down with the mouse. Place the guideline on the visible vanishing point. If a second vanishing point is visible, pull out a second guideline for it.
3. Pull similar guidelines out of the left ruler, placing them on the vanishing points.
4. Click on the other object. If you're still in Perspective-editing mode, the vanishing points of the scond drawing should appear instantly.
5. Place the mouse pointer on the vanishing points of the currently selected object and drag them to the intersections of the guidelines. The result should look something like Figure 10.12.

Extruding

There's something else new in *CorelDRAW!*. Not only can you do perspectives, blends, and envelope manipulation, but you can take a two-dimensional object and push it into three-dimensions.

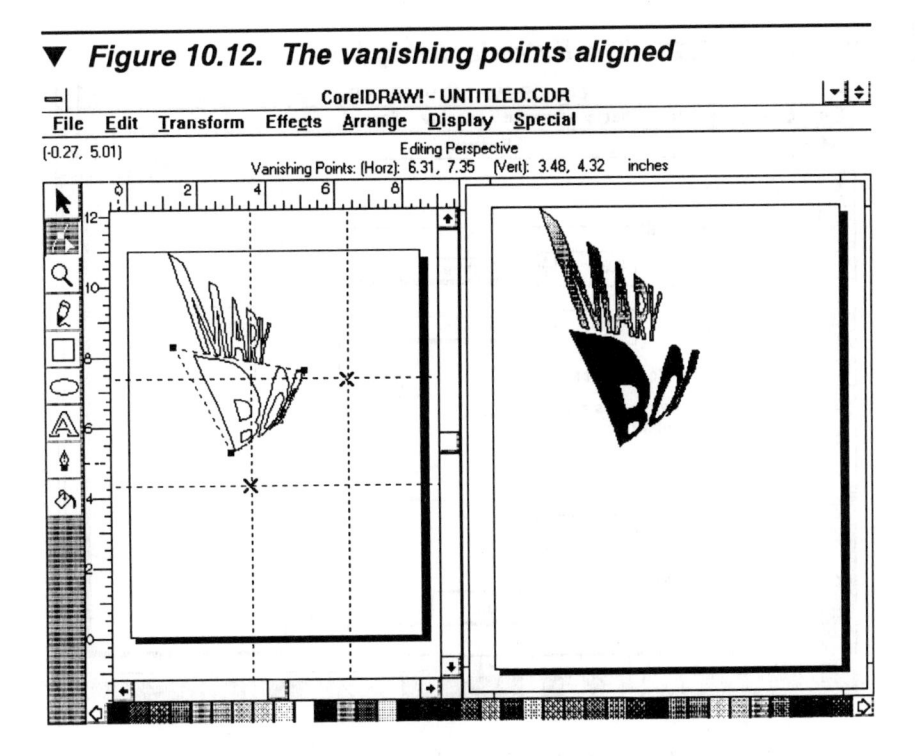

Extruding

▼ *Figure 10.12. The vanishing points aligned*

Start with a simple example. You will turn a rectangle into a rectangular solid.

1. Use the rectangle tool to create a rectangle on the page area. Fill the rectangle with a white color.
2. Pull down the Effects menu and select Extrude (or press Ctrl-E). You will see the dialog box shown in Figure 10.13.

The important parts of this dialog box are:

▲ The perspective box. With this checked, the extrusion will give the appearance of three-dimensionality.
▲ The Vanishing point (if Perspective is selected) or the Extrusion Offset (if Perspective is not selected). This establishes the direction the extrusion takes when it leaves the existing limits of the object.
▲ Absolute Coordinates (if Perspective is selected). Allows the offset to be specified according to ruler coordinates rather than relative to the object.

▼ **Figure 10.13. The Extrude dialog box**

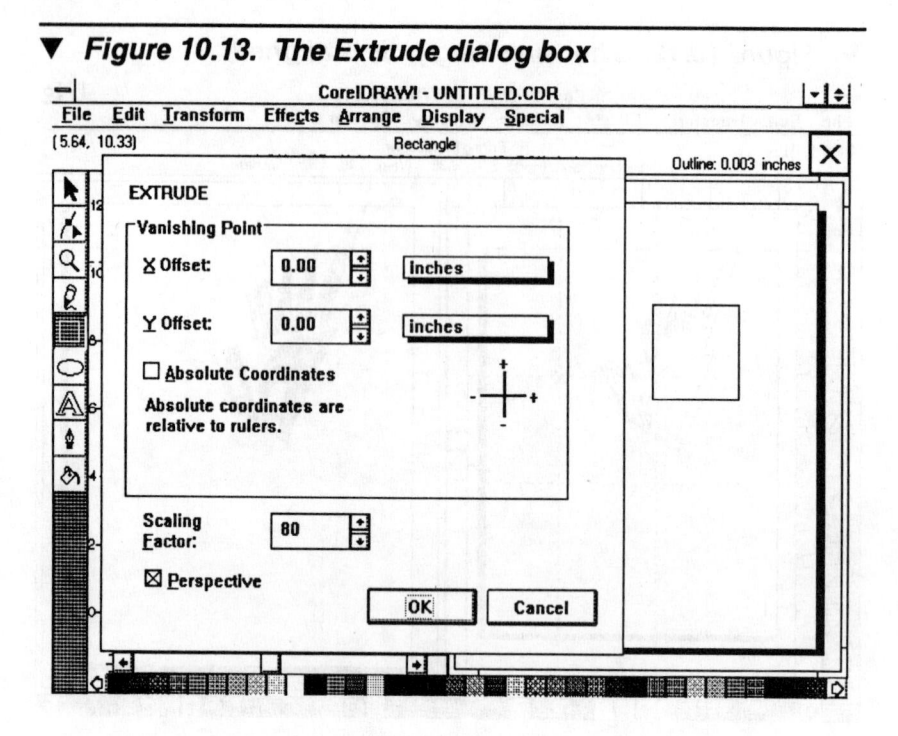

▲ The Scaling Factor tells where the second plane is relative to the plane of the screen. A value between 0 and 99 represents a position behind the object. A value between 101 and 200 represents a position in front of the object.

3. Select Perspective, with an offset of -2 inches for X and Y. Leave Absolute Coordinates turned off and set the scaling factor to 50. The result is shown in Figure 10.14.

Interestingly, the extrusion is entirely independent of the object, so once you have extruded an object, you can move the object away and leave just the extrusion behind, as is done in Figure 10.15.

Programming the Right Mouse Button

The right button of the mouse is a pretty useless thing most of the time. The only use it generally has is for selecting the arrowhead to

Advanced Topics ▲ 313

▼ *Figure 10.14. The extruded rectangle*

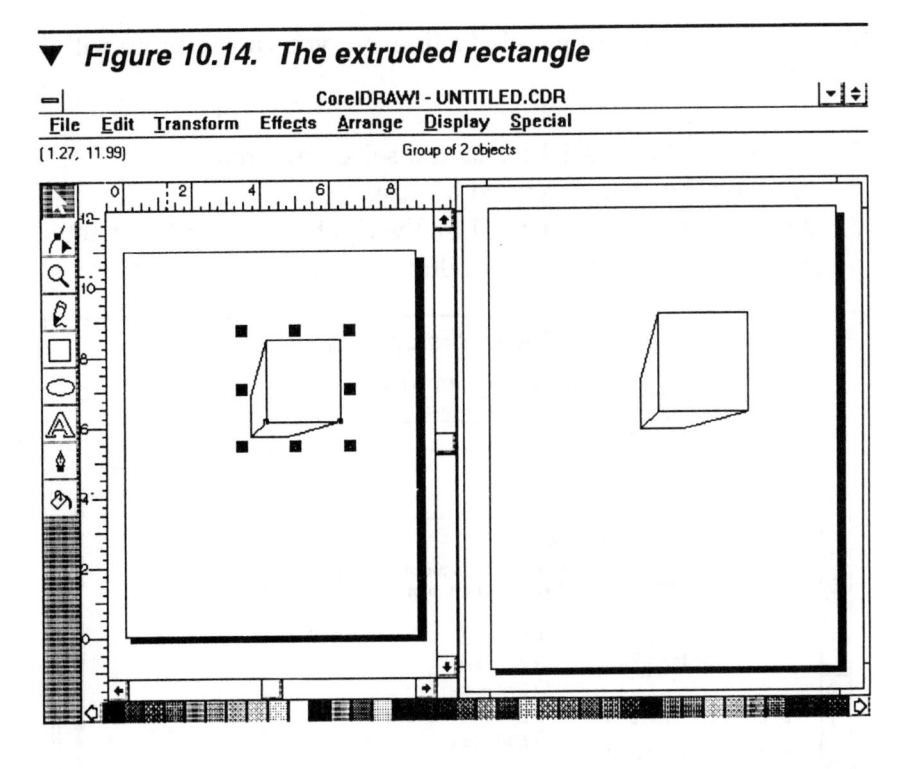

Programming the Right Mouse Button

▼ *Figure 10.15. Moving the object away from the extrusion*

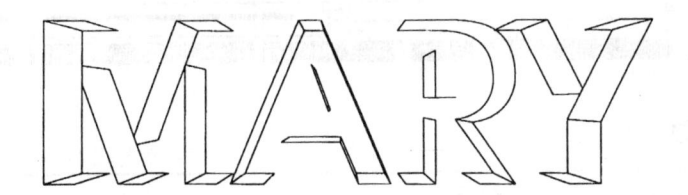

place on the terminating end of a line. But you can do more with it than that.

1. Pull down the Special menu and select Preferences.
2. Click on the button marked Mouse.
3. As you can see in Figure 10.16, the right mouse button is set to Not Used. Simply make the alternate selection you prefer.

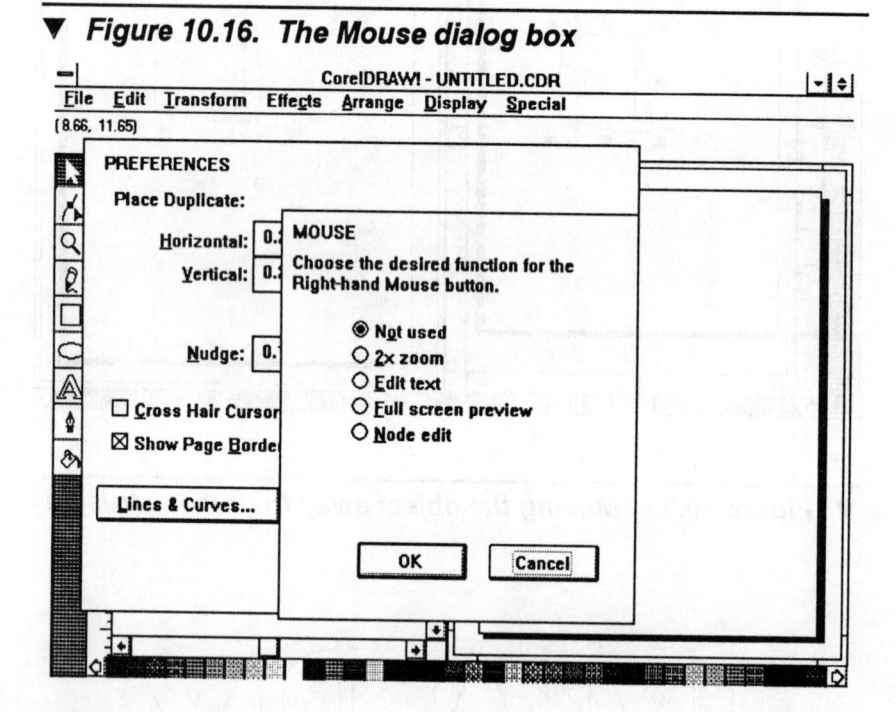

▼ **Figure 10.16. The Mouse dialog box**

TIP

Watch for changes in the way Windows uses the mouse buttons in versions after 3.0. These changes may also result in changes in the way *CorelDRAW!* uses the buttons.

Repeat

One command that doesn't fit under any other heading, but is so useful that it deserves mentioning is the Repeat command found on the Edit menu. Selecting this command has the effect of issuing the last command again. This can be a tremendous timesaver when doing the same operation to several objects on the screen.

Repeat

CHECK YOURSELF

1. Draw a rectangle and select Edit Perspective from the Effects menu. Hold down the Shift and Ctrl keys and drag the upper-right handle up.

2. Continuing check yourself 1, keep moving the upper-right handle until the vanishing point appears on the screen. Note which side of the screen it's on.

3. Draw a curving line on the screen, then select Extrude from the Effects menu. Make the offset 1-inch in both X and Y directions and set the Absolute Coordinates at 50.

ANSWERS

1. The left handle should move down.

2. The vanishing point should appear on the left side of the object.

3. The curving line should look like a ribbon.

Exercises

This exercise assumes that you have *CorelDRAW!* running and a new, blank page area is visible. If you already have something on the screen, save it and select New from the File menu.

What You Should Do	How the Computer Responds
1. Enter the text IMP in capital letters in Avalon text. Draw a rectangle around it that is about twice as tall and four times as wide as the text. The text should be roughly centered in the rectangle. If they are not aligned pretty closely, select both and use the Align command on the Arrange menu to center them vertically and horizontally. Click on the Pick tool and drag a selection rectangle around both the text and the rectangle.	1. Both the text and the rectangle will be selected.
2. Pull down the Effects menu and select Blend. In the Blend dialog box, enter 10 as the number of blend steps. Click on OK.	2. Note that most of the blend steps are broken.
3. Make sure the pick tool is selected. Drag the blend an inch to the right.	3. The blend steps will move but the original rectangle and text will remain in place.
4. With the blend steps still selected, pull down the Arrange menu and select Break Apart. Pull down the Arrange menu again.	4. Break Apart is still available, and the blend steps are still combined. Why? The programmers at Corel Systems, whether by accident or design, made blend steps so they couldn't be broken apart.

5. Press the Del key to eliminate the blend steps. Click on the original text. Pull down the Effects menu and select Edit Envelope. In the resulting menu, select the second from the bottom entry. Hold down the Shift and Ctrl keys and drag the node in the middle of the bottom of the envelope.

6. Pull down the Edit menu and select Undo.

7. Hold down the Shift key and drag the top-left corner of the envelope up to the corner of the rectangle.

8. Click on the pick tool. Click on the rectangle and press the Del key. Click on the text to select it. Pull down the Effects menu and select Extrude. In the EXTRUDE dialog box, set the offsets at 1-inch for X and Y. Set the scaling factor to 40. Make sure the Perspective check box is checked.

5. The text will expand to a diamond shape as all four side handles move outward in concert.

6. The text will return to its original appearance, but it will still be available for envelope editing.

7. Both left corners will move the same distance in opposite directions. The envelope will look a little like a ketchup bottle lying on its side.

8. The text will be made to look as if it is three-dimensional. You might want to color the extrusion (it's the part selected after the extrusion) by clicking on a color on the palette at the bottom of the screen. This will make the extrusion more distinct.

Exercises

9. With only the extrusion selected (not the text) press the Del key to remove it from the screen. Select the text. Pull down the Effects menu and select Edit Perspective.

10. Hold down the Ctrl and the Shift keys and drag the upper-right corner of the envelope about an inch upward.

9. A new envelope will appear around the text, perfectly rectangular.

10. As the upper-right node moves straight up (the effect of the Ctrl key) the lower-right node moves straight down the same distance (the effect of the Shift key).

Appendix

Quick keyboard commands

About *CorelDRAW!*	Alt-F,D	Alt-A,S	Straighten Text
Add New Envelope	Alt-C,N	Alt-A,T	Fit Text to Path
Add New Perspective	Alt-C,P	Alt-A,U	Ungroup
Align	Alt-A,A	Alt-A,V	Convert to Curves
Align	Ctrl-A	Alt-Backspace	Undo
Align to Baseline	Alt-A,L	Alt-C,B	Blend
Align to Baseline	Ctrl-Z	Alt-C,C	Clear Envelope
Alt-A,A	Align	Alt-C,D	Edit Envelope
Alt-A,B	To Back	Alt-C,F	Copy Perspective From
Alt-A,C	Combine	Alt-C,L	Clear Perspective
Alt-A,F	To Front	Alt-C,N	Add New Envelope
Alt-A,G	Group	Alt-C,P	Add New Perspective
Alt-A,K	Break Apart	Alt-C,R	Copy Envelope From
Alt-A,L	Align to Baseline	Alt-C,V	Edit Perspective
Alt-A,N	Back One	Alt-C,X	Extrude
Alt-A,O	Forward One	Alt-D,A	Auto Update
Alt-A,R	Reverse Order	Alt-D,B	Show Bitmaps

Alt-D,C	Show Color Palette	Alt-S,M	Merge-Back
Alt-D,F	Show Full-Screen Preview	Alt-S,X	Extract
Alt-D,G	Snap to Guidelines	Alt-T,C	Clear Transformations
Alt-D,I	Grid Setup	Alt-T,M	Move
Alt-D,L	Guidelines Setup	Alt-T,R	Rotate and Skew
Alt-D,O	Preview Selected Only	Alt-T,S	Stretch and Mirror
Alt-D,P	Show Preview	Auto Update	Alt-D,A
Alt-D,R	Show Rulers	Back One	Alt-A,N
Alt-D,S	Show Status Line	Back One	PgDn
Alt-D,S,S	Snap to Grid	Blend	Alt-C,B
Alt-D,T	Show Preview Toolbox	Blend	Ctrl-B
Alt-D,W	Refresh Wire Screen	Break Apart	Alt-A,K
Alt-E,A	Select All	Break Apart	Ctrl-K
Alt-E,C	Copy	Character Attributes	Alt-E,H
Alt-E,D	Duplicate	Clear	Alt-E,L
Alt-E,E	Redo	Clear	Del
Alt-E,H	Character Attributes	Clear Envelope	Alt-C,C
Alt-E,L	Clear	Clear Perspective	Alt-C,L
Alt-E,P	Paste	Clear Transformations	Alt-T,C
Alt-E,R	Repeat	Combine	Alt-A,C
Alt-E,S	Copy Style From	Combine	Ctrl-C
Alt-E,T	Edit Text	Control Panel	Alt-F,C
Alt-E,U	Undo	Convert to Curves	Alt-A,V
Alt-F,A	Save As	Convert to Curves	Ctrl-V
Alt-F,C	Control Panel	Copy	Alt-E,C
Alt-F,D	About *CorelDRAW!*	Copy	Ctrl-Ins
Alt-F,E	Export	Copy Envelope From	Alt-C,R
Alt-F,G	Page Setup	Copy Perspective From	Alt-C,F
Alt-F,I	Import	Copy Style From	Alt-E,S
Alt-F,M	Print Merge	Create Arrow	Alt-S,A
Alt-F,N	New	Create Pattern	Alt-S,C
Alt-F,O	Open	Ctrl-A	Align
Alt-F,P	Print	Ctrl-B	Blend
Alt-F,S	Save	Ctrl-C	Combine
Alt-F,X	Exit	Ctrl-D	Duplicate
Alt-Return	Redo	Ctrl-E	Extrude
Alt-S,A	Create Arrow	Ctrl-F	Fit Text to Path
Alt-S,C	Create Pattern	Ctrl-G	Group
Alt-S,E	Preferences	Ctrl-Ins	Copy

Appendix ▲ 321

Ctrl-J	Preferences	F10	Shape tool
Ctrl-K	Break Apart	F11	Fountain Fill
Ctrl-L	Move	F12	Outline Pen
Ctrl-N	Rotate and Skew	Fit Text to Path	Alt-A,T
Ctrl-O	Open	Fit Text to Path	Ctrl-F
Ctrl-P	Print	Fit zoom in window	F4
Ctrl-Q	Stretch and Mirror	Forward One	Alt-A,O
Ctrl-R	Repeat	Forward One	PgUp
Ctrl-S	Save	Full-Screen Preview	F9
Ctrl-T	Edit Text	Grid Setup	Alt-D,I
Ctrl-U	Ungroup	Group	Alt-A,G
Ctrl-V	Convert to Curves	Group	Ctrl-G
Ctrl-W	Refresh Wire Screen	Guidelines Setup	Alt-D,L
Ctrl-X	Exit	Import	Alt-F,I
Ctrl-Y	Snap to Grid	Merge-Back	Alt-S,M
Ctrl-Z	Align to Baseline	Move	Alt-T,M
Cut	Shift-Del	Move	Ctrl-L
Del	Clear	New	Alt-F,N
Duplicate	Alt-E,D	New Object Outline Color	Shift-F12
Duplicate	Ctrl-D	New Object Uniform Fill	F12
Edit Envelope	Alt-C,D	Open	Alt-F,O
Edit Perspective	Alt-C,V	Open	Ctrl-O
Edit Text	Alt-E,T	Page Setup	Alt-F,G
Edit Text	Ctrl-T	Paste	Alt-E,P
Ellipse tool	F7	Paste	Shift-Ins
Exit	Alt-F,X	Pencil tool	F5
Exit	Ctrl-X	PgDn	Back One
Export	Alt-F,E	PgUp	Forward One
Extract	Alt-S,X	Preferences	Alt-S,E
Extrude	Alt-C,X	Preferences	Ctrl-J
Extrude	Ctrl-E	Preview Selected Only	Alt-D,O
F2	Zoom in	Print	Alt-F,P
F3	Zoom out	Print	Ctrl-P
F4	Fit zoom in window	Print Merge	Alt-F,M
F5	Pencil tool	Rectangle tool	F6
F6	Rectangle tool	Redo	Alt-E,E
F7	Ellipse tool	Redo	Alt-Return
F8	Text tool	Refresh Wire Screen	Alt-D,W
F9	Full-Screen Preview toggle	Refresh Wire Screen	Ctrl-W

Repeat	Alt-E,R	Show Preview	Shift-F9
Repeat	Ctrl-R	Show Preview Toolbox	Alt-D,T
Reverse Order	Alt-A,R	Show Rulers	Alt-D,R
Rotate and Skew	Alt-T,R	Show Status Line	Alt-D,S
Rotate and Skew	Ctrl-N	Snap to Grid	Alt-D,S,S
Save	Alt-F,S	Snap to Grid	Ctrl-Y
Save	Ctrl-S	Snap to Guidelines	Alt-D,G
Save As	Alt-F,A	Straighten Text	Alt-A,S
Select All	Alt-E,A	Stretch and Mirror	Alt-T,S
Shift-Del		Stretch and Mirror	Ctrl-Q
Shift-F4	Show page	Text tool	F8
Shift-F9	Show Preview toggle	To Back	Alt-A,B
Shift-F11	Fill Tool	To Back	Shift-PdDn
Shift-F12	Outline Color	To Front	Alt-A,F
Shift-Ins	Paste	To Front	Shift-PgUp
Shift-PdDn	To Back	Undo	Alt-Backspace
Shift-PgUp	To Front	Undo	Alt-E,U
Show Bitmaps	Alt-D,B	Ungroup	Alt-A,U
Show Color Palette	Alt-D,C	Ungroup	Ctrl-U
Show Full-Screen Preview	Alt-D,F	Zoom in	F2
Show page	Shift-F4	Zoom out	F3
Show Preview	Alt-D,P		

Glossary

Alignment. This refers to the placement of objects relative to one another. *CorelDRAW!* can center objects or align them with their tops, bottoms, or right or left sides.

Archiving. Compressing files for backup storage. *CorelDRAW!* comes with LHarc, a shareware compression program. You can use this program to compress your drawings to get more on a backup disk. Just type LHARC at the command line in DOS (not in *Windows*) to see a help screen that will help you figure out how to use the program. Mosaic also has a feature that allows files to be compressed into archives.

Autotrace. A method for turning bitmap graphics into vector drawings. It looks for edges, where black borders on white, or where colors or shades of gray border on one another and places a line at this border. There is a simple autotrace within *CorelDRAW!* and a more complete version in Corel Trace.

Backup. A backup is simply a spare copy of a program or other kind of file. Prudent computer users back up their software as soon as they purchase it and back up their data files once a week. Other computer users have been known to back up as often as every day. If you fail to make regular backups, you will certainly regret it one day.

Bezier curve. A Bezier curve is a curve determined (or described) by a method developed by a French mathematician named Bezier. A Bezier is determined by its beginning and end points, its "launch angles", which show the angle at which the curve meets its endpoints and how much force or "stretch" is involved in its movement (these are represented by the control points in *CorelDRAW!*).

Bitmap. A kind of graphic that is, in essence, laid out on a grid. Individual points in the grid may be turned on (black) or turned off (white) or, in some cases, contain a number representing a color or a shade of gray. The grid may be very fine, even 300 dpi or higher, but the graphic is made up of points that don't adjust well when sized, and have no relationship with one another, making editing more difficult. The alternative to bitmap graphics is vector graphics. Raster graphics is another word for bitmap graphics.

Button. A button is a device in a dialog box in *Windows*. The most common buttons are Cancel (which means "make the dialog box go away and don't take any action") and OK ("go ahead and take action based on the settings in this dialog box").

CAD. Computer-aided design (or CAD) is the process of design with the mediation of a computer to take care of the simple tasks like file management and redrawing. CAD lets you use your imagination and never fear to make a change because it will mean redrawing everything. The CAD output can then be used to operate machine tools to create real objects that match the drawing. This is known as computer-aided machining (CAM) and you will often see these two acronyms together, as in CAD/CAM.

Check box. A check box is a device you will find in *Windows* dialog boxes. A check box is called that because when its condition is set, an X appears in its box.

Clear. Clear means Delete in *Windows* parlance. No copy of the selected object is sent to the Clipboard. The only way to bring the object back is to select Undo from the Edit menu.

Clicking. To click, press the left mouse button once and release it immediately.

Clip art. Clip art is predrawn art. Using it saves you time and effort when producing graphics. If you create the main part of the art, say a house, you can decorate it with shrubbery and lawn flamingos from a clip art collection.

Clipboard. This is a temporary storage area in *Windows*. This is where graphics go when you select Cut and Copy from the Edit menu.

Close box. The box in the upper-left corner of all windows is known as the system menu or the close box because clicking on it once calls up the system menu and double clicking on it closes the window.

Closed object. A closed object is an object whose outline is complete: the beginning point is joined to the end point. Only closed objects can be filled with patterns and colors.

Control panel. This is a program within *Windows* that is used to make settings in *Windows*. You will most often use the control panel to change the printer or printer orientation.

Control points. These are the handles used to manipulate Bezier curves. The distance that a control point appears from the end point is an indication of the strength of its influence on the curve and the angle is shown by its literal angle from a line that might be drawn to the other endpoint of the curve.

Copy. This term, as it is used in *Windows*, means that a replica of the currently selected object will be sent to temporary storage on the Clipboard.

Curve. Anything that is not a straight line is a curve. Curves take more memory and other resources than straight lines.

Cut. This term, as it is used in *Windows*, means that a replica of the currently selected object will be sent to temporary storage in the Clipboard and the original is eliminated from the screen.

Deselect. Clicking away from all objects will deselect all objects. Clicking on a selected object while holding the Shift key down will deselect it.

Dialog box. A dialog box is literally a box full of options that will appear on the screen. Some of the selections on the box may call up other dialog boxes. When you see an ellipse (...) in a menu or a button in a dialog box, that means the item will call up a dialog box.

DISKCOPY. This is a DOS command that copies every piece of information from one disk onto another, including the arrangement of files on the disk (which is not an action performed by COPY or XCOPY).

Double clicking. This is an action that involves very rapidly pressing and releasing the left mouse button twice.

Dragging. This action is accomplished by placing the mouse pointer on an object, pressing and holding the left mouse button, and then moving the mouse pointer to a new position.

Duplicate. This command in the Edit menu creates a copy of whatever object is selected, but the copy is placed on the screen rather than in the Clipboard. The duplicate is placed very near the original, but at a slight offset. You can set the offset with the Preferences command in the Special menu.

Ellipse tool. The ellipse tool will create an ellipse when it is selected and the mouse is dragged within the *CorelDRAW!* window. By holding the Ctrl key down while dragging, you can create a perfect circle.

Em. An em is literally the width of the letter M in a font. It's the widest letter and therefore the standard width to use for measuring kerning and word spacing.

Fill tool. The fill tool is used to fill objects with patterns and colors, or to remove the fill.

Font. A font (sometimes loosely referred to as a typeface) is a group of characters that share certain attributes, like weight (thickness of lines), serifs, and other components.

FORMAT. This is a DOS command that causes the computer to prepare a disk to receive data. Once a disk is formatted, it need not be formatted again, but a disk fresh out of the box must be formatted or it cannot be used.

Fountain. A gradation of color or shading across an area.

Grayed menu item. Items that appear grayed in menus (rather than black) are not available at the current time for some reason. Clicking on these items has no effect.

Grid. A grid is a set of fixed points on the screen that allows you to easily place objects at regular intervals. See Snap.

Guideline. A guideline is an extension of the ruler. You can place a guideline anywhere on the screen to indicate alignment, for example. A guideline is obtained by placing the mouse on a ruler and dragging it.

Handles. When an item is selected and the pick tool is in use, the item will be in the middle of a selection rectangle with eight handles, or tiny rectangles, around it.

Justification. This is a term that refers to the alignment of text. Full justification means that both the right and left margins are even. Some people refer to fully justified text simply as justified text. Others refer to right-aligned text as right-justified and left-aligned text as left-justified.

Keyboard shortcut. A quick way to enter a command on the keyboard that might be entered more slowly with the mouse. The appendix of this book contains many keyboard shortcuts.

Line. A line is anything that isn't a curve in a drawing. Lines have no control points, so they represent a savings in memory and other system resources over equivalent curves.

Maximize. A window is maximized when it fills the entire monitor screen. Maximize is a command on the system menu.

Menu. A menu is a list of options. Good programming practice dictates that the items on a specific menu should be related to each other or the same class of actions. Thus, all the commands having to do with disk access are available on the File menu.

Menu bar. All of the most important menus for a program are brought together at the top of the window in a line. this is called the menu bar.

Minimize. A window that has been reduced to an icon is minimized. This doesn't mean that the program is shut off. In *Windows*, minimized programs can continue to operate, though they are not generally given 100 percent of the system resources. Minimize is a command on the system menu.

Mouse. A mouse is an input device used to closely mimic the movement of the human hand on the desktop. It isn't perfect, but it's better than most of the alternatives. It's about the size and shape of a bar of soap and generally it's connected to the computer by a cable that transmits information to the computer about your movements.

Move bar. The move bar is the same as the title bar of a window. It contains the name of the operating program and often the name of the document or drawing currently in memory. If

Handles
▼
Move bar

the window isn't maximized, you can place the mouse pointer on the move bar and drag the window around by it.

Nodes. In the wire frame window, the curves and lines of the wire frame are terminated by nodes, also loosely referred to as end points.

Object. An object is an individual item on the screen. Objects can be grouped or combined, making many objects into one object.

Object-oriented. A drawing program that constructs objects and then manipulates these objects to create drawings is called an object-oriented drawing program (OODP).

Open object. An object whose outline is not completely closed is an open object. An open object cannot be filled in *CorelDRAW!* unless it is first closed.

Outline tool. The outline tool is used to perform node editing, bitmap clipping, and for working with the character attributes of text.

Page area. The central area of the *CorelDRAW!* window is partially filled with a representation of a sheet of paper. This is what is referred to as the page area.

Paint program. Paint programs are programs that manipulate screen memory. They are not object oriented and produce bitmap graphics.

Palette. A collection of colors for use in a graphic.

Paragraph text. Text that is entered in a block format is referred to as paragraph text. It is the only kind of text that can be fully justified in *CorelDRAW!*. Paragraph text makes use of a property called *word wrap* to limit the lengths of individual lines. If the text is too large to fit in the paragraph block, the excess will simply not appear on the screen or in the printout.

Paste. Paste is an item on the Edit menu that brings information back from the Clipboard and places it on the screen. The information remains on the Clipboard, so it can be pasted more than once.

Pencil tool. The pencil tool is the tool used for autotracing and freehand drawing.

Pica. A unit of measurement equivalent to approximately 1/6 inch.

Pick tool. The pick tool is the primary tool used for selecting and manipulating objects on the page. It's the arrow-shaped tool at the top of the toolbox.

Pixel. An individual dot of light on the monitor is a pixel. It is the smallest unit of graphic information available on the monitor. Paint programs manipulate individual pixels, using them to paint a low-resolution picture.

Point A unit of measurement equivalent to approximately 1/72 inch.

PostScript. PostScript is an interpreted language for describing pages. In whatever device it is used, it will drive that device to create a graphic at its maximum resolution, whether it is a 300 dpi laser printer, a 1200 dpi typesetter, or a 72 dpi monitor.

Precedence. Precedence determines the order that objects are drawn on the screen.

Preview. The preview screen shows an approximation of the graphic as it will appear on paper.

Program group. *Windows* organizes its programs according to tasks in special windows called program groups. When *CorelDRAW!* is installed, all the associated programs are placed in a special program group called Corel Applications.

Program item. The individual programs in a program group are called program items. They are icons that represent the programs.

Radio button. Certain items in dialog boxes are called radio buttons. They are like check boxes, but checking one box unchecks all the other boxes.

Raster. The raster is the beam of electrons your monitor uses to brighten the pixels on the screen. Since the pixels are, in effect, individual units of the raster, paint programs are referred to as raster (as opposed to vector) graphics.

Rectangle tool. The rectangle tool is the item in the toolbox used for creating rectangles and squares.

Registration. A registration mark is a tiny cross used to position a piece of paper or a film negative.

Restore. Restore is a screen size between maximized and minimized. It is one of the options on the system menu.

Ruler. The ruler is a literal measuring device that can be turned on at the top and left side of the *CorelDRAW!* window.

Pick tool
▼
Ruler

Selection rectangle. You can drag a selection rectangle with the shape tool or the pick tool. It is used to enclose items you want to have selected. Any items not enclosed completely in the selection rectangle won't be selected. Once an item is selected, the selection rectangle is represented by the positions of eight tiny black handles that can be used to distort or rotate the selected block of items.

Shape tool. The shape tool is used for node editing. It's the second item in the toolbox.

Skew. If you picture a rectangle being forced under pressure into the shape most people associate with the word parallelogram, you have a pretty good idea what skew is. When you skew an object, the side you are skewing moves parallel to its opposite side, which remains stationary. The other two sides "lean" to accommodate the action.

Status line. The status line is a region just beneath the menu bar at the top of the *CorelDRAW!* window that tells certain information about the selected object and the position of the mouse pointer in the window.

System menu. This menu is also known as the close box. It is a small rectangle at the top-left corner of all windows. Click on it once to see a menu of system actions for sizing the window. Also called the Control menu.

Text box. A text box is a rectangle within a dialog box where you can type information. Generally, if there is text in a text box, you can double click in the box to select the information completely. Then when you type your information, the information that existed when the box was called up will automatically be deleted.

Text string. If you click on the text tool, then click on the page area, and then enter text in the Text dialog box, it will be placed on the screen as a text string. This is distinct from paragraph text (see Paragraph text). You are responsible for making sure your lines are of the right length.

Text tool. The text tool is the tool in the toolbox that shows the letter A. It's used to place strings and paragraphs on the page area, as well as symbols from the symbol libraries.

Title bar. The title bar is the part of any window that contains the name of the operating program and usually the name of the currently open document. It's also called the move bar (see Move bar).

Tool box. The toolbox is a kind of supplemental menu bar that runs down the left side of the *CorelDRAW!* window.

Trace. See Autotrace.

Type size. A measure of the height of a letter in points (a value approximately equal to 1/72 inch).

Type style. This term usually refers to italic, bold, or bold-italic.

Typeface. This term is often loosely interchanged with the word font, although its actual meaning is not quite the same. A font is a typeface (like Times-Roman) in a particular style, like roman, italic, bold, or bold-italic. Typeface refers to all of these at once. This is a distinction that is rarely made in desktop publishing. Generally you can get away with using the words typeface and font interchangeably.

Vector. A vector is a line drawn from one point on the screen to another without reference to the raster. Oscilloscopes use vectors. The idealized way vectors trace objects on the screen is similar to the way PostScript describes them to the printer engine of a laser printer and the way *CorelDRAW!* saves its graphics. Therefore, *vector graphics* is used to refer to drawn images, as opposed to painted raster graphics.

Windows. Areas of the screen controlled by a single program are called windows. Windows contain menus, close boxes, move bars, and other features not typically found in dialog boxes. That's one way to differentiate between the two.

Wire frame. This is the bare bones of a drawing, including nothing but the outlines of objects.

Wrap. Wrap or word wrap is when text will automatically break at the end of a line.

Zoom tool. The zoom tool is the tool in the toolbox that looks like a magnifying glass. It's used to take closer looks at objects on the screen.

Tool box
▼
Zoom tool

Index

Actual Size, 172-73
Add, 90, 210
Alignment
    of nodes, 88-90
    of objects, 75-76, 323
All Fonts Resident, 127
Art
    clip, 158-61
    exporting, 151-52
    importing, 147-51
Autotrace, 152-58, 323
Auto Update, 179, 319, 320

Backups, 24-25, 146, 323
Batch Feature, 273
Bezier Curves, 84-86, 324
Bitmaps
    cropping, 211
    graphics, 2, 324
    show, 179-80, 319, 322
Blends, 256-59, 298-302
Break, 88, 204-6, 319, 320, 321

Brush Color, 254-56

Cancel, 51-52
Characters
    attributes, 320
    changing appearance of, 105-7
    changing attributes of, 287-89
    editing outlines of, 290-94
    interactive kerning with, 286-87
Charisma, 2
Clear, 93, 319, 320, 324
Clicking, 7, 324
Clip Art, 158-61, 324
Clipboard, Text from, 100-101, 325
Closed Objects, 80-82, 325
Colors
    brush, 254-56
    fill, 74-75
    and grayscale tracings, 272-73
    mixing, 260-61
    new object outline, 321
    outline, 73-74, 322

Pantone, 261-62
process, 238-39
and shape blends, 256-59
and solid fills, 82-83
spot, 236-38
See also Blends
Commands, Keyboard, 11-14, 319-22
Control Panel, 116-18, 320, 325
Control Points, 85-86, 201-3, 325
See also Nodes
Copies, Number of, 127
Copy, 92, 319, 320, 325
style from, 93-94, 320
CorelDRAW!
backup for work created with, 24-25
equipment needed for, 6
exiting, 30-35, 320, 321
explained, 2-4
installation, 20-28
keyboard commands, 11-14
mouse commands, 6-11
printing with, 124-34
program contents, 15-17
registration, 23-24
screen, 30-31, 35-54
starting and exiting, 30-35
uses of, 4-5
window, 48
Corel Trace, 265-73
batch feature, 273
creating color and grayscale tracings, 272-73
starting, 266-72
Crop Bitmaps, 211
Crop Marks and Crosshairs, 126-27
Crosshairs
See Crop Marks and Crosshairs
Curves, 325
Bezier, 84-86

convert to, 319, 320, 321
into lines, 86-87, 208-9
smoothing through nodes, 203
Cusp, 91, 209
Cutting and Pasting, 92-95, 321, 322

Default Screen Frequency, 128-29
Delete, 87, 210, 321
nodes, 87-88, 199-201
Deluxe Paint, 2
Deluxe Paint II Enhanced, 3
Double Clicking, 7, 326
Dragging, 8, 326
Drawing, 78-82
open and closed objects, 80-82
Drawings
creating, 56-60
getting rid of, 63-64
loading, 64-66
saving, 60-62
DrawPerfect, 2
Drop Shadows, 71-72
Duplicate, 93, 320, 321, 326

Editing, 66-78
adjusting text spacing, 96-98
aligning objects, 75-76
changing character appearance, 105-7
changing fill color, 74-75
changing outline color, 73-74
changing precedence, 72-73
changing preview arrangement, 111
changing text appearance, 104-5
character outlines, 290-93
creating drop shadows, 71-72
envelopes, 319, 321
existing rectangles, 66-67
existing text, 95-96
getting text from clipboard, 100-101

getting text from file, 102-4
making precise adjustments, 69-70
making text fit in text rectangle, 98-100
multiple objects, 67-69
nodes, 81, 83-92, 195-214
perspective, 319, 321
text, 320, 321
using grid, 76-77
using zoom tool, 107-10
Ellipse, Text Bound to, 278-80
Ellipse Tool, 45-46, 321, 326
Envelopes, 302-6, 319, 320, 321
Exiting *CorelDRAW!*, 30-35, 320, 321
Exporting Art, 151-52, 320, 321
Extruding, 310-12, 319, 320, 321

Files
    backups, 146
    managing, 145-66
    preparing for typesetter, 135-38
    text from, 102-4
Fills
    color, 74-75
    fountain, 229-40, 321
    new object uniform, 321
    solid, 82-83
    tool, 47, 322, 326
    using, 250-54
    vector, 215-25
    See also Lines and Fills
Film Negative, 127
Fit in Window, 173
Fit Text to Path, 277-81, 319
Fit to Page, 126
Flatness, 128
Fountain Fills, 229-40, 321, 326
Fountain Stripes, 127-28
Full-Screen Preview, 176-77, 320, 321, 322

Graphics
    resolution, 122
    types of, 2
Grids, 76-77, 326
    setup, 320, 321
    and snap, 180-85, 320, 321, 322
Guidelines, 326
    setup, 320, 321
    and snap, 185-89, 320, 322

Importing Art, 147-51, 320, 321
Include File Info, 127
Installation, 20-28
Interactive Kerning, 281-89
    changing character attributes, 287-89
    with multiple characters, 286-87

Jaggies, 2
Join, 81, 206-8

Kerning, Interactive, 281-89
    changing character attributes, 287-89
    with multiple characters, 286-87
Keyboard Commands, 11-14, 319-22

Left-handedness, 8-9
Lines and Fills, 215-64
    brush color, 254-56
    color and shape blends, 256-59
    fountain fills, 229-40
    mixing colors, 260-61
    Pantone colors, 261-62
    pen points, 243-50
    PostScript patterns, 240-43
    vector and raster patterns, 216-29
Lines Into Curves, 86-87, 210

Magnification, 168-74
    actual size, 172-73

fit in window, 173
show page, 174
zoom in, 168-71
zoom out, 171-72
Menu, 327
back, 320, 321
bar, 50-51
Merge
printing, 138-42
using, 51, 327
Mosaic, 162-64
Mouse, 327
clicking, 7
commands, 6-11
double clicking, 7
dragging, 8
for left-handed people, 8-9
programming right button, 312-14
Move, 69, 320, 321

Nodes, 328
adding, 90, 210
aligning, 88-90
attaching, 6-8
breaking, 88, 204-6
cusp, 91, 209
deleting, 87-88, 199-201, 210
editing, 81, 83-92, 195-214
joining, 81, 206-8
smoothing curves, 90-91, 203
symmet, 91-92, 210
See also Control Points; Curves
Number of Copies, 127

Object-Oriented Graphics (OOG), 2
Objects, 328
aligning, 75-76
editing, 66-78
multiple, 67-69

open and closed, 80-82
Open Objects, 80-82, 328
Orientation, 122
Outline
color, 73-74, 322
tool, 47, 328

Page Area, 47-48, 328
Palette, 47, 189-91, 320, 322, 328
Pasting
See Cutting and Pasting
Path
fitting text to, 277-81, 319, 320, 321
Patterns
creating, 320
PostScript, 240-43
vector and raster, 216-29
PC Paintbrush, 2
Pencil Tool, 43-44, 321, 328
Pen Points, 243-50
arrows, 246-47
behind fill, 245-46
corners, 246
line caps, 246
pen shape, 247
scale with image, 246
type, 245
Perspective, 306-10
add new, 319
clear, 319, 320
copy from, 319, 320
editing, 319, 321
Pick Tool, 36-40, 329
Points, Pen, 243-50
PostScript Patterns, 240-43
Precedence, Changing, 72-73
Previews, 174-80, 320-22, 329
arrangement, 111
auto update, 179

Index ▲ 337

full screen, 176-77
preview selected only, 178-79
refresh wire screen, 180
show bitmaps, 179-80
toolbox, 177-78
Printers
changing, 119-23
installing new, 118-19
selecting, 116-18
Printer Setup, 129
Printing, 115-44
with *CorelDRAW!*, 124-34
dots per square inch (dpi), 2-3
merge, 138-42, 320, 321
only selected, 126
as separations, 126
to file, 129
with typesetter, 135-38
Process Color, 238-39

Raster, 329
fills, 225-29
graphics, 2
Rectangles, Editing, 66-67
Rectangle Tool, 44-45, 321, 329
Redo, 320, 320, 321
Refresh Wire Screen, 180, 320, 321
Repeat, 314-15, 320, 321, 322
Rotate and Skew, 69-70, 320, 321, 322
Rulers, 189-91, 320, 322, 329

Scale, 127
Screen
elements of, 35-54
explained, 30-31
refresh wire, 180, 320, 321
Select All, 94-95, 320, 322
Shadows, Drop, 71-72
Shape Blends, 256-59

Shape Tool, 40, 321, 330
Show Bitmaps, 179-80, 319, 322
Show Page, 174, 322
Smooth, 90-91, 203
Snap
and grids, 180-85, 320, 321, 322
and guidelines, 185-89, 320, 322
Solid Fills, 82-83
Spacing, Text
adjusting, 96-98
Spot Color, 236-38
Starting *CorelDRAW!*, 30-35
Status Line, 48-50, 189-91, 320, 322, 330
Stretch and Mirror, 69, 320, 321, 322
Symbols, 161-62
Symmet, 91-92, 210

Text, 275-96
adjusting spacing, 96-98
changing appearance of, 104-5
changing appearance of individual characters, 105-7
from clipboard, 100-101
creating and displaying, 276-77
editing, 95-96, 290-93, 320, 321
from file, 102-4
fitting into text rectangle, 98-100
fitting to path, 277-81, 319, 320, 321
limits on amount of, 103-4
straighten, 319, 322
using, 95-111
Text tool, 46-47, 321, 322, 330
Tile, 126
Title Bar, 50, 330
Toolbox, 35-47, 331
preview, 320
Tools
ellipse, 45-46, 321
fill, 47, 322

outline, 47
pencil, 43-44, 321
pick, 36-40
rectangle, 44-45, 321
shape, 40, 321
text, 46-47, 321, 322
zoom, 40-43, 107-10, 168-74
Tracings, 152-58, 265-73
  color and grayscale, 272-73
Type, Style of, 104-5, 331
Typesetters
  preparing files for, 135-38

Undo, 51-52, 319, 320, 322

Vector, 331
  fills, 215-25
  graphics, 2
  and raster patterns, 216-29
Views, 167-93
  grids and snap, 180-85
  guidelines and snap, 185-89
  magnification, 168-74
  palette, 189-91
  previews, 174-80
  rulers, 189-91
  status line, 189-91

Windows, 10
  operation, 28-29, 331
Wire Screen, Refresh, 180, 320, 321

Zoom In, 168-71, 321, 322
Zoom Out, 171-72, 321, 322
Zoom Tool, 3, 40-43, 107-10, 168-74, 331